D0009729

... GRIPPING ... Somehow, with all she has gone through, she has managed to come to a sympathetic understanding of everyone, Americans and Vietnamese. THIS IS THE BOOK FOR THOSE WHO WANT TO KNOW WHAT THE WAR WAS REALLY LIKE."
—Frances FitzGerald, author of *Fire in the Lake*

"RIVETING!"—*Seattle Post-Intelligencer*

"PIERCINGLY HONEST ... In her ability to love without erasing contradictions and ambiguities, Hayslip shows us what real forgiveness can be."—*Booklist*

"ELOQUENTLY WRITTEN ... RIVETING ... A STORY OF TRIUMPH."—*Pittsburgh Post-Gazette*

"IT IS A TESTIMONY TO THE INTELLIGENCE, UNFLINCHING HONESTY, AND SIMPLE CLARITY OF LE LY HAYSLIP'S VOICE ... THAT THE DIMENSIONS OF HER STORY SEEM PARTICULAR ... This is one of those stories that defeat moral attitudes; to read it is to look at both the vibrantly alive face of 'the other side' and the deadly heart of war. All one can do is gaze, and perhaps bow one's head at the terrible sorrow and pity of it all." —*The New York Times*

"POWERFUL!"—*Playboy*

"A COMPELLING, EXCRUCIATINGLY PAINFUL MEMOIR that reveals the soul and suffering of a people torn by civil war that escalated into near-Armageddon."—*Kirkus Reviews*

LE LY HAYSLIP lives in San Diego, California, with her three sons. She is the founder of East Meets West Foundation, a charitable relief and world peace organization. JAY WURTS was an Air Guard pilot during the Vietnam War. He has written and edited a variety of books and currently lives in Los Angeles.

When Heaven and Earth and Earth Changed Places

A Vietnamese Woman's Journey from War to Peace

LE LY HAYSLIP

with Jay Wurts

A PLUME BOOK

PLUME
Published by the Penguin Group
Penguin Books USA Inc., 375 Hudson Street, New York, New York 10014, U.S.A.
Penguin Books Ltd, 27 Wrights Lane, London W8 5TZ, England
Penguin Books Australia Ltd, Ringwood, Victoria, Australia
Penguin Books Canada Ltd, 2801 John Street, Markham, Ontario, Canada L3R 1B4
Penguin Books (N.Z.) Ltd, 182–190 Wairau Road, Auckland 10, New Zealand

Penguin Books Ltd, Registered Offices: Harmondsworth, Middlesex, England

Reprinted with permission of Doubleday, a division of Bantam Doubleday Dell
Publishing Group, Inc.

First Plume Printing, May, 1990
10 9 8 7 6

Copyright © 1989 by Le Ly Hayslip and Charles Jay Wurts
All rights reserved. For information address Doubleday, a division of Bantam Doubleday Dell
Publishing Group, Inc., 666 Fifth Avenue, New York, New York 10103

Ⓟ REGISTERED TRADEMARK—MARCA REGISTRADA

LIBRARY OF CONGRESS CTALOGING-IN-PUBLICATION DATA
Hayslip, Le Ly.
    When heaven and earth changed places : a Vietnamese woman's
journey from war to peace / Le Ly Hayslip with Jay Wurts.
        p.   cm.
    ISBN 0-452-26417-0
    1. Hayslip, Le Ly.   2. Vietnamese Conflict, 1961-1975—Personal
narratives, Vietnamese.   3. Vietnam—Description and travel—1975-
4. Refugees—Vietnam—Biography.   5. Refugees—United States—
Biography.   I. Wurts, Jay.   II. Title.
DS556.93.H39A3   1990
959.704'38—dc20   89-13711
                                                   CIP

Printed in the United States of America

Without limiting the rights under copyright reserved above, no part of this publication may be repro-
duced, stored in or introduced into a retrieval system, or transmitted, in any form, or by any means
(electronic, mechanical, photocopying, recording, or otherwise), without the prior written permission
of both the copyright owner and the above publisher of this book.

BOOKS ARE AVAILABLE AT QUANTITY DISCOUNTS WHEN USED TO PROMOTE PRODUCTS OR SERVICES. FOR
INFORMATION PLEASE WRITE TO PREMIUM MARKETING DIVISION, PENGUIN BOOKS INC., 375 HUDSON
STREET, NEW YORK, NEW YORK 10014.

ACKNOWLEDGMENTS

THIS BOOK, like my life itself and the East Meets West Foundation, owes everything to the people in it and to those with whom it came in contact as it grew from conception to maturity. I wish to thank everyone—good, bad, or indifferent; living or dead—who appears in this book. I appreciate and honor you, because without you I could not have discovered myself or the mission of my life.

Foremost among these people I place my ancestors, father and mother, brothers and sisters, nieces and nephews, and other relatives with whom, together and apart, I have shed many tears in sorrow and in happiness. I honor, too, all Vietnamese and all people everywhere who still weep for their loved ones and hope one day to see their families reunited; and to the people of all races who have worked, and work today, so tirelessly to restore trust and compassion between my native and adoptive countries and among all nations of the world.

To my three wonderful sons—James, who first put my spoken words to paper; Thomas, who served me many bowls of rice, hot tea, and tissues during the writing of this book; and Alan, who gave me love and hugs when all I could offer in return were tears—I give a mother's love and thanks: I could not have completed my work without you. To my departed husbands, Edward, who brought me and my sons Thomas and James to safety, and Dennis, who took responsibility for us afterward, I say: your spirits have given me the strength to write. I give to you a wife's humblest thanks and hope this work has honored you.

My thanks go, too, to my co-author, Jay Wurts, who helped my memories walk and live and breathe again, and his wife Peggy, for her tangible and moral support throughout this project; to Sandra Dijkstra and Casey Fuetsch, who shared our vision; to Milton and Len Low, for the many hours they spent helping to make East Meets West a reality; to Rotarian Bill Chaffin, who first helped me share my story with others; to Peter C. Dirkx, Commander, USN (Ret.), for his kindness and advice; to David Huete for his video expertise; and Mr. Herbert Pass, veteran of another terrible war, whose understanding, compassion, and generous support has made possible much of what East Meets West has accomplished to date.

I wish also to thank Drs. Nguyen Thi Ngoc Phuong (of Tu Du Hospital, Ho Chi Minh City), Ly C. Dai and Hoang Quynh (of the Ministry of Health), Huynh Que Phuong (Chief Deputy of Scientific Research, Viet Duc Hospital), Nguyen Chi Linh (of the Ministry of Education), Nguyen Manh Hai (of the Ministry of Culture), Binh Thanh and Pham N. Quang (of the U.N. Mission), and Hoang Lien (of the Red Cross, Quang Nam) the Socialist Republic of Vietnam, for helping East Meets West establish its medical program in that country. Our thanks, too, go to Dr. John S. Romine and Diana Tracey at the Scripps Clinic and Research Foundation, La Jolla, California, and John Downs, for their support; to Stephen Graw, the U.S.-Vietnamese Aid Coordinator; to Jim Watson and Jim Robinson for their support; and to Phuong Vi, Kathy Greenwood, Mr. and Mrs. Lu Van Moc, and all my foster children and stepsons for always being there when help was needed most.

Finally, I am grateful to Jerry Stadtmiller and his wife Pat, for putting me in touch with so many U.S. Vietnam veterans who seek to heal the wounds of war through the work of our foundation; and to everyone who has served or supported East Meets West as directors, donors, advisers, and volunteers—from the physicians in Vietnam to our printers in America—for the countless tasks and many tangible services necessary to reach out and deliver to our beneficiaries the product of our dreams and labor.

L.L.H.

CONTENTS

* * *

Everything I knew about the war I learned as a teenaged girl from the North Vietnamese cadre leaders in the swamps outside Ky La. During these midnight meetings, we peasants assumed everything we heard was true because what the Viet Cong said matched, in one way or another, the beliefs we already had.

The first lesson we learned about the new "American" war was why the Viet Cong was formed and why we should support it. Because this lesson came on the heels of our war with the French (which began in 1946 and lasted, on and off, for eight years), what the cadre leaders told us seemed to be self-evident.

First, we were taught that Vietnam was *con rong chau tien*—a sovereign nation which had been held in thrall by Western imperialists for over a century. That all nations had a right to determine their own destiny also seemed beyond dispute, since we farmers subsisted by our own hands and felt we owed nothing to anyone but god and our ancestors for the right to live as we saw fit. Even the Chinese, who had made their own disastrous attempt to rule Vietnam in centuries past, had learned a painful lesson about our country's zeal for independence. "Vietnam," went the saying that summarized their experience, "is nobody's lapdog."

Second, the cadres told us that the division of Vietnam into North and South in 1954 was nothing more than a ploy by the defeated French and their Western allies, mainly the United States, to preserve what influence they could in our country.

"Chia doi dat nuoc?" the Viet Cong asked, "Why should outsiders divide the land and tell some people to go north and others south? If Vietnam were truly for the Vietnamese, wouldn't we choose for ourselves what kind of government our people wanted? A nation cannot have *two* governments," they said, "anymore than a family can have two fathers."

Because those who favored America quickly occupied the seats of power formerly held by the French, and because the North remained pretty much on its own, the choice of which side best represented independence was, for us, a foregone conclusion. In fact, the Viet Cong usually ended our indoctrination sessions with a song that played on our worst fears:

> Americans come to kill our people,
> Follow America, and kill your relatives!
> The smart bird flies before it's caught.
> The smart person comes home before Tet.
> Follow us, and you'll always have a family.
> Follow America, and you'll always be alone!

PROLOGUE

Dedication to Peace

FOR MY FIRST TWELVE YEARS of life, I was a peasant girl in Ky La, now called Xa Hoa Qui, a small village near Danang in Central Vietnam. My father taught me to love god, my family, our traditions, and the people we could not see: our ancestors. He taught me that to sacrifice one's self for freedom—like our ancient kings who fought bravely against invaders; or in the manner of our women warriors, including Miss Trung Nhi Trung Trac who drowned herself rather than give in to foreign conquerors—was a very high honor. From my love of my ancestors and my native soil, he said, I must never retreat.

From my mother I learned humility and the strength of virtue. I learned it was no disgrace to work like an animal on our farm, provided I did not complain. "Would you be less than our ox," she asked, "who works to feed us without grumbling?" She also taught me, when I began to notice village boys, that there is no love beyond faithful love, and that in my love for my future husband, my ancestors, and my native soil, I must always remain steadfast.

For my next three years of life, I loved, labored, and fought steadfastly for the Viet Cong against American and South Vietnamese soldiers.

After these initial "lessons," the cadre leaders introduced us to the two Vietnamese leaders who personified each view—the opposite poles of our tiny world. On the South pole was President Ngo Dinh Diem, America's staunch ally, who was Catholic like the French. Although he was idolized by many who said he was a great humanitarian and patriot, his religion alone was enough to make him suspicious to Buddhists on the Central Coast. The loyalty we showed him, consequently, was more duty to a landlord than love for a founding father. Here is a song the Republican schoolteachers made us learn to praise the Southern president:

> In stormy seas, Vietnam's boat rolls and pitches.
> Still we must row; our President's hand upon the helm.
> The ship of state plows through heavy seas,
> Holding fast its course to democracy.
> Our President is celebrated from Europe to Asia,
> He is the image of philanthropy and love.
> He has sacrificed himself for our happiness.
> He fights for liberty in the land of the Viet.
> Everyone loves him earnestly, and behind him we will march
> Down the street of freedom, lined with fresh flowers,
> The flag of liberty crackling above our heads!

In the North, on the other pole, was Ho Chi Minh, whom we were encouraged to call *Bac Ho*—Uncle Ho—the way we would refer to a trusted family friend. We knew nothing of his past beyond stories of his compassion and his love for our troubled country—the independence of which, we were told, he had made the mission of his life.

Given the gulf between these leaders, the choice of whom we should support again seemed obvious. The cadre leaders encouraged our natural prejudices (fear of outsiders and love of our ancestors) with stirring songs and tender stories about Uncle Ho in which the Communist leader and our ancient heroes seemed to inhabit one congenial world. Like an unbroken thread, the path from our ancestors and legends seemed to lead inevitably to the Northern leader—then past him to a future of harmony and peace.

But to achieve that independence, Ho said, we must wage total war. His cadremen cried out "We must hold together and oppose the American empire. There is nothing better than freedom, independence, and happiness!"

To us, these ideas seemed as obvious as everything else we had heard. *Freedom* meant a Vietnam free of colonial domination. *Independence* meant one Vietnamese people—not two countries, North and South—determining its own destiny. *Happiness* meant plenty of food and an end to war—the ability, we assumed, to live our lives in accordance with our ancient ways. We wondered: how can the Southerners oppose these wonderful things? The answer the Viet Cong gave us was that the Republicans prized Yankee dollars more than the blood of their brothers and sisters. We did not think to question with our hearts what our minds told us must be true.

Although most of us thought we knew what the Viet Cong meant by freedom, independence, and happiness, a few of us dared to ask what life the Northerners promised when the war was over. The answer was always the same: "Uncle Ho promises that after our victory, the Communist state will look after your rights and interests. Your highest interest, of course, is the independence of our fatherland and the freedom of our people. Our greatest right is the right to determine our own future as a state." This always brought storms of applause from the villagers because most people remembered what life was like under the French.

Nonetheless, despite our vocal support, the Viet Cong never took our loyalty for granted. They rallied and rewarded and lectured us sternly, as the situation demanded, while the Republicans assumed we would be loyal because we lived south of a line some diplomats had drawn on a map. Even when things were at their worst—when the allied forces devastated the countryside and the Viet Cong themselves resorted to terror to make us act the way they wanted—the villagers clung to the vision the Communists had drummed into us. When the Republicans put us in jail, we had the image of "Communist freedom"—freedom from war— to see us through. When the Viet Cong executed a relative, we convinced ourselves that it was necessary to bring "Communist happiness"—peace in the village—a little closer. Because the Viet Cong encouraged us to voice our basic human feelings through patriotic songs, the tortured, self-imposed silence we endured around Republicans only made us hate the government more. Even on those occasions when the Republicans tried to help us, we saw their favors as a trick or sign of weakness. Thus, even as we accepted their kindness, we despised the Republicans for it.

As the war gathered steam in the 1960s, every villager found his or her little world expanded—usually for the worse. The steady parade of troops through Ky La meant new opportunities for us to fall victim to outsiders. Catholic Republicans spurned and mistreated Buddhists for worshiping their ancestors. City boys taunted and cheated the "country bumpkins" while Vietnamese servicemen from other provinces made fun of our funny accents and strange ways. When the tactics on both sides got so rough that people were in danger no matter which side they favored, our sisters fled to the cities where they learned about liquor, drugs, adultery, materialism, and disrespect for their ancestors. More than one village father died inside when a "stranger from Saigon" returned in place of the daughter he had raised.

In contrast to this, the Viet Cong were, for the most part, our neighbors. Even though our cadre leaders had been trained in Hanoi, they had all been born on the Central Coast. They did not insult us for our manners and speech because they had been raised exactly like us. Where the Republicans came into the village overburdened with American equipment designed for a different war, the Viet Cong made do with what they had and seldom wasted their best ammunition—the goodwill of the people. The cadremen pointed out to us that where the Republicans wore medals, the Viet Cong wore rags and never gave up the fight. "Where the Republicans pillage, rape, and plunder," they said, "we preserve your houses, crops, and family"; for they knew that it was only by these resources— our food for rations, our homes for hiding, our sons and brothers for recruits—that they were able to keep the field.

Of course, the Viet Cong cadremen, like the Republicans, had no desire (or ability, most of them) to paint a fairer picture. For them, there could be no larger reason for Americans fighting the war than imperialist aggression. Because we peasants knew nothing about the United States, we could not stop to think how absurd it would be for so large and wealthy a nation to covet our poor little country for its rice fields, swamps, and pagodas. Because our only exposure to politics had been through the French colonial government (and before that, the rule of Vietnamese kings), we had no concept of democracy. For us, "Western culture" meant bars, brothels, black markets, and *xa hoi van minh*—bewildering machines—most of them destructive. We couldn't imagine that life in the capitalist world was anything other than a frantic, alien terror. Because, as peasants, we defined "politics" as something other people did someplace else, it had no relevance to our daily lives—except as a source of endless trouble. As a consequence, we overlooked the power that lay in our hands: our power to achieve virtually anything we wanted if only we acted together. The Viet Cong and the North, on the other hand, always recognized and respected this strength.

We children also knew that our ancestral spirits demanded we resist the outsiders. Our parents told us of the misery they had suffered from the invading Japanese ("small death," our neighbors called them) in World War II, and from the French, who returned in 1946. These soldiers destroyed our crops, killed our livestock, burned our houses, raped our women, and tortured or put to death anyone who opposed them—as well as many who did not. Now, the souls of all those people who had been mercilessly killed had come back to haunt Ky La—demanding revenge against the invaders. This we children believed with all our hearts. After all, we had been taught from birth that ghosts were simply people we could not see.

There was only one way to remove this curse. Uncle Ho had urged the poor to take up arms so that everyone might be guaranteed a little land on which to cultivate some rice. Because nearly everyone in Central Vietnam was a farmer, and because farmers must have land, almost everyone went to war: with a rifle or a hoe; with vigilance to give the alarm; with food and shelter for our fighters; or, if one was too little for anything else, with flowers and songs to cheer them up. Everything we knew commanded us to fight. Our ancestors called us to war. Our myths and legends called us to war. Our parents' teachings called us to war. Uncle Ho's cadre called us to war. Even President Diem had called us to fight for the very thing we now believed he was betraying—an independent Vietnam. Should an obedient child be less than an ox and refuse to do her duty?

And so the war began and became an insatiable dragon that roared around Ky La. By the time I turned thirteen, that dragon had swallowed me up.

In 1986, after living for sixteen years in America and becoming a U.S. citizen, I went back to Vietnam—to find out what had happened to my family, my village, my people, and to the man I loved who had given me my first son. I went with many memories and many questions. This book is the story of what I remember and what I found.

It is dedicated to all those who fought for their country, wherever it may be. It is dedicated, too, to those who did not fight—but suffered, wept, raged, bled, and died just the same. We all did what we had to do. By mingling our blood and tears on the earth, god has made us brothers and sisters.

If you were an American GI, I ask you to read this book and look into the heart of one you once called enemy. I have witnessed, firsthand, all that you went through. I will try to tell you who your enemy was and why almost everyone in the country you tried to help resented, feared, and misunderstood you. It was not your fault. It could not have been otherwise. Long before you arrived, my country had yielded to the terrible logic of war. What for you was normal—a life of peace and plenty— was for us a hazy dream known only in our legends. Because we had to appease the allied forces by day and were terrorized by Viet Cong at night, we slept as little as you did. We obeyed both sides and wound up pleasing neither. We were people in the middle. We were what the war was all about.

Your story, however, was different. You came to Vietnam, willingly or not, because your country demanded it. Most of you did not know, or fully understand, the different wars my people were fighting when you got here. For you, it was a simple thing: democracy against communism. For us, that was not our fight at all. How could it be? We knew little of democracy and even less about communism. For most of us it was a fight for independence—like the American Revolution. Many of us also fought for religious ideals, the way the Buddhists fought the Catholics. Behind the religious war came the battle between city people and country people—the rich against the poor—a war fought by those who wanted to change Vietnam and those who wanted to leave it as it had been for a thousand years. Beneath all that, too, we had vendettas: between native Vietnamese and immigrants (mostly Chinese and Khmer) who had fought for centuries over the land. Many of these wars go on today. How could you hope to end them by fighting a battle so different from our own?

The least you did—the least any of us did—was our duty. For that we must be proud. The most that any of us did—or saw—was another face of destiny or luck or god. Children and soldiers have always known it to be terrible. If you have not yet found peace at the end of your war, I hope you will find it here. We have important new roles to play.

In the war many Americans—and many more Vietnamese—lost limbs, loved ones, and that little light we see in babies' eyes which is our own hope for the future. Do not despair. As long as you are alive, that light still burns within you. If you lost someone you love, his light burns on in you—so long as you remember. Be happy every day you are alive.

If you are a person who knows the Vietnam war, or any war, only by stories and pictures, this book is written for you too. For you see, the face of destiny or luck or god that gives us war also gives us other kinds of pain: the loss of health and youth; the loss of loved ones or of love; the fear that we will end our days alone. Some people suffer in peace the way others suffer in war. The special gift of that suffering, I have learned, is how to be strong while we are weak, how to be brave when we are afraid, how to be wise in the midst of confusion, and how to let go of that which we can no longer hold. In this way, anger can teach forgiveness, hate can teach us love, and war can teach us peace.

PHUNG THI LE LY HAYSLIP
San Diego, California
October 1988

ONE

Coming Back

"SUFFOCATE HER!" the midwife told my mother when I came into the world.

I weighed only two pounds and looked just terrible—like a *meo con* kitten. My mother was forty-one when I was conceived, and so was very nervous about her ability to deliver a healthy child and survive. She sang heroic songs to her tight belly, ate sparingly, and worked extra hard during those months so that we both might be as strong as possible. When her bag of water broke, she was working in the fields in the midst of a winter storm. As she ran toward our house, warm fluid streaming down her legs, she cradled her aching belly and called to my father, "Trong— get the midwife!"—which he knew very well to do, having sired two sons and three daughters before me.

As a consequence, I came into the world very small but very tough. My mother answered the midwife, "I will bury her when she stops breathing. Now get out of here."

My mother was born in 1908 in the village of Man Quang on the Thu Bon river. In her prime, she was nearly five feet tall, which is very big for a Vietnamese woman. Her hair was beautiful, long, and black, and whenever she cut it, which was usually once each year, village women would gather around and offer money for the clippings, called *cai chang*. These they sold again to the city wig-makers. Hair-selling was an important way for village women to make money and my mother's long, healthy hair always fetched the best prices. Just as often, though, my mother would give the clippings to relatives and so keep the product of her body in the family. I used to grab a scrap or two myself—not for wig-money, but because it was so pretty and because it was so rare to see her with her hair down. Hard labor demanded that she always wear it up.

She had two other special signs of beauty. One was her "Buddhist ears," which, with their long lobes, showed she would live a long and fruitful life. The second was her blackened teeth, made dark from the three-day process of *nhom rang,* and strong from chewing betel nuts. Because the nut juice perked you up and kept your mouth from going dry while working in the sun, only active, strong-minded women enjoyed the habit. This showed our neighbors that she was an independent, healthy person fully capable of tending to her family.

Because villagers shun anything that's odd, my family avoided me as an infant and only my mother would hold me and tend to my needs. They said later it was because they did not want to become attached to anything so unlikely to stay in this world, but I think they secretly hoped I would die and so free my mother to care again for them. Who could blame them for that? After all, I was the youngest, I looked sickly, and I was a girl. Everybody wants sons and brothers, not daughters and sisters. I was just an extra mouth. It took three months of feeding that extra mouth before the baby around it grew to the size of an average newborn.

Owing to my extra appetite and her own middle age, my mother quickly ran out of milk. She tried to get other nursing mothers to feed me, but they were peasants too and were upset by the sight of her armful of fuzzy gristle. They had many excuses why they could not help and some, I think, were true: such as the fact that there was little enough food around for them to produce milk for their own children, let alone for someone else's. One unstated reason was that they were jealous of my mother who, although past forty, was still a beautiful and fertile woman. As a consequence, my mother milked our calving buffalo and fed me with dots of fluid from her finger. This in itself was a sign of desperation. Everyone knew that infants seldom thrived on buffalo's milk. Consequently, when I stubbornly refused to die, they gave me the nickname *con troi nuoi—* she who is nourished by god. He seemed as good a provider as anyone.

Despite my puny physique, my mother said I was very alert. She talked to me constantly and told me everything she was doing. I think that accounts for my very strong memories of her and why I bear no grudge for my family or the villagers who wished to see me die. How can I fault them for wanting my misery ended? Anyway, when I was big enough to convince people I would stay, my family took me to their hearts.

When I could walk, my sister Lan (who was eight years older than I was), would take me out to play with the other children. Once, we were playing in the dusty street when people began to scream and thunder broke from a sunny sky. The ground shook as in an earthquake and giant snakes with many heads coughed loudly. Although I didn't see them, I knew they were snakes because the villagers shouted that the "devils" were coming back. I knew they had many heads because they coughed so rapidly. I knew they were giants because they were so loud. The snakes' spittle flew into the village and splattered people with blood. When the snake-monsters came, Lan grabbed me under the arms and whisked me into one of the trenches that had been dug by the road. While we lay huddled together like burrowing animals, she sang in my ear:

> French come, French come,
> Cannon shells land, go hide!
> Cannon shells sing,
> Like a song all day!

Despite the terrifying din and dirt walls crumbling around us, she sang it like a happy washing song and it slowed my racing heart. I knew I would be safe as long as she was there.

When things quieted down, we sneaked back out like frightened mice. Sometimes, after other visits, the snakes' keepers would be in the village. The keepers were giant men who smelled bad because they were big and sweaty and often had to crawl through piles of dung. Sometimes they would pick me up, make devily faces and jiggle me, and give me cookies and some dark, sticky sweet water to drink. Some of the strangers were black, but most had white faces with the black men's marks on their cheeks. Because of these fearsome marks, we called them *ma duong rach mac,* or "slash face." They had long noses, round eyes, and wore funny hats. They carried jangly packs on their backs and enough pots and pans and knives and metal fruits on their webbed belts to be mistaken for traveling merchants. They swayed and swaggered when they walked and moved not at all like the villagers, who walked like people. In every way they resembled the demons in our stories. They had long teeth, horns sticking out every which way, faces like horses or boars, and made the noise and fire of dragons. Even the friendly ones made us sick with horror.

When we had more warning that the snake-monster was coming, my mother would pack me into a small bamboo basket (I discovered that I could fit into many small things—a handy talent) and flee with our family: sister Hai, the eldest, who was engaged; sister Ba Xuan, who was four years younger than Hai; brother Bon Nghe, who was my mother's favorite; sister Lan, who took care of me often; and brother Sau Ban, who was nearest to me in age. I was called "Bay" Ly because I was sixth-born, *Bay* meaning "six"—number names made good nicknames when there were only so many given names to go around.

Sometimes we escaped to Danang and stayed with Uncle Nhu, usually with just the clothes on our backs. During the journey we would camp in old bunkers and often had nothing to eat. My mother would hold us and rock us and sing the song of our plight:

> In our village today
> A big battle was fought,
> French kill and arrest the people;
> The fields and villages burn,
> The people, they run to the winds:
> To the north, to the south,
> To Xam Ho, to Ky La.
> When they run, they look back;
> They see houses in flames.
> They cry, Oh, my God—
> Our houses are gone—
> Where will we lay our heads?
> In our village today,
> A big battle was fought.
> Old ladies and children,
> Were sent straight to hell.
> Our eyes fill with tears
> While we watch and ask God:
> Why is the enemy so cruel?

Upon returning we discovered, true to the song, that the snake-monster had breathed on many houses and left them in ashes. Once, even our own home was burned.

On that occasion, we heard the alarm and fled in the middle of the night with no time to take anything. I was especially scared because my father soon left us and I did not see him again until we returned a week later. By then, our house was a smoldering ruin. As I climbed out of my basket, I could still hear the snake-monster snorting and bellowing in the distance. We all cried when we saw the living embers of what used to be our home. My father and mother walked past the foundation and inspected the dikes that marked our land. They seemed relieved that the earth had not been wounded too badly. Magically, my father brought our heirlooms, ancestral shrine, and some of our furniture—including his tools and farm implements—out of the forest. He had stayed behind to save what he could from the devils. Without pausing for sleep, my father and mother began rebuilding our home.

Gradually, I forgot about the snake-monster and its fiery breath. My mother carried me to the fields or I stayed at home and sister Lan looked after me. Although the land remained fertile, farming was often interrupted and the whole village came close to starvation. Sometimes we had to eat banana roots, banana skins, orange peels, or whatever else we could scavenge. My father and brothers caught fish when they could, but angling is not the farmer's art. Sometimes they went into the forest and trapped jungle rats (bigger and healthier than city rats), which my mother would fry like rabbits. But this was rare. As hunters they made better fishermen.

One day when things were really bad, my father brought home some sweet potatoes, which we all knew he had stolen. Our crop had been destroyed, they did not grow wild, and he had no money to buy them. That night, we children filled our bellies while our parents ate animal fodder: pig bran and bamboo shoots. My father hated stealing, but he hated starving his children more. Only when I was older did I realize how much my parents suffered during this time. I made a child's solemn oath to be a dutiful, perfect daughter. I would stay close at hand when I grew up and help them when they were old. I would let nothing prevent me from repaying their love.

My sister Lan took this pledge as well and for a while became my guardian angel. She kept me washed when the other kids went dirty. She sewed my old clothes while my playmates ran around in rags. She kept my hair brushed and beautiful and clean. Because of her attention, I was favored by the *ma duong rach mac* whenever they came to the village. They would be nice to me while they treated the other kids like gnats. It helped me put up with them without showing the terror I really felt.

Twice a year, in May and October, we villagers prepared the land for planting. Because these months followed the winter and summer monsoons, it meant we had a variety of natural (as well as war-made) disasters to repair: from floods and high winds to plagues of grasshoppers and the wearing out of the soil itself.

Although we grew many crops around Ky La—sweet potatoes, peanuts, cinnamon, and taro—the most important by far was rice. Yet for all its long history as the staff of life in our country, rice was a fickle provider. First, the spot of ground on which the rice was thrown had to be just right for the seed to sprout. Then, it had to be protected from birds and animals who needed food as much as we did. As a child, I spent many hours with the other kids in Ky La acting like human scarecrows— making noise and waving our arms—just to keep the raven-like *se-se* birds away from our future supper.

According to legend, god did not mean for us to work so hard for our rice. My father told me the story of *ong trang bu hung,* the spirit messenger who had been entrusted by god to bring rice—the heavenly food—to earth for humans to enjoy. God gave the messenger two magic sacks. "The seeds in the first," god said, "will grow when they touch the ground and give a plentiful harvest, anywhere, with no effort. The seeds in the second sack, however, must be nurtured; but, if tended properly, will give the earth great beauty."

Of course, god meant for the first seeds to be rice, which would feed millions with little effort; and the second to be grass, which humans couldn't eat but would enjoy as a cover for bare ground. Unfortunately, the heavenly messenger got the sacks mixed up, and humans immediately paid for his error: finding that rice was hard to grow whereas grass grew easily everywhere, especially where it wasn't wanted.

When god learned of this mistake, he booted the messenger out of heaven and sent him to earth as a hard-shelled beetle, to crawl on the ground forever lost in the grass to dodge the feet of the people he had so carelessly injured. This harsh karma, however, did nothing to make life easier for farmers.

When the seeds had grown into stalks, we would pull them up—*nho ma*—and replant them in the paddies—the place where the rice matured and our crop eventually would be harvested.

After the hard crust had been turned and the clods broken up with mallets to the size of gravel, we had to wet it down with water conveyed from nearby ponds or rivers. Once the field had been flooded, it was left to soak for several days, after which our buffalo-powered plows could finish the job. In order to accept the seedling rice, however, the ground had to be *bua ruong*—even softer than the richest soil we used to grow vegetables. We knew the texture was right when a handful of watery mud would ooze through our fingers like soup.

Transplanting the rice stalks from their "nursery" to the field was primarily women's work. Although we labored as fast as we could, this chore involved bending over for hours in knee-deep, muddy water. No matter how practiced we were, the constant search for a foothold in the sucking mud made the tedious work exhausting. Still, there was no other way to transplant the seedlings properly; and that sensual contact between our hands and feet, the baby rice, and the wet, receptive earth, is one of the things that preserved and heightened our connection with the land. While we worked, we sometimes sang to break the monotony and raise our spirits. One song my mother taught me went:

> We love the words *hoa binh;*
> *Hoa binh* means peace—first *hoa,* then *binh:*
> *Hoa* means "together" and *binh* means "all the same."
> When we're all together, no one is parted.
> When we're the same, no one's at war.
> Peace means no more suffering,
> *Hao binh* means no more war.

When the planting was done, the ground had to be watered every other day and, because each parcel had supported our village for centuries, fertilized as well. Unless a family was very wealthy, it could not buy chemicals for this purpose, so we had to shovel manure from the animal pens and carry it in baskets to the fields where we would cast it evenly onto the growing plants. When animals became scarce later in the war, we sometimes had to add human waste collected from the latrines outside the village. And of course, wet, fertile ground breeds weeds and pulling them was the special task of the women and children. The first big weeding was called *lam co lua di,* followed a month later by a second "weeding party" called *lam co lua lai.* The standing water was also home for mosquitoes, leeches, snakes, and freshwater crabs and you were never too sure just what you would come up with in the next handful of weeds. It was backbreaking, unpleasant labor that ran fourteen hours a day for many days.

When the planting was over, we would sit back and turn our attention to the other tasks and rewards of village life: from making clothes and mending tools to finding spouses for eligible children and honoring our ancestors in a variety of rituals.

On the fourteenth of each month (measured on our lunar calendar) and on the thirtieth and thirty-first of the month *(ram mung mot—*when the moon is full) we brought fruit, flour, and the special paper objects such as money, miniature furniture and clothes—all manufactured for religious purposes—into the house and burned them at our family altar. My father would then bow and pray for the safety of our property and our lives. His main concern was for our health, which he addressed specifically if one of us was sick, but he never ended a prayer without a heartfelt request for the war to stop.

But planting was only part of village life. Like daylight and darkness, wakefulness and sleep, the labors and rituals of harvest defined the other half of our existence.

According to legend, human problems with rice didn't end with the forgetful beetle. When god saw that the mix-up in magic sacks had caused so much trouble on earth, he commanded the rice to "present itself for cooking" by rolling up to each home in a ball. Of course, the rice obeyed god and rolled into the first house it was supposed to serve. But the housewife, unprepared for such a sight, became frightened and hit it with a broom, scattering the rice ball into a thousand pieces. This so angered the rice that it went back outside and shouted, "See if I come back to let you cook me! Now you'll have to come out to the fields and bring me in if you want your supper!"

That was the closest any Vietnamese ever came to a free bowl of rice.

Beginning in March, and again in August, we would bring the mature rice in from the fields and process it for use during the rest of the year. In March, when the ground was dry, we cut the rice very close to the soil—*cat lua*—to keep the plant alive. In August, when the ground was wet, we cut the plant halfway up—*cat gat*—which made the job much easier.

The separation of stalk and rice was done outside in a special smooth area beside our house. Because the rice was freshly cut, it had to dry in the sun for several days. At this stage, we called it *phoi lua*—not-yet rice. The actual separation was done by our water buffalo, which walked in lazy circles over a heap of cuttings until the rice fell easily from the stalks. We gathered the stalks, tied them in bundles, and used them to fix roofs or to kindle our fires. The good, light-colored rice, called *lua chet,* was separated from the bad, dark-colored rice—*lua lep*—and taken home for further processing. The very best rice, of course, we gave back to Mother Earth. This seed rice was called *lua giong* and we put it into great jars which we filled with water. The wet rice was then packed under a haystack to keep warm. The nutrients, moisture, and heat helped the rice seeds to sprout, and after three days (during which we watered and fertilized the seedbed like a garden), we recovered the jars and cast the fertile *geo ma* seeds onto the ground we had prepared. But this was rice we would enjoy another day. The preparation of rice to eat now was our highest priority.

When the *lua chet* was dry, we stored a portion in the main part of our house, which we called *nha tren,* or top house, because my father slept there and it held our ancestral shrine. This rice was kept in bins behind a bamboo curtain which was also a hiding place for valuables, weapons and supplies, and little kids like me when soldiers came to the village.

In the back part of the house, called *nha duoi,* or lower house (because the mother and children slept there), we had an area of open floor where we would eventually conclude our labor. Once the brown rice grains were out of their shells, we shook them in wide baskets, tossing them slightly into the air so that the wind could carry off the husks. When finished, the rice was now ready to go inside where it became "floor rice" and was pounded in a bowl to crack the layer of bran that contained the sweet white kernel. When we swirled the cracked rice in a woven colander, the bran fell through the holes and was collected to feed the pigs. The broken rice that remained with the good kernels was called *tam* rice, and although it was fit to eat, it was not very good and we used it as chicken feed (when the harvest was good) or collected it and shared it with beggars when the harvest was bad.

We always blamed crop failures on ourselves—we had not worked hard enough or, if there was no other explanation, we had failed to adequately honor our ancestors. Our solution was to pray more and sacrifice more and eventually things always got better. Crops ruined by soldiers were another matter. We knew prayer was useless because soldiers were human beings, too, and the god of nature meant for them to work out their own karma just like us.

In any event, the journey from seedling to rice bowl was long and laborious and because each grain was a symbol of life, we never wasted any of it. Good rice was considered god's gemstone—*hot ngoc troi*—and was cared for accordingly on pain of divine punishment. Even today a peasant seeing lightning will crouch under the table and look for lost grains in order to escape the next bolt. And parents must never strike children, no matter how naughty they've been, while the child is eating rice, for that would interrupt the sacred communion between rice-eater and rice-maker. Like my brothers and sisters, I learned quickly the advantages of chewing my dinner slowly.

When I was old enough to help, I spent every day in the rice fields with my mother. While we worked, she taught me everything I had to know about life. In the West, for example, people believe they must "pursue happiness" as if it were some kind of flighty bird that is always out of reach. In the East, we believe we are born with happiness and one of life's important tasks, my mother told me, is to protect it. It seemed strange to me, then, when the Catholic teachers told us that little babies were "born in sin" and must spend their lives struggling miserably to overcome it. How can one be happier than a little baby? They come into the world with nothing and could not be more pleased about it. How long must a pious rich man live to be happier than a baby?

Among the other things my mother taught me was how to be a virtuous wife and dutiful daughter-in-law: how to bring myself to my husband as a virgin and how to take care of the family I would have one day. I remember once, when soldiers were in Ky La, my mother and sister mixed red vegetable dye with water and stained the crotches of their pants. They said it would make the soldiers think they had their periods and discourage any ideas of rape. Unfortunately, a few soldiers didn't care what stains were on a woman's pants, but that was every girl's risk in Ky La. My mother taught me, too, that even when soldiers weren't around, child-bearing and menstruating women were not as clean as men or old ladies. We had to use the side doors of temples or churches and wash our layered, bloodstained underclothes before the sun—which bore on its face the image of our male god—came up to be offended by our *mau co toi*—the blood of sin. No wonder they called it the "woman's curse."

I learned from my mother, too, that a good wife needn't care too much about her husband's wealth provided she protected what wealth he had. Although we had no mortgage or utility bills, coming up with cash for necessities (like material for clothes and incense for worshiping our ancestors) or luxuries (like beer for my father) was the wife's responsibility. My mother raised extra produce in her garden and sold our fattest ducks in the market. If she could afford to buy a bit of gold or jewelry, she would bury it immediately in the yard. Whatever she couldn't make, she had to buy, so she became very handy and thrifty. Whatever she bought, she saved, and on more than one occasion, I would learn, her savings meant the difference between life and death.

Because I was her youngest child, she told me about her life as the youngest daughter in her family. Her maiden name was Tran Thi Huyen, which she refused to surrender to become a wife. Her father died when she was five and her mother, who could not cope with four children in addition to a full day's work in the fields and responsibilities to her in-laws, followed him to the grave within a year.

Hearing this, I became very worried for my own parents and one day while my mother and I were pulling weeds, I asked how my grandfather died. I knew this would comfort me because my father was so strong and grandfathers were always old and sickly. What harm could come to a strong young man?

She responded, "He was killed in the war, of course."

"So my aunt Thu raised you?" I asked.

"Yes, but only until she married. When she moved out, my little brother Khan cried and cried. He thought they were going to put her in a basket and carry her away like they did our mother."

I laughed at the foolishness of little boys. Perhaps it was wise they were encouraged to go to school while most girls were told to stay home. They certainly needed the education. I asked her again about her oldest brother. He was famous in our family for his training in the city.

"Nhu was first in our family to go to school," she said, "although it was usually on an empty stomach. None of us could eat until the evening when Aunt Thu would bring dinner out from her house after her own day's work in the fields. There I would be in her yard, waiting with Khan in my arms and Nhu at my side. We must have made a pretty picture—three skinny little kids waiting to see what we were getting to eat!"

"Aunt Thu must have been very tired, taking care of two families." I tried to sound sympathetic, but it seemed like the highest luxury to have someone bring food to you, even if it was your only meal. As the youngest girl, I always had to help fix dinner while my brothers played. Sometimes it didn't seem fair.

My mother laughed without humor. "Thu was good to us, but her chores were over when she brought our food. For me, the night's work was just beginning. I still had to take the food home, make dinner, feed everyone, and clean the house. Then, I had to be mother to little Khan and usually to Nhu as well. That meant mending and tending and giving them love and listening to them complain even when all I wanted to do was collapse in a heap. And of course, duty required me to pay your aunt Thu back. I helped her in her husband's field whenever I could leave our own farm unattended."

"How long did you have to do that?" I copied my mother's stance in the muddy water, planting my feet like a woman warrior. Her strong back swiveled easily at the hips. Her arms churned like a tireless machine. Together we hurled the defeated weeds into shallow baskets—slain soldiers for a funeral pyre. When dry, they would be burned for kindling in the kitchen.

"As long as I can remember. We never had enough to eat and our clothes were always tattered so I depended on Aunt Thu. Eventually, your uncle Nhu went to higher school in Danang city. He got a good job and started a family of his own. That's where your six Danang cousins come from. I still had to care for Khan, even though he wasn't so little anymore and pulled all kinds of pranks. I used to go down to the cemetery and visit my parents' graves and ask them what to do about him."

"Would they answer you?" Being a woman warrior was harder work than I expected, so I rested on my basket.

"Most of the time. Come on, Bay Ly—*mau len lam co di!* Do you think that grass will pull itself?" She nudged my arm and I hopped to it. "They reminded me how important it is for a girl to have a mother. How else will she learn to be a lady, eh? Who else will tell her how to do her chores? When you marry, your mother-in-law will become your second mother—your boss. If you can satisfy her as a maid, she'll think you are a suitable wife for her son. Remember, your husband comes first—is served first at the table—then the children, and then you. You will learn to serve your mother-in-law tea with two hands, as is proper. You will invite, and not call, her family and yours to dinner. You will bow your head to honor them even as you bend your back to serve them. You will not interrupt your husband when he is speaking, even when he is wrong. When you have passed probation, you will earn more privileges and respect—do you think those things are free? Eventually, your mother-in-law will come and pay homage to me. She will tell the whole village what a fine mother Le Ly has. You see, your father's mother had no one to compliment for his fine wife. So I had to relay those compliments to my mother's grave."

"How did you meet my father?" The weed soldiers on my side of the furrow were winning. Reinforcements—my mother's strong fingers—sloshed through the water to help.

"We met working in the fields, where do you think? A lot of young men were interested in me then, I'll tell you!"

For the first time that day my mother's rhythmic, unrelenting work pace slowed. She smiled even though I hadn't said anything funny. "Actually, fate brought us together. Uncle Khan had just moved out and I finally had some time to myself. I even thought of traveling. But I saw your father working in the paddy next to mine, and he saw me. I had no parents for his matchmaker to approach, so I just let word get around that I was available. I found out his name was Phung Trong. He was the next-to-youngest child in his family. His father was wealthy—at least for a village man. He had several plots of land. Even so, everyone said Phung Trong was not spoiled at all, but gentle and kind. No one even commented on how handsome he was, which made me believe the other things they said about him. I was very lucky to marry him."

"Did you have a fancy wedding?"

"No. I had nobody to give me away, so what would be the point?"

She told me how she moved in with my father's family to begin a three-year probation as a wife. The first lesson she learned was that perfection is a slippery pig. Although she was soon convinced of her own worthlessness, as is necessary in training a wife, she drew few complaints from her mother-in-law. Unfortunately, this silent praise was rain on a fallow field because her own mother could never hear it. Still, she worked hard and made her mother-in-law's life easier. Her new husband, my father, was happy, too. Because they had chosen each other, and had not been paired by ambitious parents, my mother and father had the hope of love between them. This was neither usual nor necessary for newlyweds. Nonetheless, my mother tried hard to please everyone. After all, she had no family to run back to.

"So you had babies—" My statement of fact turned into a question. "Where did your babies come from? Where did I come from?"

My mother's reaping fingers did not miss a beat. "From the same place your brothers and sisters came from: Mother's navel. I still have your cord in a box at home to prove it."

My wet fingers probed under my shirt to that mysterious, lumpy hole in my belly. I wondered how old I would be before babies of my own began popping out of it. From the corner of her eye, my mother saw my anxious look.

"Don't worry," she said. "God makes babies and puts them inside your belly. You'll have plenty of warning."

"But Father says I'm his little girl too—"

My mother grunted, "Men are always taking credit for god's work, aren't they? And the work of women. That's why I tell you and your sisters *dung gan dan ong*—stay away from the man, eh? Especially when you're in bed. When a man comes near, that's god's signal to make a baby. That's why your father and I sleep in different rooms. How many brothers and sisters do you want? The men sleep where they belong: in the front room to guard our ancestors' shrine. Besides, where would my Bay Ly sleep, if not with her poor old mother and sisters?" The rough fingers tickled my navel and I fell on my bottom in the shallow water.

Many years later, in 1963—the year the Viet Cong came to my village—American warplanes bombed Man Quang. It was at noon, just when the children were getting out of school. My aunt Thu and her pregnant daughter-in-law were making lunch for her husband and four grandchildren when the air-raid signal blared. They all jumped under the wooden table and sheltered the pregnant woman with their bodies—even the little kids. A bomb fell in Aunt Thu's front yard—on the place where my mother and her brothers used to stand when they were children expecting food. Hot shrapnel tore through everyone except the pregnant woman. Aunt Thu and one of her grandchildren were killed. The passing fragment left only a weeping hole where her generous heart had been.

At the funeral, my mother cried and I tried my best to comfort her. Aunt Thu's husband was in the hospital with two broken legs, and two of her four sons were absent because they had already died in the war. The same was true for both of Uncle Khan's boys. None of Uncle Nhu's children could come because they all worked for the government in Danang and although we would have welcomed them, the rest of the village—all loyal to the Viet Cong—would not.

We went home with what was left of Aunt Thu's family and buried her in the yard. Because the pregnant daughter-in-law was too shaken to care for her children, my mother made me stay with them for a week. Normally, I wouldn't have minded, even though I didn't want to be like a daughter-in-law in the pregnant woman's house or have to be "mother," like my mother had been, to three children who were not my own. The reason I minded was that I was afraid of Aunt Thu's ghost. Lying mutilated in a shallow grave a few feet beyond the door, her angry spirit might seek vengeance on the living—*ma di Thu o duoi ma hien ve!* I feared the circle of her tragic life might draw me in, because I was her niece, and I would not escape the hardships she had suffered. I was also alarmed and angry at the way fate had rewarded her. How could these things happen to such a good person? I wanted to be a good person, too, but I also wanted to live. The two did not seem to go together.

Just before the French war ended, I discovered who the enemy was. I realized they weren't magic devils after all, but men of another race. Still, I did not find the knowledge comforting. It meant that people, not monsters, made war. It made me suddenly aware that the human sadness in Ky La was not natural, or the ordinary way of the universe.

This melancholy filled the air like dust and choked everyone, drawing endless sighs and tears. Although I did not know all the forms of our Buddhist religion, I knew more or less what each ceremony meant. Everywhere people wept at altars or burned incense for the dead. The fields and crossroads were littered with crude shrines put up to honor loved ones who had been killed in the war. The message of heartbreak was written clearly on every face and was loud in the sobs of every voice. My own heart grew heavy despite my baby toughness.

Some of the dead, mostly older people, had been privileged to die in almost natural ways: of starvation, of drowning in a river while fleeing a battle, of exposure while sleeping unprotected in the fields, of failed hearts and tired souls worn out by too much trying. But most were killed by weapons wielded by the French and their Vietnamese allies. Of these victims, most were children no older than myself. I began to wonder why I was spared while so many of my playmates, neighbors, and relatives were not. Try as I might, I could not feel special enough to deserve such treatment. I simply felt lucky. Having to depend on so undependable a protector as luck only increased my discomfort, but I didn't know how else to feel.

We found ourselves praying more often, trying to calm the outraged spirits of all the slain people around us—like the ghost of a twenty-five-year-old pregnant woman who was killed by the French and sang lullabies to her dead baby in the cemetery; or a boy I knew who was blown up, and cried in the wind for fate to send a replacement victim so that he might be allowed to go home. Slain soldiers used to parade around the cemetery, too, but whenever we kids got close, they evaporated into the mist.

At night, my family would sit around the fire and tell stories about the dead—both distant ancestors and people recently killed. Such stories all followed a common pattern, like acts of a play or the rules of a poem. The teller must always specify how the victim died, usually in great detail. We had water ghosts—*ma nuoc*—people who died by drowning. We had *ma le*—shiftless ghosts who liked to frighten people simply because they had nowhere else to go or no great spiritual task to accomplish. We also had *ma troi*—ghosts who flew through the air (not all of them do, like Western ghosts); and *mai dai*—ghosts who are as stupid after death as the person was in life. When this preliminary scene-setting was done, the teller must recount what the dead person was like before he or she died, even if it was only a guess. These stories used to frighten me until I learned they were concerned more with the qualities of the deceased person's spirit than the grisly facts of his or her death. Because the manner of death influences each person's life among the spirits, the teller cannot leave out any detail, especially if the death had been sudden and violent. Consequently, I began to think of the supernatural—of the spirit world and the habits of ghosts—the way others might think of life in distant cities or in exotic lands across the sea. In this discovery, I would later find I was not alone.

Once, my mother told me about our neighbors.

"If they are neighbors," I asked, "why can't we see them?"

"You will never see them if you look for people," she said in a tone that made me feel like a very silly little girl—as if I had been looking for fish in the sky or birds underwater. "You must learn to look for spirits. And to look for a particular spirit, you must know something about who the person was and how he or she died."

I told her I was ready to learn.

"Well, when the French Legionnaires came to the village one day, we all ran off, as was our habit. The Frenchmen, as was their habit, took this to mean that the village was filled with Viet Minh, and so took extra care to search for enemies. On this day, the only two people who did not hear the alarm were our neighbors. The husband was out back cutting wood and the wife was inside doing chores. They were young, newly married, and daydreamed a lot.

"Moroccans came to their house quietly. They burst in and surprised the woman. The soldiers had been disappointed in their search and were pleased to find a victim on which to show their anger. They ripped away the woman's clothes and threw her to the floor. She fought and screamed, of course, but she could hardly resist. Her husband, coming back from the thicket, heard her and dropped his firewood. He ran in the back door, still holding his hatchet, and beheld them raping his wife. He, too, was no match for the soldiers, who disarmed him easily. They laughed at the way he fought and taunted him like bullies. Several of them carried him, still screaming for his wife, outside where they pinned him down by his hands and feet. Like butchers preparing a pig for market, they separated his limbs at the joints, one by one, using the husband's own hatchet. When they were through, they went back into the house and waited their turn at the wife. When all were finished, one soldier put a gun to the woman's head. He asked if she wanted to be killed with a bullet or if she wished to join her husband. Naturally, she chose her husband, so they took her outside and repeated their mayhem on the wife. Fortunately for her, after hacking away her limbs only at the knees and elbows, their officer called and the soldiers were obliged to leave. Fortunately, too, she was a very strong woman. When we returned, she had enough strength left to tell us what had happened before her spirit joined her ancestors. We gave them the best funeral we could, which wasn't much because we feared the soldiers would come back."

"So how do you recognize their spirits?" I asked even though I feared the answer. I couldn't see why anyone would want to look at dismembered ghosts, even if they had been neighbors.

My mother read the thoughts in my face and gave me a sad smile. "You can still see them around their house, mostly at night, begging for food and water. And don't worry—they are whole as can be. The wife's hair is long and tangled with twigs, and her face, although sad, is full of strength. The husband however, looks very forlorn, because he failed to do his duty and protect his wife and his house. His eyes are always downcast."

"Why do they beg? Weren't they farmers like us?"

"They died without leaving children to worship them—to bring cakes and paper money and burn incense for them. Do you think we do these things for no reason?"

But the "slash face" Legionnaires, I eventually found out, were not the only death-bringers our village knew.

The Viet Minh, the *bo doi* "soldier boys" who were the followers of North Vietnam's Ho Chi Minh, fought the French to win Vietnamese independence. Because Ky La was midway between North and South, we villagers had characteristics of both regions. We were more serious than many in the warmer South, but not so stern as people in the North. Consequently, many villagers supported the Viet Minh even though they had Southern relatives who favored the French. As a result, the Viet Minh lectured us often; like wary parents who were not sure how their children would behave when they were gone. They reminded us of our ancient duty to repel the invaders. They explained that anyone who died fighting for justice would not fall into an untended grave.

The Viet Minh went out of their way, at first, to behave like villagers and not like soldiers. They did not rob and pillage like the mercenary Moroccans. They did not shoot people by accident or torture them for amusement, although suspected collaborators were dealt with harshly. More than once, French partisans were found bound and gagged in their houses, with grim red smiles cut wide on their throats. Sometimes the executions were public. The Viet Minh would ask us, "How can these Vietnamese who side with the French betray their own race?" We could not answer this question, so we cheered with them for Uncle Ho. We knew that even though we fought against the colonial government, we were not traitors to our country. After all, the Free French themselves had resisted both the Germans and their own Nazi collaborators in World War II. Our situation was no different. If anything, we felt the French should be ashamed of themselves for lording over a land that was not theirs.

Although I was too young to do anything against the French, I remember my sisters getting ready—cleaning up, brushing their hair, and practicing each night—to sing and dance for the Viet Minh fighters who lived around our village. Despite their stirring words, the songs always made me sleepy.

> Remember—a young boy growing up
> Has seen his fatherland suffer.
> Because of that, I will be brave!
> I will lead the valiant
> From Chu Lai to Vinh Dien and Trang Son Mountain
> And scramble from the ocean ashore
> To dry my courage in the sunlight of victory!
> I will race our flag to King Nghia Hoi
> Who builds our base camp at Can Vuong.
> Our voices we carry to battle!
> With bare hands we destroy the enemy!
> Central citizens resisting the French!

My sisters also prepared rice balls, bandages, and other things the fighters would need in the field. Each evening, a Viet Minh representative came to the houses of sympathetic villagers and took our gifts to the battle zones. We were never paid for these provisions, but then, neither were the Viet Minh paid to fight on our behalf. Pay makes a soldier a mercenary, we thought, and money for supplies turns patriots into profiteers. The peasants of Ky La had not yet learned to think of war as a business.

My mother was more than patriotic. She had a secret tunnel dug under her bed and once in a while I saw her or my father pass supplies into it. I never knew if the tunnel dead-ended below the house or if it led somewhere. I did know that the Viet Minh spent most of their time underground, which made them very difficult to find, even if you were a friend. The villagers kept them fed and clothed because if they appeared aboveground during the day they would be shot like rats by the French. Even though they were mysterious, I did not fear them as I feared the Legionnaires. Unseen, they protected us like our ancestors.

Or so I thought.

My oldest sister, Hai (so-called because she was firstborn—her given name was Ngai), was born in 1931 and was married with a child of her own when the war was nearly over. When her daughter, baby Tinh, was only three days old, Hai's husband, Ba Lac, was arrested by the French for "suspiciously" carrying some stalks of rice along the road. Of course, the soldiers never notified the next of kin when someone was taken into custody—especially if they were accused of being Viet Minh. Consequently, our first sign that something was wrong was when he did not show up for dinner on the day he was arrested.

In these circumstances, it was customary for the whole family to go down to the local prison, Don Pho Xanh, and scan the barbed-wire compound to see if the missing relative were among the inmates. Fortunately, Hai's husband was alive, but even from a distance we could see he had been badly beaten. The Moroccan guards sent us away with a hoot when we tried to communicate with him through the wire.

That Sunday, when family visits were allowed, Hai took little Tinh in her arms and my mother gathered me up, too, and we set off to take food to Hai's husband. When we got to the prison, we joined a long line of villagers who were there for the same reason—home-cooked meals being the only real food most prisoners received during their incarceration, which sometimes lasted for months.

When we finally worked our way to the head of the line, Hai called her husband's name and held up Tinh to the wire so he could see his little daughter through swollen eyes. With great effort, he hobbled to the fence where the ever-present guards let him take the sack of food and change of clothes Hai had prepared. Although her husband wanted desperately to talk, a big Moroccan quickly muscled him away with the barrel of a gun. We sat around the edge of the compound for a long time, just staring at Hai's husband, until the prisoners were ordered back into the shelters. After that, we went home.

The next day my sister was so upset she couldn't speak to any of us. She tried to be brave, but the thought of having to raise a daughter alone stole her senses and she could only cry and curse the French through her tears.

Some months later, word passed that the French would be releasing some prisoners in order to win favor among the villagers. Naturally, we all hoped Hai's husband would be one of those released—and why not? He was innocent of any crime, and although he thoroughly disliked the French, he was certainly no fighter.

On the day of the rumored release, Hai loaded herself up with food and clothes and my mother put Tinh and me in bamboo baskets on opposite ends of a shoulder pole and we all set out for Don Pho Xanh prison. When we arrived, the clearing around the fence was packed with people, and we wound up waiting hours in the hot sun before anything began to happen.

Finally, a big convoy of military trucks drove into the compound. Like cattle, the prisoners were herded from the shelters and loaded onto the trucks, which then rolled back onto the highway. The crowd shouted—fearful and disappointed—and spilled around the gate, each family shoving the next for a glimpse of a loved one, or to throw supplies into the beds of the moving trucks. When the one with my brother-in-law rumbled past, Hai raised little Tinh into the air, waving her like a flag, while my mother tossed food at her forlorn father.

In a matter of minutes, all the trucks were gone and we were left, silent and sad, in the baking heat. Gradually, the families dispersed—to their homes or to the fields. Tinh began crying and I cried too and we started back for Ky La, stopping every once in a while for a long glance down the dusty road in the direction of the trucks.

Days turned into weeks and we heard nothing—not even rumors—about the convoy's destination or the fate of the prisoners. After a few months, Hai's life settled into a solemn routine, tending the house she had shared with her husband and working in the fields while my mother and sisters helped take care of me and baby Tinh. If a woman's husband went away with the army or Viet Minh, went to look for work in the city, or, like Hai's husband, was sent to military prison, she could be left for many years to raise her children alone. Relatives tried to help, but parents and adult brothers and sisters usually had troubles of their own.

Even so, Hai and Tinh were luckier than some. Children who were orphaned went to the nearest relative and became part of that family, even to the extent of taking a new family number-name to signify their place in that household. If a wife died and the husband lived, it was customary for the man to remarry as soon as possible to provide a mother for his children. No man was believed capable of earning a living and raising children at the same time, although, as my sister was finding out, this was regularly expected of women in the same position. (My mother once pointed out a village man who spent an unusually long time choosing a second wife and said, *"Hmph! Ga trong nuoi con!"* (There goes a rooster who thinks he can hatch chicks!)

These second marriages often created more problems than they solved, however, because few women accepted stepchildren as their own and the man, if he had offspring by a previous wife, almost always preferred the original children—singled them out for favors and property—over his children by the second marriage. Consequently, most motherless kids wound up with grandparents and aunts and uncles rather than single fathers, and were better off because of it. This is one reason several generations of the same family—and all their brothers and sisters—tended to live in one place. The more family members living around you, the better your chances of weathering a storm—especially when those problems involved little kids.

When a child reached eighteen, he or she was old enough to establish a separate household, though few children were encouraged to do this. Our motto was "Water the sapling to sit in the shade"—meaning that everything we did for our children was aimed at preparing them to help us in our old age. Because, as children, we grew up knowing that we ourselves would count on our own children for support in later life, we did not resent this burden. No weapon or torture terrified peasants more than the prospect of losing their children.

Traditionally, farm mothers bought gold and jewelry for their children at a tender age so that girls could have a small dowry and boys could buy the tools and livestock they needed to support a family. Marriages were arranged by parents with an eye for the spouses' compatibility, security, and improvement of the family's position in the community. To choose a spouse yourself and marry only for love was considered a terrible folly—in the same category as gambling away an inheritance or accidently setting fire to your house. This put the relationship between husbands and wives on a business-first basis: that business being survival and the preservation of the family and the link with one's ancestors. Because of this, respect between husband and wife was more common than affection, although it could grow into the kind of devout family love that characterized the strongest couples.

This focus on duty before heart often led village men to mistreat their wives. In fact, wife-beating was so common it was accepted as a necessary way for men to blow off steam and, oddly enough, keep the family together—for we believed the main reason men abandoned their families was because of bad karma: they had lost all hope of living a happy life. Like the extremes single mothers sometimes went to for survival, we accepted wife abuse without condoning it—as an unfortunate but sometimes inescapable part of life, like hard work and disease. Consequently, women seldom left a healthy husband voluntarily; too much was riding on everyone playing his or her part no matter what. If a married woman felt abused, she had only to look at an unmarried cousin or widowed sister to learn what life without a man was like. "Better to sell cheap than not sell at all!" the saying went. If my parents, for example, had wanted me to marry a bad-tempered man, I would have had to accept it—no ifs, ands, or buts. If he beat me, nobody would say anything to him about it, least of all my parents. Everyone would assume it was my fault, because keeping a husband satisfied would have been my primary duty. To run away or go to outside authorities to get a divorce would have been unthinkable—a betrayal not only of my duty to my husband, but to my parents as well. In fact, people who took it upon themselves to violate our most important customs also were expected to turn their backs on their families, just as their families were expected to reject them in turn. Given our peasant society's desire for safety and tradition, such rules made perfect sense to us, no matter how illogical they seemed to outsiders. From the cradle, we Vietnamese had learned to respect all forms of authority: parental, religious, governmental. To fit in, we had to respect the rights of others. Telling us how to observe these rights was the natural role of fathers, priests, and officials, and our duty was to obey them. Because boys had to support a family and fight wars, they were forgiven many mistakes. Because girls received the benefit of their menfolk's labor and sacrifice in battle, they were expected to do nothing wrong. Fair or not, this was the basic contract that bound our village together. Before the Americans came, it seemed to work well enough.

So my sister Hai tried to make a full life with only half a family. In 1954, when the peace treaty was signed with the French, word came that her husband had been sent directly from prison to Hanoi—where many Viet Minh sympathizers had been assigned to keep them from causing trouble in the South. Not long after that, she heard a rumor that he had found another woman and had started a second family. My mother tried to get Hai to remarry—to ease her burden with little Tinh and protect her from pesky, randy soldiers—but Hai would hear none of it. Waiting patiently for rice to grow or mountains to fall or lost husbands to come back was also the Vietnamese woman's way.

All in all, Hai waited seven years for her husband to return. In 1963, she and her daughter Tinh moved to Saigon in search of a better life.

My oldest brother, Bon Nghe (called "Bon" because he was the third child born), was even more patriotic than my mother. When the Viet Minh war ended in 1954, the country and many families like ours were split in half. Bon told our parents that he, along with my sister Ba's husband, and many other village boys, must go to Hanoi for two years. He said some men had come to the village from the North with Ho Chi Minh's instructions that the country's young men should go to the capital to receive what he called their "national language education." My father accepted this, but my mother was mistrustful, as well as deeply hurt. I think she was torn between her patriotism and her natural desire to keep her children close.

She had been working in the fields when Bon gave her the news so she stopped what she was doing and went home to make lunch, even though it was too early. She called us all in and we were surprised to find sweet rice, a special dish eaten only at holidays, on the table. While we ate, my mother cried. After the meal, we all went back to work and my mother prepared for Bon's leaving. Late in the day, Ba's husband came over to say good-bye. Because many young men were going North that night, the whole village turned out in the streets. The political odor of the journey was lost among the pleasant smells of farewell feasts.

After everyone had gone, I frequently asked my parents about Bon. "When is he coming back? What is he going to do?" They always answered soberly that he was simply away at school, although the two years turned into three, four, and five. Every once in a while I would catch them whispering about Bon, who was referred to now as *"con tap ket ra bac"* (our Hanoi son), or by me as "my Hanoi brother."

One night many years later, after the new Viet Cong war had started, I heard my parents tell a neighbor that Bon had finished his schooling and was the leader of a North Vietnamese Army reconnaissance team. They seemed relieved that he would not be involved in heavy fighting, but would serve his country by spying on the enemy. Stealth and concealment would be his weapons. To do his job, he must stay alive. Still, he was a warrior in time of war and by now we had learned that anything that had to do with the North had to do with continued suffering and dying. Everyone wanted peace, but Ho Chi Minh would settle for nothing short of victory.

Although we never said it, we all believed we would never see Bon again.

MORNING, MARCH 30, 1986:
THE KOREAN AIR DEPARTURE GATE,
LOS ANGELES INTERNATIONAL AIRPORT

I promise my boys I will come back, but who can be certain? My oldest son, Jimmy, a strong young man with a Vietnamese father he's never seen, blinks back tears. My youngest son, Alan, cries openly—the way he did when I left him on his first day at school in San Diego: a scared little boy whose mother was going away, perhaps forever. My middle son, Tommy, born in Vietnam but now a good American teenager, has pretended his classwork is too important to see his mother off at the airport; although that mother knows he's probably too proud to have his brothers see him cry. Like all the men in my life, they feel more than they can show.

Still, I know just what they are going through. I, too, want to see my mother again. A Vietnamese daughter's duty is to care for her parents; to be close when she is needed. I have not seen or spoken to my mother for almost a generation. An ocean and a war have come between us. I ask my boys, "Wouldn't you do the same thing for me?" They are good sons and answer yes, even though their teary eyes make it clear they wished that I, as my mother's child, was less dutiful than they.

"What if the Communists won't let you out of the country?" Jimmy asks. He knows all about my life before coming to America. He knows that the Vietnamese father who sired him twenty years before is expecting me in Saigon, a place now called Ho Chi Minh City. He knows I left Vietnam with a Viet Cong death warrant on my head. "What if they throw you into prison?"

"Then I will get by in prison, eh?" I rub his clean black hair the way all boys hate their mothers to do. I said I would get by—survive and do the best I could—because it's true. That was how I've lived all my life. Because of that, I am surprised my American boys think I would say such a thing just to cheer them up. I cannot say what I really fear: that I will be imprisoned as soon as I step off the plane and see neither my mother nor my sons again. I will save those tears for the window of the big jet airplane. Instead, I say what I said to little Alan a few years ago in that frosty American school yard: *"Me di nghe con."* (Your mother loves and leaves you.)

Like my journey to America sixteen years before, my return to Vietnam looks to be a bumpy trip. Around me in the 747, passengers read inattentively or sleep the fitful sleep of people in between. Their clothes are loose and twisted like the rags on refugees. Their too-small pillows and blankets make uncertain beds. They try to look composed as the big plane shudders in rough air. The pilot's voice comes on the speaker to remind us that by crossing the International Date Line, we have sacrificed a day to the miracle of jet travel. Of course, we will regain it coming back. Coming back always sets things straight.

The UN mission of the Socialist Republic of Vietnam gave me a short list of things I could take into that country from America. It did not read like a tourist's guidebook, but a shopping list for Sears: one bicycle, two radios, one sewing machine, one hundred yards of material, five cartons of cigarettes. You could also bring your camera and film, medicine for

T W O

Fathers and Daughters

AFTER MY BROTHER BON went North, I began to pay more attention
to my father.

He was built solidly—big-boned—for a Vietnamese man, which meant
he probably had well-fed, noble ancestors. People said he had the body
of a natural-born warrior. He was a year younger and an inch shorter
than my mother, but just as good-looking. His face was round, like a
Khmer or Thai, and his complexion was brown as soy from working all
his life in the sun. He was very easygoing about everything and seldom
in a hurry. Seldom, too, did he say no to a request—from his children
or his neighbors. Although he took everything in stride, he was a hard
and diligent worker. Even on holidays, he was always mending things or
tending to our house and animals. He would not wait to be asked for
help if he saw someone in trouble. Similarly, he always said what he
thought, although he knew, like most honest men, when to keep silent.
Because of his honesty, his empathy, and his openness to people, he
understood life deeply. Perhaps that is why he was so easygoing. Only a
half-trained mechanic thinks everything needs fixing.

He loved to smoke cigars and grew a little tobacco in our yard. My yourself, and as many U.S. dollars as you could carry. Uncle Ho's young socialist republic, for so long the implacable enemy of Uncle Sam, seems very hungry now for his dollars. It is not surprising. Vietnam is a new state and American money is the mother's milk of nations. The Vietnamese seem willing even to forgive a long-lost daughter—one who has absented herself from her family and her people—in order to get more of them. Or, perhaps in my case, they have something else in mind.

One cannot enter the new Vietnam straight from the United States. Like neighbors too proud to renounce a feud, both nations depend on matchmaker countries like Thailand to reconcile their peoples. So it was that the final leg of my journey back to Vietnam—to my village, my mother, and my past—must begin in Bangkok. It is here that people from the West going into Vietnam can pause and collect their final documents, gifts, thoughts, and determination before proceeding further. It seems a good idea. I am traveling alone. I have no allies to help me should I run into trouble. I am not a politician. I am not even certain of the reception I will receive from the one man who knows I'm coming: Jimmy's father, Anh.

I look out the window at the shiny, cloud-dotted water below and Anh's handsome face and strong body fill my mind. Of course, it is the memory of a teenage girl's first love that paints the picture. The twenty years between us have changed the world. How much less can they have changed the object of that girl's first love?

I look down at the ocean and wonder how he has fared since the Communist government took over. The brief letters I have received from him in anticipation of my trip are wholly without life—words written for a censoring bureaucrat, not for me. They spoke of schedules, visas, and required documents, not love—even for his unseen son. At best, they reeked of caution, or of fear.

mother always wanted him to sell it, but there was hardly ever enough to take to market. I think for her it was the principle of the thing: smoking cigars was like burning money. Naturally, she had a song for such gentle vices—her own habit of chewing betel nuts included:

> Get rid of your tobacco,
> And you will get a water buffalo.
> Give away your betel,
> And you will get more paddy land.

Despite her own good advice, she never abstained from chewing betel, nor my father from smoking cigars. They were rare luxuries that life and the war allowed them.

My father also liked rice wine, which we made; and enjoyed an occasional beer, which he purchased when there was nothing else we needed. After he'd had a few sips, he would tell jokes and happy stories and the village kids would flock around. Because I was his youngest daughter, I was entitled to listen from his knee—the place of honor. Sometimes he would sing funny songs about whoever threatened the village and we would feel better. For example, when the French or Moroccan soldiers were near, he would sing:

> There are many kinds of vegetables,
> Why do you like spinach?
> There are many kinds of wealth,
> Why do you use Minh money?
> There are many kinds of people,
> Why do you love terrorists?

We laughed because these were all the things the French told us about the Viet Minh fighters whom we favored in the war. Years later, when the Viet Cong were near, he would sing:

> There are many kinds of vegetables,
> Why do you like spinach?
> There are many kinds of money,
> Why do you use Yankee dollars?
> There are many kinds of people,
> Why do you disobey your ancestors?

This was funny because the words were taken from the speeches the North Vietnamese cadres delivered to shame us for helping the Republic. He used to have a song for when the Viet Minh were near too, which asked in the same way, "Why do you use francs?" and "Why do you love French traitors?" Because he sang these songs with a comical voice, my mother never appreciated them. She couldn't see the absurdity of our situation as clearly as we children. To her, war and real life were different. To us, they were all the same.

Even as a parent, my father was more lenient than our mother, and we sometimes ran to him for help when she was angry. Most of the time, it didn't work and he would lovingly rub our heads as we were dragged off to be spanked. The village saying went: "A naughty child learns more from a whipping stick than a sweet stick." We children were never quite sure about that, but agreed the whipping stick was an eloquent teacher. When he absolutely had to punish us himself, he didn't waste time. Wordlessly, he would find a long, supple bamboo stick and let us have it behind our thighs. It stung, but he could have whipped us harder. I think seeing the pain in his face hurt more than receiving his halfhearted blows. Because of that, we seldom did anything to merit a father's spanking—the highest penalty in our family. Violence in any form offended him. For this reason, I think, he grew old before his time.

One of the few times my father ever touched my mother in a way not consistent with love was during one of the yearly floods, when people came to our village for safety from the lower ground. We sheltered many in our house, which was nothing more than a two-room hut with woven mats for a floor. I came home one day in winter rain to see refugees and Republican soldiers milling around outside. They did not know I lived there so I had to elbow my way inside. It was nearly supper time and I knew my mother would be fixing as much food as we could spare.

In the part of the house we used as our kitchen, I discovered my mother crying. She and my father had gotten into an argument outside a few minutes before. He had assured the refugees he would find something to eat for everyone and she insisted there would not be enough for her children if everyone was fed. He repeated his order to her, this time loud enough for all to hear. Naturally, he thought this would end the argument. She persisted in contradicting him, so he had slapped her.

This show of male power—we called it *do danh vo*—was usual behavior for Vietnamese husbands but unusual for my father. My mother could be as strict as she wished with his children and he would seldom interfere. Now, I discovered there were limits even to his great patience. I saw the glowing red mark on her cheek and asked if she was crying because it hurt. She said no. She said she was crying because her action had caused my father to lose face in front of strangers. She promised that if I ever did what she had done to a husband, I would have both cheeks glowing: one from his blow and one from hers.

Once, when I was the only child at home, my mother went to Danang to visit Uncle Nhu, and my father had to take care of me. I woke up from my nap in the empty house and cried for my mother. My father came in from the yard and reassured me, but I was still cranky and continued crying. Finally, he gave me a rice cookie to shut me up. Needless to say, this was a tactic my mother never used.

The next afternoon I woke up and although I was not feeling cranky, I thought a rice cookie might be nice. I cried a fake cry and my father came running in.

"What's this?" he asked, making a worried face. "Little Bay Ly doesn't want a cookie?"

I was confused again.

"Look under your pillow," he said with a smile.

I twisted around and saw that, while I was sleeping, he had placed a rice cookie under my pillow. We both laughed and he picked me up like a sack of rice and carried me outside while I gobbled the cookie.

In the yard, he plunked me down under a tree and told me some stories. After that, he got some scraps of wood and showed me how to make things: a doorstop for my mother and a toy duck for me. This was unheard of—a father doing these things with a child that was not a son! Where my mother would instruct me on cooking and cleaning and tell stories about brides, my father showed me the mystery of hammers and explained the customs of our people.

His knowledge of the Vietnamese went back to the Chinese Wars in ancient times. I learned how one of my distant ancestors, a woman named Phung Thi Chinh, led Vietnamese fighters against the Han. In one battle, even though she was pregnant and surrounded by Chinese, she delivered the baby, tied it to her back, and cut her way to safety wielding a sword in each hand. I was amazed at this warrior's bravery and impressed that I was her descendant. Even more, I was amazed and impressed by my father's pride in her accomplishments (she was, after all, a humble female), and his belief that I was worthy of her example. *"Con phai theo got chan co ta"* (Follow in her footsteps), he said. Only later would I learn what he truly meant.

Never again did I cry after my nap. Phung Thi women were too strong for that. Besides, I was my father's daughter and we had many things to do together.

On the eve of my mother's return, my father cooked a feast of roast duck. When we sat down to eat it, I felt guilty and my feelings showed on my face. He asked why I acted so sad.

"You've killed one of mother's ducks," I said. "One of the fat kind she sells at the market. She says the money buys gold which she saves for her daughters' weddings. Without gold for a dowry—*con o gia*—I will be an old maid!"

My father looked suitably concerned, then brightened and said, "Well, Bay Ly, if you can't get married, you will just have to live at home forever with me!"

I clapped my hands at the happy prospect.

My father cut into the rich, juicy bird and said, "Even so, we won't tell your mother about the duck, okay?"

I giggled and swore myself to secrecy.

The next day, I took some water out to him in the fields. My mother was due home any time and I used every opportunity to step outside and watch for her. My father stopped working, drank gratefully, then took my hand and led me to the top of a nearby hill. It had a good view of the village and the land beyond it, almost to the ocean. I thought he was going to show me my mother coming back, but he had something else in mind.

He said, "Bay Ly, you see all this here? This is the Vietnam we have been talking about. You understand that a country is more than a lot of dirt, rivers, and forests, don't you?"

I said, "Yes, I understand." After all, we had learned in school that one's country is as sacred as a father's grave.

"Good. You know, some of these lands are battlefields where your brothers and cousins are fighting. They may never come back. Even your sisters have all left home in search of a better life. You are the only one left in my house. If the enemy comes back, you must be both a daughter and a son. I told you how the Chinese used to rule our land. People in this village had to risk their lives diving in the ocean just to find pearls for the Chinese emperor's gown. They had to risk tigers and snakes in the jungle just to find herbs for his table. Their payment for this hardship was a bowl of rice and another day of life. That is why Le Loi, Gia Long, the Trung Sisters, and Phung Thi Chinh fought so hard to expel the Chinese. When the French came, it was the same old story. Your mother and I were taken to Danang to build a runway for their airplanes. We labored from sunup to sundown and well after dark. If we stopped to rest or have a smoke, a Moroccan would come up and whip our behinds. Our reward was a bowl of rice and another day of life. Freedom is never a gift, Bay Ly. It must be won and won again. Do you understand?"

I said that I did.

"Good." He moved his finger from the patchwork of brown dikes, silver water, and rippling stalks to our house at the edge of the village. "This land here belongs to me. Do you know how I got it?"

I thought a moment, trying to remember my mother's stories, then said honestly, "I can't remember."

He squeezed me lovingly. "I got it from your mother."

"What? That can't be true!" I said. Everyone in the family knew my mother was poor and my father's family was wealthy. Her parents were dead and she had to work like a slave for her mother-in-law to prove herself worthy. Such women don't have land to give away!

"It's true." My father's smile widened. "When I was a young man, my parents needed someone to look after their lands. They had to be very careful about who they chose as wives for their three sons. In the village, your mother had a reputation as the hardest worker of all. She raised herself and her brothers without parents. At the same time, I noticed a beautiful woman working in the fields. When my mother said she was going to talk to the matchmaker about this hard-working village girl she'd heard about, my heart sank. I was too attracted to this mysterious tall woman I had seen in the rice paddies. You can imagine my surprise when I found out the girl my mother heard about and the woman I admired were the same.

"Well, we were married and my mother tested your mother severely. She not only had to cook and clean and know everything about children, but she had to be able to manage several farms and know when and how to take the extra produce to the market. Of course, she was testing her other daughters-in-law as well. When my parents died, they divided their several farms among their sons, but you know what? They gave your mother and me the biggest share because they knew we would take care of it best. That's why I say the land came from her, because it did."

I suddenly missed my mother very much and looked down the road to the south, hoping to see her. My father noticed my sad expression.

"Hey." He poked me in the ribs. "Are you getting hungry for lunch?"

"No. I want to learn how to take care of the farm. What happens if the soldiers come back? What did you and Mother do when the soldiers came?"

My father squatted on the dusty hilltop and wiped the sweat from his forehead. "The first thing I did was to tell myself that it was my duty to survive—to take care of my family and my farm. That is a tricky job in wartime. It's as hard as being a soldier. The Moroccans were very savage. One day the rumor passed that they were coming to destroy the village. You may remember the night I sent you and your brothers and sisters away with your mother to Danang."

"You didn't go with us!" My voice still held the horror of the night I thought I had lost my father.

"Right! I stayed near the village—right on this hill—to keep an eye on the enemy and on our house. If they really wanted to destroy the village, I would save some of our things so that we could start over. Sure enough, that was their plan.

"The real problem was to keep things safe and avoid being captured. Their patrols were everywhere. Sometimes I went so deep in the forest that I worried about getting lost, but all I had to do was follow the smoke from the burning huts and I could find my way back.

"Once, I was trapped between two patrols that had camped on both sides of a river. I had to wait in the water for two days before one of them moved on. When I got out, my skin was shriveled like an old melon. I was so cold I could hardly move. From the waist down, my body was black with leeches. But it was worth all the pain. When your mother came back, we still had some furniture and tools to cultivate the earth. Many people lost everything. Yes, we were very lucky."

My father put his arms around me. "My brother Huong—your uncle Huong—had three sons and four daughters. Of his four daughters, only one is still alive. Of his three sons, two went north to Hanoi and one went south to Saigon. Huong's house is very empty. My other brother, your uncle Luc, had only two sons. One went north to Hanoi, the other was killed in the fields. His daughter is deaf and dumb. No wonder he has taken to drink, eh? Who does he have to sing in his house and tend his shrine when he is gone? My sister Lien had three daughters and four sons. Three of the four sons went to Hanoi and the fourth went to Saigon to find his fortune. The girls all tend their in-laws and mourn slain husbands. Who will care for Lien when she is too feeble to care for herself? Finally, my baby sister Nhien lost her husband to French bombers. Of her two sons, one went to Hanoi and the other joined the Republic, then defected, then was murdered in his house. Nobody knows which side killed him. It doesn't really matter."

My father drew me out to arm's length and looked me squarely in the eye. "Now, Bay Ly, do you understand what your job is?"

I squared my shoulders and put on a soldier's face. "My job is to avenge my family. To protect my farm by killing the enemy. I must become a woman warrior like Phung Thi Chinh!"

My father laughed and pulled me close. "No, little peach blossom. Your job is to stay alive—to keep an eye on things and keep the village safe. To find a husband and have babies and tell the story of what you've seen to your children and anyone else who'll listen. Most of all, it is to live in peace and tend the shrine of our ancestors. Do these things well, Bay Ly, and you will be worth more than any soldier who ever took up a sword."

Before I was twelve and knew better, I played war games with the children in my village. These games were popular because we had been taught since birth that the legendary king, Dinh Bo Linh, had won his crown by excelling at such things. So, like children everywhere, we copied what we admired. Some of us pretended to be Republican soldiers (who were just like surly policemen), while others would be Viet Cong, whom we supposed were only gangsters. When one force was too badly out-numbered, some of us switched sides, although others refused to play the game at all unless a certain person was "the enemy" or was "on my side"—whichever side that happened to be on that day. The old war between the Viet Minh and the French seemed a lifetime away (it had been many years since Ky La had seen fighting and the village, in fact, had been renamed "Binh Ky" by the new Republic as part of its total break with the past), and armies of this new war, the Viet Cong and the Republic, were both filled with Vietnamese. "How bad can this be?" we asked ourselves during rests between mock battles. "A family feud? A spat between brothers?" We had seen plenty of those in our own families. We could not imagine such a war to be real.

Still, I never enjoyed the game. When I played a Republican, I always imagined that the laughing face at the end of my stick-rifle was my brother Bon Nghe, who had gone to Hanoi and who might one day come back to fight around Ky La. When I played a Viet Cong, I could think only of my sister Ba in Danang, who, being married to a policeman, locked her door every night out of fear of "those terrorists" who blew up power stations and cars and took potshots at the officials for whom her husband worked. I could not accept the idea that either my brother or sister must somehow become my enemy.

In school, the pressure to take sides was enormous. Our teacher, a villager named Manh, who was paid by the government, asked us, "What will you do if you see a Viet Cong, or hear about someone who's helping them?" We answered in chorus, "Turn him in to the soldiers!" Manh praised us for our answer and told us that the Republicans would pay our families big rewards for every Viet Cong we helped them capture. Still, when we played among ourselves, there was no shortage of Viet Cong fighters, and the children who pretended to be Republicans usually did so halfheartedly.

In 1960, Madame Ngo Dinh Nhu, the sister-in-law of Ngo Dinh Diem and first lady of our country, came to a nearby village with the idea of organizing the local children—and particularly its young women—into Republican defense brigades: the *Phu Nu Cong Hoa,* "women warriors" who would repel the Viet Cong terrorists. Along with my teenage brother, Sau Ban, I drilled with the other youngsters at school—although Sau Ban looked out for me and showed me how to handle our training weapons safely and made sure I didn't volunteer for anything that would get me into trouble. We learned new patriotic songs proclaiming our loyalty to the Republic and took target practice with rifles that were quickly confiscated when we were finished. We heard lectures about how to keep ourselves safe from the Viet Cong, then acted out what we had learned in little plays in which the enemy was always defeated and President Diem and Madam Nhu (represented by posters on sticks) walked among us dispensing candy and congratulations.

About this time, too, my mother began to worry about my "Hanoi brother" Bon Nghe. She made several trips to Danang, to see my uncle and listen to war news on the radio. Each time she brought back a stack of newspapers which either I or Sau Ban (being the only ones left in our house who could read) relayed to my father as best we could. The news was seldom reassuring. Viet Cong were being arrested all over the place and many more were being killed by airplanes and attacks by Republican soldiers. My father looked so discouraged by this news that I sometimes regretted the gift of reading. How useful is a skill that doesn't plant or harvest rice and makes the ones you love unhappy?

To make matters worse, Republican soldiers were now a familiar sight in our village. Unlike the French, they tried to be kind and often helped us in the fields. Although I was just a flat-chested girl of twelve, I liked the way these handsome young men looked at me and teased me and shared their rations when it was time to eat. My mother warned me away from them, though, telling me I would endanger the family if I talked too much. "What business is it of theirs," she would say, "about who married who, or whose relatives worked where and for how long?" I had yet to learn that in the war that was about to begin, many people would be killed simply because they were related by birth or by marriage to the wrong person—someone who was an enemy to the person who held the gun.

Because of what my mother said, I came to see all those handsome young Republican soldiers as criminals who might one day murder my brother Bon Nghe. Now, whenever they came to the village, I hid in the fields or, if that's where the soldiers were, in my house. A few who had befriended me earlier would stop outside and call my name, but I always stayed out of sight. When my mother went to the door, they would ask about her family and she would say, in a voice that was heavy with sadness, "Yes, I have a daughter, but she is out working"; or "Yes, I have a son, but he is with the military." When the soldiers inquired further, she would use the peasant's best defense: ignorance and fatalism. "No, I don't know his branch of the service"; or "Yes, he sometimes comes to visit, but who knows when he'll come again?" That the visits were only in her memory during the tearful dark of midnight was also none of the soldiers' business.

The first time I saw a Viet Cong fighter close up it was just about dark and I was cleaning up our kitchen. I happened to gaze out the window to the house next door, which (although it was owned by Manh, who had been my teacher) was often used by villagers for gambling. Without a sound, a half-dozen strangers scampered into Manh's house and then shouted "Nobody move!" The oil lamp in Manh's window went out and people began running from the house. At first I thought it was Republican soldiers raiding the gamblers, as they had done several times before, but it soon became obvious that this was not that kind of raid.

Manh was the last one out, led at gunpoint with his hands atop his head. I could hear his familiar voice arguing with the strangers: "But— I don't know what you're talking about!" and "Why? Who told you that?" I leaned into the window to get a better view when I saw one of the strangers standing just outside. He wore black garments, like everyone else, and had on a conical sun hat, even though it was already dark. His sandals were made from old tires and his weapon had a queer, curved ammunition clip that jutted down from the stock like a banana. He seemed to be keeping an eye on the dusty road that ran by Manh's house and he was so close to me that I was afraid to run away or even duck down for fear that he would hear me.

Suddenly one of the strangers barked an order in an odd, clipped accent (I found out later this was how everyone talked in the North) and two of his *comrades* prodded Manh to the edge of the road. I could still hear Manh begging for his life when two rifle shots cut him short. The strangers then ran a Viet Cong flag up the pole that stood outside our schoolhouse and left as quickly as they had come. The leader shouted over his shoulder: "Anyone who touches that flag will get the same thing as that traitor!"

The guard who was standing by my window glanced over and gave me a wink, showing he knew I had been there all the time and had learned the lesson he had come to teach; he then followed his troop into the night. The handsome, cocky face beneath the sun hat reminded me of my brother Bon Nghe, but it stimulated me the way my thoughts of brother Bon never did.

By now all the villagers were out of their houses, staring curiously into the darkness and chattering wildly among themselves. Manh's wife ran with her relatives to the road and retrieved his body while his six children—two of whom had been my playmates—looked after them, too stunned to leave their house or even to cry. Finally, the youngest called out her father's name and ran off, just as my own father's hand fell upon my shoulder.

"Bay Ly," he said quietly—with none of the alarm I heard in the other voices. "Do you know what you've just seen?"

"My teacher—" I said, suddenly aware of the catch in my throat, "they killed him! The Viet Cong shot him! But he was nice to us! He never hurt anyone!"

"He was Catholic," my father said, sounding like a teacher himself. "And a follower of President Diem. He talked too much about how Buddhists were ruining the country."

"But we're Buddhists, Father! He never said bad things about us!"

"No." My father cradled my head against his chest. "But what he said endangered others—and some of those people lost their lives. I am sorry for Manh and his wife and children. But Manh's own careless words got him into trouble. We'll give him a decent burial, but you remember what you've seen—especially when you think about talking again to the soldiers."

On the very next day, the Republicans came back to Ky La—more than we'd ever seen—with trucks full of steel girders and cement and barbed wire. They chopped down the Viet Cong flag and told the farmers to build defenses around the village. The ditches left over from the French occupation, now overgrown with weeds, were made deeper and bamboo trees were cut down to make spikes and watchtowers. During the weeks of construction, the soldiers told us to stay indoors and keep our houses dark at night. As soon as the sun went down, the Republicans set up ambushes around the village and waited for the dogs to bark—a sure sign that intruders were lurking outside.

But nothing happened. After a while, the Republican troops pulled out and left us in the hands of the "Popular Force"—the *Dan De*—local villagers who had been given small arms and a little training in how to use them. Because the war seemed to leave with the soldiers, the PF officials declared peace and Ky La, despite its new necklace of stakes and barbed wire, tried very hard to believe them.

Unfortunately, the peace didn't last very long. A few days later, my father awakened me in the middle of the night and took us to the place where the Republicans had left their biggest cache of materials, including some long metal poles. Within a few minutes, we were joined by most of our neighbors. One PF officer said, "Here—take these poles and hide them so that the Republicans won't find them. Our fighters need them for protection against enemy tanks."

Without further discussion, we took as many poles as we could carry and hurried off to bury them outside our house. "Oh yes," the PF officer added. "If you have a watchdog, give him to a relative out of town or boil him up for supper. We can't have any dogs barking the next time our freedom fighters come to the village!"

Although I wanted badly to ask my father what was happening, I obediently helped him carry some twenty poles to our house. By the time we finished burying them, a huge bonfire had been started in a clearing behind our house, with most of the villagers—including the children—collected around it. In the light of the dancing flames, I recognized the handsome Viet Cong soldier who had winked at me on the night my teacher Manh was killed. He just strolled along, cradling his weapon, wearing the amused smile I'd seen many young men wear when they eyed pretty girls at the market. The Viet Cong cadre, and many of the villagers, piled onto the fire everything the Republicans had given them to defend the village—bamboo stakes, fence posts, and thatching from the watchtowers. The only thing that was spared was the material from our half-completed schoolhouse.

"Save the school!" the cadre leader told us in his funny Northern accent. "Your children need their education but *we* will teach them what they should know. The first thing they must learn is that on this night, Ky La was saved." He gestured to the black-uniformed troops around the fire, "We are the soldiers of liberation! That is how you will call us. We are here to fight for our land, and our country! Help us stop the foreign aggression and you will have peace. Help us win and you will keep your property and everything else you love. Ky La is *our* village now—and yours. We have given it back to you."

As he spoke, another soldier ran yet another Viet Cong flag up the pole beside the schoolhouse.

"Know where your bunkers are, comrades, and be ready to fill them soon! The battle is on its way!"

The Viet Cong soldiers who had up to this time been everywhere in the village—ripping down the Republican construction and prodding the villagers out to the meeting—now fell into ranks behind their leader. As they moved into the jungle, the leader turned and told us, "Down the road you will find two traitors. I trust they are the last we will see in Ky La. We must leave now, but you will see us again."

Everyone in the crowd looked at everyone else, wondering which two had been taken. When the Viet Cong were out of sight, a few men began putting out the fire, afraid it might spread to the houses, but most simply went back to their homes. A few minutes later, we heard gunshots on the road to Danang. My father and some others went out to bring back the bodies but as we had already guessed, one was the younger brother of Manh—a victim because of his family connections. The other was a village busybody—a veteran of the Viet Minh, who, after a long imprisonment, had become a government informer. He came to our house often and asked my mother about my brother Bon, making her—and all the other mothers who had sons in the North—worry for their lives. Now the informer himself had been informed against and I felt, deep in my young girl's heart, that he, like Manh, had gotten what he deserved. It was my first taste of vengeance and I found that revenge, like the blood that once ran from my nose during our war games on the playground, tasted sweeter than I expected. It made even a puny little farm girl feel like someone important.

The next morning, as we buried the two victims, the Republican troops returned. This time they came into our houses and searched for evidence that might link us to the enemy. The soldiers drafted some workers and made them clean up the remains of the bonfire the Viet Cong had left. They interrogated everyone, separately and together, to find out what had happened and, more importantly, what was going to happen next. They were especially displeased with the PF officers and arrested one of them—the wrong one, we noticed—and drove him away in a jeep. Like everyone else, I said nothing. The man was never seen in Ky La again.

When we were finally allowed to go back to the fields, the Republican patrols went with us and herded us home again at sunset. Although some of the soldiers who spent the night in the village offered to buy our food, most just took what they wanted. In the course of a single evening, we watched a whole month's rations go down the soldiers' throats. Still, my father reminded me, there were worse things they could have done.

That night, I slept with my mother while my father and brother Sau Ban and several Republican soldiers slept by the door. I had a terrible dream of ghosts floating through the village and into our house and into my mouth and nose and I couldn't breathe. I woke up to find my father's hand over my face and his voice whispering for me to lie still. He held me a long time—not for comfort, but to keep me from moving—and I went back to sleep. In the morning, the soldiers were gone and word passed quickly that a half-dozen Republicans had been murdered in their sleep—throats cut from ear to ear. *"The dogs—where are the dogs?"* I heard a Republican officer cry in dismay. He wondered what had happened to the watchdogs of Ky La.

The infiltration and midnight murders seemed to unnerve the Republicans, and thereafter they stayed in the village only during the day. As soon as they were gone and the sun had set, the Viet Cong came back with loudspeakers and called everyone from their homes. At first, we assembled cautiously, not knowing what to expect, but soon their plan was clear. The children were organized into committees to watch for informers and to run messages between the villagers and Viet Cong in the field. The able-bodied men who were excused from duty with the guerrilla militia were organized into labor squads to dig tunnels that would allow the Viet Cong to pass into and out of the village without being seen. Families were ordered to build bunkers for their own protection and to have coffins ready, as if for the elderly, to be used for Viet Cong casualties after a fight.

Although this gathering didn't break up until dawn, we held a family meeting as soon as we got back to our house. My mother would go to Danang to buy powder for cement and my father and brother and I would start digging a bunker beside our house. We would make it as close to the front door as possible so there would be no delay in finding it when the shells began to fall—even during the night. We made no secret about our project, and worked on our bunker with the help of neighbors even when the Republicans were around. We dug down about three feet and went out two feet from the house and then dug down again. The idea was to make the entrance go down, then over, then down like the letter "Z" so that flying shrapnel and bullets couldn't get us from above. When my mother returned with the powder, we made plates of cement and held them along the bunker walls with the poles we had stolen from the government.

After three days' work, we covered the roof of our bunker with straw and sand and took in the things we'd need: an oil lamp, a bucket of water, a big jar to use as a toilet, a packet of dry rice, and some old pillows and a blanket for bedding. Because our house was at the edge of the village and the first place people working in the fields would run to when the fighting started, my father insisted that our bunker be big enough for extra people. Because of this and because of the extra care my father always took with everything, our bunker became a model for others in the village and was considered one of the safest.

While we villagers prepared our bunkers, the Viet Cong also had us make things for them. Because children like me were smaller and more agile than men, we were often called on to prepare or put finishing touches on booby traps and decoys. We received special training from the Viet Cong on what to do and usually finished our work by oil lamps or when the full moon was overhead, always listening for the sound of helicopters or the hollow "click" of rocket launchers that was our signal to dive for cover. The sand outside the village was easy to shovel and we soon had a system of trenches along the roads both into and out of Ky La. On the paths used most frequently by the Republicans, the Viet Cong put cartridge traps (which were bullets held over a nail that discharged when you stepped on them), punji pits (which were spiked boards set knee-deep into the ground—when stepped on, they broke in half and sent poisoned barbs into the soldier's legs above his boots), and trip-wire grenade traps of every type. Some fighters even filled coconuts with gunpowder and made pulling fuses for them, too, although these were pretty dangerous, even to their makers. Surprisingly enough, although we knew how deadly these traps could be, we kids had no second thoughts about helping the Viet Cong make them or put them into place. To us, war was still a game, and our "enemy," we were assured, deserved everything bad that happened to them.

When the Republicans finally returned, however, nothing we planned worked out. Because some villagers stayed loyal to the South, many of our secret self-defense force fighters were identified and hauled off to jail. Those who weren't caught were put to work filling in the trenches we had just dug or were required to help the soldiers expand the family bunkers so that Republican troops could use them. When most of our labor for the Viet Cong had been undone, they raised the Republican flag and one officer made a speech about how they had saved us from our enemy. Despite all our work for nothing, we were grateful at least that a battle had been avoided. Unfortunately, this happiness, too, would not last long.

Because they distrusted us, the Republicans made a fortified camp in Ky La before going into the jungle to look for Viet Cong. Many Republican soldiers were killed on these sweeps because they carried so much equipment—bedding, entrenching tools, and rations—and so were clumsy as well as noisy. They preferred to walk where the ground was easy and high and dry and made perfect targets for their enemy, who cut them down from hiding.

The Viet Cong on the other hand were small, quick, and carried nothing but a weapon, some ammunition, and a little dry rice. This kept them safe in battle, but it meant their day-to-day life was miserable. When they were hit, they had only herbal medicine to treat their wounds. When they were killed, their bodies were not removed, like the Republicans' were, for a decent burial at home. Usually, we peasants had to roll them up in mats and stick them in shallow graves before the authorities found them. When the Republicans caught us around a dead Viet Cong fighter, we had to act like we didn't know what was going on. We would tell the soldiers that nobody knew who the dead person was, even though his family might be standing right there, holding back their tears. We would claim the dead man was a vagabond or someone from another village. "Would you soldiers like to haul him away for us?" *No, they would not.* So we'd bury him ourselves and the relatives would mourn in secret. Unlike the Republicans, the Viet Cong fighters received no pay and their families seldom got pensions when they were killed. Wives lost husbands, parents lost sons, little kids lost fathers, and all had to pretend as if nothing happened. The government came after the Viet Cong with boats, planes, tanks, trucks, artillery, flamethrowers, and poisons, and still the Viet Cong fought back with what they had, which was mostly cleverness, courage, terror, and the patience of the stones.

When the Viet Cong could not be found (they spent most of their time, after all, hiding in caverns underground with entrances hidden by cookstoves, bushes, false floors, or even underwater by flowing rivers themselves), the Republican soldiers took out their frustration on us: arresting nearby farmers and beating or shooting them on the spot, or carting anyone who looked suspicious off to jail. As these actions drove even more villagers to the Viet Cong cause, more and more of our houses were modified for Viet Cong use. The cadremen told us that each family must have a place in which liberation troops could hide, so my father dug an underground tunnel beneath our heavy cookpot which could house half a dozen fighters. While my father and other villagers worked on their tunnels, we children were taken to a clearing beyond the village graveyard, on the threshold of the swamp, where we were taught revolutionary songs. One of the first we learned was in praise of Uncle Ho—Ho Chi Minh —who, we were told, awaited news of our heroism like a kindly grandfather:

> The full moon shines on our land,
> So that we can sing and dance
> And make wishes for Uncle Ho.
> Uncle Ho—we wish you a long life!
> We wish you a long beard that we can stroke
> While you hold us in your arms
> And tell us how much you love us and our country!

We were also taught what we were expected to do for our village, our families, and the revolution. If we were killed, we were told we would live on in history. We learned that, like the French, men of another race called *Americans* wanted to enslave us. "Their allies are the traitorous Republicans of Ngo Dinh Diem!" the Viet Cong shouted. "Just as our fathers fought against the French and their colonial administrators, so must we now fight against these new invaders and their running dogs!" We learned that cheating, stealing from, and lying to Republican soldiers and their allies were not crimes, and that failing to do these things, if the situation demanded it, was treason of the highest sort. Girls were shown the pattern of the Viet Cong flag—half blue (for the North—the direction of peace), half red (for the bloody South), with a yellow star (for the union of yellow-skinned people) in between—and told to sew as many as they could for use in demonstrations or whenever one was asked for by a fighter. Even when the hated Republicans were in our village and our flag could not be displayed, were were to fly it proudly in our hearts. We then sang songs to celebrate those brothers and fathers that went north to Hanoi in 1954. I sang loudly and thought of Bon Nghe and knew he would be proud.

Although it was nearly dawn when I got home from the first meeting, my parents were still awake. They asked what I'd been doing and I told them proudly that I was now part of the "political cadre"—although I had no idea what that meant. I told them we were to keep an eye on our neighbors and make sure the liberation leaders knew if anyone spoke to the hated Republicans. I told my mother to rejoice, that when her son— my beloved brother Bon—came back from Hanoi, he would be a leader in the South, just as the leaders of our own cadre had been trained in Hanoi and now were helping our village gain victory over the invaders.

Although my mother was not sure that my involvement with the cadre was a good idea, she seemed happy that through them, somehow, Bon's return might be hastened. My father, however, looked at me with an expression I had never seen before and said nothing. Although Ky La's first big battle had yet to be fought, it was as if he had seen, in my shining, excited, determined little face, the first casualty of our new war.

It was a hot afternoon and I was tending our water buffalo in the fields, prodding it left and right with a bamboo stick and daydreaming when the motor noise began. The sound of trucks and jeeps was now so familiar in Ky La, especially during the day, that nobody paid any attention to it except as a reminder to keep to his own business and make sure that business was as far as possible from the Republicans.

But this motor noise was different. Like a tiger growling in a cave, the hollow noise became a roar and our buffalo grunted and trotted without prodding toward the trees. Steadily, the roar increased and I looked into the sun to see two helicopters, whining and flapping like furious birds, settle out of the sky toward me. The wind whipped my clothes and snatched the sun hat from my head. Even the ankle-deep water itself retreated before the down blast of their terrible beating wings. What could a puny girl do but fall down on her knees and hold fast to mother earth?

To my surprise, I did not die. Almost as quickly as it arrived, the roar spun down and the dying blast of wind and water gave back the heat of day. As I raised my eyes, the dull green door on the side of the ship slid open and the most splendid man I had ever seen stepped out onto the marshy ground.

He was a giant, even bigger than the Moroccans who occasionally still haunted my dreams, but crispy clean in starched fatigues with a yellow scarf tucked into his shirt and a golden patch upon his shoulder. The black boots into which his battle pants were bloused shone bright as a beetle's shell.

Still cowering, I watched his brawny, blond-haired hands raise binoculars to his eyes. He scanned the tree line around Ky La, ignoring me completely, and chewed the lip below his scrubby mustache. In a husky voice, he said something in his queer language to another fair-skinned soldier inside the door, then dropped the field glasses to his chest and climbed back inside his machine.

Instantly, the flap-flap-flap and siren howl increased and the typhoon rose again. As if plucked by the hand of god, the enormous green machine tiptoed on its skids and swooped away, climbing steadily toward the treetops, the second craft behind it. In seconds even the hollow growl was gone, replaced by my father's voice.

"Bay Ly—are you all right?"

I looked up at him from my knees. My face must have revealed my wonder because his expression of anguish turned quickly to relief—and then to anger.

"The *may bay chuong-chuong*—the dragonflies—weren't they wonderful!" I blurted out what was in my heart.

My father cupped my face roughly and cleared the wet hair from my eyes. "Wonderful? Hah! They were *Americans!* You risked your life hanging around here while they landed. Even our buffalo has more sense than you!" He raised me to my feet. My legs were still wobbly with excitement.

"But didn't you see them, Father?"

"Yes—I saw them. So did everyone else. So did the Viet Cong. Now go catch your ox and take him home. It's almost lunchtime."

Only when I retrieved my hat and stick and began spattering across the field to the trees did I notice that other people were staring in my direction. At supper that evening, my father had not only lost his anger, he actually seemed pleased.

"Father—why are you smiling?" my mother snapped. "Your daughter was almost killed today by Americans. The propellers could have chewed her up and spat her all the way to Danang. What's wrong with you?"

My father put down his bowl. Little rice grains stuck to his chin. "I'm smiling because I'm told we have a brave woman warrior in our house —although she'd better be more careful if she wants to be around for New Year's, eh?" He mussed the stringy black hair on my head.

"What are you talking about?" my mother asked.

"Oh, haven't you heard the news? It's the talk of Ky La: How little Bay Ly stood her ground against the enemy's *may bay chuong-chuong cua My huy*. She didn't budge an inch!"

"That's what the neighbors are saying?" My mother couldn't believe that her lazy, absentminded daughter could have done anything so grand.

I didn't have the heart to tell them it was awe, not courage, that nailed my feet to the ground when the Americans landed. In time, we all would learn the wisdom of standing still at the approach of Americans—the way one learns to stand still in the face of an angry dog. Before long, any Vietnamese who ran from American gunships would be considered Viet Cong and shot down for the crime of fear.

Although Americans had been in the village before and now came more frequently to Ky La, we children never got used to them. Because they had blue eyes and always wore sunglasses, a few of us thought they were blind. We called them *mat meo*—cat eyes—and "long nose" to their backs and repeated every wild story we heard about them. Because the Viet Cong, when they captured them, always removed the Americans' boots, (making escape too painful for their soft, citified feet), we thought we could immobilize the Americans by stealing both their sunglasses and their shoes. How can a soldier fight, we reasoned, if he's not only blind but lame?

Still, the arrival of the Americans in ever-increasing numbers meant the new war had expanded beyond anyone's wildest dreams. A period of great danger—one we couldn't imagine at the time—was about to begin.

The Viet Cong, too, sensed this grave development and stepped up their activities. In our midnight meetings, which were now held more often, they told us how to act when the Americans and their Republican "lap dogs" were around.

"What will you do when the enemy sleeps in your house?" the cadre leader asked.

"Steal his weapons!" we answered in chorus. "Steal his medicine! Steal his food!"

"And what will you do with what you steal?"

"Give it to you!" The village children laughed happily and applauded our own correct answers. Whenever we turned something in to the Viet Cong—even something as small as a mess kit or pocketknife—we were rewarded like heroes. Handmade medals were pinned to our shirts and our names were entered on the Blackboard of Honor.

My name quickly rose on the list because the Republicans in our house were so careless. We lived on a rise of ground near the fields and swamps and because it was easy to see in all directions, the soldiers there would relax. A few of us stole firearms—automatic rifles and pistols—but the Viet Cong seldom used them because the ammunition was different from the kind they received from the North. What they really wanted were hand grenades and first aid kits—things any fighter could use—things that were in perilously short supply. Once, I stole a hand grenade and hid it in a rice container that also held *man cau* fruit, which looks just like pineapples. My father discovered it by chance and his mouth fell open when one "fruit" he grabbed weighed so much more than the others. He buried it in a secret place and lectured me sternly about taking such chances, but I didn't care and promptly stole another one as soon as I had the chance. We kids used to laugh when a careless Republican got chewed out by his superior for losing such equipment. The fact that those things might lead to new deaths on both sides, including women and children in our own village, never occurred to us. For us, the new war was a game for earning medals and an honored place on lists—ideas we had been taught to honor for years in the government's own school.

Of course, every once in a while, one of us would get caught. If the stolen thing was a bit of food or clothing, the soldiers would just box our ears and take it back. But if it was a weapon or a piece of expensive equipment, the child would be arrested and taken away, to be tortured if she did not tell the soldiers what she knew about the Viet Cong. One friend of mine—a girl named Thi, whose parents "went north" when the war began—was about two years older than I was and very clever. Because she lived with her grandmother and there were no men around, the Republicans often used her house as a base and were very careless with their gear. One afternoon, she stole not only several hand grenades, but a large Republican machine gun. Unfortunately for her, she was caught when the soldiers found her struggling with a box of heavy ammunition and was spirited out of town in the officer's jeep. The Republicans never publicized these arrests because they were ashamed to admit that so many peasants in our village were against them. It was easier for the suspect to "just disappear," like the wayward equipment itself.

The cadre leaders were very clear about how we were supposed to act if we were threatened with capture. Because we knew where many secret tunnels were hidden, we were told to hide in them until the Viet Cong could help us. If they could not, we were expected to commit suicide— using, if need be, the weapon or explosives we had just stolen. Our deaths would mean nothing if they came after torture; only by dying in battle or by our own little hands would we be immortalized as heroes. This had been programmed into us by the Viet Cong and our own ancient, heroic legends, so we never questioned it for an instant. We didn't realize the Viet Cong were more concerned about terrified children giving away their secrets than guaranteeing our places in history. Loyalty was something the Viet Cong always worried about—more than battles or American bombs—and I would one day find out just how dangerous these worries could make them.

Eventually, the children my age and older went to fight for the Viet Cong. As you would expect, few parents approved of this, even the ones who hated the Republicans and Americans the most. Many parents, including my own, begged to have their children excused but few exceptions were made. Fortunately, because I was my parents' last daughter (my brother Sau Ban, by this time, was away in Saigon working with the youth construction brigade) and because my father had worked so diligently to build bunkers and tunnels for the Viet Cong in our village, and because my eldest brother Bon Nghe had gone to Hanoi, and because I had already proved my loyalty and steadfastness on other occasions— including the arrival of the American helicopters—I was allowed to remain at home and perform other duties. In a solemn ceremony, I was inducted into the secret self-defense force and told I would be responsible for warning the Viet Cong about enemy movements in my village. After a battle, I was to help the nurses tend our wounded and report on enemy casualties. Although I was disappointed that I could not join my friends in combat, I was proud to be doing a job so similar to that of brother Bon Nghe.

My main assignment was to keep an eye on the stretch of jungle that ran between Ky La and the neighboring village. As usual, my father played an important role in keeping me safe and alive. He would stand on the high ground behind our house—the same ground on which he had first instructed me about my duty to Vietnam—and relay my signal to the Viet Cong sentinels at the far edge of the forest. If Republicans or Americans were inside the village, he would take off his hat and fan himself three times. If the enemy was approaching the village, he would fan himself twice. If the coast was clear, and no enemy troops were around, he would fan himself once. This system, my father told me, had been used by the Viet Minh and was very effective. It allowed me to stay near the village where I would be safer and less suspect, and permitted the adult, my father in this case, to take most of the risk by giving the signal himself. If the system went wrong and some Viet Cong were killed, he assured me that his, not mine, would be the next body found on the road to Danang. Similarly, if the Republicans figured out the signals, he would also be killed—but only after being tortured for information. Although I was still blinded by my young girl's vision of glory, I began to see dimly what a terrible spot the war had put him in. For me and most other children, the new war was still an exciting game. For my father, it was a daily gamble for life itself.

As the war around Ky La dragged on, the Viet Cong established regular tasks for the villagers. One week, our family would cook rations for them—although the Viet Cong never asked for anything special and refused to take food if it meant we would have nothing ourselves. The next week, it might be our duty to sew clothes: to repair old uniforms or make new ones—sometimes with the parachute silk taken from captured fliers or from the wreckage of an American plane. As standing orders, young girls like me were supposed to make friends with the Republicans and steal their toothpaste, cigarettes, and other sundries that were welcomed in the jungle. To make sure these false friendships didn't blossom into real ones, we were reminded during our midnight meetings of the differences between our liberation soldiers and the Republicans and Americans who fought them.

"The imperialists and their running dogs," the cadre leader said, shaking his fist in the air and showering spit on those nearest him, "have aircraft and bombs and long-range artillery and ten men for every one of ours. We have only rags and rifles and those supplies we carry on our backs. When the Republicans and Americans come to your village, they trample your crops, burn your houses, and kill your relatives just for getting in the way. We respect your homes and the shrines of your ancestors and execute only those who are traitors to our cause. President Diem gives you foreign invaders while Ho Chi Minh promises you a free

Vietnam. The Republicans fight for pay, like mercenaries, while we fight only for your independence."

As much as we disliked the wartime dangers, we could not argue with what the leader said. For every American who yielded the right of way to us on the road, many more bullied us like cattle. For every Republican whose politeness reminded us of our sons and brothers, there were others who acted like pirates. Whenever it was safe to do so, we organized demonstrations and walked from village to village in our area, waving the Viet Cong flag and shouting slogans to our neighbors. We cursed the "Republican lapdogs" and told the safely distant Americans to get out of our country. It was helpless rage that drove us, but it made us feel better and seemed to even the odds, if only in our hearts. Unfortunately, on one occasion, those terrible odds—and the awful reality of the war— finally caught up with me.

It was during one of these demonstrations, on a hot windless night, that a Viet Cong runner came up and told us the Republicans were about to bombard the area. Everyone ran to the roadside trenches and the Viet Cong themselves disappeared into the jungle.

At first, the shells hit far away, then the explosions came toward us. Flares drifting down on parachutes lit up the sky and threw eerie, wavering shadows across my trench. The bombardment seemed to go on for hours, and as I lay alone in my hiding place, flinching with each explosion, I began to worry about my family. I had a terrifying vision of my house and parents coming apart as they rose high on a ball of flame. I had a powerful urge to run home, but somehow I overcame it. Leaving the trench before the shelling stopped would have been suicide—even silly young farm girls knew that.

When the explosions stopped, I stretched out from my embryonic coil and poked my head out of the trench. The night air smelled terrible— like burning tires—and splintered trees and rocks lay all over the road. From the direction of Ky La, a big force of Republicans were coming up the road, rousting civilians from the trenches. It was illegal to be outside after dark, even in your own village. To be away from your local area on top of that was all but a confession of being a Viet Cong.

I lay in my burrow and tried to decide what to do. All I could think of was our two neighbors, sisters named Tram and Phat, whose two brothers had gone to Hanoi while a third had stayed in Ky La. The Ky La brother was arrested and tortured by Republicans because of his connections to the North. When he was released, the first thing he did was kiss his family good-bye and slash his wrists. This so shocked and angered the sisters that they became staunch supporters of the Viet Cong. When the Republicans came back to arrest them, the sisters let it be known they were hiding in their family bunker, too afraid to come out. The soldiers, of course, went in after them. When they crawled inside the bunker, they saw the sisters sitting together, calm as can be, each holding a grenade without its pin. Their small hands were clasped around the safety handle, ready to release it should either of them be bothered. The soldiers, fearing to shoot them and thus set off the grenades, scrambled to get out. But the sisters released the grenades anyway and perished with three of their enemies. The next day, their mother buried what was left of her daughters beside her son and went out to work in the fields. The Republicans followed her and, fearing to get too close to the last member of such a dangerous, desperate family, shot her down from behind the dikes.

I did not have a weapon, but it would be easy enough to goad the soldiers into shooting me, or, for that matter, to grab the barrel of one rifle and pull it against my chest. Still, I did not want my own mother to die because of my heroism or bad luck. Over and over in my head I repeated her advice for just this situation: *If you're too smart or too dumb, you'll die—so play stupid, eh? That shouldn't be too hard for a silly girl who lets herself get caught! Act like you don't know anything because you are young and stupid. That goes for either side, no matter's who's asking the questions. Play stupid, eh? Stupid, stupid child!*

When the soldiers finally lifted me from the trench, muttering and covered with dirt, they must have thought I was simpleminded or shell-shocked by the explosions. Instead of questioning me or beating me or shooting me on the spot, as they had done with some others, they tied my hands behind my back and pushed me into a truck with other people from the parade and drove us all to the nearest jail.

From the truck we were led to a room with no furniture and told to wait silently. One by one, the guards took people to another room for interrogation. I was the fifth or sixth to be taken, and until that time, no one before me had come back. Because I hadn't heard shots, I was foolish enough to think they had been released.

When my turn came, the guards hustled me down a corridor to a windowless cell with a single electric light bulb hanging from the ceiling. A young Vietnamese soldier with many stripes and decorations made me squat in the middle of the floor and began to ask simple questions like "What is your name? Where are you from? Who is in your family?" and, most importantly, "What were you doing so far from your home in the middle of the night?" I answered each question like a terrified little girl, which, as my mother had promised, was not difficult. I said I sneaked away from home to follow what sounded like a feast-day parade. The people in the parade said we were going down the road to see a play. I told the soldier I was always getting into trouble like this and asked him to please not tell my parents because my father would whip me and my mother would—

The soldier's blow stopped my clever story and almost knocked me out. The next thing I remember I was being jerked up by my hair with my face pointed up at the light bulb. The interrogator asked again, in a rougher voice, what I had been doing away from my village. Sobbing, I answered again that I had heard a parade and followed it to see a play. I didn't mean any harm to anyone. I only wanted to see the play and have fun—

The guard behind me lifted me by my hair and I yelped and he kicked the small of my back—once, twice, three times—with his heavy boots. I now screamed as loud as I could—no acting!—but he kept me dangling and kicked me some more, my scalp and back on fire. Each time I tried to support myself, the soldier kicked my legs out from under me so the more I struggled the worse it hurt. Finally I went limp and the guard dumped me on the floor. The interrogator screamed his questions again, but I could only cry hysterically. He hit me a few more times, then pulled me up by my tied hands and shoved me out the door. The guard took me down the hall and into a big room that had been divided by bamboo bars into a dozen tiny cages. They thrust me into one of them—a space not big enough for even a small girl like me to stand up or stretch out in—and padlocked the door.

For a long time I simply lay sobbing on the cage's bamboo floor. My tears stung the welts rising on my face and my back was beginning to throb. With my hands still tied behind me, I rolled upright against the bars. The room smelled like a sewer and when I focused my eyes I saw that a single drain at its center was used as the toilet for the cages. At once I recognized some people from the demonstration, although nobody was from my village. What we all had in common, though, was the badge of interrogation: purple eyes, puffed foreheads, mouths and noses caked with blood, teeth chipped or missing behind split lips and broken jaws. Like the interrogation cell, the dingy room had but a single unblinking light bulb from which even closed eyes offered no relief.

I began to feel desperate pain now in my lower back and bladder. Afraid I would wet my pants, I hiked down my trousers and relieved myself shamelessly on the floor. I watched the stream of frothy liquid tinged with red meander down the drain and I almost fainted. I had never seen blood in my urine before, and assumed it meant I was dying.

Still, the painful river inside me flowed on, blood or no blood, and my little girl's bottom sank to the bars and I sat there shivering, peeing, and crying—careless of anyone—wanting only my mother and my bed and an end to this terrible nightmare.

After crying myself out, I went to sleep. The next thing I knew the door of my cage banged open and strong hands dragged me by the ankles toward the door. I was put on my feet and shoved down the hall toward the interrogation cell, which, just by my seeing its door, almost made me vomit. By the hazy light at the end of the hall I knew that the sun had come up—perhaps to mock my misery—on a beautiful summer day.

Inside the airless cell, however, everything was midnight—except for the harsh, unsleeping bulb. But a different, older soldier greeted me now and, to my astonishment, he ordered the guard to untie me. My little joints popped as I stretched out my arms and rubbed the welts on my wrists.

"Con an com chua?" (Have you eaten?), the soldier asked politely.

I didn't know how to answer. The question might have been what it seemed—a jailer's inquiry about the status of an inmate. But the question was also the formal greeting made between peasants from the earliest mists of time in a land where food was always scarce. I chose the most traditional, politest answer possible.

"Da con an com roi" (I have already eaten, thank you), and cast my eyes down at the filthy floor. It seemed to satisfy him, although he said nothing more about my breakfast.

"Sergeant Hoa tells me you were most uncooperative last night." The soldier circled me slowly, inspecting my wounds, gauging, perhaps, which weeping cut or puffy bruise would render pain—and therefore answers —most quickly. He paused, as if expecting me to dispute Sergeant Hoa, then said, "Anyway, all that's in the past. Others have told us everything we want to know about last night. All you need do is confirm a few details, then we can get you cleaned up and back to your family—perhaps in time for lunch, eh? You'd like that, wouldn't you, Le Ly?"

My heart leaped at the sound of my name spoken kindly on this strange man's lips—as well as at the prospect of seeing my family. As my surprised and hopeful face looked up, I saw he was reading a piece of paper— perhaps Sergeant Hoa's report from the night before. Possibly, it contained a good deal more.

"Yes, I would like to go home," I said meekly.

"Good. Well now, Le Ly, let's talk a moment about the Viet Cong hiding places around Binh Ky. We know about their tunnels beneath the haystacks and their rooms behind the artillery shelter south of the village—" He trailed off, hoping, perhaps, that I would add some other places to his list. "By the way, why *were* you in the trenches last night?"

"I jumped in to escape the explosions."

"Of course. And why were you outside at all?"

"I woke up and saw a parade pass our house. I joined it without waking my parents and was told we were going to see a play. We were almost to the playhouse when the explosions began. I got scared and jumped in a trench. I was too afraid to go home because I thought my parents would spank me."

"I see. And what was the play about?"

I was quiet a moment, then said, "I don't know. I didn't see it."

"Just so. And who was to be in the play?"

"I—I don't know that either."

"Tell me, Le Ly, do you know this song?

> We are so cheerful and happy,
> We act and sing and dance,
> Vietnam's stage is in sunlight,
> Because Uncle Ho fills us with joy.

"I know that song," I replied, "but you sang the wrong words. The song I know goes:

> We are so cheerful and happy,
> We act and sing and dance,
> Vietnam's stage is in sunlight,
> Because Ngo Dinh Diem fills us with joy.

My little girl's voice, choked with fear and bruises, must have sounded funny because the soldiers in the room laughed loudly. Perhaps I was the first peasant girl they'd met whose father knew two versions of every political song.

"Do the Viet Cong ever come to your village, Le Ly?"

"Yes."

"And what do they look like?"

"They look like you—except they wear black uniforms."

The soldier lit a cigarette. He was quiet for such a long time that I thought he was going to hit me. Instead he said, "We'll talk again, Le Ly." He nodded and the guard took me back to my cage.

I stayed in the cage two more days. Every morning, a prison worker would splash water on the fetid floor and every evening we were given one bowl of rice with a few greens or pork fat mixed in to sustain us. We were allowed to drink three dippers of water each day and had a few minutes every afternoon to walk around in the compound. Prisoners were forbidden to speak, even in the cages, because the soldiers feared we would coordinate our stories or make plans for breaking out. Given our pathetic condition and the many soldiers and guns that surrounded us, I had trouble imagining how anyone could fear us. Of course, that was exactly why the soldiers worried. The Viet Cong were famous for turning innocent situations into danger for their enemies. Because of our reputation and the countermeasures it demanded, neither jailers nor inmates could relax.

Each night I was taken back for interrogation with Sergeant Hoa and each time he asked fewer questions and beat me longer and with more fury. Each morning I was taken to the cell where the second soldier—always kindly and fatherly and good-natured—would show horror at my wounds and ask me different questions about the Viet Cong and life around Ky La. Compared with Sergeant Hoa and the endless hours in the stinking bamboo cage, these sessions were almost pleasant and I found it harder and harder to play dumb and avoid telling him about my family, whom I now missed very much.

On the third day, after a particularly bad beating the night before, I was summoned for what I thought would be my morning interrogation, but instead was led down the hall toward the shaft of daylight where I found my mother and my sister Ba's husband, Chin, who worked for the government police force in Danang. Despite the toughness I tried to cultivate in prison, I ran weeping to my mother while Chin talked to a soldier about my release. My poor mother, who looked ten years older for my absence, inspected my oozing wounds distastefully—like a shopper sizing up a bad melon. Although I could see she was in almost as much pain as I was, she said nothing, but kept a grim straight face for the soldiers. If I had fooled my jailers into thinking that I was just a naughty, runaway child, my mother's hard look must have convinced them that the beatings I suffered in jail would be nothing compared with the punishment I would get from this heartless woman at home.

Outside, Chin gave me a nasty look and departed on his bicycle. When we got on the bus that would take us near our village and had ridden about a mile, my mother could contain herself no longer and wept as I had done that first night in my cell. She told me Chin was angry at having been disturbed to help his country in-laws, especially since his own house might now be watched and his loyalties questioned because of his shadowy relatives. Although I felt sorry for him, I was so happy to be free that his future troubles—or even my own—just didn't seem to matter.

LATE MORNING, APRIL 1, 1986:
THE EMBASSY OF THE SOCIALIST REPUBLIC
OF VIETNAM, BANGKOK

I sit on a bench across the street and a block away from the new Vietnamese embassy. Over the top of my newspaper, through my sunglasses, I watch the entrance to the building—a tall wall surrounding a blue wooden house and compound filled with tropical plants—a demure façade for a shy new country. For such a crowded city, the traffic—whizzing cars and motorized rickshaws called *tuktuks*—on the divided street is very light. Thai vendors and a few mothers with children squat in doorways breathing air that is sickly sweet with ginger and exhaust. I am trying to be patient; to figure out exactly what I should do next.

Yesterday morning, after my arrival in Bangkok, I went through the decorative iron gate to visit the embassy—but presented neither my passport nor the letters I had received from the Vietnamese mission in New York. I did not even tell them my name. I was pleasant, polite, and breezy. I said I was shopping nearby and wanted information about tourism. I spoke only English, which implied that I could have been from anywhere. Maybe they thought I was a bored and wealthy Thai or Malaysian or even a Filipino housewife looking for a new way to spend her Yankee money. They were happy to oblige.

While they collected the tourist information, I waited at the counter and listened to the clerks talk Vietnamese among themselves. I felt a stab of homesickness and a tingle of excitement. These were people from my homeland. Perhaps they had been there as recently as last week. It was all I could do to keep from blurting out questions: "What's the news from Danang? Have harvests been good on the Central Coast? Does anyone know of old so-and-so who used to live on Tu Do Street in Saigon?" But it was not yet time for a reunion. When I left my village in 1965, my name was on a Viet Cong death list. When I left Saigon in 1970, at age twenty, I was known to many as a black marketeer. Either of these crimes would be enough to land me before a Revolutionary Tribunal, no questions asked. If there was one thing the cadres hated worse than traitors, it was war profiteers. The fact that I was neither would be beside the point. Suspicion alone was enough to convict you.

But the clerks' conversation was routine. They were more concerned about where they would go for lunch than interrogating a silly lady tourist. Surprisingly, I found their bureaucratic indifference a healthy sign. I was handed a pamphlet and a stack of forms. The receptionist smiled like a travel agent. I left the building quickly before I became too trusting.

My next stop was the American embassy. The difference between the two buildings was enormous. The Vietnamese embassy had looked like a middle-class Thai house. The waiting area offered a threadbare couch and wooden chairs. Pale walls were decorated with portraits of Ho Chi Minh and pictures of happy peasants riding bicycles, toting rice sacks, and pounding steel in backyard foundries. Only the Communist flag and brass nameplate outside the door let you know you were in a government building and not the field office of some second-rate Asian insurance company.

The American embassy, on the other hand, was majestic and imposing. A sculptured eagle, wings outspread and beak gaping, lorded over a cluster of flags. It was in a nice residential neighborhood and set well back from the street. A wrought-iron fence, concrete terrorist barriers, and young marines in tapered shirts guarded the entrance. Inside the carpeted entryway, the staff wore suits and greeted you with quiet dignity, like bankers. A young couple—an American serviceman and a Thai woman—talked excitedly ahead of me in line: he on his way back to an old life in the States, she on her way to a new one as his bride. It looked just like Saigon in 1970. Would they be married a year from now? Who could say. One beauty of America, among its many other qualities, is that nobody asks.

The political attaché spoke with me for half an hour in his office. He was a young man—too young to have been in the war—and I wondered how much he really knew about anything. His opinion about my trip, nonetheless, was clear. I should not go. The Vietnamese Army was still fighting in Cambodia and against the Chinese to the north. Travelers coming out reported dire poverty in the countryside and the beginning of unrest in the cities. The Communist government, adept at war, had grossly mismanaged the peacetime economy. Like Mao's cultural revolution in China, all the wrong people had been jailed after "liberation" in 1975. Apprentice machinists had been put in charge of factories. Junior tellers ran the Central Bank. Party loyalty and ideological purity meant more than technical competence or skill. Bureaucrats from the North displaced the local PRG (the former civilian Viet Cong) leaders and made all decisions in the South.

The attaché painted a very grim picture. Only Americans on official business had visited the country lately, and none of those were Vietnamese. It would be foolish for me to go.

I thanked the officer for the briefing and headed back to the hotel. My head was spinning. Once again I was caught in limbo—between heaven and hell—and didn't know which way to turn. Although friends and a few reporters in San Diego knew my itinerary and anticipated date of return, their cheery faces turned glum when I actually began the trip. Even though I had corresponded with Jimmy's father, Anh, in Saigon, his careful response to my inquiries could be interpreted many ways. He may even have believed the letter was a trick—an attempt by the government to trap him in the act of collaborating with the enemy. From the Vietnamese mission in New York I had received a list of official contacts and rules about my visit, but it was unlikely they had checked deeply into my background. That sort of thing would be accomplished once my visa application and passport were in the hands of their embassy at a regional port of entry. Weighing all the evidence, I had few reasons to be confident and many more to be afraid. I had only two choices: be gone or be patient. Give up or give god—or luck or fate—a chance to help me.

So I sit anxiously on my bench overlooking the Vietnamese embassy.

The little voice which has guided me with reasonable success so far in life is telling me to go slow; but it has nothing much to say about which direction that slow pace should take me. I am waiting for a sign that will confirm or dispel my fears. I know from experience that such a sign can take many forms. Sometimes it is just a feeling that pops into my heart —the offspring of prior emotions. Sometimes it is an action I can observe: I meet a person, hear a conversation, or see something usual in an unusual way—and suddenly the puzzle makes sense. I must be vigilant to recognize these signs, but not so inquisitive as to increase my troubles. I must be brave but not too bold. I must let the hand of fate or luck or god guide me as it will, as children are guided by parents, but I must decide which way I will be led—like a girl pulling her cautious mother toward the lion house at the zoo.

I look past my paper for the hundredth time, and see a well-dressed Caucasian woman hand in hand with a little girl enter the embassy building. *Of course.* Now it is time to go. Without hesitation, I put my paper down and race across the brick sidewalk. Bystanders look at me noncommittally. Perhaps I am not the first Vietnamese survivor to contemplate her fate on this poor bench.

Inside, I fall in line behind the woman and the child—a scrub-faced little girl about eight—who wait their turn behind a tall, distinguished-looking European, who had entered a few minutes before. Gratefully, I notice that none of the clerks from the previous day are on duty. If I go ahead and apply for my visa, at least I won't have to deal with suspicious stares.

We stand for several minutes and I search for some pretext to speak to the woman. The little girl is restless, so the mother tells her to sit down on the couch and look at a magazine. She speaks English—*English English*—and I assume that she is British. The girl brushes by me. I smile after her and then at the mother. It is an excuse to start a conversation.

"You have a beautiful daughter!" I tell her.

The woman's face lights up, "Oh—she's a corker all right. Bit of a trial at this age, though. Are you applying for papers?"

She is an Aussie—as much "American" as I can hope to find in a place like this. I relax but keep up my guard. The smile on my face is easier to hold.

"Papers?" I play dumb. "Oh, you mean visa for Vietnam? Well, I have these forms—" I fumble in my purse for the documents the clerks gave me the day before. The Australian lady touches my arm like a sister.

"Oh, put those away, luv. The mister and I just got back from Hanoi and I can tell you they've got a clerk for every paper they give you. Act like you don't understand and the counterman will do everything. It's better that way. Then one official can write down exactly what the next one wants to see."

"You've been in Hanoi?" Perhaps this wonderful woman has traveled south as well!

"Oh yes. We lived there for years. The mister's in machine parts—you know, lathes and drills and all of that."

The distinguished-looking man at the counter angles toward us. Although he wears an expensive suit, he does not look American—or even Australian. He averts his eyes, but I can tell he is trying to overhear our conversation. Perhaps he speaks English too.

"Excuse me," I say to her quietly, "is that the mister?"

"What?" She glances at the man, then back toward me, blushing, and fingers her necklace nervously. "Oh no—although I wouldn't mind if he was." She gives me a gentle, bawdy nudge. "No, Dickie's still in Vietnam, clearing up odds and ends with the business. He'll be out at the end of the week. In fact, I'm here to complete his travel papers now. To tell you the truth, I think he's reluctant to leave the country. Nostalgia, you know."

"He was Australian GI?"

"Yes. A construction engineer. Two tours. One in '69 and one in '70.

Speaks the language like a native. Fell in love with the place, I think. It's a shame what happened to those people during the war. I mean, the rubble around Hanoi and Haiphong—it's enough to make your heart break. You're from the North—?"

It is an innocent question—an invitation to share in the conversation —the usual traveler's small talk I would be happy to make if I were a usual traveler. I am convinced this woman is who she says she is, but my heart pounds nonetheless. The man at the counter is straining to hear us. I would much prefer it if this were a private conversation.

"No—no, no," I answer quickly, smiling, wilting. "Not from the North." That is no revelation. As soon as I spoke Vietnamese, any native would know that much. "Your husband," I continue, changing the subject, "he had no troubles traveling in Vietnam? I mean, having been an allied soldier? You were not followed or questioned?"

"Oh, bother!" The woman fans away my question as if I had been her daughter complaining of bad dreams. "Hanoi's as safe as Sydney. Safer, I think, since they don't have our drunks and pickpockets! And they treat us like royalty. They've always had a yearning for Western things—even with all those Soviets hanging about. I'd go back again tomorrow."

The clerk who had been stamping papers at the counter disappears into an office and the well-dressed man suddenly turns and takes each of us by the arm. It is a gentleman's grip though, not a policeman's, and it feels oddly reassuring. He steers us away from the counter, back toward the couch where the little girl sits yawning over an agricultural journal.

"I beg your pardon, ladies," the man says with a soft European accent. He introduces himself as Per, a Norwegian emissary to the UN's technology training mission in Vietnam. "I couldn't help overhearing your conversation. I hope you will keep your voices down—yes?"

The Aussie lady looks offended. "I'm sorry. I didn't know we were disturbing you!"

The man shrugs pleasantly. "Oh, you are not disturbing me. Quite the contrary. Still, you would like to continue your conversation in the lounge? Perhaps outside? It's such a pleasant day!"

In a flash I know what the gentleman means. Gratitude floods over me. "Thank you," I say. "A woman traveling alone always appreciates good advice."

"You're going alone to Vietnam?" Per asks. "To Hanoi?"

"No. To Saigon."

"You mean Ho Chi Minh City," Per smiles. "You should be careful about that, too. Our friends behind the counter are very touchy about some things."

"I suppose I need a guide." I turn to the Aussie woman, who now seems as charmed as I am by the man. "It's too bad you and your daughter are not going back. We could travel together."

"Well, luv, p'rhaps you've found a better guide! Why don't you take my place in line? Hildy and I have the whole afternoon. It was a pleasure meeting you both." She shakes our hands. "Good luck on your trip!"

She joins her daughter on the couch and pulls out a paperback from her purse—an American spy novel. Cloak-and-dagger is fun, but only when it happens in books. I think Per and I gave her the creeps.

"You have been to Vietnam before?" I ask Per.

"To Southeast Asia many times, but to Vietnam—no. This is my first trip," he smiles warmly. "The UN sponsors technical schools around Ho Chi Minh City. We've had a sizable staff in the South for almost a year now. I've been dispatched to see how they're doing."

The clerk returns to the counter with Per's paperwork.

"Look," Per says to me softly, "I don't know who you are or what you have in mind, but I would be happy to tell you what I've heard about conditions inside the country. To tell you the truth, I've been hoping to run into someone who knows the customs and language. Possibly a returning Vietnamese national—?" He looks at me appraisingly but I say nothing. "Anyway, I'm flying in day after tomorrow. Perhaps we can lunch at my hotel—it's just down the street."

Although my tired eyes are seeing double, this pleasant, helpful, fatherly man looks like a gift from heaven. I accept. We leave when his business is finished.

At the hotel's restaurant I ask him more about his agency. He gives me his card and explains the UN mission's work—training young men and women to be technicians. What he says about the country is all secondhand information—rumors and gossip and the party line dispensed at official briefings—but it seems to match what the Aussie lady had said. Although I have no way of knowing the truth behind his words, the way he says them seems sincere. I try to be friendly and keep fear out of my voice, but he notices now how I have turned every question about myself back on him. Eventually, the moment of truth arrives.

"You are from the South—" Per says. It is half question and half statement. "Come on," he smiles, "you aren't the first South Vietnamese expatriate I've met. You all have the same lost-puppy look in your eyes. You want to go home but you're afraid of what you'll find. That's nothing to be ashamed of."

My guard is down and it shows on my face. Despite myself, I give him an embarrassed smile. "I come from a little village near Danang. You probably haven't heard of it. It was called Ky La in the time of the French, and Binh Ky by the old Republic."

He admits that he has not. He then tells me what else he has guessed about me. He comes so close to the truth that for a moment, I think he has spoken to someone who knew me from the States. It seems foolish to play coy any longer. I tell him my story as briefly as I can, although his earnest questions keep us at the table another two hours. Per is no fool. He agrees I am pressing my luck. Only some deep reservoir of good sense or good fortune has kept me from announcing myself prematurely to the officials.

Although talking to Per has reassured me a little, we do not go back to the Vietnamese embassy. Instead, we go together to the U.S. embassy where he offers to sit with me while I talk again with the American officials. He will compare what he hears with what he has been told about the country and give me his objective opinion. It seems a logical plan.

When we come out of the meeting I am shaken but unmoved. The attaché is still worried about my safety. Per says I should expect that sort of attitude from my country's government. After all, they are in business to keep Americans safe in foreign lands. If they can persuade me to cancel my trip, I would avoid even the slightest peril, so it profits them to paint as bleak a picture as possible. The State Department runs a "tidy ship." They are less concerned than I am about finding my family and discovering what has happened to my village, my country, and my life. They don't worry if the fate of a few Vietnamese peasants means anything to anyone now. There is an official version of the war and its aftermath and they have a policy toward the socialist republic. Who could expect them to say anything different?

Still, Per agrees that I should take precautions. I fill out a lengthy State Department form about my itinerary, my contacts in Vietnam, and when I am supposed to come back. I am given a list of names of people to ask for in case I get into trouble. It is an impressive list, but it seems little more than a kind of bureaucratic "rabbit's foot." The Viet Cong and North Vietnamese were very effective during the war about getting whomever and whatever they wanted. I have no reason to think they will be less efficient now that they run the country.

Before we leave, the attaché asks—for his own information, of course —if there is any reason I might be held captive. I answer, "The best reason of all. I have promised my father's spirit that I will tell everything I have learned to my family, my people, and the world."

"You are writing a book?" The attaché raises his eyebrows.

I answer, "Yes."

He shakes his head sadly and wishes me luck.

Per drives me back to the Royal Hotel in his rented car. As we drive, I feel relieved and thankful. He confesses that it is not his habit to intrude on other people's conversations or affairs. He admits, too, that the new Vietnamese Government still seems mistrustful of his organization. Humanitarian motives don't make much sense to them. He says, "Humanitarianism to them is neither 'dialectic' nor 'material'!" and laughs as if he had made a joke. I don't understand what he means, but the sour official face and deep distrust the Vietnamese Government shows outsiders seem in keeping with what little I'd heard about them. He admits, too, that he thinks they are testing him—following him around and monitoring his calls, conversations, and correspondence—to see if he is really who and what he claims to be. They find it impossible to believe that anyone from the West could be interested in helping the Vietnamese people while their government is communistic.

When he drops me at my hotel, I thank him for everything and kiss him good night on the cheek like a dutiful daughter. In my room, I treat myself to a soak in the luxurious bathtub. I do not know what to expect in Sai— I catch myself now and say "Ho Chi Minh City, HCMC, HCMC" for practice—but I am certain that luxuries like these will be few and far between.

I dry myself with a fluffy towel and put on my pajamas. I climb into the king-size bed, too exhausted to unpack or do anything but switch off the light and settle in for a long and glorious sleep.

As I close my eyes, I feel more confident in my mission. Per and I will return to the Vietnamese embassy tomorrow and supply pictures for our visas, which, when accompanied by my papers from New York, should be quickly granted. There should be no reason to worry further until we touch down in Vietnam, and then I will be traveling with a respected humanitarian as my ally to speed me through my first encounter with state officials.

Still, even with the help of good omens and good luck, something troubles me inside. Providing saviors in the form of fatherly strangers who are willing to interrupt their lives in order to help others may be the way of fate, but it is also the way of governments who wish to ensure that certain people do certain things.

My eyes pop open in the darkened room. My tired brain—that little voice that refuses to be silent—slips into gear. What did I really know about Per other than what he himself has told me? Why should I accept his word without question when my instincts tell me to lump him together with glib-talking State Department officials, brash Aussie mothers, and slyly careless embassy clerks?

"Bay Ly, Bay Ly!" My father's voice, a thousand years old and very distant, hums in my head. "My little peach blossom—what have you gotten yourself into?"

The spirit voice laughs easily—warmly. I close my eyes onto blackest black I have ever seen, smile with him, and fall asleep like a baby in his arms.

THREE

Open Wounds

Mid-morning, April 3, 1986:
Bangkok International Airport

THE AIRPLANE taking us to Ho Chi Minh City is a cold cylinder, a long box—a coffin—waiting for takeoff. Try as I might, I do not feel lucky. Per sits beside me, calm and masculine in his dark suit, well-trimmed beard, and cologne. Still, I am not reassured. This morning, putting on my *ao dai* (the traditional high-necked, long-paneled Vietnamese dress) like a sacrament, packing my suitcase, sharing a hurried break-fast with Per, and then riding in his car to the airport—all this passed in a fog. Now, his fatherly presence, once so comforting, only reminds me that it's a man's world and that men make war. Both have caused me more than enough trouble in my life.

The Air France jetliner lumbers forward, engines screaming. I take Per's hand and squeeze it for all I'm worth.

"Here, here, Le Ly," his male voice says soothingly. I can't see his wry smile because my eyes are stuck shut. He covers my hand with his own. "Just relax, eh? You're going home."

Home! Home is a place you find in your heart, not on a map. People are raised to think their native country is their home, but that's not always true. Coming back a changed person to a place whose people live differently from the way you knew is another kind of homecoming. American vets coming back from the Vietnam war knew this only too well. Now, their feelings are mine and I don't like those feelings one bit.

All Vietnamese and most Americans know about Saigon. Saigon was called Paris of the Orient by the French, and like her sister city in Europe, she was sultry and sulky, brash and noisy—the yin and yang that produced everything the war became for both sides. For the North, she was the symbol of Western decay: a town of whores, corrupt politicians, and greedy citizens who measured themselves more by their resemblance to their foreign masters than by fidelity to their ancestors. For the South, she was a shimmering oasis in a desert of fear and poverty. For many Southern peasants to "go to Saigon" was a passport to unimaginable wealth and excitement.

Twenty-one years ago, almost to the day, a skinny, barefoot farm girl clad in black pajamas, an old overshirt, and a torn straw hat stepped out of the hell of her village onto an antique propeller plane at Danang, and out again onto the ramp at Saigon's Tan Son Nhut airport—America's biggest air base of the war—and into heaven. After the black-and-white life of the countryside, it was as if I had been transported to the Land of Oz—tossed into a kaleidoscope of whirling sound and color. I had exchanged the clean sea breeze of the village for hot wind that reeked of gasoline, perfume, hamburgers, Southern noodles, and tear gas. My tiny world of peasants and soldiers was replaced by an enormous universe of citizens in fancy clothes, sputtering motorbikes, and a million voices chattering in a hundred different dialects. It was as if the whole planet had come to Saigon for the game of war: some as spectators, some as players—but all with cash in their pockets, liquor on their breath, and the footsteps of death behind them.

But if the blare of Saigon's music and the roar of her traffic drowned out the cries of war in the countryside, so did it obscure the buzz of insects in a quiet dusk and the laughter of children coming home to a feast of love in their parents' arms. Saigon, for me, was such a place: both saving mother and painted, jealous sister. I have no idea now which of these will greet me on our reunion.

While Per holds my hand and tries to make me feel better, my thoughts fly ahead of the airliner: back to a time when the war with America—when the name of America itself—was a darkening cloud on Ky La's horizon.

* * *

WHEN I ARRIVED back at Ky La after my first arrest, Republican and American soldiers were everywhere. Although there had been a few funerals after the bombardment, the Viet Cong warning had saved many lives and the government troops were angry and discouraged at their inability to locate the enemy.

In the absence of fighting, the Republicans and Americans tried harder to "pacify" our village, distributing food and cigarettes, and taking our wounded civilians to GI hospitals. Still, the government soldiers who wandered too far were soon discovered with their throats slashed or with a bullet between their eyes. Whenever they heard gunshots or found more victims, the Republican and American forces would deploy and pepper the area with gunfire, artillery shells, and air strikes. Because the Viet Cong were always low on ammunition and had to make every shot count, they seldom attacked unless they were sure of victory. Because they had so much of everything, the Republican soldiers seldom counted their shots and called most attacks a victory. This pull and tug soon settled into a kind of routine for fighting the war: Viet Cong attack, government counterattack, period of calm, then Viet Cong retribution and another round of fighting.

Unfortunately, this routine came to an end about six months after my return from the district jail—just before the New Year's holiday. Convinced by the enemy's sloppy tactics that the allies were ripe for defeat, the Viet Cong decided to mass for a major attack against Ky La—a "bloody nose" for the government delivered by schoolchildren and militiamen that would be felt all over Vietnam.

First, because everyone went visiting during New Year's, our major holiday of Tet, the Viet Cong used the week of extra traffic to smuggle weapons and troops into the area. Some rode in coffins during fake funerals or right along with the corpse if the funeral was real. Others changed clothes with the pallbearers and sneaked into the village undetectd by Republican sentries. Code words were passed by people who pretended to be drunks shouting or singing in the streets. Village girls were told to prepare extra food and bandages because the battle was supposed to last three days and casualties might be high. Old men and women said extra prayers while those few younger men left around made coffins or ran off to join the Viet Cong so that they would not be left out of the victory.

Two girls I grew up with who had gone off with the Viet Cong earlier in the year now came back for the battle. When I saw them just before the fight, I could hardly believe my eyes. They had undergone training in Hanoi and were tough as old army boots. They snapped orders and wore their weapons the way Saigon girls wore jewelry. They said the attack had been planned to the last detail and rehearsed in the jungle using models of the village. Their battle code, as always, was simple: "When the enemy attacks, we withdraw. When he stands, we harass. When he is tired and disorganized, we attack. When he withdraws, we pursue." I tried to talk to them about village things—teenage-girl things, like handsome boys and local gossip—but they were not interested. War, for them, was more than a name on a blackboard or a bottle cap medal for stealing some soldier's watch.

Finally, on the evening when the Republican garrison and their American allies were getting ready to move out—to be replaced by another unit—we got word the attack was coming. My father gave the warning signal from our house—it was a careless poke with his broom at our roof—something the Republican sentries, who were always watching, never suspected. The signal was passed from house to house until everyone knew to take shelter after dark. For us, the trick would be to get into our family bunker without being seen by the soldiers. Because this was not always possible, we knew we might have to pass the night in the tunnel beneath our cookstove, as we had done before, praying—wide-eyed and terrified—while the shooting went on outside.

And as fate or luck or god would have it, the attack began too soon, catching the villagers, as well as the enemy, off-guard. Out of the shadows beyond Ky La, mortar rounds screamed in and exploded on the Republican convoy. Viet Cong fire teams inside the village popped out of their hiding places and raked the streets with bullets while the Viet Cong main force began advancing through the darkened fields.

When the shooting started, I was at a neighbor's house delivering some first aid kits I had hidden in a basket. They were for the Viet Cong riflemen the widow woman let hide in a tunnel underneath her bed. The first explosions knocked us down and when I tried to get up, the woman's bed flew back and knocked me down again as three Viet Cong fighters scrambled up to their positions. In the street outside, the Republicans and Americans dove for cover and began firing blindly, not knowing where the enemy shots were coming from.

The Viet Cong in the room started shooting and the noise from their guns was so loud I saw double. They were supposed to be snipers but it sounded like they were firing at anything and everything that moved— just like their terrified opponents outside. How many allies shot allies and Viet Cong shot Viet Cong we never knew but the melee was murderous and nothing but chaos—a riot of shouts and screams and terrible, ear-crushing thunder. Time and again machine gun bullets ripped through the poor woman's house and covered us with splinters, but miraculously no one was hit. The floor itself vibrated with the rhythm of battle—spent cartridges and pottery shards danced around our heads—and I finally covered my ears with my hands and coiled up like a baby: too terrified to move—to slide to safety in the hole where the Viet Cong had come out—or to even think about doing it. I was too terrified even to pray. All I could do was hug my head and curl up like an almost-squashed bug and wait for it all to be over.

Then, as if my unsaid prayers were answered, everything got quiet. When I dropped my shaking hands and raised my head, I saw that the Viet Cong in the room were gone. The door to the house was open, and outside, smoke billowed like an oily black caterpillar down the street. The widow woman beside me looked up too, but she was too shocked or scared to move. I crawled to the door and peeked out. Across the street, an army truck lay on its side against a house which it had set on fire with burning gas. A treasure-trove of government supplies—backpacks, tools, spilled cartons of rations, and bits and pieces of wrecked equipment—lay everywhere on the road, along with several crumpled bodies. In the distance, I could hear gunfire crackle and the steady *whump* of mortars; but here, the battle of Ky La seemed over.

Like a little black cat, I hopped to my bare feet, grabbed a first aid kit, and darted out the door. I crouched on the warm earth for a moment, making sure nobody saw me, then scampered down the street in the direction of my house. All I could think of was finding my parents and returning to the safety of our bunker.

Before I got very far, I came to a half-dozen bodies sprawled in the light of the burning truck. All were villagers or Viet Cong but only one was still alive—I could tell by his groans. I didn't see any Republican or American casualties—there must have been many—but it was their custom to remove their dead and wounded as soon as possible, even in the middle of a fight.

As far as I could see the survivor had two wounds: a big shrapnel tear in one shoulder and a bullet hole in the chest. I put a compress on the shoulder as I had been taught to do in our midnight meetings, but the chest wound was sucking air and, although I timidly poured what little antiseptic I had all over it, I knew from my first aid lessons that the poor man would not live long enough to be tended by a doctor. I tried to cover the bullet hole with a bandage but the man twitched and yelled and coughed blood so badly that I got scared and backed away. I watched him squirm for a minute, deciding what, if anything, I could do, then finally closed the lid of my stolen American first aid kit, crawled back, and said a little Buddhist prayer in his ear, and left him to his ancestors.

Near our house at the edge of the village the battle was raging much closer. The Americans and Republicans were fighting fiercely in the paddies—I could see them leapfrogging to and fro in the failing light. Flares began popping overhead and covered the fields with an eerie blue light while gun muzzles flashed like fireflies in the darkness below the trees. Overhead, helicopters and warplanes began to arrive—traced by their fiery exhaust and the deafening noise of their engines. Explosions from their bombs and rockets began to rip the jungle. Soon the whole field was lost in acrid smoke.

I found my parents hurriedly burying two dead Viet Cong fighters and although their hearts rejoiced at seeing me, we had no time for greeting. As I helped my mother roll one badly mutilated body in a mat, I noticed that the strangely unmarred face staring back at me was the handsome, cocky Viet Cong fighter who had winked at me that night the Viet Cong first came to Ky La. My heart rose to my throat and my arms became like lead.

"What's wrong, Bay Ly?" my mother snapped. "Do you want us to get caught? Hurry—cover him up!"

Hiding my feelings as I had seen the other women do, I gently covered his face and lifted—embraced—the body's head while my mother took the feet. Together, we lowered him into the dark hole my father had dug and covered him up with earth.

The fighting raged for the rest of the night and although the Viet Cong never controlled the village, they claimed later to have killed over fifty enemy soldiers at the cost of only eight. When morning finally came, my mother and father and I climbed out of our bunker to watch the sun rise on our battered, bullet-pocked home. Our mouths were dry as the dusty street but we were too tired to drink—too exhausted even for sleep. Our job now, as it had always been, was to clean up and rebuild our lives with whatever the war had left us.

For the next few days, the Republicans and Americans poured troops and firepower into the jungle around Ky La—a raging elephant stomping on red ants too far down in their holes now to feel the blows. The Viet Cong had planned a three-day battle, but they had underestimated the colossal numbers of men and arms the enemy was willing to commit to prevent Ky La from falling into their hands. Inside the village, soldiers went from house to house, tearing everything apart to find the Viet Cong hideouts. Where anything suspicious was found, the house was burned and its occupants tied up and taken away for interrogation. Two thirds of my village disappeared this way: in smoke and prison trucks during those first days after the battle. So little was left that even the Viet Cong soon lost interest in Ky La as a prize of war. Instead, they turned their attention to the one thing they knew they could gain no matter what: a grip of terror on the survivors.

Despite—or perhaps because of—the terrible battle, the Viet Cong cadremen took even harsher steps to control us. They began by killing those they suspected of spying for the enemy, usually by taking the accused from their houses in the middle of the night and shooting them in the street—leaving the bodies for relatives to discover. Later, when government forces weren't around, the Viet Cong called villagers to special justice meetings—*moi chi di hop*—during which they held kangaroo courts for the accused and shot them afterward. Everybody knew these trials weren't trials at all but warnings to make sure we did what we were told. To us, the trials simply gave the Viet Cong the excuse they needed to kill more and more villagers for smaller and smaller crimes.

Naturally, these trials made us stay on our toes and we were careful not to talk to the wrong person or go to the wrong place at the wrong time. After a while, our fear of the Viet Cong—of false accusation by jealous neighbors or headstrong kids—was almost as strong as our fear of the Republicans. If the Republicans were like elephants trampling our village, the Viet Cong were like snakes who came at us in the night. At least you could see an elephant coming and get out of its way.

One consequence of the increased killing by both sides was the growing number of parentless children. Many of them found homes with relatives, in Ky La or more distant places, but many others were reduced to scavanging in the fields and garbage dumps, begging, or stealing from farmers. They wandered around, alone or with other orphans, looking as miserable as they were. Sometimes they played with the other kids, only to stop when they remembered their situation and move on like little ghosts. Most of the time they just hung around like old people, waiting for something good or bad to happen: for a little food or affection to come their way, or for death—sudden or slow—to release them from their suffering.

The oldest child in each family was responsible for providing for that family once the parents were gone. Sometimes this responsibility included vengeance for the father's death. I think many killings in the war, all over Vietnam, came from this alone. Too few of us were able to leave hurt behind and seek life instead of death. Too many of us were willing to die, and not enough were willing to live, no matter what. I finally began to realize that *this* was what my father meant when he called me a "woman warrior" so many years before. A woman may do many things, but the first thing god equipped her for is to bring forth and nourish life, and to defend it with a warrior's strength. My task, I was beginning to see, was to find life in the midst of death and nourish it like a flower— a lonely flower in the graveyard my country had become.

At times these killings were so frequent—from vendettas against informers or fighting among old rivals, as well as from patrolling soldiers —that anyone nearby, including children or old women, was collared into burying the dead. More than once while working in our fields, I heard gunshots and hit the deck. When it was safe to look up, I would see people running to a dike or to the middle of a paddy where a dead villager would be sprawled in the mud. We would stop our work and drag the person to a space of dry ground and dig an instant grave. We even stopped wondering which side had done the killing. Someone might say, *My ban*—killed by Americans, or simply *dich ban*—killed by the enemy, without taking the time or risk of specifying which enemy it was. As months of this went by, we children gradually lost our appetite for the "game" of liberation. We were, after all, just kids. We could take only so many sleepless nights, endless hours in musty bunkers, unjust beatings at the hands of soldiers, and terror at the Viet Cong trials before all we wanted was for things to return to the way they had been before the new war started. Of course, a child must grow up—she can't stay an infant forever; just as a war, once started, grows from infancy to assume a life of its own—one so terrible that even the parents who spawned it no longer claim it for their own.

When our enthusiasm for resisting got too cool, the Viet Cong simply turned up the heat. By the second year of this new war, we could not go to another town or talk with anyone from outside the area without first getting permission from the cadre. If a stranger came to the village— even someone's long-lost relative or an orphan from another district— everyone wanted to know who it was and how long he or she was going to stay. Life in the village had gone from love and distrust of no one to fear and mistrust of everyone, including our neighbors. It was okay to visit your friends and relatives, but if you stayed too long, the cadre leaders were sure to ask about it later. If you stopped for a ladle of water, they asked why you chose to stop at that particular house and why you lifted the ladle in that particular way. And there was no doubt who was answering those questions—warping every innocent act to make it appear to be a threat: it was the younger children. They had studied the example of older kids like me and wanted to be heroes. They wanted to get their names on the Blackboard of Honor, even if it cost them, now and again, a neighbor, aunt, or sister.

Unlike suspicion, however, food and money were in short supply. Girls were expected to gather wild fruit and firewood and sell it in the market to earn money for Viet Cong clothing, medicine, cigarettes, and anything else the soldiers needed. The Viet Cong also wanted us to keep a record of every animal we slaughtered so that our tithe of rations could be computed. This was especially troublesome during times of feasting for our departed ancestors. We needed permission from the cadre leaders to consume anything more special than our daily fare and permission was not always granted. Finally, my parents decided it was simpler just to eat all our food outside so the neighbors could count what we ate and reassure the Viet Cong we were not feasting in secret. We agreed that nobody should waste food or clothing or have luxuries while our countrymen were suffering to rid us of invaders. But we also knew that the reason they were fighting—the reason they were *supposed* to be fighting—was to preserve our ancient rights and independence. When the Viet Cong began to condemn us for practicing what they claimed to be protecting, we began to suspect—at least in our hearts—that the new war we began with high hopes was over, and that another sort of war had begun.

On a February morning in 1964, shortly after I had been released from the district jail after my first arrest, I was on sentry duty in Ky La. It was unusually chilly and a heavy mist hung in the valleys on three sides of the village. My shift had started at sunrise—about an hour before—and I knew it would be a long day. The older woman, Sau, who was supposed to be my partner, had not shown up. The Viet Cong were very careful about scheduling the teams of sentries upon whom so much depended. Usually, a team consisted of one mature woman and a girl, or two women—but never two girls, for the temptation to daydream or gossip was too strong and there was always the chance that something unusual would happen—something not foreseen by detailed Viet Cong instructions—which would require quick action and good judgment. Occasionally, Viet Cong inspectors would check us if the area seemed safe—Loi and Mau were the fighters detailed most often to my shift, and we had an easy, friendly relationship. But today, even the birds stayed shivering in their nests.

The fog that morning made everything drippy and caused the world to collapse to my feet. To make matters worse, the white air absorbed all sounds from the village and ever since I arrived I had heard a faint moaning and grinding which my predecessors (the sentries from dusk till dawn) had attributed to mountain spirits.

Consequently, I put my bucket (we always carried a pail or basket to avoid suspicion) on a piece of dry ground beneath the big tree that was our station and made myself a fortress against the ghosts: sitting hunched with my arms over my knees; peeking between them and the brim of my useless sun hat at the watery wall of air.

After what seemed like half the morning, the ground gradually opened around me—ten meters, twenty, finally a hundred and more until the fog touched the dikes at the edge of the field and the trees beyond the road to Phe Binh loomed out of the mist like giants. It was then that I saw the teeming mass of soldiers on the road—Republicans, hundreds of them. The moaning had been their voices, muffled by the fog; the grinding, the soldiers' boots on the rocky road.

Panicked, I jumped up—but saw I had no place to go. The troops were already past my station and almost inside the village. If I ran either way—toward Ky La or away toward the Viet Cong—I would surely be cut down. If I stood still, or attempted to hide among the rocks, I would not only let the Viet Cong walk into a trap, but be caught in the crossfire myself. In the blink of an eye, my situation had gone from nervous boredom to one so desperate that only a desperate act would save me. Despite my terror, I forced myself to walk nonchalantly toward the road, right into the soldiers' teeth. Every few paces, I bent to pick up a sweet potato or low-lying berries that grew around the field, and put them in my bucket. When I got close enough to see out of the corner of my eye the soldiers watching me from the corners of their eyes, I hummed a little tune and paused even longer and more often. *Surely,* they must think, *there is no more loyal Republican than this happy little farm girl out gathering her family's breakfast!*

By good acting or good luck, nobody bothered me and when I was completely past the troops and within a stone's throw of the swamp (the direction from which the Viet Cong usually came), I dropped my bucket and peeled off the top two of the three shirts I always wore. The top shirt—the one I would wear all day if nothing happened—was brown. Any Viet Cong seeing it would know that conditions were clear in my sector. The second shirt was white, which I would show if anything suspicious had happened—like a helicoper loitering in the area or a reconnaissance team passing through. The bottom shirt, the one I wore now, was all black and meant that a major threat was around—a fully armed patrol or convoy of troops headed in my direction.

As it turned out, a woman I recognized as a Viet Cong scout was coming down the road from the direction of Bai Gian carrying a shoulder pole with two buckets. Her presence meant that the Viet Cong were on the move and probably close behind her. If she was doing her job properly, she would be looking for me in the fields, which were now barely visible through the mist. Sure enough, she scanned the horizon as she walked, then stopped when she saw that I was not at my station. Slowly, she looked around until she saw me in my black shirt pretending to pick berries by the road. Quick as a wink, she unshouldered her pole, pretended to have trouble with one of the ropes that held the buckets, and scuttled back in the opposite direction.

My legs went limp with relief. By giving my signal in time, I had prevented a Viet Cong massacre. But there were still hundreds of enemy troops between me and the village. I had no alternative but to continue playing the innocent schoolgirl.

When my bucket had a respectable load of potatoes and berries, I walked back toward Ky La. The Republicans by now were beginning their sweep through the fields and the quarter-mile of road between me and the village was almost clear. The further I went, the faster I walked until I dashed the last few steps to my house. Inside, my father greeted me with a sigh of relief. He had looked for me on the hillside when the fog lifted and, seeing I wasn't there, became frantic. I told him about the soldiers and the close call with the scout and he told me to change my shirt quickly so that, in case of trouble, the soldiers who saw me couldn't identify me as the girl beside the road.

We then got our tools and went out to watch the situation—but we didn't wait long. The Republican and American soldiers were back within hours, angry because their mission had been spoiled. They sent squads through the village rounding up women who fit my description. Although most girls ran away, I just stood there with my father, trusting my new shirt and loyalty act to get me through. Unfortunately, I had already pushed my luck too far that wintry day. A squad surrounded us at once and I was arrested, along with three other girls, and blindfolded. My hands were tied behind my back and as the soldiers led us to a truck, my father tried to convince the sergeant in charge that I had only been out gathering breakfast, but the soldiers pushed him away and threatened him, too, with arrest if he didn't stop interfering.

The ride to Don Thi Tran prison was unpleasantly familiar. I prayed that my old tormentors would not be on duty when I arrived—especially Sergeant Hoa. I hoped I would be kept in the arrival area instead of the awful cages, and that my sister Ba's policeman husband could be summoned from Danang before I was called for interrogation. To my surprise, all my wishes came true.

The holding room was full of prisoners—mostly girls—and because I had not been charged with anything specific, my priority for interrogation was low. Besides, as I had already learned, the questions and answers were always the same: *Why were you arrested?* "I don't know." *How old are you?* "Fifteen—I'm just a little kid." *Have you seen any Viet Cong?* "Yes." *What do they look like?* "They look like you, but with black clothes," and so on. The problem with their questions was that you could answer most of them honestly, even if you were a cadre leader yourself, and not get into trouble. For most of us, including the district police who inherited us as prisoners, the mass arrests after a raid were little more than a game. The worst part was being held captive while a sweep was going on. The troops would herd us together and make us wait in the hot sun without water or permission to go to the toilet—sometimes for most of the day. We often wondered why heavily armed soldiers worried so much about us women and children, but by this time, experience had taught them never to turn their back on a villager—no matter how skinny, little, or harmless she appeared.

Late the next morning, Ba's husband, Chin, arrived on his bicycle and gave the prison commander an order for my release. When I came out from the cell, both the commandant and my brother-in-law scowled at me.

"The logbook shows you've been here before, Phung Thi Le Ly," the commandant said sourly. "Your brother-in-law vouched for you then, but you can't seem to stay out of trouble. Well, I promise you both that if you're picked up again, even a note from the President won't get you out! Now get out of here! *Di ve*—both of you!"

I could see Chin was even more angered by the commandant's chewing out than by the trouble I had caused him. When we were outside, he pulled me up by the shoulders and gave me a good shaking.

"Look, you little troublemaker," he barked, "I'm finished with you and your whole family! I don't care if we're related or if Ba Xuan cries to high heaven about her poor little sister. You tell your mother and father that I'm finished risking my job for you. One day the soldiers will catch you doing something really bad and then we'll *all* go to prison—this policeman's badge won't mean a thing! Do you understand me?"

I nodded yes and he got onto his bicycle and pedaled away, ringing the bell irritably at some people who blocked his path.

It took me an hour to walk home, and when I got there, the soldiers were gone and the village was buzzing about my exploit.

"You're a hero, Bay Ly!" my mother told me. "The Viet Cong are calling a meeting tonight in your honor!"

It was true. Shortly after sundown, the villagers crept out of their houses and went into the swamp where the cadre leaders were already waiting by a roaring fire. When everyone had gathered, the woman with the shoulder pole testified that I had risked my life by walking right through the enemy column to find a place to give my signal. Next, the cadre leader proclaimed that his small band of fighters would probably have been wiped out by the Republican force, which meant that I was indirectly responsible, too, for saving his own life.

"To honor you, Miss Le Ly," he said, grinning in the firelight, "we will do much more than write your name on the blackboard. We will teach all the children in the village to sing the 'Sister Ly' song in your honor."

The original "Sister Ly" was a Viet Cong fighter who killed many enemies and was very famous, although she was eventually arrested and never seen again. It was Viet Cong practice to dedicate such patriotic songs to a hero's namesake when that person distinguished herself—but it had never before happened in Ky La, and the honor, for such a young girl, was unprecedented. The cadremen passed out papers with the following song printed neatly across it:

SONG FOR SISTER LY
Sister Ly, who comes from Go Noi,
Where the Thu Bon washes the trees,
Has defeated the horse-faced enemy.
Her daily rice she could not eat
Without hearing the tortured prisoners.
Although the moon is covered with clouds,
Her glory will shine forever.
One day we heard Sister Ly
Was in prison—tied up hand and foot.
Beaten by day—tortured by night
She sings "Mother don't cry.
While I live, I still struggle.
Comrades, please save your tears,
Sister Ly is still living,
And her struggle will go on forever.

After the cadreman had led the children through a few choruses of this song, he added: "Miss Le Ly is now assigned the honored task of teaching the young children how to serve the fighters who defend them. She will teach them how to resist their captors in jail—as she has done twice herself—so that they may follow in her glorious footsteps."

The villagers all clapped and the little kids, who were always the most enthusiastic at these meetings, cheered with them. My mother beamed proudly and although my father smiled too, I could see by his eyes that he was worried. He realized that my notoriety might very well put me in more danger over the next few months than any of us had bargained for.

During the next few days, I carried my song sheet around with me constantly, even though I had already memorized the words. I diligently taught our neighbors' children all the Viet Cong songs I knew but told them never to practice them at home, where Republicans might be listening. In the fields, we played the "Viet Cong game" and they all ran and hid and I praised those who were hard to find and made those whom I discovered too easily keep practicing until I had to shout for them to come out. It was just like my old war games at school, except now everyone was on the same side.

One afternoon, at a time that was usually quiet, I was resting in a hammock under the shed that housed our water buffalo, humming "Sister Ly" to myself, when I was completely surprised by a Republican patrol that appeared out of nowhere by the roadside. I could tell from their camouflaged uniforms, red scarves, and painted faces, as well as by the crispness and silence of their movements, that these were not ordinary soldiers, but *linh biet dong quan*—South Vietnamese Rangers. These special forces were seldom seen in our area, and when they were, bad trouble always followed. Where the regular Republican troops feared to go, these tough, clever fighters walked right in. Whenever I saw them, my mind filled with half-forgotten images of *ma duong rach mac*—the "slash face" legionnaires of my most terrifying childhood memories. Now, these ghosts from my past had materialized for real and their weapons were pointed at me.

I rolled out of my hammock and glanced involuntarily at the hillside, wondering why the danger signal had not been given, but it was too late for heroics. One camouflaged trooper stepped up and grabbed me by the collar. The paper with the Viet Cong song on it fluttered to the ground from under my shirttail.

"What's your name?" the soldier demanded.

I stammered an answer and prayed the paper would go unnoticed.

"Hey, look," the soldier beside him said. "She dropped something!"

The first soldier picked up the paper, studied it a moment, then looked me straight in the eye. "Where did you get this, girl?"

"I—I found it—"

"Where?"

I turned and pointed to the swamp.

"You mean somebody gave it to you?"

"No! I found it blowing in the wind. There were lots of them flying around. Just ask the other kids. They all have one too!"

More soldiers crowded around to look at the paper and I could already feel their fists and rifle butts beating me. I chewed my lip and tried to look innocent even though I wanted to cry.

Finally the first soldier shook the paper in my face and said, "You know what we do when we find trash like this?"

I shook my head, wide-eyed with terror.

"We do this!" He took out his lighter, flipped open the top, and in seconds my little song was reduced to ashes. "Wrap her up," he snapped to a subordinate. "We'll take her into the village."

Again, my hands were tied behind my back and I was shoved down the road to Ky La. As we went, more of these camouflaged, fast-moving troopers darted out of the bushes and from behind trees and dikes into the fields. Moments later gunfire broke out but it did not sound like a battle until I arrived with the rest of the villagers at the holding area behind our house. There we were held at gunpoint while Republican helicopters swarmed overhead and landed beyond the trees. Within the hour, thick smoke rose above the distant jungle. "Bai Gian—" the word passed quietly. "The soldiers are attacking Bai Gian!"

Bai Gian was a peaceful forest hamlet tucked in among coconut, orange, and mangrove trees with freshwater pools and waterfalls that were a haven for animals and birds and the many people who used to go there just to enjoy the scenery. It was also a very wealthy place with big houses and people who bore the honorary surname *Cuu,* which meant "village elder." Because it was so quiet and hard to reach, the Viet Cong often used Bai Gian for recreation, and because the Viet Cong were usually lurking nearby, the Republicans avoided it like the plague. That was before the special forces took an interest in the place. When all was said and done, not only Bai Gian, but its poorer, neighboring suburbs and most of its sister village of Tung Lam would be reduced to ashes.

Near sundown the troops came back and, although the battle was continuing, they apparently felt safe enough to let us go back to our homes. My hands were untied and with my parents I went immediately to our bunker where we lived on emergency rations for two days while troops and tanks and airplanes widened the battle zone around Bai Gian.

On the third day we came out. Although the air was hazy from dust and smoke, the sunshine felt good and we were glad to leave the musty bunker, which now smelled of our collective waste and sweat. Rumor had it that the rangers had trapped a few Viet Cong away from their sanctuaries, but the ordinary troops who came in to press the attack had suffered heavy losses. Consequently, the soldiers mopping up after the battle were in a vengeful mood.

While the other troops withdrew, these soldiers stayed behind to question us for clues to the enemy's sanctuaries. When the temporary camp by my school was too full to admit more prisoners, they set up assembly-line interrogation stations in the street and sometimes openly beat the villagers who didn't give satisfactory answers. This caused us to worry even more because such actions showed the soldiers no longer cared about our good opinion. Ominously, they seemed to talk about us the way we talked about our barnyard animals on the day they ceased to be pets and began to look like supper.

Near sundown, when all but a score of Republicans had withdrawn, the last of the soldiers began shooting at random, hitting people and animals that were unlucky enough to be caught in the streets. Others looted houses near the center of town and set them on fire with lighters and gasoline. By the time they had finished, the fire had spread to outlying buildings and over half of Ky La was in flames.

My father and the other village men spent the rest of the night battling the fires as best they could. My mother went from house to house giving food to survivors and consoling several women who had been raped and beaten by departing troops. For my part, I remained in our house and watched over the little children whose parents could no longer care for them. I dressed burns on tiny hands and put bandages on cut legs and bloody heads. The kids' terrified eyes stared back at me in the light of their own burning homes as if they expected the heroic Miss Ly to bind up their breaking hearts as well as their battered bodies. As much as I wanted to raise their spirits, I couldn't think of anything to say.

One little boy with bad burns on his arm saw that I was distressed. In the saddest, smallest voice I ever heard, he began to sing the "Song for Sister Ly." I knelt beside him and, being careful not to disturb his arm, hugged his head and chest so hard that his song turned into sobs. Within moments, all of Ky La's children were wailing as their village and child-hood innocence came crashing down around them. Although I could silence Miss Ly's song—which now seemed to me obscene—I could not silence the children's pain. For the pain itself was a voice; a voice that had risen above Ky La as a chorus of deathly smoke.

For several weeks after the three-day battle, the Republicans bombarded the area around my village—attempting to do with aircraft and artillery what ground troops had failed to accomplish: drive the Viet Cong away or slaughter them in their hiding places. Although the aerial attacks didn't occur every day, they happened often enough and with so little warning that we seldom went into the fields, and even then what we found usually did not make the risk worth taking. The paddies would be littered with rubble—upturned trees, shattered rocks, and charred craters where bombs or artillery rounds went astray. Those crops that weren't pulverized were scorched by the blast and lay withering on stalks like embryos cut from the womb. Dead animals lay rotting in the sun—water buffalo with stiff legs and bodies bloated as big as a car; disemboweled pigs and the remains of jungle animals that had run out of the forest to escape the gunfire only to be ripped apart by the explosions. Every now and then, too, we came across some dead humans—charred like wooden dolls fished from an oven, blackened arms cocked in an eternal embrace with their ancestors.

For the most part, the soldiers ignored civilian and animal casualties and we had to dispose of them as best we could to prevent disease from infecting the living. By the time we cleared our fields of rubble and buried the victims, another attack would usually begin or it would be dark and time to go back to our homes. Like it or not, we had become part of the endless machinery of terror, death, and regeneration.

One afternoon during this long campaign, some families were brought to Ky La from Bai Gian after what was left of that once-beautiful village had been converted to a "strategic hamlet," requiring half of the people to move to a more secure location. Because the bombings and periodic sweeps by Republican and American soldiers had suppressed Viet Cong activity in our area, Ky La was considered a "pacified" village, although government troops seldom spent the night here and when they did, it was always under arms.

Among these refugees reduced to begging was the family of Cuu Loi, the second wealthiest man in Bai Gian and an old friend of my father's. Cuu Loi's number-eight daughter, Thien, was about two years older than I was and a little bit shorter, with the much darker skin typical of people from that area. She was a quiet girl and we always got along well because I loved to talk and, after several years of war, there was a shortage of listeners in the village—the teenagers having gone off with the Viet Cong, the Republicans, or to shallow, premature graves. Thien was also a Viet Cong supporter, but had been arrested more often and (although she wouldn't speak of it) had been tortured more intensely and more frequently than I had. When I saw her again after the destruction of Bai Gian, she had the lackluster eyes of one who had seen and suffered too much. She clung to me for security just as I clung to her for companionship—although I could never make her safe anymore than she could substitute for my own lost brothers and sisters. Anyway, for the time being, we were all that each other had.

Cuu Loi repaired an abandoned house next to Uncle Huong, who lived at the edge of the village. For several weeks things went well—Thien's mother set up a garden and tended some hens that we gave her. Her father worked the land next to ours and we girls spent many pleasant hours together helping each other do chores. One night, however, our unaccustomed good luck ran out. Cuu Loi went out after dark to relieve himself and was shot dead outside his door. To make matters worse, no one could claim or examine the body until daybreak—such were the dangers from the government "cat" while Viet Cong "mice" were around our village.

When I went to Thien's house the next morning, it had already been surrounded by troops. After a few minutes' questioning about her father, Thien was arrested once more and taken away in a truck. When she came back two days later, she had been beaten quite badly and could hardly move or speak. I nursed her at our house because she was my friend and because her mother now had to labor in the fields without a husband. Over the next six weeks, Thien was arrested again and again, and each time returned in worse shape than before. Although she was always quiet, she now said nothing at all, and even my mother—who had never particularly liked Thien's family owing to their wealth and high station—began to pity her. As it turned out, she could have saved her pity for us both.

After one evening of particularly intense bombardment, Thien and I were rousted by soldiers from a roadside trench into which we had jumped to escape the shells. As soon as we climbed out, I knew we were in for trouble. The soldier who shone the flashlight in my face was none other than the Republican ranger who had burned my song a while before.

"Didn't we arrest you on the road a few weeks ago?" the ranger said. "Yes—you're the girl with the filthy VC songbook!"

"No, not me—" I protested.

He shone the light at poor Thien, whose face was still raw from a QC (Quan Canh, the Republican military police) beating administered a few days before. "Then maybe, it was you—"

"No—not her either!" I interrupted. "She's from Bai Gian. She's only been in the village a little while!"

"Bai Gian!" the soldier spat. "That shithole is full of VC! Here"—he called to his corporal—*"bat no Di!* [arrest them both!] Two more Charlie for My Thi."

A pair of rangers quickly put us on the ground, frisked us for weapons, and tied our hands; but cold terror at the very mention of My Thi had already paralyzed us like a punch to the stomach. My Thi torture camp—the maximum security POW prison outside Danang—was run by the army, not the district police. It was a place even the toughest Viet Cong couldn't talk about without wincing. While the rangers hustled us back to the village with the day's haul of prisoners, we were all too terrified even to whisper among ourselves.

For about twenty minutes Thien and I rode down the bumpy, darkened road with a half-dozen others, mostly grown-ups I didn't recognize. Although we were in a walled compound when we got out, I recognized the sounds and smells of China Beach immediately. My Thi was a huge camp containing many American-built shacks—some for prisoners, some for guards, some for purposes I did not want to know. As soon as we were off the truck, QCs descended on us like vultures and hustled us off to different places. I was led to a small bare cell where I would spend the rest of the night alone—listening to guards shuffling up and down the hall and, when they went away, to the roaring surf beyond the brightly lit perimeter.

In the morning, I was awakened by human screams. I got off the plywood board that served as a bed and crouched on the cement floor, covering my head to block the sound. Perhaps, if I looked small and pathetic enough, the guards would leave me alone. Such was the state of reasoning even one night in My Thi produced.

Within an hour two guards came to my cell and pulled me into the corridor. They didn't even wait until I was in the interrogation room to brutalize me, but banged me against the walls and punched me with their fists, shouting threats and accusations as we went. Inside the interrogation room, which was at the end of the same long building as my cell, I was shown a number of implements on a table in front of me. There were some electric wires hooked up to a hand-cranked generator, scissors, razor blades, and knives of various shapes (like the kind a surgeon uses), and buckets of soapy water which I knew were not for washing.

Without even asking me a question, the interrogator ordered: "Put your hands on the table!"

As soon as I did, the guards strapped down my wrists and the interrogator clipped a wire to each thumb. He turned the crank casually a few times and flicked a switch the way someone else might turn on a radio. A jolt of electricity knocked my legs out from under me and the entire room went white. A second later I was hanging from the straps, clambering to stand up. My lips were tingly and I could see my fingers twitching in the harness.

"So—you see we're not playing games!" the interrogator said, leaning on the table. "Tell me quickly: Why were you and the other girl hiding in the trench?"

"We jumped in to escape the explosions—"

"*Liar!*" The interrogator slammed the table. "There was a battle going on! You are *phu nu can bo*—VC cadre girl! You were carrying supplies! Where is the ammunition hidden?"

"I don't know anything about ammunition!"

"Then what were you doing on the battlefield? How many battles have you been in, eh? What is your rank?"

"Please! I'm just a little girl! I haven't done anything!" His hand hovered near the crank and I instinctively pulled against the straps. But instead of turning on the electricity, he picked up a short-bladed knife.

"Do you know what these are for?" he asked.

"Yes. I've seen them before."

"Has anyone used them on you?"

I hesitated before answering, "No—"

"Good." He put down the knife and stood up quickly. "Release her."

To my amazement, the guards unbuckled the straps. I backed away from the table like a wary animal and rubbed my wrists.

"Go back to your cell. Think about what these things could do to your body. How would your boyfriend or husband or baby like you without nipples, eh? Or, perhaps, I'll cut some skin off your ass for some sandals, or maybe throw a few of your fingers to the guard dogs. You think well about it, Miss Viet Cong hero—then when you're called again, come prepared to tell me everything you know!"

The guards pushed me to the door and down the hall to my cell. I knew it was as useless to worry about the torture the interrogator described as it was to try and figure out ways to outsmart him. If I was to survive, I must play my own game—not his. Experience had taught me that if you answer one way long enough, it ruins your tormentor's game. After all, for most of them, it's just a job (just like my job now was to be a prisoner). No workman wants to work harder than he has to—especially for no reward. Even a sadistic interrogator has better things to do than terrorize dumb schoolgirls when there is nothing left to learn. With my mind reassured by that plan, I had the luxury of stretching out on my small board and thinking about Thien—wondering where she was, what was happening to her, and what would be left of her should she ever be released. How hopeless it must seem to her—to be in a place like this without a father to grieve for you, work for your release, or greet you when you came back.

The next morning the same two guards took me from my cell, but instead of going back to the interrogation room, I was taken with two other girls whom I did not know to an alley between the buildings where a post was set into the ground. We were ordered to stand against the post, each facing a different direction, while one guard tied us fast with a rope. I had no idea what they intended to do with us—we were too close to the buildings to be set on fire and if they intended to rape us, we would not be left clothed with our legs immobilized by rope. I concluded that, with no interrogator present, we three had, for some reason, been singled out for punishment—and that punishment was to stand under the hot sun, without water or toilet, for the afternoon. Compared with the knives and scissors, there were worse ways we could have spent the day. Besides, feeling the other girls' shoulders against my own was comforting, and after a few moments we found our fingers were locked together in mutual support. Unfortunately, the post held other perils besides the sun.

As soon as we were were tied up, one guard brought out a can and began to brush something sticky all over our feet. When I looked down, I saw that the whole area between the buildings was covered with anthills—the small black kind whose bites stung worse than bees. Within minutes, our sticky feet had attracted dozens of them and the girls beside me were screaming and trying to drive them off, but the ropes prevented us from raising our legs. For some reason, I alone had the presence of mind to stand still. *The ants want honey, not me,* I thought, as if it all made perfect sense, *so I will stand still and let them have it.* The more the girls beside me struggled, the more the ants attacked them. The longer I stood still, the higher I could feel the hundreds of little legs on my skin—tickling the fine hair of my body, crawling along my crotch and buttocks and down the backside of my knees—but the fewer times I was bitten. To make matters worse, the guards had gone on about their business and the girls had no one to appeal to with their screams and I had nobody to impress with my self-control. And so we occupied ourselves, shrieking and pulling against the ropes or trying to hold still, while the shadow of the pole crept from one building to the other.

After several hours, our perspiration had carrried away most of the honey and we were no more to the ants than what the post had been before. The guards came back and looked us over, smirking at how our legs had become swollen and purple as berries.

"Have our patriotic ants made you girls any smarter?" one of them asked, looking directly at me. "Are you ready to talk now to the interrogator? Huh? Answer me!"

"I'm ready to go *home!*" was the only reply I could think of.

The soldier laughed and went away. A few minutes later he came back with a bucket of water. Gingerly, he rolled up his sleeve, fished around in the bucket, and brought out a glistening water snake about half the length of his arm. This he promptly dropped into my shirt, and repeated the act with two more snakes for the other girls. I knew from their appearance that the little snakes weren't poisonous, but their bite was painful and the awful slithering—as they probed my waist, breasts, armpits, and neck trying to find a way back to the water—was, in its own way, worse than the ants. Besides, whatever patience or self-control I could muster had long ago been exhausted. I screamed at the snake, then screamed at the guards, then screamed at the sky until the noon blue turned black and my voice was reduced to a squeak.

After sundown, the guards untied us and threw water all over us to get rid of the honey and ants and to help them recover their snakes. I was taken again to the interrogator's room where the previous day's encounter was repeated. This time, the interrogator tried to trick me by asking the same question several different ways, banging the table whenever my answer was wrong. "Where do the Viet Cong hide?" he would ask. "I don't know," I would answer. "Okay then, if you don't know where they hide, tell me where they come from!" Then, "If you don't know where they come from, tell me where they go!" and so on. Next he asked if I ever stole weapons and ammunition and went down the list of other commonly pilfered items: first aid kits, clothing, and rations. My only defense was to answer all his questions the same way ("No," "I don't know," and "I don't understand") and avoid playing the interrogator's game: giving measured answers to trick questions which would only whet his suspicions and draw me closer toward the deadly instruments he reserved for his final assault. In the end, he just threw up his hands and had me taken to my cell.

When the door slammed shut I found myself in darkness with a hollow heart, sick stomach, and itchy legs. I lay down on my hard little bed and tried to make sense of what was happening. I truly believed this interrogator was at last convinced I had nothing to hide, but his realization of this was no guarantee of a speedy release—now, or ever. The army had many interrogators and one suspect held in prison would be one less Viet Cong to worry about in the bush. Already, in the few times I had been moved around the camp, I recognized several people from the village—people who had disappeared years before and who, very likely, would call My Thi their home until the end of the war, or death, released them.

The next morning, however, I was taken neither to the interrogation room nor to the torture post, but to the front gate where I was escorted through layers of fences, barbed wire, and curling concertina to the sandy headlands and told simply to "Go home!"

Dumbfounded, I could only stand there and watch the soldiers go back into the compound, wondering why and how I had been so miraculously released. It then occurred to me that perhaps Thien had been released too—maybe ahead of me—so I ran as fast as I could for the road to Danang and my sister Ba's house, where I could get cleaned up and eat a meal before beginning the long walk home.

At Ba's house, however, I was surprised to find my mother waiting for me.

"How did you know I would be released?" I asked her. "Nobody gets out of My Thi in three days!"

"Well, you do, little miss hero—and it cost me more than you can count!" She immediately began inspecting me for damage, her face angry, relieved, and sad all at once.

"Chin got me out?" I didn't believe my policeman brother-in-law could have such clout, let alone such a monumental change of heart—as well as character.

"Chin? Don't be silly! He has no influence in a military camp. He wouldn't even handle the bribe for fear of a corruption charge on his record! No, I had to go to my nephew, Uncle Nhu's son—the Republican lieutenant. He couldn't act directly, but he knew someone I could approach. It cost me half your dowry, but I suppose you're worth it—" She took me by the ear and twisted me around, inspecting my backside for wounds. "Well, I can see you're in one piece. Wash up and I'll take you home before anything else can happen."

As it turned out, there was no more dangerous place we could have gone than Ky La. As soon as we entered the village, I could tell everything had changed. People—even old neighbors—avoided my glance, then stared at me as I passed. That night, the Viet Cong held a rally, but the messenger didn't come to our house. "Just stay at home tonight," my father counseled with a worried look on his face. "It's going to take a while for them to decide what to do."

"Decide about what, Father? Are they angry with me?"

"They're suspicious because nobody gets out of My Thi so quickly—even for a bribe."

"Then why don't we tell them about Uncle Nhu's son?" I asked innocently.

"That would be even worse." My father shook his head. "Then they'd know we had blood ties to the Republicans. Just sit still for a while and let things calm down."

But things didn't calm down—they went from bad to worse. Because the Viet Cong (and because of them, the villagers) didn't trust us, we no longer got warnings about Republican raids or Viet Cong reprisals. When troops appeared, our only defense was to stand still and so we were frequently questioned when Americans and Republicans came to the village—contact that only strengthened the Viet Cong's suspicions. To make things worse, our obvious estrangement from the villagers made us even more trustworthy in Republican eyes, and our house was often spared while the other homes were ransacked. Even my own father, in his attempts to protect me, wound up increasing my danger. He was certain I would not survive another arrest (Thien, in fact, still hadn't come back) and forbade me to go to the fields. Instead, he did all my work himself, even those chores I customarily did for the Viet Cong—delivering rations and making up first aid kits. My absence, however, only convinced them even more that I was cooperating with the Republicans. My father argued that I was sick—first to the Republican soldiers, who remembered me from their patrols, and then to the Viet Cong, when they asked about my absence. Of course, no one believed him, and I could see from his expression each night that the noose around my neck was also tightening around his own. I decided I could not let anything happen to my father because of me.

The next morning, I took my hoe and left the house before my parents, determined to put in a good day's work in front of everyone. On the way, I passed six Republican soldiers, who, having grown more friendly toward me over the last few weeks, only waved. I ignored them, stuck my proud nose higher in the air, and went about my business. Unfortunately, I soon heard their boots on the soil behind me.

The faster I walked, the faster the crunching followed. I forced myself not to look back, but I knew they were behind me. A moment later I heard shouts, followed by the crackle of gunfire, and hit the dirt. But the

soldiers weren't firing at me. Instead, they were all shooting furiously into the bushes beside the road. A second later, they charged forward and I heard one yell that they had hit two Viet Cong fighters—killing one and badly wounding the other. Apparently, the Viet Cong were in the process of setting up an ambush and, afraid the soldiers had seen them, tried to run away. Some of them made it, but these two did not.

Now I could hear the Republicans chatter excitedly. They were pleased with their trophies, but wondered if I was a Viet Cong spy sent to lure them to an ambush. One of them started to come after me, then stopped, looked around, and went back to his buddies. Without further delay, they took their prisoner and scuttled down the road the way they came, worried, apparently, that a bigger force of Viet Cong lurked somewhere in the forest.

Now I had no doubt that my days with the Viet Cong were over. Not only had I mysteriously escaped the notorious My Thi prison, but I had just been seen leading a Republican squad toward a Viet Cong position. Nobody would be interested in my side of the story. Nobody would be interested in the truth. The same "facts" were there for everyone to see and truth, in this war, was whatever you wanted to make it. And, as if all this wasn't bad enough, I had brought it on by disobeying my father. I was a disgrace and liability to everyone. I didn't deserve to live.

With tears streaming down my face, I stumbled down the road to our paddy and began working like a robot. As self-inflicted punishment, I would expose myself to whichever side wanted to shoot me first. *Giet toi di*—go ahead! My heart shouted silently, *Kill me! My life is over. What more do I have to lose?*

But no one attacked me that morning in the paddy—nor that afternoon. My father went to work in another field and the villagers ignored me, as usual. At the end of the day I just went home. The winter air seemed chillier than usual and even the setting sun and calling birds held no warmth for me. Workers hurried to stuff a last few bundles of rice into their baskets before the light was gone; the kids, ducks, and chickens all jammed around their houses waiting to be fed. Pigs squealed and dogs barked but their familiar sounds no longer gave me comfort. When I got home my mother asked me where I'd been.

"Working," I told her in a sullen voice, and began sweeping the house while she prepared our evening meal.

"Your father will want to speak to you," she said, and made it clear that she, too, was displeased with my disobedience. I didn't mention the skirmish by the road.

Furiously, I swept a cloud of dust out our front door and onto the feet

of two callers who had suddenly appeared in the dusk. I apologized and looked up into the faces of Loi and Mau—the two Viet Cong fighters who had been my supervisors on sentry duty. Normally, I would have been pleased to see them. Now, their hard faces made the broom freeze in my hands.

"Miss Ly," Loi, the oldest, said formally, *"Moi chi di hop."* (You must come to a meeting.)

Because we had been excluded from meetings since my release, my first reaction was one of gratitude: I was being accepted back by my comrades!—or at least was being given a chance to tell my side of the story.

"Who is it?" my mother called.

"Loi and Mau," I replied in an eager voice. "I'm supposed to go to a meeting!"

My mother came to the door with terror in her eyes. She studied the stony Viet Cong faces a moment, then said, "Give me a minute. I'm coming with you—"

"No!" Loi held up his rifle. "Miss Ly comes alone!"

I looked at my mother and a lump of fear rose in my throat. Still, there was no way to argue with Loi's rifle.

"I'll tell your father." My mother hugged me tightly, then gave me up.

As we walked through the darkened street, Loi in front and Mau in the rear—as guards would escort a criminal, not a hero—our neighbors glanced with hate from their windows. "Now you're going to get what you deserve!" their eyes seem to say. "Spy! Now you'll see what we do to traitors!"

"Where are we going?" I asked Loi, trying to keep the panic from my voice.

"Chi im di!" (Shut up!) he replied. "The prisoner may not ask questions."

Prisoner! Mo toa oan nhan dan—So I am going to my trial! Of course, the Viet Cong "people's court" followed only one script and had only one ending—I had seen enough of them to know that. As we left the settled area and the gloom of the forest engulfed us, my mind raced for an answer—what to say, what to do, to convince them of my innocence? Somehow, even the cold efficiency of the My Thi torture factory seemed more just than this. At least the government kept you alive in order to give you pain, and where there's life, I had learned, there's always hope.

After marching awhile, I could see we were headed for a thatched cottage near Phe Binh where children's education meetings were often held. My old girlfriend Khinh used to live there—she had a crush on

my brother Sau Ban and came around often before the youth corps took him away. Now, seeing the cottage again reminded me of Khinh; and Khinh, of my brother Ban. By the time we got to the clearing, my eyes were so full of tears I could hardly see the front door.

Inside, about twenty people were seated in a circle around the floor. One of the cadre leaders, a strident woman named Tram, was in the middle of a speech. Loi stopped me at the door and I felt Mau grab my hands and begin tying them behind my back. As he did so, I recognized an old family friend—a man highly regarded in the village—get up and leave the meeting. He squeezed past me in the doorway and for a second our eyes met. Oddly, there was no hint of reproach in his glance—not even the kind of fear that would drive a loyal friend to abandon me in my hour of need. Instead, the eyes were friendly—almost joking—as if this were all some kind of prank. I was too stunned by his manner—by the events of the day—to call out for help. And so the only man who might have saved me in what was obviously my trial for life slipped wordlessly into the jungle.

Feeling more helpless than ever I turned my attention to Tram's belligerent speech. I saw at once from her flame-red cheeks and raspy voice that this would not be a prosecution, but a denunciation.

". . . So, I ask you, what should we do with a woman who betrays our revolution? What should be done with a woman who spies for the enemy and betrays her comrades in the field? What have we done to such people in the past?"

"Execute her! Kill her!" some voices piped back. "Teach her a lesson all traitors will learn from!"

Two things happened now that were very odd. First, it struck me that Tram never once mentioned my name—only "a woman" who has done this and that. Second, although my hands had been tied and my escort made it clear I was a prisoner, I had not been thrust into the center of the room—the usual place for the condemned at a Viet Cong trial. Did the people at Tram's meeting really know it was Phung Thi Le Ly she was denouncing? Or was this some other meeting to which I had been summoned merely as a warning? Or—worst of all—had Tram and Loi and Mau simply decided to take the people's justice into their own hands?

"There, do you hear that, Miss Ly?" Loi whispered menacingly in my ear. "The sentence is death!"

Tram had stopped speaking now and was staring at me with hard, pitiless eyes. All of a sudden I was pulled backward out of the house and hustled down a narrow path toward Rung Phe Binh—the swamp at the edge of the village. Loi and Mau were moving quickly, as if they were afraid of being followed or of not finishing their mission fast enough. This too was unusual. All executions heretofore had been in front of a crowd. Who would profit from my lesson if my little body simply disappeared into the swamp? Such was the work of gangsters, not the liberation army—but still, I would be just as dead. It was all too confusing and horrifying to think about—and time for thinking, or anything else, was running out.

The hard dirt turned mushy beneath our feet and I felt flying bugs and dangly branches and tall grass brush against me in the dark. Eventually we came to a neck of ground that led to a weedy island in a part of the river that had been dammed for irrigation. It had always been a pleasant, vital place—full of birds and fish and frogs—I had played there many times with my brother Sau Ban and kids from school. Now, the ragged, moonlit brush and scruffy trees bobbed ominously in the wind and the black water, like the gauzy air, was silent and foreboding.

We splashed across the swampy ground and plowed through the brush to a clearing among the trees. In the middle of the clearing was a hole —a grave—with two shovels stuck into the loamy soil. There was no question about where we were headed. All I could think of was my mother and father—had someone from the meeting gone to tell them what was happening? *Maybe they're on their way to save me right now!* How would they take the news of my death? I was the last child in the family—everyone else had been lost to the cities or the war. I knew my father couldn't live without his family around him. The bullet that killed me might just as well pass through his heart. *So this is how I will repay him as a Phung Thi woman—a woman warrior—by lying dead in a swampy grave!*

Loi pulled my tied hands up sharply, buckling my legs, and I fell to my knees beside the grave.

"Well, Miss Ly, you know why we're here," he said, almost casually, as if we were about to go fishing or pick some fruit.

I heard the bolt slide up and down in his rifle, chambering a round. I swayed on my knees, trying to think of something to say—*anything*— that would keep me alive a little longer. While I fretted, another part of my brain wondered what my *ma ruoc hon*—the ancestral ghost who would escort me down to hell—would look like. Would she be beautiful and filmy, like the Christian death-angels I had seen in the Catholic picture books? Or would she be harsh and painted, like the Buddhas that guarded Marble Mountain? I concentrated on my breath—on taking in and letting out the stuff of life. Living things breathe and as long as I could feel my own breath I'd know I was alive. I closed my eyes, took in a deep, quivering, lungful of air, and—

Loi's heavy sandal kicked me over onto my side.

Although the air was cool, the sand on my cheek still held the warmth of day. I lay there relishing the sound of the wind and the croaking frogs and—somewhere far away—a barking dog and wailing baby. I opened my eyes and through the brush I could see the village oil lamps come on across the river: *ngon den treo truoc gio*, I thought—the lamp before the storm—like the light of life, so terribly hard to spark and so easy to put out. If a lamp glowed in my parents' house, it would mean my father was home—banging his head against the wall, raging at his impotence to save his daughter. My mother would be shrieking in his ear, *What are you doing? Do something!* I can hear him answer in a voice that's thick with pain, *"Dap dau vao tuong chet!"* (I cannot, so I must break my head upon the wall!)

Around me, the swamp creatures went about their nightly rituals— spinning webs, setting traps, stalking prey—and I knew I was only one of many beings on this island who would not see the morning sun. Here is where I would stay. My little bones would become a part of this tiny island for the rest of time—my spirit a mournful howl in the wind. With dirt in my eyes and mouth and hair, I was already becoming part of Mother Earth.

Loi's strong hand plucked me out of the sand and I teetered again on my knees. He forced my head out over the yawning grave.

"Do you see that?"

"Yes," I said in a weary voice.

"What is it?" he asked.

"A grave—"

He yanked my hair savagely. "Stupid girl! It's *your* grave!"

"It's my grave—" I repeated tonelessly.

"Do you know that the enemy is with your parents right now?"

"No."

"Do you care about your parents?"

"Yes."

"Okay then. You answer my questions honestly and maybe they'll stay alive. Why did you lead the soldiers to our comrades this morning?"

"I didn't lead them. I was just going into the fields and they followed me. Why won't you believe me?"

"What kind of deal did you make to get out of My Thi prison? Did you promise them some Viet Cong ears for their belts?"

"I don't know what you're talking about. My mother bribed an official—"

"Why did you lead the enemy to our ambush?"

Loi repeated all his questions as if I hadn't answered. I repeated all my answers as if I didn't care. There was no point prolonging things. I was ready to die.

"Bah!" Loi hit the back of my head and I fell over. I closed my eyes and chanted a prayer.

"What's this?" Loi asked sarcastically, "Our hero Miss Ly is afraid to die?" His rifle barrel bit into my temple like a drill, pushing my head further into the sand.

My heart shouted silently into the night, *Why don't you do it—bastard! What are you waiting for?* and I prepared for the shattering explosion that would return my spirit to the well of souls, to come back at another time and place to a better life.

Suddenly, the pressure of the gun barrel went away and Loi turned around. I heard him whispering with Mau, then his moon shadow fell over me again.

"Hey—hero! Do you want to live?"

My heartbeat, reduced to a trickle—no more than the sap in the trees whose roots would soon surround my corpse—began to pound in my head. My eyes flickered open. For a second, I almost resented my body's desperate desire to live after my soul had made its peace with eternity. But I was just a little girl and living flesh, as it must, won out. I prayed that I would find the right words.

"My life is in your hands—"

"What the hell does that mean?"

Before I replied, I thanked god for my extra breath—my extra time. Whatever happened, I knew I must try to calm things down—to keep Loi from jerking the trigger even by accident. In as soft a voice as I could muster, I said, "I mean I won't ever talk to the enemy. I have been shamed enough in the village."

"You hear that, Mau?" Loi turned and I heard Mau laugh like a ghost. Loi's hands wrapped around my ankles, twisted me onto my back, then grabbed my collar and jerked me to my feet like a puppet. He removed his peasant's hat and tossed it to the sand. His rifle was gone, but a knife gleamed evilly in his hand. He looked me up and down the way a butcher eyes a roast.

Now they're going to do it! I thought. *He's going to stab me! He doesn't want to waste a bullet!* Like an alarm, my spirit voice cried to my mother and father, blotting out all sounds in my head except the pounding of my heart. My skin broke out in sweat, clammy as a fish. Leaves rustled at the edge of the clearing and I noticed Mau had disappeared. *What's happening? What are they up to? What*—

Loi knocked me flat on my back. When I opened my eyes, the shadow of Loi's face—inches away, grotesque and distorted, scarcely human—blotted out the stars. I rolled my head from side to side, trying to escape his face and evil breath.

"All right, you fucking traitor—!" His rough hands tore down my pants. His weight went away and he stood astride me in the moonlight, frantically unbuttoning his pants. "But if you tell anybody about this, we're going to kill you for real!"

New terror rose inside me. I wriggled like a crab—flopped like a fish—toward the grave, for the safety of the hole, but with my hands tied behind me and my feet tangled in my pants and Loi's fence-post legs holding me fast, I couldn't move.

"God—*no!*" I shouted "Mother! Father! Please—no!"

Loi's hand covered my mouth, "Shut up, you little bitch—!" The hand went to my neck and stopped me from sliding and what felt like a big, blunt thumb pressed urgently between my legs. A second later it was as if the knife itself had cut my crotch. Loi's hips pumped furiously and his fingers tightened around my throat, choking me till my vision sparkled. I went limp and prayed that when this was over, Loi would at least have the kindness to kill me quickly. What choice would he have now? *None.* In Viet Cong eyes, he was now as much a criminal as me. I prayed my father would find my grave. Certainly, my lingering, shrieking soul would guide him to it like a beacon and I would then have a casket and funeral as I deserved. But not this. *Not this!*

Loi's hand relaxed and breath flowed back in my body. He pulled away, staggered to his feet, and raised his pants. His face, though dim in the moonlight, was still revolting. He hawked up some spittle and spat it over me. I turned my head and rolled to one side, pulling my quivering knees up to my chin. I tried to think but my brain was as numb as my body.

I have been raped—I now knew the horror that every woman dreads. What had been saved a lifetime for my husband had been ripped away in less time than it takes to tell. Most horrible of all was that the act of making life itself had left me feeling dead. The force of Loi's twisted soul had entered me and killed me as surely as his knife. He could shoot me now—I wouldn't even feel the bullet.

Mau was next to me. He untied my hands and gently turned me over. "Le Ly," he whispered, as if afraid to be overheard, "listen to me. If you live, do you promise to never tell anybody about what happened?"

I pulled up my pants and stared into the younger man's face. "I didn't deserve this, Mau," I said bitterly.

He didn't answer. I saw Loi across the clearing, urinating into the bushes. Loi called over his shoulder, "She's going to tell her family, isn't she?"

"No," Mau shouted. "She's too ashamed. Aren't you, Le Ly?"

I didn't say anything. Loi came back and picked up his rifle.

"Okay," he said. "We could've killed you for your crime, but we didn't. Consider yourself lucky. What happens next is up to you. If you ever say anything about this to anyone at all, we'll wipe out your whole family. Do you understand?"

I nodded sullenly.

"Okay," he sniffed loudly. "Now get the hell out of here!"

I started to jump up but Mau held me fast.

"No, wait," Mau said. "She can't go home tonight. Even if she doesn't talk, Tram will skin us for letting her go."

"You're right." Loi thought a moment, then said to me, "Hey, hero! Don't you have an aunt who lives near here?"

He meant my cousin Thum, Uncle Huong's daughter. Thum had two brothers who went to Hanoi and her house was sometimes used by the Viet Cong to hide supplies. "Yes," I said, averting my eyes—I couldn't bear to look at him, "in Tung Lam."

"Okay then, we'll take you there for the night. But say one word to her about any of this and we'll burn her house down with both of you inside! Now get up. Get moving!"

Painfully, as if I had been on the sand for a thousand years, I got up and straightened my clothes. The grave still lay open beside me, but it was now no more threatening than a post hole or a bunker. What Loi had killed in me could not be buried; yet I already felt its weight—like a shoulder pole or tumor—on my soul. My bottom stung and was wet with my virgin blood and Loi's seed, and as I walked bowlegged toward the old boat used as a ferry on the far side of the island, I felt filthy and wanted only to bathe in the river and pray at the ruined pagoda that loomed darkly above the trees outside Tung Lam.

But there would be time for all that later. In fact, my whole life now seemed burdened with time: time I would not spend with a husband for whom I had been ruined; time free of happy children that I would never bear. Curiously, despite the paralyzing fear I had felt only moments before, I now longed for the bullet that slept in Loi's rifle.

We took one of the canoes the villagers kept tethered to the bank and paddled onto the river. I could easily see the lights of Tung Lam through the trees ahead, and behind and to the east, the lights of Ky La, which was now circled with flares and aircraft.

"The Americans are back," Mau whispered, pointing to the lights.

Loi sniffed the chill air and wouldn't look. Certainly, the allies would return in force after the morning's skirmish and chances were good that Loi and Mau would be in battle again before tomorrow was over. An hour ago I would have felt sorry for them. Now I silently relished the moment of their death.

We tied up the boat on the opposite bank and moved quietly through the brush—no place at night was one hundred percent safe, even for the Viet Cong—and knocked on the door to my cousin's house. It swung open and I saw Thum with a baby in her arms. Loi pushed her aside and went in, rifle cocked and ready. There was nobody home except Thum and her three children.

"Bay Ly!" Thum was surprised to see me, "What are you doing here this time of night?"

"Never mind," Loi answered for me. He pointed the gun at my cousin. "Come inside."

Loi and Mau went in and talked with Thum while I shivered on the porch. A few minutes later the fighters came out and started off for the jungle.

"So remember," Loi said over his shoulder to Thum, "mind your own business and give her a place to sleep. We'll come for her in the morning."

Thum looked me up and down and could see from my pale face, rumpled clothes, and shivering body that I had been through an ordeal. "Come on, Bay Ly," she said softly, "come and sit by the stove. Have you eaten?" She called to Loi, "Don't worry—she'll be fine."

Thum took me inside and poured some water for me to wash. Although she never said so, I could see she thought I had been assaulted by soldiers—beaten up and maybe molested. "Those damned Republicans!" she swore under her breath, confirming what I had already guessed Loi told her. "Damn all of them to hell!" I was too tired and too afraid of Loi's threat—and too ashamed—to contradict her. All I wanted now was sleep.

I wrapped myself in a blanket and lay on the bed while Thum's children did homework around the stove. It was a warm, peaceful scene and my eyelids began to sag. Just as I was about to go to sleep, someone knocked on the door.

Thum answered it and I heard a male voice. I opened my eyes and saw Thum look at me, then step back from the door. Mau came into the room and said, "Miss Ly, you must come with me."

With every joint on fire, I threw back the blanket, got up, and trudged after Mau like a zombie. Just outside the house, I stopped and asked, "Where's Loi? Where are you taking me? What's going on?"

Mau looked back with his little boy's face and motioned me forward, "Come on. Just a little further. I've got something to tell you."

I sighed, but I figured that without Loi around, Mau at least could be trusted. I knew he felt bad about what Loi had done. Maybe he wanted to apologize. Maybe he had already reported Loi to Tram, their hard-nosed lady commandant, and Loi himself had been arrested. Maybe Mau couldn't stand the thought of a comrade so vilely degrading a hero of the liberation—let alone a young girl from their own village—and killed Loi himself and had come now to tell me I could rest easy.

When we were just beyond sight of Thum's house, Mau whirled around and pushed me down on the jungle floor. I squealed and covered my face, expecting him to beat me, but instead he sat on my stomach and aimed his rifle at my head.

"I'm—I'm sorry, Miss Ly"—his voice quivered more than mine—"but this is something I have to do!"

My god—here it comes! I swallowed hard and closed my eyes. I tilted my head upward to give him a better shot. I didn't want him to miss or just wound me. I wanted him to end it—to end all this, to end everything now all at once. This was god's mercy. I would wait for peace no longer.

But Mau didn't fire. Instead, rough male hands again tore down my pants. I opened my eyes to see Mau struggling feverishly with his belt, the rifle crooked absently in his arm. It would have been easy to disarm him—to knock the gun away and crush his testicles with my knee and run back to cousin Thum's—but what then? I could take the gun and shoot him, but would that save me from Viet Cong retribution? Would hunting down Loi and splattering the sand with his brains restore my lost virginity? Would accusing the two Viet Cong who wronged me make the cadre leaders think I had wronged the Viet Cong any less?

Drugged by too much hate and fear and confusion, I just lay back and let Mau do what he had to do. Unlike Loi, he did not spit on me and curse my womanness when he finished. Rather, he seemed like a sad little boy who, believing he was not a man, settled for the imitation of manhood Loi had shown him. That I was the stage for this poor show made no difference; for by now I knew I was no more than the dirt on which we lay. The war—these men—had finally ground me down to oneness with the soil, from which I could no longer be distinguished as a person. Dishonored, raped, and ruined for any decent man, my soiled little body had become its own grave.

When Mau was done, he got up, buttoned his pants, and offered me his hand. Slowly, dizzily—like falling in a dream—I put on my pants and got up without his help. He walked me back to Thum's house, then ran when she opened the door.

"What happened to you?" Thum asked, looking at the leaves in my hair and the dirt on my just-washed face.

"Nothing." I didn't even give her the courtesy of a decent lie. "Mau had something to tell me."

I went back to bed and Thum put out the lamp. I could hear her children asleep around me like warm puppies. While I began the endless wait for sleep, I tried to plan what to do in the morning, but it all seemed so pointless and futile. Either Loi and Mau would come, or they would not. Either I would be raped again, or I would not. I might be arrested again by the Viet Cong, or perhaps by the Republicans—but what did it matter? The bullets of one would just save bullets for the other. I no longer cared even for vengeance. Both sides in this terrible, endless, *stupid* war had finally found the perfect enemy: a terrified peasant girl who would endlessly and stupidly consent to be their victim—as all Vietnam's peasants had consented to be victims, from creation to the end of time! From now on, I promised myself, I would only flow with the strongest current and drift with the steadiest wind—and not resist. To resist, you have to believe in something.

LATE MORNING, APRIL 3, 1986:
WESTBOUND OVER THE KAMPUCHEA-VIETNAM BORDER

Per, having gotten up to use the toilet, returns to his seat and apologizes for being gone so long. He says he ran into another worker from his UN agency at the back of the plane and stopped to chat. I tell him not to worry about me; I am a big girl whose eyes are wide open. I thank him for his help so far and assure him I am quite content with my situation. I have decided to let go of useless worry and put myself in the hands of god, who has done okay by me so far. Why shouldn't I trust him for another couple of weeks?

"Good," Per says, and jots down some numbers on the back of his calling card. "I'm glad you feel that way because my colleague just told me something you should know. It seems another Vietnamese woman—a refugee from the South who just came back for a visit—was jailed for six weeks by the Communists. It seems she owed the government three thousand dollars from the war. Even after she signed a promise to pay, they wouldn't let her go; not without interrogation. I gather it was not a pleasant experience."

Per gives me the card, but with my heart now pounding behind my eyeballs, I can hardly see the writing.

"Here are some people to call if you get into trouble," Per says. "Forget the list the embassy gave you. These people are fixers. They know the system—the policemen and *bo doi*. If anybody can help you, they can."

He must have seen how pale I got because next he covers my hand and says, "But don't worry. I'm sure you'll be okay."

The pilot announces in French that we'll soon be landing in Ho Chi Minh City and thanks us for flying with his airline, Air France, flag carrier for the country our hosts had taken such trouble to throw out when I was little. America, at this moment, never seemed so far away.

Below us, the spotty clouds open up and I can see the jungle canopy, broken here and there by clustered roofs, terraced paddies, and the veinlike tributaries of the Mekong River. After a while, I notice the flat-topped buildings and low-rise tenements that mark the outskirts of Ho Chi Minh City.

Per sorts through the papers in his portfolio, his mind already on the day ahead of him. I take a brush from my purse and begin using it on my hair. It does not need grooming after the short airplane ride, but it reminds me of the way my mother used to brush my hair and I calm down. The farm girl butterflies are still in my stomach, just as they had been two decades before on my arrival in Saigon, but now it's excitement of a different sort. My girlish anticipation is tempered by a woman's prudence. My rosy vision of a joyful homecoming is tinged by the filter of unhappy memories. *Of course,* the State Department man had said, *things will be different than you remember.*

The new Saigon now stretches out before us and the jetliner banks again, rolls level, and lands in hazy sunshine. The wild winter monsoon has weeks ago given way to hot, dry winds presaging summer. As we turn off the runway, I press my nose to the window and strain to see the once-familiar surroundings of the old American air base. My joy and curiosity, however, don't last.

The jet blast of our engines sends clouds of dust curling over the once well-tended lawns of Tan Son Nhut. The buildings themselves, along with the blockhouses and towers once filled with military policemen, have lapsed into disrepair—unwanted orphans of foreign invaders. Workmen lie napping where rows of GIs once waited in nervous lines for trucks to the front, or in green bags and aluminum coffins for the last ride home. All along the runway, rows of camouflaged American warplanes—originally lined up like eagles for inspection—now sit in rusty heaps, their new masters unwilling or unable to care for them.

I see these once-terrifying birds of prey—*may bay sau rom,* fighter bombers with their brood of corroded bombs stacked around them like broken eggs—and I am filled with grief. For me, it is worse than if time has stood still; it is as if time has gone on and left the war in a cocoon behind it. I could care less about the waste of American money the old machinery represents—what mother laments a broken sword that can no longer kill her babies? No, I realize suddenly what these useless things —these scabs on the wounds of war—must mean to a people who still lack hoes and tractors to till their soil. What a victory! To capture busloads of bombs and truckloads of ammunition when what they needed were buses to haul workers and trucks to take their produce to market! I consider the *total waste* those rusting hulks represent—not just for their own sake, but for what they might have been—and I am close to tears. The spirit of war that once animated them has fled, fled even the trees and grass and buildings of the airport, and for that I am grateful. But is it peace or merely a different kind of war that has been left in its place?

"Le Ly," Per asks softly, "are you okay?"

I feel the tears streaming down my face but there's nothing I can do. I feel the scrawny little farm girl that I was, the jaded city girl I would become, my father and Aunt Thu and brother Ban and a thousand other spirits from the war all crowding in my seat. I can only nod my thanks to this kind man. I fear to speak because I don't know which spirit voice—angry, kind, understanding, forgiving, or vengeful—will answer. Per deserves better than that. They all deserved better than they got.

The airplane stops and the people around us begin gathering their things. I blot my cheeks and try to let that happy farm girl take over Le Ly Hayslip. As we move down the aisle, the airliner no longer seems like my coffin but a mother's womb delivering me to a new life in *noi chon nhau cat ruon*—the land where we bury our umbilicus. I step through the metal door and into the sunlight. The peasant farm girl drinks in Saigon's hot, wet air—yes, *Saigon*'s, not Ho Chi Minh City's!—and a big smile blooms across her face.

Lightheaded, I feel Per's strong hand on my arm. We descend the metal stairs in stark sunshine and board a shuttle bus for the short ride to the crumbling gray terminal. I notice now that at least half the passengers are foreign-born—a good sign. It is unlikely the government will harass me with so many outside witnesses.

Inside, the spacious terminal is like a haunted house. All the old ticket counters, service windows, and concessions are boarded up. Although it seems incredible, we are the only people in the building. The attendant leads us like a chain of ants, all laden with bags and boxes, to the customs dock at the end of the terminal. There, we encounter our first *can bo,* the Vietnamese officials, and I feel my muscles tighten.

Obligingly, we make little queues at each desk. I am relieved to see a number of U.S. passports pop out of briefcases, pocketbooks, and jackets. While we inch closer to the desks, I look ahead to a stone-faced, elderly Vietnamese official and his young assistant, who are screening passports, and realize the old saying is true: no matter how bad you think things are, someone somewhere is worse off than you. How much would that old man and his teenage assistant give to trade places with me for even a day, despite my fears, to enjoy a taste of life in America? The more I think about this, the less fearsome the bureaucrat becomes.

Per and his UN associate clear the checkpoint and go on to the luggage inspection tables. I step up next and hand the old man my papers. The official looks me up and down in my *ao dai,* then reads my visa—stamped by the government's UN mission in New York and countersigned by the Vietnamese embassy in Bangkok.

"Another Vietnamese-born American," he sighs. "Well, you at least haven't forgotten your origins!" He gives me the closest thing to a smile I have seen on his face so far. When he gets to my name and picture however, he pauses. He looks at me again, then whispers to his assistant, who runs off. The young man returns leading another Vietnamese official in a faded uniform. The old man drags my suitcases and boxes to the side.

"But—don't you want to inspect my luggage?" I hear the panic in my own voice. Most of the passengers have cleared passport control and are now filling out customs forms, or negotiating taxicabs into town. Between those who have "made it" and me, I see only the boy and the uniformed officer walking resolutely toward us.

When they arrive, the old agent gives the officer my passport. The man is a gristly, muscular fellow who looks like no stranger to trouble.

"Miss Phung Thi Le Ly—?" he asks, then screws up his eyes at my alien last name, *"Hai-sall-ipp?"*

"Yes, that's me—" I give him a nostalgic smile. And why not? My life is passing before my eyes!

The man reaches into his jacket. "This is for you."

He returns my passport along with a slip of paper. It is a typewritten notice—stamped, dated, signed, and countersigned in good bureaucratic form—telling me to report to a certain government office upon arrival. Although it does not give a reason, my fears supply the answer.

"Yes—I see, I see." I stall for time because I don't see at all. I'm at a loss for words. I look at the man. "But it doesn't say why."

"Moi chi di hop," the man says flatly, and my heart almost stops. *Come to a meeting,* he says—just as I had been summoned to the people's court of revolutionary justice. Now, more than twenty years later, I don't know what shocks me more: hearing the summons again, or the party's long memory.

"I will fetch our car," the man says, and departs. The teenager stays at my elbow, watching me intently.

Per has been wrestling with forms and only now notices that I've been detained. He comes over and asks, "What's wrong, Le Ly? Why aren't they letting you through?" For an instant, I am too numb to answer. He takes the note from my trembling hand. Black thoughts take over my mind. *I will never see my three boys again—*

"It's all in Vietnamese," Per says. "Does the government want money from you?"

They want my life— This can't be happening!

"Dem thit nop mieng hum," I say finally, too dizzy to separate the blur of languages and images that spin through my head.

"I don't understand—" Per says. "What does it mean?"

"Dem thit nop mieng hum—" I repeat and take back the note. "It's an old village saying. *The meat has been brought to the tiger."*

FOUR

Losing the Way

Noon, April 3, 1986:
Tan Son Nhut Airport,
Ho Chi Minh City, Vietnam

I WIPE THE TEARS from my face and put the terrible notice in my purse, snapping the clasp with finality. No more weeping. I must think clearly. I must get in touch with my higher self—that more-than-conscious inner voice that seldom speaks with words. I chide myself for giving in to self-pity in a dangerous situation. Even Le Ly the simple farm girl would not have been so stupid. Lack of awareness breeds surprise, and surprise, panic. And panic is the enemy of survival. If nothing else, wars make you appreciate what's important.

The chattering voices around me fade away and I replay every detail of my encounter with the officer, searching for clues in his tone of voice, in his choice of words, in the note shoved up at me like a gun, cruel and threatening.

I rip into my suitcase and retrieve a stack of papers: dull correspondence, rules and regulations for the trip sent to me from the Vietnamese mission in New York. Frantically, I plow through the forms, looking for one dimly recollected bit of information—my life raft in the storm that's beset me.

"Here it is—" I stretch the letter between trembling hands. Amid the fine print about rules and procedures, I read one almost forgotten footnote: "Upon arrival, visitors receiving entry authorization from the United Nations mission will be briefed on travel conditions by the Vietnamese National Committee. Transportation from the visitor's port of entry will be provided if available."

Warm blood flows back to my fingers and toes and I laugh but it's more like a choke.

"Of course!" Per's relief is almost as great as mine. "You applied for your visa through New York! The note that fellow gave you—it's an invitation, that's all. They just want you to come to a travel briefing!"

With wobbly legs, I go to a bench and sit down. I read the UN paper again and compare it with the notice. The Vietnamese writing is in a Northern dialect so I have trouble understanding every word—but they seem to match. I don't believe it! Did I really think this trip would be a holiday? Did I panic because of a guilty conscience—did I *really* believe I owed my life to the Viet Cong, payment for a crime I didn't commit? Or am I just too excited about seeing Anh again—too preoccupied with memories of a girl's first love to think through details that, in a place like this, can mean the difference between safety and danger?

Per looks at me curiously. He must think this flighty female has no hope of caring for herself. I notice that without the beard, with eyes of another race and in another time, the expression could be Anh's. It was the way he first beheld me when I came to serve his household, and later—to share his spirit and his life.

* * *

WHEN I TURNED THIRTEEN and was blessed with the woman's curse of menses, my parents betrothed me to Tung, a sixteen-year-old boy from the neighboring village of Tung Lam. My father was quite happy when he announced the marriage contract—intended to be consummated three years hence with rites, drums, gongs, and feasting with all our relatives. For him, it was another step toward fulfilling my destiny as a Phung Thi Chin—a woman and woman warrior who would, with her womb now as well as spirit, link his ancestors to the generations that would follow. My mother was not so sure. She had other married daughters and because I had been the family's baby for so long, was unsure that I would be capable of winning my future mother-in-law's approval.

"What does a baby know about raising other babies?" she muttered to herself. "How can Bay Ly take care of a man when she can barely take care of herself?"

For my part, I was uninterested in destiny or responsibilities. I only wanted to see more of this boy who was to be my husband—to see if he was as beautiful as the husband in my dreams or as kind and wise as my father. Tung was three years older than I was and was a graduate of the local elementary school, which meant he was qualified to be a teacher himself. I first saw him on the night Manh was killed, when Tung and his father came to us for shelter, afraid the Republicans were after them. After that, we saw each other only at a distance, although he sometimes walked by my house on his way to teach the first- and second-graders and stared at my window longer than was polite. For my part, I would sometimes stare at his house, which was occasionally visible across the river in Tung Lam, and fantasize about the life we'd have together, but these daydreams never got too romantic. In our society, marriages were arranged like business deals and I would have to make do with whomever my parents selected. Consequently, I came to think of Tung more like a distant cousin who would one day share my roof, than the prince of a young girl's dreams. As it turned out, this detachment spared me tears I could ill afford to shed.

Shortly before my fourteenth birthday, in 1963, Tung joined the Viet Cong and was soon thereafter reported missing in action and probably killed. That was typical of the war—nobody knew anything for certain, and even our Tung Lam relatives couldn't verify his death. Because Viet Cong fighters were buried as soon as possible after a fight, and because the cadre leaders seldom admitted their true losses, there was a chance we would never know what happened.

So, on the long, cold hike through the night to catch a bus to Danang—at the beginning of my exile from Ky La to escape the further wrath of the Viet Cong—I asked my mother what would happen if Tung turned up alive at the end of the war. Although I had come home after my night at Thum's and told her promptly about the mock trial and my almost-execution, I revealed nothing of my double rape. Although this was mostly to safeguard my parents' lives (Loi, after all, was fully capable of carrying out his threat), it was also due to shame. Because part of me still wanted to believe it never happened, the other part of me went on fantasizing about things that might have been. From that perspective, a dead fiancé was the best suitor I could have, even though I might be cursed with *song trong mong ao*—dreams haunted by Tung's restless, unfulfilled spirit. Still, despite her ignorance of my true condition, my mother told me to be silent. She was as bitter about things as I was numbed by them.

"Don't torture yourself with impossible dreams," she said, hustling me along by the hand. "You're an exile from your home. The village has turned against you. You can forget about living a normal life. And forget about outlasting the war, eh? The war will go on forever. The village—the whole country—must have done something terrible for fate to punish us so much. But that's our karma. If you're lucky, you'll go to your ancestors before you have to suffer anymore. That's the best any of us can hope for these days—a quick end and better luck in another life!"

In Danang, we discovered that my brother-in-law, Ba's husband Chin, would have nothing more to do with me. My last adventure with the provincial police had almost cost him his job and my mother was forced to promise that we would ask him no more favors. It was all she could do to convince him to let me stay in my sister's house for a week—just long enough to find another place to live.

Fortunately, it was only a couple of days before Ba found me a job as housekeeper with a family that lived on the outskirts of Danang. In exchange for my bed and board, I looked after the children while the husband (a petty district official) worked and the wife ran a general store at the front of their property. They had five children very close in age and because the mother worked nearby and the grandparents lived in the adjacent house, help was always close if I needed it.

In the evenings, I would take the family's dishes outside and wash them with the woman's sister, who also lived next door. She was about my age and within weeks we became good friends. After doing the dishes on Fridays, we would run down to the Catholic church and check the weekly casualty lists the priest had nailed to the door. This was the only news we got from the countryside (because she was so young and I was just a servant, nobody told us anything) and I thanked god each time the list went up with names I didn't recognize. Each week the list got longer, though, made worse by a second civil war that had broken out between the Catholics and the Buddhists, and after a while I began to worry about my parents. I felt guilty for my life of relative safety in Danang, although I didn't know how long it would last.

My employer was a sloppy fat fellow who, although he was only forty, looked older than my father. He generally ignored me when his wife and his children were around, but when their backs were turned, he leered at me and made comments that could only have one meaning.

One hot afternoon when the children were all sleeping, he came back for lunch and told me to go to the front of the house and see if his wife was still working.

"Do you want me to call her for lunch?" I asked stupidly.

"No—don't say anything," he snapped. "Just see if she's busy."

When I returned, he was dressed only in his undershirt and shorts and was drinking a bottle of beer. I told him the store was open with a long line of customers waiting. As soon as I said this, of course, I knew it was a mistake. For a long time my boss had wanted to get me alone, undisturbed by his wife or children, and I could tell from his expression that this was just the opportunity he wanted. He sat on a beat-up kitchen chair and motioned me over. Reluctantly, I compiled.

"Come here, Le Ly," he said with his oily voice. "Have you ever tasted beer?"

I said no, I hadn't, and he insisted I stand next to him and take a long drink from the frosty bottle. The brown liquid tasted as bad as it looked and I coughed a mouthful all over his chest and the rising lump in his underpants. His lust shrank quickly and one of the kids started crying and I ran from the room to take care of her. When I came back out, baby on my arm, both my master and his clothes were gone.

That night my friend and I checked the casualty lists, as usual, and returned with the dishes in our baskets. I said good-bye to her on her doorstep and stopped by the store to see if my mistress needed anything before I went back to the house. There was a long line outside (people were hoarding food because of the religious riots) and she said to tell her husband she could not close up for an hour. I groaned when I heard this and steeled myself for an evening of dodging his advances until his wife got back.

Although the shop had electric lights (it was next to the street and used city services), the vacant lot that connected the store to the home was unlighted and dotted with trees. Even though the children played here during the day, it was a creepy place at night and I hated to walk through it alone. This time, my fears were justified. As I passed the last big mulberry tree an arm reached out and caught me by the neck. The dishes went crashing and I tried to scream but a hand covered my mouth and threw me backward on the dirt. Instantly, a heavy man was on top of me and while one set of sticky, chubby fingers covered my mouth, another groped under my shirt. A beery voice slurred, "Oh, come on, Le Ly! Don't fight me! I can make things nice for you! Just hold still!"

It was my employer—the fat toad had gotten drunk and decided to waylay me on my way to the house! My thoughts froze midway between

terror and disgust. *This can't be happening—! Not again!* Although my instincts told me my life was not in danger—at least at the moment—I
reacted as if the playground were a battlefield. My stiffened fingers jabbed
his throat and as the beery breath choked off, I kneed him as hard as I
could. When his hands finally dropped, I wriggled free and ran to the
house.

When he staggered in a few minutes later, I was surrounded by his
children. I gave him a piercing stare but he was in no mood for trouble.
He cursed and gave me a rude gesture and went to bed. When his wife
came home later, I was chewed out for breaking the dishes and told I
would have to replace them. I didn't tell her what had happened, since
I couldn't leave without my mother's permission and I didn't want to
make things worse by starting a fight between my bosses—one that would
probably end with my being kicked out. Having a place to live—even
with a bad boss and an unjust debt—seemed better than being homeless.

Nonetheless, I sent a note to Ba the next day telling her that my job
was a "bad situation getting worse" and that she should send for my
mother right away. From the time of my attack to the time my mother
got me, I stuck close to my friend next door or huddled among the kids.
Because it was hard to do these things and do my chores at the same
time, the wife complained to my mother that I had become a lazy worker.
Still, she knew her husband well enough to let me leave without paying
for the dishes.

After we left, I told my mother what had happened and she commanded
me never to speak of it. "What do you want people to think," she asked,
looking at me as if everything had been my fault, "that you are a husband
tease and a tattler? No. Never anger the people who feed you. We'll go
see Uncle Nhu. Maybe he can keep you under control."

At Uncle Nhu's I fared little better. Although I was soon living with
a hard-working family of honest people, watching their happiness day in
and day out only made me miss my parents more. I had trouble sleeping
and my stomach sometimes hurt, even though I had plenty to eat. Whenever I could, I ran errands to the market just to see if I could find anyone
from Ky La who would give me some news from home. Unfortunately,
most villagers knew that I had been condemned by the Viet Cong and
so were reluctant to talk to me, even in the city. Most of the time they
just turned their backs and ignored me when I approached.

One day a nine-year-old boy for whom I used to baby-sit came to the
market with his parents. Because I knew the parents would reject me, I
followed them secretly until I could signal the boy from hiding. He smiled

when he saw me and dashed forward with outstretched arms. Although she didn't see me, I heard his mother call him back but his father said, "Never mind—let the boy have fun. He'll be back when it's time to go."

After giving each other a hug, I started to take him by the hand—to go sit under a tree where he could tell me all the news—but he pulled away and said with a worried face, "Le Ly, you've got to go home. Something terrible's happened to your family!" Before I could find out more, he ran back to his parents, afraid, like the others, to be seen with the "traitor Miss Ly."

I went back to where I worked and cried for the rest of the day. Perhaps the boy had been sent by the Viet Cong to lure me back, I wondered, utterly possessed by my fears. *Perhaps my parents were already dead!* I just couldn't stand not knowing. But going back was worse than risky—it could mean death for my mother and father if things were really okay. I decided to ask Uncle Nhu for advice.

"Don't go!" my uncle said, shaking his head. "Aren't you in enough trouble already? Besides, the government has checkpoints on all the roads and the Viet Cong control the countryside. Don't make things worse for yourself. Just wait for your parents to come to you."

But waiting, I decided, was not for Phung Thi women. I concluded that my uncle Nhu had grown soft and feeble living in the city—even one so poor as Danang—and was beginning to think like an old man. I asked him for some food to give my parents, then went to my employers and told them I was leaving. At sundown the following day, I set out alone for Ky La.

Winters are cold and wet on the Central Coast, and a storm had been raging since morning. It was a bad time to be outdoors anywhere, even for the Viet Cong, and so it was a perfect time for my march to Ky La. Unfortunately, what was usually a half day's walk in fine weather was made longer not only by the storm, but by the circular path I had to take. Although I had made many unpleasant trips between Ky La and Danang—as a child fleeing the French or on demonstrations for the Viet Cong—none was as miserable as that one night alone in the jungle, hills, and swamps. At once I lost my sandals to the mud and the soles of my feet were cut by jagged rocks in the darkness. In the marshes, sharp-bladed saw grass sliced my hands while crabs nipped at my feet and leeches drank blood inside my clothes. Driving rain stung my skin like bees and wind roared through the hills in gusts so strong I was stopped several times in my tracks. By the time I reached Ky La and daylight had turned the angry sky gray, I had lost not only my gift of food but most of my clothes and a good deal of skin.

Like a miserable caterpillar, I crawled on my belly below the dikes until I reached some reeds a stone's throw from where my father was working in the fields.

"*Cau!*" (Father!) I gave a feeble cry.

"Eh? *Ai do?*" (Who's there?) My father brandished his hoe as if it would protect him from flamethrowers and bazookas. If I had been an enemy, given all the weapons around Ky La, the ground beneath him would already be scorched. Sometimes I wondered what went through his head.

"It's me—Bay Ly!" My hoarse whisper in the drizzle made me sound more like a little kid than ever, and that smallness made me angry.

Fortunately, my father was smarter than I remembered. As soon as he saw my pathetic face among the reeds, he turned his back and continued hoeing. Too many eyes might be watching to make a proper reunion. "What are you doing here?" he asked the empty field.

"I came to see you and Mother!" My original grand idea of saving them now seemed preposterous even to me. All I wanted was to be safe and warm and fed.

My father smiled the way he smiled when I was a very little girl and did equally stupid things. "Well, you've seen me," he said, trying to sound serious, "and you'll see your mother when she comes to visit you in Danang."

"But the little neighbor boy—the one I used to baby-sit for—said you and Mother were in big trouble! I thought our house had been destroyed!" Even as I spoke, of course, I could see our home sitting quietly in the rain.

"Well, you thought wrong, didn't you?" My father chopped at a weed. "Listen, Bay Ly—everything's under control. When it's lunchtime and everyone's in from the fields, I want you to go to the house. Your mother will be there and will give you something to eat. But you can't stay in Ky La. It's too dangerous. After dark, you'll have to go back to Danang."

That noon, my mother welcomed me with hugs and tears, then boxed my head for coming back. While I dried my hair by the fire and dabbed my cuts and put on warm clothes, she cooked a hot meal and told me about her troubles.

"The Viet Cong think you're hospitalized in Danang," she said, chopping sweet onions. "They were angry at the guards for taking pity on you and angry at me for helping you escape. To make amends, I was appointed village watchdog in your place. I was told to watch the road between here and the jungle and give a signal if the enemy approached."

She stopped talking a moment, as if she were still sorting things out in her mind, then said, "About a week ago, two Viet Cong fighters were killed by a Republican patrol that sneaked into the village. Nobody knows how the enemy got here—maybe through one of the old tunnels. Anyway, they blamed the village watchdogs, including me. Now I'm under house arrest."

I started to ask her what that meant, but she just put my food in front of me and said, "There—now you know everything. Be quiet and eat your meal."

But her red eyes and long face told me there was much more to her story than that. Later in the day, when she was out tending the chickens, I asked my father what really had happened. He shook his head sadly.

"Your mother didn't tell you? Well, I'm not surprised. She still won't talk about it, even with me." He dug at his crooked teeth with a bamboo toothpick. "It seems your mother came back from the fields and found some Republican soldiers in our house. They knew she was a sentry and made her stand in front of the window facing the swamp. They told her to signal 'all clear' so that some Viet Cong would come into the village. Of course, she didn't signal anything. She just stood there and waited, hoping nothing would happen."

My father glanced out the window to make sure my mother was still occupied with the hens. "About dusk, two Viet Cong came out of the forest. It was stormy then, just like now, and they walked with their heads down into the wind so they couldn't see where they were going. They were almost to our door when your mother finally yelled, but it was too late. The soldiers rushed out to capture them but the two fighters resisted and were killed. I think you knew them. One was Loi—the tall fellow, the cadre regular. The other was old what's-his-name—you know, the little guy who followed him around. Mau—that's who it was."

My god! They were the Viet Cong guards who raped me! I could not tell my father about this terrible coincidence—even my mother didn't fully know what happened. As much as I felt gratified by the news, I was afraid my bitter exaltation would be reflected on my face, so I quickly covered my cheeks with my hands as if overcome by grief.

"I'm sorry if they were your friends, Bay Ly. At least they were spared a death by torture." My father caressed my hair, then continued, "A couple of nights later, the Viet Cong came back in force and arrested everyone who'd been on watch. They went through the village shouting 'Come to a meeting!' and paraded your mother and four other women, hands tied, to a clearing outside Bai Gian. They even tied my hands so I couldn't interfere and told your uncle Luc to come along as a witness. When we got there, the leader accused each woman of collaborating with the enemy. When he got to your mother, she replied that she had given a warning, but had simply shouted too late. The leader slapped her and said she should have sacrificed her life, if necessary, to save the fighters.

"So the cadre leader pronounced them all guilty and lined them up on their knees in front of the crowd. One by one, he walked down the line and blew their brains out with his pistol. Your mother was last in line. When he got to her and put the barrel behind her ear, I closed my eyes and started praying. But your uncle Luc jumped out and told the cadre leader to stop. He asked how a woman who sent her oldest son to Hanoi could even think of betraying her country. He said, 'Huyen has six nephews and two sons-in-law right now out fighting the enemy—how dare you accuse her of treason!' You have to remember, Bay Ly, Uncle Luc is well known to the cadre. He's supported them for years and helped their saboteurs in Danang. His appeal gave the cadre leader time to realize what he was doing. He had just killed four of the five village mothers he had arrested and killing them all, without showing any mercy, might have turned the people against him. So he eased the hammer down and told your mother to get up. He said that for her, the revolution would be lenient and he paroled her to Uncle Luc. He said she had to stay within a hundred paces of our house and not associate with our neighbors."

My father let out a long sigh. "With that, the meeting was over. The other families buried their women and Luc and I took your mother home—she was too shaken to walk by herself—where she's been ever since. So you can see, you're safe enough if you stay inside. Nobody comes anymore to visit. But the cadre leader told Uncle Luc he wants you back after your wounds have healed. He says your sentence has also been commuted from death to hard labor in the cause of liberation."

"Do you believe him?"

"I believe he wants you back. What happens after that—who can say?"

Our life in Ky La had finally become intolerable. That moment on her knees—the four crumpled bodies beside her, the cocked pistol behind her ear, eternity staring her in the face—had turned the world upside down for my mother. She no longer understood what the war, truth, or justice were about. She had even lost those few simple joys a peasant woman gleaned from a hard life in the countryside. She became a shadow woman, ostracized by neighbors and confined to her house, garden, the nearby well, and a stretch of dusty road a hundred paces in either direction. She used to walk to the limit of her prison like an old dog at the end of its rope and just stand there, pressing against the unseen bonds that held her. I think she secretly hoped that she would one day be seen stepping across that invisible line and the long-delayed shot would ring out, releasing her miserable spirit from the hell of Ky La for the harmony of life with her ancestors. It was a death wish I myself had felt after my own conviction, rape, and reprieve. Everyone thought we should be happy escaping Viet Cong justice; but there is something about a borrowed life that can never be fully lived. It was the first of many upside-down feelings I would try to understand in the months and years ahead.

During these weeks I wandered between Ky La and Danang like an orphan, sometimes staying with my sister Ba, sometimes with Uncle Nhu; sometimes as a housekeeper when I could find a proper family with extra children and extra food. But my soul was restless and gnawing pains in my stomach became a constant companion. When it seemed safe (and later, whether it seemed safe or not), I went to Ky La and visited my parents, even though they seemed a little closer to the grave each time I saw them.

Finally, my father could bear our life in limbo no longer. He went to Uncle Luc, who was our warder, and asked him to petition the Viet Cong for our release—our pardon—in exchange for exile to another place. My father never told me how this bargain was struck, but he woke us up one night and told us to get dressed. My mother and I would be going to Danang and from there by plane to Saigon where my sister Hai and other friends would help us "find a situation"—a place to live and a way to earn a living. He had made a deal for our lives, but it meant that we must go far away and not come back—at least until the war was over. It meant too that he must remain behind—to keep our land and worship the ancestors its soil protected. These things—the crops, the jungle, the livestock, the incense on our altar—would be his only companions. I knew from the look in his eyes that the burdens of exile would fall as heavily on him as on us.

We did as my father commanded; my mother reluctantly, because she was leaving the place where she had raised her family and lived most of her life; me, with great relief and growing excitement. I was fed up with the terror and privation of wartime village life and hated both the Viet Cong and the government for what they had done to me and my family. I also knew that Saigon was every country girl's vision of nirvana.

Although my sister Hai had lived in Saigon for several years, the best stories I had heard about the place came from Bich, a beautiful girl a few years older than I was whose father had gone to Hanoi with my brother Bon. Because Bich was so loyal to the Viet Cong, they helped her move to Saigon where she first worked as a housekeeper and then as a bar girl to spy on the Republicans. When she came back to Ky La in 1962 to visit her mother, it was as if she had returned from another planet.

Her beautiful black hair, which had always been very long, was now piled up like a beehive on her head and made brittle as a bird's nest with hair spray. While we sat together one evening, dangling our toes in the river, she told me about such marvels as flushing toilets and streets so long you had to take a bus to go from one end to the other. She said women wore *makeup* and brassieres and high-heeled shoes to make whatever they had look better and to help men distinguish one woman from another. She had begun to learn English (*"Everyone* speaks English in Saigon!") and from her work as a bar girl could mix forty kinds of drinks. She regularly wore clothes that left her shoulders and arms and thighs and the tops of her breasts exposed, which scandalized me because she had always been so sweet and proper in the village. In Ky La, we girls were taught to hide our bodies and our feelings from men. We did nothing to make ourselves look prettier, for pretty in wartime meant danger— although for some girls it also meant money. Only when I asked further about this did I learn the difference between real prostitutes and women who simply looked like prostitutes to please their men. I was happy to learn this difference because Bich's way of life sounded exciting and although I desperately wanted to wear makeup and fancy clothes, I didn't want to become a hooker and suffer the scorn such women earned. Besides, what they did did not seem fair to the men who were their customers. Why would a man pay a woman to go through the act of making babies, I reasoned, and then end up without a child for all his trouble? Perhaps such men went to prostitutes because they were so stupid. Anyway, Bich told me other things as well: about drugs and con men and ladies who took young country girls off buses when they arrived in Saigon and turned them into slaves—but little of that made sense and the place still sounded like heaven, particularly when she said the war had not yet come to that city.

My mother and I left Ky La in the middle of the night and neither of us looked back. We caught the old bus to Danang, where my sister Lan bought our airline tickets with some of the money my mother had saved for my dowry. Since I knew I could never be a proper bride, saving gold now for a marriage seemed a terrible waste, so I would have been the last one to complain.

We boarded the refugee plane with a host of other peasants. (Officials, Americans, and wealthy Vietnamese all flew in military planes or in the modern airliners that crisscrossed the sky at all hours of the day and night.) I was barefoot and wore only my black peasant's pajamas, an extra shirt given to me by my sister, and a farmer's sun hat, which was my only souvenir from Ky La.

The ride in that shaky old propeller plane was, of course, the high point of my young life. Even my mother, who had seen her share of airplanes when she and my father helped build the original French airstrip at Danang, wore a silly, terrified grin most of the trip. For me, however, the flight was much more than a thrilling ride. When we left the ground and banked gently over the ocean, it was as if I was seeing my homeland for the very first time—taking it all in at a glance like god in heaven— and I felt my first true sense of peace. The pale sky seemed infinite and I was climbing toward it like a celestial spirit. The shiny blue ocean with its ribbon of surf, the patchwork of paddies and dusty lots and lumpy green hills all grew smaller in my eyes the way a mother dwindles in the eyes of her growing daughter. In those few moments, I soared above and beyond all the tragedies I had known. That wonderful sense of climbing above and leaving things behind would come to me again and again in my life and I would train myself to listen for its secrets. Although I did not realize it at the time, that flight and those feelings brought with them something else, something I had never experienced in Ky La, something even my wonderful parents—who knew everything about life and duty —could not, for their own heavy burdens, give me: the simple feeling of *hope*.

Unfortunately, such feelings rise like morning mist and evaporate too quickly. In a short time, we were circling to land at Tan Son Nhut and the immense and frightening city of Saigon was spread out below us like a gray-green carpet of welcome.

Safely on the ground, our airplane taxied—nose in the air like a snooty bird, waggling its tail back and forth as it went—past rows of green and brown warplanes bristling with bombs and rockets and covered with GIs in T-shirts or no shirts at all. When we stopped, the sea bird's silver door dropped open and we vomited out of its gullet like a sickly catch, stumbling over each other to be first for the luggage, first for the toilets, and first on the buses for the half-hour ride into town.

Because our baggage was our clothes, my mother snaked through the crowd and got us seats on the Air Vietnam bus ahead of everyone— despite the way her silly teenaged daughter kept stopping to gawk at the terminal's shops and restaurants; at the handsome, well-dressed men of every race, and beautiful women in swirling *ao dai,* who floated like water lilies among them.

Our Saigon bus (which was much nicer than the rattletrap that ran from Ky La to Danang—a good omen) took us past ancient French plantations with columned houses, broad lawns, and rows of palm, eucalyptus, and banana; past enormous Buddhist temples, swept clean and

swathed in banners (a welcome contrast to the rural temples that had
been bombed and neglected in the war); and, in the city itself, miles and
miles of traffic—cars, trucks, buses, convoys, taxis, jeeps, motorbikes,
siclo pedicabs, and bicycles—in front of the bus and behind it, beside it
and on the sidewalks, in the alleys and on the curbs—some even driving
into the buildings beneath giant garage doors! It was all too much for
one farm girl to take in at one sitting. When we got within walking
distance of our family's friends, my head hurt as much as my bottom
from the constant stopping, starting, and staring.

We got off the bus at Ham Nghi Street and took a *siclo* to a block of
seedy tenements that were, up to that time, the grandest buildings I'd
ever seen. The people who received us had moved from Ky La to Saigon
many years before, when I was a toddler, and although my mother greeted
them like relatives, I felt I was in the house of strangers—made stranger
still by their city ways. Their narrow apartment was cramp-crowded with
useless funiture and decorations. Their family shrine, with candles and
incense pots for each departed soul, was not well kept, which showed
impiety for their ancestors. Their children, which included one boy about
my age, were very impolite. They didn't bow to their parents and interrupted them all the time. Consumed by the strange new things and odd
smells and the spectacular view through their filthy window, I only half
listened to my mother's explanation for our sudden appearance, and her
attempts to discount the nasty rumors that had preceded us. *Yes, Trong's
okay. No, we weren't wiped out by the Viet Cong—where did you hear that?
Oh, don't listen to her! Well, it's all a misunderstanding. We'll only be in
Saigon awhile. Can you fix us up with a place to stay? Bay Ly is an experienced
housekeeper. Yes—she pleased a wealthy official when she worked in Danang!
He had a very demanding wife, you bet! Oh, ten children? No problem. Bay
Ly will have them calling her "auntie" before the first day is out. Do you
think they'll have a bed for me?*

Despite all the chitchat, my mother was begging from these sterile city
people and I began to feel that everything here would be wrong. My head
ached and my stomach hurt and all I could think of was my father. In
Ky La, good luck or bad, everybody knew us. We had land and roots
and a connection with our ancestors as well as the people around us.
Here, we were less than the wind—vagabonds with only the clothes on
our backs—ghosts who, unlike real people, had no place to sleep or even
a way to keep ourselves fed. I also found myself at the receiving end of
lusty glances from their teenaged boy (I had seen that look before!), who
smoked cigarettes like his father and complained loudly about this and

that and laughed rudely at my mother's country accent. Still, he was part of Saigon and Saigon's magic was too new and powerful to leave me anything but intoxicated.

My mother and I spent our first city night on their kitchen floor, curled around each other like dogs. The next day we went calling on everyone we knew or had heard about in Saigon. No matter who these people were, their life in the city had a certain sameness about it—different from Ky La, but identical to each other. The husbands were always harried and too busy, even with the menial jobs most of them had, to spend much time with their families, preferring instead to go gambling or drinking with friends and servicemen. The mothers were harried too, and too busy with gossip and shopping to worry about their children (who were all ungovernable anyway) or their husbands—who either beat them like tyrants or ignored them completely. The children were either angels in Catholic school uniforms or hoodlums, there was no in between. Some of the older children, the mothers told us, were hard-working students or held down jobs with the government or local businesses; and each family, of course, had a son or cousin or uncle in Republican uniform— as witnessed by the framed photographs (sometimes draped with black bunting) of smooth-cheeked young men in service caps that sat on every mantel, if they were alive; or near every household shrine, if they were not.

During one of these visits, we found someone who thought she knew where my sister Hai was working—as a cook for a wealthy household. Unfortunately, the woman did not know how to find her but promised she would try.

That evening, we went "home" and did chores to repay my mother's friend. Later on, while the women talked, my mother's friend suggested that Thai, the teenage boy who had been making cow eyes at me since I arrived, take me for a ride on his moped and show me some sights. I was reluctant to leave my mother, but the thought of motoring through Saigon's streets with the wind in my hair was too much to resist. I borrowed some clean clothes from Thai's sister and brushed my hair as best I could, trying to make myself look as I imagined Bich might look in all her Saigon finery. Thai wore a white, short-sleeved shirt (the pocket of which contained his ever-present pack of cigarettes), a pair of expensive slacks, and shiny shoes. With his hair slicked back he almost looked like a man and I felt very grown-up as I bowed good-bye to my mother and he ignored his and we slipped through the door toward god knows what.

As we cruised down the brightly lighted, crowded street, Thai bragged

about all the money he made on the black market and I believed him. Beginning with the motorbike, he had nicer things, including a watch and a camera, than anyone I had known, and a cocky way of walking and talking that I used to associate only with people who held rifles in their hands.

After a while Thai suggested we go see "a movie" in "a theater." I said I had no idea what this was and after shaking his head in amazement at such a country simpleton, he explained that a theater was simply a big warehouse where people go sit in the dark and watch a play consisting of moving photographs. Although this still didn't make much sense (and I wasn't sure I wanted to sit in the dark with Thai or anyone else I had met so far in Saigon), the chance of seeing the inside of one of the city's great buildings and witnessing a miracle like moving pictures was too good to pass up.

Inside the theater, Thai bought us a snack and we tiptoed on the sticky floor past rows of knees to a pair of folding seats. When the lights went down, white dots sparkled on the screen and the loudspeakers came alive and people, thirty feet high, began to walk and speak and I felt Thai's arm steal around my shoulder. When I tried to pull away he pointed out that every other couple in the theater was doing it—fondling each other and kissing—and that it was the tradition, part of what seeing movies was all about. At first, the gigantic images were startling—almost hypnotic—but when the novelty wore off, the noise from the loudspeakers and the odd mix of smells, the rancid exploded corn Thai made me eat, and the unspeakable *strangeness* of it all began to make me sick. I tried to get up but Thai held me in my seat and tried again to fondle my shirt. My experience with such things to this point in my life, of course, had been anything but pleasant. Any man who had been closer to me than my brother Sau Ban or my father had either rape or molestation on his mind and I was in the mood for neither—regardless of Thai's "tradition." When he wouldn't quit, even after my loud complaint that drew stares from the people around us, I deflected his advances in the only way I knew how—the way I'd been taught to defend myself by the cadre trainers in Ky La, the way I had defended myself from my lecherous employer in Danang. Although the sound of his head hitting the seatback in front of us was terrible, I knew only his mannish pride had been hurt. I rushed from the theater—apologizing politely to the ghostly faces whose toes I ran across—and went back to the tenement. Everyone but Thai's mother was surprised to see me back so soon. Of course, I said nothing about my host's terrible behavior. When Thai returned some hours later, every-

one was asleep, but I could hear him telling his parents that the "Viet Cong bitch" was in the city on a terrorist mission and that if they were smart, they'd kick us out before all of them were arrested.

The next morning, my mother's friend politely told us that with relatives coming they would have no more space to share. If word had not come at noon that my sister Hai had been located, we would have spent the next night on the streets.

Hai had gone to live in Saigon in 1963 at the age of thirty-one after giving up hope of ever seeing her "Hanoi husband" again. Her Catholic employer came from North Vietnam after the French war ended and, being the kind of hard, clever workers that region was famous for producing, the employer's family made lots of money in the funeral business—helped along, no doubt, by the widening war and the elaborate, costly rituals associated with Catholic and Buddhist rites. But Hai's life as a servant was strictly regimented and, even as a cook, she enjoyed no special privileges. Her world was confined to the kitchen and her room, and occasionally the market. It was only because the rest of the household was enjoying their customary afternoon nap that Hai was able to steal away long enough to see us. Because we wished to keep our visit private, we had no option but to meet Hai on the street corner outside our host's apartment. The cold anonymity of the street, however, was nothing compared to the chilliness of Hai's welcome.

"So, how much of the rumors are true?" this slightly tough big city sister, whom I had not seen for two very eventful years, asked without even giving us a hug.

"Rumors?" Our mother fanned away the ghosts of the Viet Cong's allegations before they could haunt the whole conversation. "Oh, they're nothing. Bay Ly got herself in trouble with Uncle, that's all. So did I. But it's all a misunderstanding. Don't worry about it. What we need now is a situation. Bay Ly's a good worker—don't let her skinny arms fool you."

My mother took my hand and, even though my stomach was really hurting now (although we had just had lunch), she tried to make me stand tall and look as strong as she claimed.

"A misunderstanding." Hai did not sound convinced. "Well, I've got to be careful. I could get in real trouble just talking to you. I've heard some stories—"

"*Stories!* From who? Ba? You can't believe everything that girl says. Not that she lies, but she only listens with one ear. She always has, even when you two were growing up. But we didn't come here to argue

about Ba. Whether we deserve it or not, god's punishing us—and your father, too."

"How is Father?" Hai asked.

"Your father's okay," my mother said solidly. "Of course, he didn't look so good when we left him. It's not usual for a man's whole family to be pulled out by the roots, leaving him all alone. He started off with six children and a wife to take care of him and now he's all by himself. God knows what he'll look like having to eat his own cooking—" Her eyes began to water but her voice remained steady. "Anyway, Bay Ly needs some help and you're her sister. What can you do for her?"

Hai laughed bitterly. "Mama *Du,* you don't understand. I'm just a cook—a maidservant. I'm not even allowed in my boss's living quarters. I can't give you a job."

"Then at least take Bay Ly for a visit, eh?" my mother said. "She's got no place to stay. Oh, I can get by with friends, but she needs a place to rest. Her stomach's been acting up and I don't want her to get sick. Just take her for a couple of days."

I left my mother standing pathetically on the street corner and followed Hai's fast, long-striding steps to her employer's house in a fancy neighborhood. As soon as we got there, my stomach began hurting so much I could not stand up. Hai put me to bed—her own bed—and when she finished her work that night she came in, put down a mat, and slept on the floor beside me.

After a day or two, I felt well enough to help Hai with her chores, but her employer did not like the idea of a housekeeper having a guest, even one who helped out, and I was told to leave the next day. Fortunately, Hai learned there was a temporary vacancy at a nearby house—a maid was needed to fill in for the regular girl who was on leave to see her family. Unfortunately, I barely lasted a day. As an ignorant farm girl I had no experience with indoor plumbing and cleansers in plastic bottles and the poor woman who hired me spent half her time correcting my mistakes and the other half yelling at me. All I could think of was the roaring pain in my stomach and how much I wanted to find my mother and get all of us back to Ky La.

When I finally saw my mother again, I told her that Grandma Phung had appeared to me in a dream and told me to go back to Ky La. This was one of the few times in my life that I lied to my mother, but I was desperate enough to try anything. Without my mother knowing it, I tried to borrow money for the trip from some of the people we stayed with, but everyone just smiled sympathetically and turned me down. I even made a plan to walk the whole distance, but I had no idea where to begin—how to get out of Saigon, let alone to Quang Nam province.

Finally, when I could keep food down no longer (and what little I did eat went right through me), my mother asked Hai to take me to a doctor. We went to Binh Dan—one of the free public hospitals that dotted the city—and after I was given a drink of pasty water and had my picture taken with a cold, clanky machine, we were told I had a small sore in my stomach—an ulcer—a hole where my little body was eating itself up out of homesickness, anger, and despair.

They put me in a ward with other sick refugees and Hai went back to her job. My mother brought me sweet rice (said to be good for bad stomachs) from Hai's kitchen and slept on a mat by my bed. She stayed with me constantly and was so helpful to the staff that the nurse who attended me offered her a job as housekeeper to her parents, a position that worked out very well and saved both of us a night on the streets when I was discharged later that week.

By this time, my mother, too, was getting fed up with our lonely, hand-to-mouth life in Saigon. She decided to go back to Danang and try to convince my father to live with us in the city. When she got back a few days later, she had little to say except that he could not—would not—come with her. She gave me a letter which had been dictated by him to one of the village children who could write.

"From Phung Trong to his number-six child," it began in good formal style, "Greeting. Your mother has told me about your suffering and sickness in Saigon. I know you miss me and want to see me very much, as I miss and want to see you. I am very lonely without my wife and children. Our neighbors shun me because of our troubles and there is no one here to share a duck feast and make me laugh. Still, I must stay and work our farm, because if I leave our land it will belong to somebody else. Also, this is the place where our ancestors are buried. I cannot neglect their graves. I know you will be disappointed that I cannot come and live with you, but I know you will understand. You are a brave Phung Thi woman and must choose life no matter what."

Somehow, my father's letter did more to heal my wounded stomach than all the doctor's medicine. I realized now that I could no longer follow my old life's path and that I must accept the new one I'd been given. Realizing that, my body stopped its own civil war against itself and I found that, before too long, I was almost as strong as my mother claimed me to be.

Soon after my mother's return, the nurse who befriended us helped us apply for jobs as servants in the household of a wealthy family who were building a new home in the neighborhood. The husband, named Anh, owned several textile factories and his wife, Lien, was born of a noble family related to Cambodian kings. They would share a magnificent townhouse with his parents, who would occupy one wing, and their two boys, who were young enough to need a nanny, which was to be my job. Because the children's grandparents were also in need of servants, the nurse believed my mother could probably work for them and so remain close enough to supervise the activities of her young unmarried daughter. In every way it seemed the answer to our prayers.

Before reporting for the interview, the nurse washed both of us up and Hai brought me some clean clothes. Although I wanted desperately to wear an *ao dai,* beehive, and high heels, the nurse convinced me that my simple dress was better. "Country fresh still counts," she said, plucking her borrowed lipstick from my hand. "You'll thank me later."

We finally presented ourselves for inspection on the street in front of Anh's green five-storied house. The uniformed steward checked us first for lice, then led us inside where we were introduced to the mistress and master as they finished their lunch at an enormous carved table.

Lien, the wife, was a frail, intelligent-looking woman with blue eyelids and short, blue-tinted hair. She wore blood-red lipstick and a hint of rouge on her cheeks which made her look like a death angel on an elegant bier. Still, although I couldn't call her pretty, she had a regal look and managed to smile pleasantly when we peasants bowed before her.

As I straightened up, I saw the husband watching me intently. It was not the leering stare of the lecher in Danang, nor the lusty look of Thai in the theater. Rather, it was a man's expression of interest—direct and earnest, and maybe a bit amused. He had high cheekbones, sculpted hair, a narrow chin almost as delicate as his wife's, and eyes like deep-set jewels. His gaze added heat to the already too-hot day and I felt lightheaded. Perspiration broke out above my lips, which I nervously dabbed with my sleeve. I prayed he would look away before I fainted.

Lien questioned my mother briefly about our past, learning little beyond the name of our village and my superb abilities as a baby-sitter, then said simply, in a rather unpleasant, high-pitched voice, "They'll do." Assured that I could lift ten automobiles and collar twenty children at a time, I was told that I would nanny two well-behaved, aristocratic boys who would hardly need attention at all. To our relief, they took my mother too, as second housekeeper in the grandparent's wing of the house.

As promised, the boys were no trouble to care for. They spent most of their time at school or with a steady stream of tutors and playmates until dinner was served in the evening. I had more trouble learning my way around the new European bathrooms and how to cook in a modern kitchen (with gas and electricity!) and use something other than river water to wash our clothes. I found I had plenty of time to visit with my mother and help her with her chores, which, being the second housekeeper, were almost as light as mine. There was a cleaning girl for every floor, a cook and scullery maid, a handyman, and two chauffeurs: one for the master's limousine and one for the mistress's Mercedes, which was kept parked in a garage below the house. According to custom, all servants lived on the top floor and I shared a little room with my mother until a cubicle adjoining the children's suite was prepared for me. When our old clothes wore out, replacements were furnished by the master, along with two hearty meals each day, in addition to which we received a small monthly stipend that my mother began hoarding immediately to send to my father in Ky La.

For three months things were perfect and I couldn't imagine a finer life. The master would leave for his office at sunup and I would prepare the children for school. Later in the morning, the mistress usually went shopping or visiting and I sometimes went with her—being privileged to ride in the Mercedes and carry her things or attend her while she took tea with the rich ladies of Saigon. At noon, the family took a two-hour nap which was when the servants ate—usually leftovers from the family's lunch. In the late afternoon, the master would come home, to be greeted formally by his wife and children, then retire to his study. Because the family ate their meals in the big kitchen before we did, I had to manufacture reasons to see this handsome man who had saved us from the streets. Sometimes I glimpsed him from the top of the stairs, only to flutter away in embarrassment when his almond eyes caught mine. Other times I found excuses—a squabble between the children or a message from a tutor—to address the mistress in his company and our eyes would meet and my legs would turn to jelly and I would scamper from the room, ashamed of my little game but powerless to stop it.

One evening, when Anh had driven himself to the office and was working late, and everyone else—including Lien—had retired, the steward instructed me (because I was the only servant who lived on the lower floor) to admit the master when he returned by opening the steel garage door below the house. For an hour I sat perched on a chair in the kitchen, ready to run downstairs when I heard the car outside. But the hour was late and growing later. I tried to occupy myself with another favorite game: imagining I was the lady of the house—commanding servants and buying clothes and having beautiful babies with the man with beautiful eyes—

I awoke with a start. The almond eyes were looking down on me above a crooked smile. Anh's jacket was over his shoulder and his tie was loose around his neck. The steward was standing next to him, tying his robe and scowling like a demon.

"You'll be punished for this, Le Ly!" he snapped. "Why, making the master open his own garage—whoever heard of such a thing?"

My sleep-soggy brain was too stunned to answer. My mouth just gasped like a carp's with unspoken apologies.

"Oh, don't be too hard on Le Ly." Anh's manicured hand stroked my hair. I melted like a cat beneath it. "It's been a long day for everyone. Run off to bed now and let's not hear anymore about it."

"Well, girl! Didn't you hear the master?" The steward nipped my ribs with his fingers and I scuttled, tears welling, to my room.

Over the next few weeks, Anh worked late many nights, and I always begged the steward for a chance to correct my mistake, but without success. Finally, when the steward was away overnight, I convinced the first housekeeper to let me swap chores, and I took up my treasured post by the stairs. This time I would not imagine things but march around the room and stamp my feet whenever I felt sleepy.

Near midnight, I heard the big car turn into the driveway. Peeking through the curtains, I watched Anh's tired face glance up from the steering wheel to see if anyone had heard him. He must have had a terrible day and I decided to restore his spirits. I dashed downstairs and rolled the big doors open with a flourish. It may have been my imagination but I think his face lit up when he saw me. He parked the car and got out wearily.

"Well, well—Le Ly!" He smiled his handsome smile. I presented my head for its stroke, but he just walked past me. Even so, the faint scent of his body was so exciting it almost knocked me over.

He took a few steps into the house, stopped, looked around, then turned back toward me. I climbed the stair and shut the door as quietly as I could and made sure to bolt it as the steward had showed me. Without saying a word, Anh held out his hand. I didn't know what it meant— or what he had in mind—but I wanted to take his hand, kiss it, and hold it next to my heart forever. I stepped forward and looked at the floor. The strong hand caressed my hair, then slid gently to my shoulder.

He pulled me close and held me. Not knowing how to respond, I timidly slid my arms under his jacket and felt his strong back through his shirt. We must have stood like that for several minutes: me, hugging him the way I imagined I would have hugged Tung or the unlucky, cocky Viet Cong soldier who was killed in the battle; him, holding me the way I imagined he held his wife, stroking my hair and caressing my face. I felt his fingers lift my chin and his warm lips covered my own. It was a long, sad kiss—not solemn, but heartfelt—and we ended it by hugging each other like lost children.

Just as unexpectedly, he pulled away, and said, "Good night, Le Ly. Forgive me."

I went to my room but as tired as I was, I couldn't go to sleep. I rolled my pillow into Anh and clung to him as I tried to figure out my feelings. Although by age fifteen I had been threatened, beaten, shot at, molested, and raped by men, I had never before been kissed by one—not as a woman; not as a wife. Anh excited me, but he scared me too. I had no idea what these confused new feelings could mean. I wanted to ask my mother, but knew I must not. She would forbid me to see Anh again in this way and I knew such an order would kill me as surely as a Viet Cong bullet. To her, it would be a question of survival—of staying in this wonderful house. To me, it meant survival too, but survival of a different sort. Somehow, I knew that keeping my curious new feelings alive was the most important thing I could do. If, on that plane from Danang, I had discovered hope, I was now close to discovering what hope was for. It seemed a mystery on which my life depended.

EARLY AFTERNOON, APRIL 3, 1986:
IN THE CUSTOMS DOCK,
TAN SON NHUT AIRPORT, HCMC

With our forms filled out and signed and stamped and countersigned and counterstamped, we lug our baggage out onto the sidewalk and prepare for the trip into town. The gristly officer waits with his car— ironically, a big American-made station wagon—and holds the door for me as if I am a queen while his driver loads my things in the back.

Before I get in, I walk over to Per and shake his hand like a brother. (I want to give him the biggest hug ever, but that would not be so good in Vietnam!) He is off to a different part of the city—to a different destiny from the one we briefly shared. I am sorry to see him go and feel a hole in my soul where this kind man's spirit has been.

The short drive to Saigon is depressing. The messenger from the committee calls out points of interest—deserted streets lined with unrepaired buildings partly hidden by brown eucalyptus, scrubby palms, and dying bushes—but I don't see them. I am a prisoner of my feelings. The sidewalk outside the terminal had been filled with shabby, desperate-looking

people—most of them women and teenagers; most of them black marketeers. Of course, black marketeers are nothing new in Vietman. We
developed the profession to a high art during the American war. But now
that timeless trade has taken on an ominous color. The women and
children who assail us—who hang on our car like beggars—ask our
names and claim to know our relatives. They promise to take us to
our loved ones for a handful of American dollars. They ask what's in our
boxes and promise to pay top *dong,* sight unseen, for anything made in
the West. Some offer to buy or sell gold, Chinese antiques, dope of all
kinds, *dong* at a top rate, not to mention radios and cameras and sex with
any object we can name. Their shrill, fear-driven voices make the dusty
air unhealthy and we crank up the windows to be rid of them—preferring
stifling heat to their all-too-human howls. I think about my old girlfriend
Bich—how she tried to explain the miracles of Saigon to that simple Ky
La farm girl—and wonder how I myself would go about explaining San
Diego and the interstate highway system and shopping malls and desktop
computers and fast-food chains and automated teller machines to these
people—or to my family. It is as if I have been asleep, enjoying a beautiful
dream for sixteen years, while these people have lived a waking nightmare.
Things *have* changed, but not as I had imagined. Saigon has gone from
a bejeweled, jaded dowager to shabby, grasping bag lady in less than a
decade. The desperate faces that peer back at me hold souls that plead
for mercy and deliverance. But just as I did when I left Vietnam in 1970,
I avert my eyes—look away and look out for number one. Isn't that how
people survive?

Eventually I begin to chat with the officer—finding out by careful small
talk what life is like in the city. "First of all," he replies, "I'd take off
that jewelry if I were you. There are still lots of unreformed people in
Saigon. They'll take your rings and the fingers with them. Yes, I'd get
rid of all that stuff. Put it in your suitcase and forget you brought it." It
is amusing to hear this party functionary still refer to Saigon as *Saigon.*
I am glad I did not do as well in my Ho Chi Minh City drills as Per
required.

We pull up at the old Continental Hotel, now renamed the Khach San
Huu Nghi, and I follow the officer like a timid sister through more black
marketeers to the reception desk. All prices are given in U.S. dollars as
well as *dong,* but that's no surprise. Why should the official vendors be
less greedy for that mother's milk of nations than the unofficial ones out
on the street? Although compared with the black market rate, the official
dollar exchange seems little more than legalized theft, I buy five thousand
Vietnamese *dong* with a single ten-dollar bill. The clerk smiles but checks

the bill closely to see if it's real. Under the watchful eye of his comrades, he enters the serial number in a logbook and rings for a porter to take my bags.

I am led by two clean-cut young boys to my room. They are filled with questions about America and I answer them as best I can, although I'm sure my words sound more like fairy tales than a travelogue. Still, they soak up everything the way dry seeds soak up rain. I reward each with a pack of cigarettes—worth far more than the Vietnamese currency the clerk encouraged me to "use with the locals."

They close the door on the odd-smelling room—the place stinks of gasoline!—and I collapse on the narrow bed and survey my new quarters. Over the foam-rubber mattress lies a single military blanket which I'm sure I won't use even on Saigon's coolest night. On the tiled floor next to the bed I notice a pair of hotel sandals—remnants of more gracious days—and on the other side an armoire for my clothes. Next to the window, I am given a small writing desk for sending postcards (on the first stage of their three-week journey to the States) and beneath that a steam radiator, which will see even less use than the blanket. Across from the radiator is a battered coffee table with two chairs. On the table is my complimentary copy of *Nhan Dan,* the Communist party newspaper, and an ashtray bearing the emblem of the old Continental—complete with French writing—but it is not for holding ashes. Instead, it is filled with insecticide to ward off mosquitoes and I am reminded once again of exactly where I am. At least that explains the terrible stink that fills the air. I would be happier with bugs.

I go into the almost-modern bathroom, dump the insecticide, and wash my face with a well-used bar of soap. I am pleased to find the hot-water tap actually produces hot water.

After napping and freshening up, I go out for dinner at a noodle shop across the street. ("Not good but the best around," the desk clerk apologizes in advance.) The surly proprietor takes my order for rice soup and returns with a covered bowl. Because of a shortage of ingredients—mostly a lack of pork—the broth, when I finally taste it, is thin and flavorless. Despite my jaded American taste, I lift my cup in delight. *It is not good, but it is good enough!* It is the kind of food I grew up on. Suddenly, the poor surroundings—victims of the war like everyone and everything else—don't seem to matter. I am a country girl in American clothes giggling at the sheer, animal pleasure of overcoming hunger. I almost feel at home.

Happy-full with thin rice soup, I hail a *siclo*—one of the bicycle-powered pedicabs that have replaced nearly all of Saigon's taxis—and climb in, determined to do a little sight-seeing before I go find Anh. My driver is a wiry, underfed man, like the officer at the airport, and covered with grease and sweat. He grins with splayed, horsey teeth and, also like the officer, calls out both old and new names for the once-familiar streets as we ride by. He seems to know everything about the old city and, judging from his appearance, has probably seen much of Saigon's wartime history firsthand. I ask him his age. "Twenty-three" he replies proudly, and I sink back in my seat, shocked and sickened. Nearly the same age as my oldest son Jimmy, this fellow was only a little boy when I left Saigon and not yet a teenager at liberation—yet he looks as old as a grandfather! I regret that I carry only cigarettes, and not vitamins, for tips. I wonder for a moment if this fellow, cleaned up and checked out and better fed, would look much different from my son pedaling his bike on a college campus.

Soon we are heading down Truong Minh Gian Street, which as I remember from the old days, was a hangout for GIs on the prowl for drinks, girls, gambling, and drugs. The last time I saw the place it was lit up like Las Vegas: full of people and cars and neon lights. Now, the only lights we see come from a few oil lamps in windows; and the only people, vendors and families scrambling home in the dusk.

I tell the *siclo* driver to stop at a hole-in-the-wall shop, just about to close, and I buy us both a cup of *nuoc mia*—sugarcane juice that is called the Vietnamese soda pop—taking care not to flash my money around too much. While we refresh ourselves, the driver continues to talk, but mostly about things that are wrong: the ever-present police (who watch the wrong things—not robbers and pickpockets, but "unreformed Republicans"), neighborhood informers, not enough food and electricity, and the necessity for everyone to work at two jobs or use the black market to get by. "And the biggest employer is still the army," he laments, "eleven years after the war! Do you think they'll ever make peace with the Chinese and Cambodians? What would they do with all those soldiers?"

I suddenly notice how dark it is and remind myself that I must still find Anh's house at a new, unfamiliar address. My horse-faced driver says "No problem!" and we pedal on for half an hour through darkened streets. Because electricity is in such short supply, Saigon suffers from rolling blackouts and one after another even the few well-lighted streets we pass go dark. Still, the night air is warm and the rhythmic pedaling comforts me. I let my mind wander pleasurably to memories of Anh and a night very much like this one almost twenty years before—

* * *

I FINALLY FELL ASLEEP with my Anh pillow when a rap on the door woke me up.

At first I thought it was someone coming to fetch me the way my mother and I had been summoned at night during an earlier stay with our friends. We were told to get dressed and, along with some others, were taken to a tenement where a Communist meeting was going on. The Viet Cong were recruiting servants to spy on government officials and industrialists, steal supplies, and, when necessary, to plant explosives around the city. We weren't sure how much anyone really knew about our past, so we played country dumb. We told them we were still too scared of the big city to go anywhere on our own. For once, it was smarter to stay bumbling peasants than to play liberation heroes and they left us alone for "smarter fish." Still, after my own bout with homesickness and war-weariness and the hospital, I understood why so many refugees went to these meetings and volunteered to help them out. Lonely, scared, and missing their families, they couldn't resist the companionship and sense of purpose offered by the "comrades."

With this in my mind, then, I was surprised and exicted when the door opened not on some sour-faced cadreman—but Anh.

"I'm sorry to wake you, Le Ly," he said softly. "I couldn't sleep after this evening."

"Neither could I."

"May I come in?"

I stepped back and his handsome figure, clad only in a robe, slipped through the airy darkness. We sat on the edge of my bed—the only place in my small room to sit—and he took my hands in his.

"I don't want you to misunderstand," he said. "I love my wife. I love my children. It's just that—this is a very bad time, eh? The war—" He smiled and caressed my hair. "Well, what would a young woman like you know about the war?"

I only looked down shyly. My heart was pounding too fast to tell him what I did or didn't know.

Finally, he took me in his arms. I felt his muscled back again through his robe and my young body ached to pull him tighter—to pull him closer to me than any man before. But if that time was to come, it would not be tonight.

He kissed me gently on the lips, kissed my fingertips, and apologized for disturbing me. He went out and closed the door behind him. I sat on my bed in the darkness, amazed that a rich and handsome man—a prince in every way—could care so much about the feelings of a poor country girl. I listened to his quiet steps as he went down the hall to rejoin his sleeping wife.

Over the next few weeks, Anh spent more time working at home—whether it was because of me or the state of his business or dangers in the city or the demands of his frail wife (who, the steward said, suffered from a heart condition), I'll never know. I only know that I bloomed like a flower from his warmth and gained understanding and courage as I watched him—and he watched me—as we went about our daily living.

My mother, of course, was not blind to these changes in her daughter. She talked more often about the poor health of our mistress—*What a shame it would be if her husband was found with another woman. What would happen to her darling children?* More than once she talked to me about the sanctity of marriage, even though I knew such a marriage would never be my own. She couldn't see how it broke my heart to be caught in this dilemma—to accept Anh's love, wrong another woman, and endanger his fine family; or reject him and not only risk our own position but lose this small bit of happiness I had finally found in life. What was I to do?

Finally, on a balmy night a few weeks later, Anh came again to my room. Although I had heard his gentle knock only once before, I recognized it instantly, so often had I replayed it—wished for it—in my mind. This time he came in without speaking, kissed me as he had that first time in the foyer, and led me to the bed. He undressed me slowly and eased me onto the too-small bed, his body covering me at once like a fragrant, muscular blanket. His hands were warm and urgent as he caressed me with rising passion. Although I had been taken by men twice before, I soon discovered just how ignorant I was about love between men and women. I thanked fate or luck or god for sending me such a gentle teacher and for the joy I knew my spirit would find in his arms. As Anh entered me, the feeling I had dreaded since that awful, endless night in the swamp gave way to a curious repose. With this wonderful prince inside me, there was no room for hate. I caressed him and loved him in return and held him to me as if he were my husband.

I don't know if Anh believed I was a virgin when he made love to me, but my quiet tears afterward—of relief, of thanksgiving—may have helped him think it. He lay beside me stroking my hair and comforting me until I went to sleep. When he left, I woke up and raised my head but he had already slipped through the door. I knew he was going back to his wife but this time I didn't care. I cupped my small hand where he had been and held his seed like a treasure for the rest of the night, dreaming of a family and Anh in the sunshine and no war. Unseen by either of us but known to our spirits, our souls had joined, as had our bodies, and within the year the fruit of that perfect moment would come back as a perfect son.

Evening, April 3, 1986:
Somewhere in Saigon

My *siclo* threads its way through several well-lighted compounds, then descends into seedy neighborhoods I would have avoided even by day. Certainly, these are not places I would expect to find Anh and his high-born family.

"Are you sure you know where you're going?" I ask the driver over my shoulder.

"No problem—" he replies, but his breathless voice shows he is no longer inclined to talk.

We snake back and forth, covering and re-covering our tracks, but always plunging further into darker, more forbidding zones of the city. I clutch my only valuable—my purse—close to my chest, then realize what a tempting target it makes, even in the dim light of the oil lamps, and stick it behind my legs. I twist around in the seat and say, "This is no good. Take me back to the hotel and I'll try again tomorrow."

"No, no," he replies without looking down. "We'll find it."

It occurs to me he might be worried about losing his fare. "I'll make sure and wait for you in the morning." I try to sound enthusiastic, like we are some kind of team whose members should look out for each other and not try anything sneaky. "How does eight o'clock sound?"

"No, no, missy. Sit still!" His tongue slavers over his donkey teeth and he pedals even faster.

I fall back in the seat and think briefly about jumping out. But the cab is moving so fast and what if I did escape? Where would I go? If the driver is honest, but just grumpy and tired, I would be worse off than before. No—we are in this together, he and I, whatever happens. All I can promise is that, one way or another, I will be one passenger—or victim—he never forgets.

The buildings narrow around us like trees in a jungle or high stones in a canyon. Although there are few people in the street, I feel the spirits of the neighborhood—inhabitants and victims of the war—close in around me: repressed, desperate, and hostile. The squeaking pedals become more oppressive as the seconds tick by and I begin to hear my own blood rushing in my head. Still, if my driver means me harm, he's had plenty of opportunities to do it. Unless, of course, he is looking for a convenient place to hide my body. Or, perhaps, he has confederates in some alley. Perhaps he—and they—have something more than robbery or murder on their minds—

Stop it! I tell myself. *You're losing your head—just like at the airport! Paranoid—that's what you are! It's this place—your memories—the ghosts!*

Just as I talk myself out of such chilling, foolish, silly, nonsensical, and nonproductive thoughts, the *siclo* turns a corner and breaks hard. We have driven into a blind alley and stopped.

FIVE

Losing Love

Late at Night, April 3, 1986:
Somewhere in Saigon

THE PEDICAB DRIVER dismounts his bike but finds I am ahead of him on the pavement. He seems startled to see me standing there—legs planted firmly, tiny fists on my hips like Mighty Mouse. But trouble, it turns out, is the last thing on his mind.

"I'm lost." He waves a hand wearily. The lines of sweat and grease on his face make his head look like a skull. "You stay with the cab, missy. Keep out of sight—for your own good, eh? I don't want anyone to rip off my *siclo*. I'm going to knock on some doors."

Thank goodness the darkness keeps him from seeing how relieved and foolish Mighty Mouse looks. I almost feel like kissing his dear animal face. Almost.

"Okay," I say. "Leave the cab here, but I'm coming with you."

Halfway down the block is a local apothecary—an herbal drug-seller doing business out of his shabby house. If anyone knows the neighborhood, it will be the herbalist. We are almost to the shop when the door swings open and a boy carrying a bag of ice comes out, headed for his bicycle. My driver snags his arm and asks if the boy knows where to find the address I've been given.

The boy looks at us nervously. Though he's almost a teenager, his face is as delicate as a girl's. He holds his precious icebag close, guarding it against the bigger man.

"I know where it is," the boy answers cautiously. "Why do you want to know?"

"Such cheek!" My driver raises his hand, but it's a playhouse gesture. "That's Saigon kids for you!" the driver says. "Everyone talks like an official!"

"Listen, boy"—I take the child's narrow shoulders—"I only want to visit the family that lives there. It's okay. I'm a friend who's come a very long way." The boy looks at me intently. Even in the moonlight, his puppy eyes seem familiar. A spooky feeling tickles my stomach. "Anyway"—I let him go—"why do you care so much about that address?"

"Because I live there," the boy answers.

"My god—what's your father's name?"

"Anh. My mother's name is Yen. Do you know them?"

I hug the boy like a long-lost aunt—a great homecoming hug, breathless and amazed. He must be convinced by now I'm crazy. "Well, come on," I cry, "take us to them! We'll follow with our *siclo.*"

The boy is still wary of this crazy lady and her thug and mounts his bike quickly. He peels away, then slows down, stops, and looks over his shoulder, waiting for us to follow. I think he's grateful to be spared a ride home by himself in the dark.

The driver pedals quickly now, turning left and right as the boy precedes us through a rat's maze of streets that finally opens onto a residential road lined with run-down houses. I watch the boy's black hair bounce and recall the jewel-like eyes and sharp chin—all features like Anh's and a little like Jimmy's too. I hope my gushy greeting wasn't too much for him. I don't want to seem too pushy or impolite, despite my excitement. I suppose he thinks that if this crazy lady really is his auntie, he'll just have to put up with her and do the best he can.

I sink back into my seat. *Put up with things. Do the best you can.* If I had an epitaph for those last months in Anh's house back in 1966—and a benediction for what lay ahead—it would have to be those words.

* * *

THE DAY AFTER Anh and I made love was fine and sunny, although my longing glances and kittenish smiles aimed in his direction were not returned. I could see he felt guilty, so I kept my mind on my chores. This didn't bother me during the day because Lien was around and he had another role to play. Besides, there was always plenty of work to be done for the children or with my mother. But at night I grew lonely; especially because I had washed myself carefully and brushed back my hair and sweetened my breath with mint leaves stolen from the kitchen in hopes that Anh would come to see me. Yet Anh did not come—not on that night or the next, or on any other night that week. The following two weeks he was out of town ("Touring his factories," was the steward's terse answer to my inquiry) and for two weeks after that he was back on his late night schedule. Because I was starting to feel tired all the time (and because I was surprised and hurt that Anh made no effort to talk to me) I didn't volunteer for doorman's duty and gave up trying to catch his eye on those few occasions when our paths crossed.

During this time I began to serve Madame Lien as companion as well as baby-sitter. She had a weak heart (the penalty of blue blood, the cadremen would say) and her physician discouraged her from sleeping with her husband—the second boy was unplanned after the close call of the first. Because she often felt bad at night, I sometimes gave her massages in the evening and sang little songs from the countryside to calm her down. I even performed some intimate duties for her, such as washing her underclothes—which for Vietnamese is a strictly personal task, even among the wealthy—and washing her hair when she was too tired. Although I did these things initially out of guilt—to pay her back with kindness for what I did with Anh, I later looked forward to them for their own sake: to help a poor woman who, despite her riches and position, was cursed with pain as a constant companion.

One morning about six weeks after my night with Anh, I got up early to wake the children and became so ill I could barely stand up. My stomach turned inside out, but it was not the pain of an ulcer. I did not even make it to the first-floor toilet but vomited on the expensive tiles outside my door. The chief housekeeper answered the children's screams and helped me to my room. She put me onto my hard wooden bed and called my mother.

Although I had been surrounded all my life by pregnant women in the village, I paid little attention to what they said about carrying and bearing children. Who wanted to hear about aches and pains when there more exciting things to think about—such as boys and battles and miraculous places like Saigon?

My mother took one look at me, pressed under my ribs (it wasn't my ulcer), smelled my breath (it wasn't poison), and asked if I'd had my period yet (I hadn't), and knew instantly what was the matter.

"Well, Bay Ly, now you've done it!" she said when the housekeeper left. "You weren't satisfied with a perfect life in a wonderful house, were you? You had to seduce the husband—make him stray from his wife. Now look what it's got you!"

"That's not the way it happened!" I protested. "Anh cares for me. He *loves* me!"

Yet even as I spoke, I knew Anh's actions over the past few weeks had been anything but loving. The garden of bliss I'd nurtured in my heart wilted before the hot blast of my mother's logic.

"Love you? He's just a lusty landowner—a billy goat in a house full of nannies! Do you think a pretty girl means any more to him than any other possession? And now you're going to have his bastard child! Perfect! Well, you'll just have to get rid of it, won't you?" She tucked the blanket close around my neck, almost choking me. "You'll go see the herbalist tomorrow. I'll tell you what to ask for."

The next day, I was able to keep my food down long enough to make the short walk to the local druggist. I couldn't come right out and admit that I was pregnant, so told him I had missed my period and wanted something to get me started. The herbalist checked my palm, as was the custom, then gave me *thuoc pha thai*, the Chinese herbs for women's complaints. I took a double dose of the terrible stuff for a week but all it did was make my morning sickness worse. I even tried jumping down the stairs, hard on my heels one step at a time, in order to jar the embryo loose, but I gained nothing but sore feet and a warning from the housekeeper to be quiet.

By the end of the third month, my condition was beginning to show and because the tiny soul inside me made such a hardy claim to life, I began to feel like a coward and bully for trying to kill it. By the end of the fourth month, I gave up my attempts to miscarry. Somehow, I came to believe that my love for Anh and the recent kindness I had shown my mistress would cause her to accept me in my predicament and help me as I had helped her. All that was left for me was to make my peace with god for my attempts to abort the unseen life inside me. Late one afternoon I sneaked into the living room to say prayers of expiation to Anh's ancestors in front of his family portraits. Unfortunately, my act had been observed.

"What are you doing, Le Ly?" Lien asked quietly. Her blue-lidded eyes looked straight at the potbelly under my tunic. Although there was no longer any reason to deny my condition, I could not see involving Anh.

"I am expecting a child," I said timidly.

"Yes, I know. We learned it from the herbalist."

I looked up at her, startled and confused.

"Oh, don't look so surprised, Le Ly. The herbalist recognized you and told our neighbor, and the neighbor told our steward right away. Did you think you could fool the old fellow with your little girl's story? Anyway, the druggist took care of you despite yourself. He gave you *thuoc bac*—a medicine to make the baby stronger and keep it safe from other potions you might try. The only question that remains to be answered is: who is the father?"

I looked down at the floor. "A boy. Someone I met at the park. You don't know him."

"And why were you burning incense?"

"At first I didn't want the baby and tried to kill it. Now I accept it. I was praying for atonement."

"In front of my husband's ancestors?"

This question flustered me. "I—I didn't know what else to do, Madame Lien. The boy is Catholic, like you. I am Buddhist."

"I see." She was holding her left arm with her right hand as I had seen her do when her heart was bothering her. Perhaps she was just trying to restrain herself. Her voice, even more high-pitched than usual, now sounded like cracking china. "Well, Le Ly, I have another explanation. I believe the father of your baby is my husband."

"Oh *no,* Madame Lien! Anh—the master—would never—"

"You will be silent." It was more a wish than a command. She raised the hand she was holding and I thought she was going to strike me. Instead, she touched my chin with a feather soft, long-nailed finger and tilted my head toward the light. Tears pooled in her eyes but she did not cry. I think she was trying to imagine Anh and me together. "Yes," she said finally. "I suppose that's what he sees in you." I didn't know what she meant, but the long fingernail ran down my cheek, building pressure as it went. It did not draw blood, but I felt its heavy mark upon my skin.

"You know I am not well, Le Ly," she continued, "but I have given my husband sons—beautiful boys—as fine as any woman could have given him. Don't think"—she trailed off, perhaps afraid to excite herself further, then said firmly—"don't think you won't pay for what you've done. Come. My husband will be home shortly. We'll wait for him in the parlor. And call your mother. I'll want to speak to her as well."

My mother acted thunderstruck when she heard Lien's accusation; not so much to show humiliation, which was expected, but from what seemed to be genuine sorrow—empathy from one woman to another who knew what betrayal was like.

"Of course," Lien said, after hearing my mother's apologies, "you and your daughter will have to leave the house at once." Her manner was no longer one of bottled anger, but cold and ominous, like poison in a teacup. Hearing this last part, my mother seemed to lose her womanly compassion.

"Leave?" she blinked. "But why? Nobody knows about this but you! Let people think the father is some delivery boy—or better yet, a soldier! Yes, of course. Servicemen bother Bay Ly all the time in the market. You've seen it yourself."

"That's impossible. *I* know, and that's enough. Besides, you know men. They're like dogs pissing on a post. If they go once, they'll go twice. They come back because it's got their scent—they've marked it as their property. And Anh would come back too—the next time your little bitch goes into heat."

"But Bay Ly's no threat to you! She offers nothing for a proper man!" My mother's desperation was showing. She was talking now like I wasn't in the room, like I was a just a troublesome animal—a stray cat caught spraying the mistress's nice furniture—and it hurt me more than all the herbalist's potions and police beatings combined.

"She's just a country girl—an ignorant, foolish, stupid child," my mother went on. "She'll make no claim on your husband. She's just a nanny—a maid who'll never be a bride! Don't think anymore about it! She's nothing! Insignificant!"

She went on and on and never once looked at me to see the tears rolling down my face.

"Absolutely not," Lien said resolutely. "I won't have her in my house. Not as a nanny, not as a housekeeper—"

"Then as number-two wife!" My mother's voice reeked of desperation.

"What? You're crazy!"

"No! As second wife—as concubine to the master! As your *slave,* Madame Lien, eh? Yes—to kick around, to warm your husband's bed when you have better things to do. Why waste your health on a man's rutting when you can leave it to a pretty girl, eh? Yes, Bay Ly's pretty —and she's already caught your husband's eye. And you know the custom. You'll still be number one; the first wife. The law's on your side—"

I was on my knees beside my mother's chair, grabbing at her legs. "Mama *Du—please—*" I was sobbing so hard I could hardly breathe.

My mother spanked my hands as though I were an unruly child, though I could see through my tears that her face was more anguished than mine.

"You straighten up, Bay Ly!" she said harshly, sliding down from her chair. She shook my shoulders again and again until we were both on our knees, weeping together on the floor.

At that moment the garage door rumbled open below us and Anh's car pulled into the driveway. We tried to compose ourselves and sat down. When Anh came in, I couldn't bear to look at him, but I imagined the expression on his face.

"We have something to discuss," Lien said with her ice-pick voice.

Anh nodded, went from the room, and returned a few moments later without his jacket and with a highball in his hand. He stood by the window and sipped it slowly while he listened to Lien's story.

". . . As a consequence," she concluded, "Le Ly and her mother must go. Today. Before supper. Right now."

Anh stared out the window awhile, then looked down at us. It was so much like the glance he gave me when we first met that I almost burst out crying again.

"Yes," he said finally, "the child is probably mine. You tried to get rid of the baby?" He was looking at my mother.

"Of course!" she said. "But your seed, master, is too strong. It's taken hold too fast—and now, it seems, it has hold of Bay Ly too. She has made her peace with god and your ancestors and intends to see things through. And that's all we're asking of you, Master Anh. Some consideration from you and Madame Lien for our position. Just put up with things, at least until the child is born. Help us get by the best we can."

"I see," Anh took a hard swallow from his drink. "Well, I won't throw you into the street. But I can't ask my wife to share her roof with you. I suppose I can put you both in an apartment until the baby is delivered. After that, we'll see—"

"Not in Saigon," Lien said.

Anh shrugged, "Well then, how far away do you want them?"

She looked at him squarely, "I don't know. How far can you drive in a day?"

Anh drained his glass. "All right. I'll send them back to Danang"— my mother began to object, but he raised a hand—"with enough money to keep you going until the baby's born. I'll send a check every month—"

"To a bank or to a relative," Lien interrupted. "I don't want you to know their address. That's an absolute condition."

"You'll . . . *have* . . . enough money to live on," Anh said. "My steward will make the arrangements."

My mother could not easily refuse these terms without revealing why we were afraid to go to back to Danang, so she was forced to accept his solution.

"Of course, Bay Ly will come back to Saigon eventually," my mother said to Anh later, after Lien had left the room. She spoke to him in the voice I had heard her use on her sons-in-law. "After the baby is born, she will come back. Don't forget her. She'd make an excellent second wife. She's strong as well as pretty. Don't forget her, now. Promise you won't forget!"

I didn't see Anh again after that. The children said he was traveling but the housekeeper whispered that he had taken an apartment near his office until we were gone and everything quieted down. The steward gave us some money and said we had a few days to make arrangements for our departure, but the atmosphere of the house was so cold and the air so full of hate—not just from Lien, but from most of the staff as well, that my mother and I got up the next morning before breakfast and took a *siclo* to the family with whom we'd stayed when we first arrived.

As we rode one last time through Anh's elegant neighborhood, my mother talked bitterly to herself. "Well, there goes everything we worked for! And what will your father say, eh? I always knew Trong would regret the way he coddled you! Well, now we're out of the pot and into the fire! *Do con hu! Do con ngu! Do con dai!* Stupid, spoiled, foolish child! It's bad enough to have a rotten daughter whom no one will marry— now I have a bastard child thrown into the bargain! And, of course, everyone will blame me! Isn't a mother supposed to protect her daughter from such things? Just tell everyone your husband's in the service. Tell them he's a soldier from Saigon—and from a good family, too! Oh, what a beautiful wedding you had! Yes—that's what we'll tell them! That's how we'll get by!"

For the first time in my life, I wished my mother was somewhere else—or even dead. It was a horrible thought—I'd never had it before —but it gripped me now as strongly as the living thing inside my belly. True, she stood by me, caring for the sick little animal no one else wanted, but somehow that wasn't enough. I was becoming a mother myself and realized that, deep down, a mother can do nothing else. I wanted to cry, but all my tears had been shed over Anh. I wanted to rage, but my hatred for the war and the Viet Cong who raped me had already consumed my blackest thoughts. I wanted to forgive, but I did not know how. I was too frightened of the future. I could only sit back in the *siclo* and caress my swollen belly. While my mother spewed venom at the pitiless world beyond, I hummed a little tune to the spirit inside my womb—just as

my mother had done for me, to toughen me up and make me worthy—
and swore to god that it would see better days.

LATE AT NIGHT, APRIL 3, 1986:
ANH'S HOUSE, HCMC

The sweet-faced boy parks his bike by a single-story house surrounded
by a ramshackle wall. With his bag of ice, he bangs through the gate
shouting, "Father! Father! A visitor! A lady's come to see you!"

I know from my earlier letters that Anh and his first wife, Lien,
divorced sometime after liberation in the late 1970s and that what the
revolution didn't cost him, the divorce ultimately did. He moved in with
his girlfriend, a woman named Yen (who had been his secretary), and
added five children to his family—one of which must be our handsome
little guide. All of a sudden, I begin to worry about what other surprises
I will find inside.

I climb down and turn to my driver but he is already putting one of
his filthy cigarettes between his lips. "I know," he says. "You want me
to wait. Go ahead—check it out. No problem."

Inside the outer wall, the concrete yard is wide enough to accommodate
a car, which, in better times, it used to hold. The yard is cluttered with
the usual spoor of a working-class family: a bicycle wheel, a wooden
stepladder, potted plants, and scraps of furniture waiting to be mended.
The porch light is on (thank god the neighborhood's been spared the
blackout!) and I see a man come through the iron-barred door toward
me. His narrow shoulders droop inside his T-shirt and a comfortable
"spare tire" rides over the elastic on his boxer shorts—the bottoms of
which are connected to his shuffling, sandaled feet by an old man's toothpick legs. The eyes in the shadowed face glow like the moon above us.

"Who is it?" the man asks in a wavering voice. "Who's there?"

I answer like a nervous schoolgirl. *"Anh Hai—!"* I call out, trying to
sound careless and pleasant. *"Hello, brother Anh!* Bay Ly—your *little
sister*—is here!" I know he can see me clearly because the porch light is
on my face, although his is still in shadow. In the middle of the path we
stop, a short breath apart. I look up into the moonlit face and see that
it's Anh all right—though the sculpted features of the man I knew have
softened with age. There are bags below the eyes and sagging skin beneath
the once sharp line of his jaw. I watch those wonderful teardrop eyes go
round with amazement.

"Bay Ly—" he whispers incredulously, "how did you get home? I thought you'd cable before you arrived!"

"I didn't come with a group," I answer, swimming in his gaze, grinning like a teenager. "I came on my own. You know me."

Yes, I can see from his warming smile he did. I can see it despite all our years apart. I can see he recognizes the mother of his American son.

"Well, come in—come, come!" He takes my arm and escorts me to the door. "Wait," he says, "your driver—I'll pay him and send him away."

"No, no. I asked him to wait. It's so late—I don't want to disturb your family. I just wanted to let you know I was here—to see you and make sure you were real. I'll go back to the hotel—"

"Oh no. I'll run you home in a little while. I'm a man of means, eh?" Anh's wry smile makes it clear he appreciates the irony of his own joke. "I have a Vespa—yes, a two-seater! Hard to find in Saigon these days! I'll zip you back in a flash. But first we'll have a visit. Look"—he gestured to the boy and his bag—"we even have ice now for cool drinks! Come on!"

I tell Anh to go ahead and I return to my *siclo*. When the driver sees me, he takes a final drag on his cigarette and pinches off the glowing ember, which falls to the ground. His thonged feet grind it out and he puts the butt in his pocket for later.

"Listen," I say, "you can go home now—and thank you so much!"

"You'll be okay, missy?" He scans the neighborhood doubtfully.

"I'll be fine. I'm old friends with the family. Thanks for looking after me." I give him three thousand *dong*—much more than the usual fare, even for a whole evening's work—and a pack of Marlboros. Which is the fare and which is the tip?—I let him decide. He stuffs the loot in his pocket, bows politely, and pedals off.

While I pay the driver, Anh slips on some long pants, combs his hair, and alerts the family to his visitor. The tiny house is comfortable but crowded with old memories: pictures from Anh's mansion, framed photographs of relatives and unframed posters taped to the wall—all reminders of the ripe old days before liberation. While he pours two glasses of *sim fruit,* purple juice just right for the balmy night, he explains what's happened to him since the end of the war.

"You know, Lien took most everything in our divorce," Anh says matter-of-factly. "I had to sell the house, the cars, you name it."

"How is Lien?" I ask, sensing Anh still feels compassion for the woman who bore him sons.

"Oh, she's doing all right. She has a boyfriend and lives in a nice little studio on the other side of town. She takes medicine for her heart and seems to be doing okay. You know, she appreciates the kindness you showed our boys when they came to America after liberation."

"They're good boys," I reply. "I'm glad they survived that terrible boat ride. They'll do just fine." I try not to take pleasure from Lien's downfall—even though I know the loss of wealth and prestige hurts her far more than Anh. Fate and her own bad heart have made her suffer enough. In addition to chronic illness, her karma was to stay on and fight to keep her husband and mansion and all the misfortune that went with them, until she lost them in the end to Yen, a younger rival, and the Communist revolution. Because she sent me from her house in 1966, my life took a turn that eventually brought me to America and I can only be grateful for that. I'm sure she was surprised when she heard I helped her boys when they arrived "fresh-off-the-boat" in 1981—refugees from Communist reeducation, privation, and weeks of seasickness and pirate attacks in the South China Sea. Perhaps we both learned something new from the way our lives continue to touch. Compassion flows from what you do *right now*—future intentions don't count.

Anh continues to tell me about my homeland's recent history. "After liberation, I had to give my company to the government—but everybody else was doing it too, so I didn't feel so bad. At least it kept me employed and out of the reeducation camps. I moved here—to Yen's house—in 1978. After that I've been just a humble worker like everyone else. Funny, isn't it?" He puts more ice in my fruit juice. "Our positions now are so opposite. You're a rich American—"

"Oh, hold on," I laugh, "I'm not a rich lady—but I've done okay. I own a restaurant and some houses in California. But no limos—no servants—" I trail off, feeling too well dressed and well fed to feign poverty for this poor man. I find no pleasure in seeing my prince brought down.

"Tell me, Bay Ly," he says soberly, "how is our son?"

I look into the strangely foreign, strangely familiar face—still handsome but worn out, like Saigon itself—and reply, "Jimmy's fine. He's a strong young man—beautiful and kind like his father. And smart as a whip. He's studying computers at the University of California in San Diego. He's a good son. And he's an American. I brought some pictures to show you later."

Anh's children by his second wife now appear with their mother. The polite teenagers standing before me have the slightly defeated look I have seen everywhere in the city. But even without nice clothes or preparation for company, they are beautiful—as I imagine Anh had been at that age. I know Anh must still feel wealthy with his wonderful family intact. Yen is a plumpish matron with strong bones, a wide, sensuous mouth, and broad shoulders. She greets me warmly.

We talk awhile and I learn more about Anh's situation and the conditions I'll find on my trip. He has trouble believing the U.S. Government has let me come freely to Vietnam and his suspicions sound strangely like my own fears about the Communists—at least to this point in my trip. Everyone, he says, is talking about the Vietnamese invasion of Cambodia—a war to keep the infamous Khmer Rouge at bay and out of Vietnam's southern provinces. But after early victories in 1979, the war bogged down into an endless struggle against guerrillas in the Cambodian countryside—"Vietnam's Vietnam," Anh calls it without smiling. He doubts that the government will be able to fulfill its promise of bringing its soldiers home by 1990.

"The Cambodian war has wrecked our economy," Anh says forlornly. "The North knew all about fighting a war, but very little about waging peace. Nobody's surprised the invasion's gone on for so long. It keeps peoples' minds off their problems at home. Now, the soldiers from the American war—the *dirty war*—are retiring. Hanoi wants a new generation of young men for the army. Even my middle boy, who's of prime military age, may be called." Tears now come to Anh's eyes. "Haven't they had enough fighting? Is that the only thing we Vietnamese are fit for in this world? No! I can't believe that!"

I tell Anh I know nothing about politics. I tell him I didn't come here to criticize anyone. I only want to see my family and try to make sense out of what's happened in my life. I don't want my visit to upset anyone, as I can see it's upsetting him. I smile and make a show of noticing on my watch how late it is, but they need no reminding. It's been a long day—one of the longest in my life—since my breakfast with Per in Bangkok. I am running now on sheer willpower.

I say good-bye to Yen and her beautiful children and give them small gifts of American chewing gum and candy, which they receive like New Year's toys. I long to show Yen the snapshots of Jimmy I brought from the States—how I, too, can raise a fine, handsome son for Anh—but I know it would be impolite. After all, although she calls herself Anh's "third wife" out of deference to me, I know she has stuck with this man through his divorce and downfall from wealth and power, through the aftermath of war and revolution—years I spent growing comfortable and secure in America. It is enough to share the joy I have found in life without rubbing her nose in her own misfortune. Sometimes it's an act of compassion simply to do nothing.

Outside, Anh rolls a dented gray Vespa into the porch light, climbs on, twists the key several times, and nurses its cranky motor to life. In the hands of a driver who knows the way exactly, our return to the hotel is much shorter than the journey that brought me from it. As I sit behind Anh, arms twined around his comfortable middle-aged body, I imagine the troubles and joys he has seen since our one perfect night together. I rest my head on his back and watch Saigon streak by in a blur.

At the Continental, we sit for a while in the lobby and I show Anh my photos of Jimmy. I present the snapshots year by year so he can see his son grow up. I watch his face change as the infant becomes a boy, the boy a teenager, and the teenager, a handsome young man. It occurs to me that as I show Anh the pictures, my own life is also on parade. I realize now, as I watch Anh enjoy the son he's never known, how much Anh has truly become my brother—not husband, not lover—but one part of the wholeness I have always sought in life. It reminds me of the first time I realized such a special relationship, such wholesome love, was possible between men and women—between a sister and a brother— between me and the brother who immediately preceded me into this world and who, as fate or luck or god would have it, was the first in my family to precede me into the next.

* * *

MY BROTHER SAU BAN (whose nickname Sau means "fifth child" —his given name was Ban) was born in 1944 and so was already five years old when I was born. In age, he was closer to me than any other brother or sister and I think this nearness made our relationship special from the start. It was from Sau Ban, as much as from my father, that I learned about men—how to talk to them and see them as people rather than silly boys or husbands. Although my much-older brother Bon Nghe was born in 1937, he was a grown man as far as I was concerned. When he went to Hanoi in 1954, it was more like losing a father—particularly because my mother, like most Vietnamese women, idolized her oldest son. My life with younger Sau Ban wasn't like that at all.

When I was little, Sau Ban used to take care of me when my sisters Hai or Lan weren't around. Because I used to scamper off and play adventurous games with the boys instead of practicing housework with the girls, this was more often than my mother knew. Sau Ban taught me how to compete with the schoolboys in volleyball, although they teased him unmercifully about the kindness he showed his baby sister and nicknamed me *Buon Ut,* which is Vietnamese for tagalong. In foot races, he often slowed down just enough to allow me to beat him. When we sailed our crude, coconut-husk toy boats on the pond, he always made sure mine stayed free of the reeds to catch the wind. In the summer, when the French war was worst, Sau Ban would go down to the swamp and hunt lizards for me to eat—sometimes the only real food I would have all day, and he never ate anything himself until he was sure I'd had enough.

But his concern for other people didn't start and stop with his family. Every year Sau Ban helped the village men rescue lowlanders from the winter floods and brought them to our house for food and shelter until the water receded. I also remember Sau Ban climbing fruit trees to help elderly people get food, or running errands for farmers who forgot their tools or needed to send a message home. All this he did cheerfully, with no expectation of reward, the way he did his other work, which was always diligently done and finished on time. In this way, he was very much like my father, although he looked more like my mother: tall, for a Vietnamese, and husky.

Sau Ban was also very talented and if his spirit had come to earth any place else, he would certainly have been an artist. Using only charcoal from our fire or spare paint left over from a government project, he created beautiful images of the village, of the hills and rivers around it, and of the people—particularly the children—who lived there. His canvases were broken boards, scraps of cloth or paper—anything that came to hand and was not useful for something else. I used to think that the beauty Ban added to these common objects made them the most valuable things in Ky La.

Because we spent so much time together and because Ban was naturally a giving, fun-loving person, he wound up spoiling me rotten. When my chores got too hard and I asked Sau Ban for help, he would not only help me, but finish the work himself so I could go play with the other children. This help included homework, too, from the government school we both attended from eight to noon and two to five each day. Ban always woke up first and did his homework, stopping only to make breakfast for my father and mother before they went to the fields. He also made our school lunches—usually rice balls wrapped in banana leaves—and even when he began leaving early to go to advanced school in Khai Tay, my lunch would always be waiting for me when I got up.

If I didn't feel like going to school (which was more often than it should have been), I would just go to my favorite play places away from the village. Because my mother seldom looked for me herself, that task usually fell to Sau Ban. Of course, knowing all my secret hideouts, Ban always found me in minutes, but it was just to make sure I was safe. He only made me go to school if there was something important going on, like a test or a visit by government officials or a celebration he knew I would like. When I turned eleven and the older schoolboys began to notice me, Sau Ban often ran back from Khai Tay to escort me home. Being pestered by boys was one of the reasons I played hooky as often as I did, but I never told Sau Ban about it. He would have beat them up or caused trouble with their parents, and it just seemed simpler to stay away.

All in all, the years with my sisters and Sau Ban were among the best of my life. Ky La then—between the French and American wars—was a childhood paradise, full of tropical birds and buffalos; dogs and chickens and pigs we called our pets; rushing rivers to swim in; and wide fields where we could run and laugh and be with our families. We had fresh rain to cool us down and a hot sun to dry us off—in short, everything little kids needed to grow up happy and strong and full of love.

Even the villagers had high hopes for a lasting peace. In 1955, Premier Ngo Dinh Diem had won a national referendum in the South and, while he organized the government as its new president, negotiated with Ho Chi Minh for the terms of a truly national election. Although we peasants assumed the winner would be crowned king (we couldn't conceive, after all, of any other form of government), we believed Vietnam would gladly accept either leader—provided it meant a free and independent country. Unfortunately, that happy dream was not to be.

When President Diem was assassinated in a conspiracy, the new government redoubled its efforts to recruit the nation's youth to the Republican cause. Because Sau Ban by this time was an apprentice bricklayer —the best one in Ky La—he was called away with the youth brigade to help the government construct what it called "double strategic hamlets" (villages with two layers of defenses) and a number of "new life" hamlets—places where peasants were sent when their old villages had been overrun by Communists.

With Sau Ban away more often than he was home, my parents began to argue—about me, my sisters, and the future of our family.

"The Republicans were here today," my father said one time at dinner. "They asked why Bay Ly wasn't out with the youth brigade doing work to defend the village. I told them she was our only child now and we needed her to take care of our farm."

"Hmph!" my mother grunted, giving me the evil eye, "for all the help she is around here! Maybe we *should* send her off with Sau Ban. That would teach her the value of a good day's work!"

"Don't joke like that," my father said.

"Who's joking?" my mother replied, clapping down her rice bowl. "Bay Ly's got to do her share like everyone else. She thinks she's some little princess—too good for chores, too busy blinking her eyes at those good-for-nothing schoolboys—"

"Mama *Du* that's not true!" I objected. "The big boys bother me all the time now that Sau Ban is gone. I only—"

"You be quiet, little princess!" My mother spanked me lightly on the forehead. My father was up from his place and grabbed my mother's wrist.

"Don't you *ever* hit her again, do you hear me?" he yelled, and flung my mother's arm away. "Won't you be satisfied until *all* my children are gone—sent away to Hanoi or Danang or Saigon or god knows where else? Bon Nghe has been gone for eight years! Lan has been gone for two and Hai for almost one—although it seems like they've all been gone for twenty! Now Sau Ban, my last son, has been taken by the government. You really want Bay Ly to join him? Are you that anxious to get rid of your family? I thought you wanted them back! All this crying all these years for Bon Nghe—well, do you mean it or don't you?"

"I *do* want my babies back—" My mother's tears began to flow.

"Or do you want it to be like when I met you, eh?" My father's face was purple—I had never seen him so upset! "You were all by yourself then—with nobody to look after you, to care whether you lived or died. Is that what you want? Maybe you're tired of your husband, too? Maybe I should go join the army!"

My mother ran from the house and I did too. She went to Uncle Khan's but I could only go to one of the play places I used to visit with Sau Ban. I wished with all my might that he would come back; having Sau Ban home always made things perfect. When I finally went home, my parents had made up and were worried that I had run away. My father took me and my mother into his arms and cried with us and said, "All I want is to see my children! If I can't have my family around me, what's the point of going on?"

The next morning, my mother told me in private, "Your father is going to make himself sick without your brothers and sisters. We've got to get Sau Ban back. We've got to get Lan and Hai to come back too, even if it's only for a visit."

As soon as she could, she went to Danang and had Uncle Nhu send telegrams to everyone: "Come home at once, your father needs you."

A week or so later, I was coming back to our house from the well when I saw Sau Ban riding down the road on a bicycle. I dropped the bucket, spilling water all over the ground, and ran to greet him. He got off, grinning as if he hadn't a care in the world, and lifted me into the air, giving me the biggest hug a girl ever had. When he put me down, I saw that his bike was loaded with treasures from the city—from Saigon!—where his crew had been working when Uncle Nhu's telegram arrived. He pushed his bike through the heavy sand toward our house and told me what had happened.

"Hai and Lan got their telegrams when I did," Sau Ban said. "We thought something terrible had happened—that father had passed away or something—"

"Oh no," I said, still breathless from seeing my brother, "he's only going crazy. He'll be better when he sees you. He misses everyone very much."

"Good. I told your sisters I'd come home first and see what's going on. It's not safe to travel in the countryside these days. I didn't want them to take the risk unless it was really necessary."

Naturally, my father was happy Sau Ban was back, but his health was very bad. It was as if seeing Sau Ban made him miss his other children even more. He fell sick within a day of Ban's arrival and the next day my mother got sick too. With both of them unable to work, Sau Ban and I did everything ourselves: worked in the fields, tended the animals, prepared the meals, cleaned the house, and looked after our ailing parents. (Sau Ban was the only man I knew, besides my father, who did not shrink from women's work—and did it better than many wives.) But Sau Ban worried, as usual, that I would get too tired or neglect my schoolwork, so he tried to do my chores too—but this time I wouldn't let him. I did everything my mother usually did, from pounding our laundry clean on river rocks to taking spare food to neighbors who had problems of their own. In the evening, Sau Ban and I would kneel by the bamboo mats on which our parents slept and pray they would be spared. Afterward, we would go outside and sit under the stars, where Ban would tell me about his adventures traveling around the country building houses and roads. Making things always seemed to make Sau Ban happy and making useful things—big and pleasing things—made him happiest of all. The stories he told of his creations always came out of him like songs.

When our parents recovered, my mother gave Sau Ban some things to take to my sisters and he set off on his bicycle—smiling and waving as if his dangerous journey to Saigon was no more than a trip to the market. Unfortunately, the joy of Ban's visit only made the pain of his leaving worse. We ate dinner that night in silence—nobody felt like saying anything, even to argue. Afterward, my father went outside and smoked one of the cigars Sau Ban had brought him and cried his eyes out to the stars.

For the next few months, things went along much as they had before, although the Republicans were beginning their buildup in Quang Nam province and we saw soldiers more often in Ky La. Occasionally we got letters from Hai or Lan or Sau Ban telling us what they were doing, or word from a friend or relative who had seen them, reassuring us that they were fine. On Sau Ban's eighteenth birthday, however, the situation changed.

Until now, Sau Ban's youth had kept him out of the service, even though his height and husky build had sometimes caused people to challenge his age and accuse him of dodging the draft. Now, he had to register with the military and because he believed his chances of escaping army service would be better in Ky La, he quit his construction job and returned to live in the village.

Unfortunately, Republican soldiers had arrived in Ky La two days before he got home. The Republican military police checked his papers when he arrived and told him to report to Danang for a physical examination and to answer questions about his past—preliminaries for induction. Either way, Sau Ban knew he would wind up in uniform: a soldier's or a prisoner's.

This bad news upset everyone. We couldn't imagine Sau Ban having to fight against his brother or our friends who had joined the Viet Cong. For that matter, I couldn't imagine gentle Ban killing anyone at all, no matter which side the person favored. My mother proposed a solution.

"You'll just have to go to Hanoi, that's all," she told him. "Perhaps the war will end while you're in training. If it doesn't, at least you won't wind up helping the invaders against your own people."

Although Sau Ban and my father reluctantly agreed with her plan, it was much easier said than done. When my older brother Bon Nghe went north, it was after the French had been defeated. Thousands of people trekked north and south as part of the postwar settlement. Now, all routes north of Hue had been cut by the government. The only way to join liberation forces from the South was to be a part of those forces already —to gain access to their secret routes and enjoy the protection of their fighters. It meant that Sau Ban would have to make contact with the local Viet Cong and go north on the difficult and dangerous Ho Chi Minh Trail.

To launch our plan to save Sau Ban, my mother went to Danang and purchased black material, rubber sandals, and a sun hat—the uniform of the Viet Cong—which my father buried in our yard as soon as she brought it home. She then cooked some food—sweet rice and black beans—and preserved them with salt for Sau Ban's journey. My job was to make sure everything looked normal around our house; to conspicuously tend the chickens and drive our water buffalo to and from the fields ("Don't let it be seen at our house during the day," my father said. "That's the surest sign that something's wrong!"). I had to sing loudly and act like a carefree little kid even though my heart was breaking at the thought of losing Sau Ban the way I had lost my other brother.

The next day Sau Ban, my parents, Uncle Luc, and I went into the fields as if to work. Everyone was loaded down with tools so that Sau Ban wouldn't stand out with his provisions for the journey. In the part of our paddy that was closest to the swamp, my mother, father, and uncle fanned out and scanned the places where people might be watching. When the coast was clear, Sau Ban dropped his tools, gave me a quick hug, said, "Don't worry, I'll be back after my training—be a big girl and take care of our parents," then slipped into the swamp. The hardest part was having to keep on working as if nothing had happened, even though I knew that might be the last time we would see Sau Ban. When I finally glanced at my parents, silent tears were streaming down their faces, which were as stony as the rocks they dug up with their hoes.

That night nobody could eat and we went to bed early, knowing sleep would ease our sorrow. About midnight, though, we were awakened by somebody in the house.

"Sau Ban!" I cried, overjoyed to see my brother's figure silhouetted against the window. He grinned as though nothing had happened, picked me up, and gave me a squeeze. My parents woke up too and were less happy than shocked. Obviously, something went wrong.

"I couldn't get through the swamp," Sau Ban said. "There were too many soldiers. Only birds and moles can get out of Ky La. I'm sorry. I failed."

"No," my mother said. "If it takes a mole to escape, then we'll turn you into a mole. Uncle Luc has contacts with the Viet Cong. We'll ask them to send an escort. They have secret tunnels all over the place. It'll take a little longer, but it's worth it. If anyone can get you out, they will."

I had never seen my mother so determined about anything. Only later did I realize how difficult this time had been for her. My father was useless at planning anything—he wanted Sau Ban safe but he didn't want him to fight for either side. He only wanted his family close by. Sau Ban wanted to please my parents, but he couldn't think of himself as a soldier.

So my mother, despite her own breaking heart, had to be strong for everyone.

It took Uncle Luc a few days to get his message to the Viet Cong and a few days more to receive their answer—a set of times and signals they would use if and when they could send an escort. During that time, my father reburied Sau Ban's uniform and told him to hide in the house and not set a foot outside—a necessity that pleased me immensely.

Finally, word came that some Viet Cong were coming and Sau Ban should get ready to go. All night we sat by the door, watching and waiting, but nothing happened. Just before sunup, Uncle Luc came running down the road and ducked into our house. He was sweaty, dirty, and out of breath.

"It's no good," he said, gasping and trembling. "The escort didn't make it. They got caught outside of town. I barely escaped myself. Now police and soldiers will be everywhere, trying to find out what's going on. Pray to god the two fighters don't crack under torture. If they do, we're all finished!"

By now even my mother agreed that the Republican noose around Ky La was too tight for Sau Ban to escape. We decided to stay alert and keep Ban hidden for the next few days and see what happened. Happily for us, no soldiers came to question us or arrest us. Although we never knew what happened to the Viet Cong escort, it's likely they died under torture. It was hard to believe these strangers died on a mission to save my brother—a man they had never met—but such was their need for fighters and the goodwill of the people at this early stage of the war.

Anyway, this delay changed everything for our family. As my mother resigned herself to the idea that Sau Ban might eventually be drafted ("I can always desert," he told her, smiling happily as was his way. "Lots of soldiers get lost and switch sides every day!"), my father seemed to regain his interest in life. He told Ban to think about living, not dying, and to get by as well as he could before fate or luck or god took matters out of his hands. My father convinced Sau Ban that he should get married and, if he could, impregnate a wife so that his seed—*their* seed, the line of the Phung men—might continue if Sau Ban were killed. (We still had no news about Bon Nghe in Hanoi—if he was living or dead, married or single, a father or a man without children. Looking back, I can understand how important it must have been to my father to feel assured that a son would live long enough to continue his family line.)

Unfortunately, finding a bride (even the hurry-up, wartime kind) was the mother's duty, not the father's, and my mother felt scarcely up to it.

She sent word to relatives in Man Quang that her youngest boy was about to go into the army and needed the best mate they could find in a hurry. Man Quang, my mother's native village, was bigger than Ky La and a good source of mates for both sexes. There were still enough unrelated people to make good babies and by the time they reached marrying age (which was sixteen or seventeen for a boy; fourteen or fifteen for a girl) the shortcomings of all the local children were well known by the matchmakers. Within a week, word came back that at least one candidate—a motherless girl named Nham, who had been raised by her father and aunts—would be worth my mother's effort to come and inspect.

In the countryside, potential brides are evaluated no less carefully than a new buffalo, pig, or bicycle. After all, a wedding extends two families as well as making them smaller by one daughter or one son. First, my Man Quang aunt and my mother made a social call on the girl's family, and while they chatted about local events, they inspected the condition of the house (especially the cooking area) to see if she had been raised to prize cleanliness and domestic responsibility. They also found a pretext for checking the household water barrel, too, for it was by custom the daughter's job to keep it filled, and a half-full tank or one that was full of stagnant water showed better than a proud father's boasts just how good a worker she was.

If the family passed these tests, it was time to observe the girl herself: to see if she flirted with village boys, disobeyed her parents, or failed to show proper respect to older people. If the daughter turned out to be chaste, obedient, and mindful of tradition, it was customary next to obtain her birthdate and consult the village shaman for an astrological reading —to see how well her natal fate and personal characteristics matched her prospective husband's. Only when all this was found acceptable did my mother formally raise the question of marriage and ask to interview the girl. It's possible all this was done by Tung's parents to evaluate me as a wife, but if they did, I didn't remember it. Such topics were fit for family conversation only if they involved a son, and Sau Ban's engagement was always bigger news than mine.

My mother returned from her home village very satisfied with what she'd found out. Nham seemed well raised, diligent in her duties, and anxious to please my mother—which would be, of course, her prime duty after marriage. (New husbands are the worst people to evaluate a wife, my mother told me. Like young dogs, they are either so in love with the wagging tail that they ignore the muddy paws, making the wife lazy; or they mount her or beat her so often that they eventually find even a good woman—and hence all women—beneath contempt, making her bitter.

Only a mother-in-law has both perspective and compassion enough to turn a young bride into a wife.) Because my mother had been denied the chance to do these things for her firstborn son, she was doubly determined to do them right for her second. On the strength of her recommendation, then, my father and brother applied to the authorities for *di coi mat*—permission to go to Man Quang to propose a contract of marriage.

Their visit was short and when they returned, my brother told me all about it. First, he said, Nham was told only that day she was being considered for marriage, let alone a marriage that would take her from her village. When Sau Ban finally met her, he discovered she was rather short (they were a curious pair, Sau Ban being so tall), but she was light-skinned and pretty and seemed to have a good heart, an independent spirit, and strong enough bones to deliver healthy Phung sons. Second, Nham and her family were alarmed that the wedding would take place so soon—within the next few months instead of three years hence, the traditional engagement time—although their shock was relieved when they learned our father owned several rice paddies, which made us seem wealthy. (Her father owned none, but worked on a relative's farm for a share of the harvest—as many did during and after the rule of the French.) Consequently, Sau Ban was considered a worthy suitor and my father presented *cau trau*—an areca nut wrapped in the leaf of the betel tree—and the proposal was accepted.

It was now a race between the receipt of Sau Ban's draft notice and the wedding. My mother began working on the red wedding dress—the mother-in-law's traditional gift to the bride (for which she would pay dearly in future toil!)—and my father made plans for the ceremony and feast that would follow.

During the intervening weeks, my mother taught my brother all the things she considered important for a new groom to know: "Don't sleep with Nham when she has her period, no matter how strong the urge takes you. And be sure to tell me if she was a virgin the first time you do it—that's very important. She'll be hard to get into and you'll find a little blood on the bed even if she doesn't cry. Some girls fake all that and we have to know if we can trust her family. Tell me, too, if she has any funny habits. A good woman should just lie there and let you do what you want—but she mustn't be too interested in men."

My mother prepared me, too, for my role as *em chong*—the sister-in-law who helps the mother police the marriage in its early years. (Normally this was the oldest sister's work, but because we were short not only on marriageable sons but daughters, I inherited the task.) I was supposed to befriend the bride and report to my mother how she acted when her mother-in-law wasn't around. "Is she a complainer or a nagger? Does she fulfill her duties willingly and look for new ways to please her in-laws, or does she wait to be told? All these things you must tell me, Bay Ly. I can't be everywhere at once and Sau Ban will be like every other new husband—too softheaded to get his marriage off on the right foot!" To all these things Ban and I just answered "Yes, Mother," or "No, Mother." Tradition required that we respectfully agree with what she said—but not necessarily do anything about it.

The wedding was held in October 1962, on a rainy day (considered good luck in the Orient) and was attended by thirty people—a large party for wartime. That night, Sau Ban and Nham slept in the lower *nha duoi* house while my mother and I shared a bed on the other side of a thin partition. For half the night, we heard them talking in low voices and sometimes giggling and sometimes getting very quiet. I whispered to my mother, "Can they make a baby just by talking about it?" I thought something more dramatic was supposed to happen. For once, my mother said nothing but only smiled and pulled me close like a baby and told me to go to sleep. I think she was too anxious for a grandson to accelerate the work unwisely.

During the next few months, my association with Nham, far from leading us to the roles of inmate and informer, made us the best of friends. Part of this was due to my natural reluctance to "turn in" a girl so close to me in age who was simply doing what girls our age do naturally (complain about too much work and wish our lives were more romantic), and part was due to my promise to my brother to stick up for Nham when she was unjustly accused simply to test her mettle.

In December, my sisters Hai and Lan came back to celebrate New Year's and because my sister-in-law was passing her wifely tests and the family (mostly) was reunited, my father was the happiest man in Ky La. Unfortunately, his joy was not to last.

In February, Sau Ban's draft notice arrived and he decided to return with Hai to the city. He reasoned that it would be easier (and safer for our family) if he left Ky La in the company of a relative rather than trying again to sneak out on his own. When the authorities caught up with him, he would be far away and, perhaps, in a place where he could more easily contact the Viet Cong. Although nobody especially liked this plan, it at least gave us a chance to give Sau Ban a proper farewell. As we would all find out later, the luxury of such formal rites—of saying good-bye to loved ones, celebrating a marriage, holding funerals—would be one of the first things we would lose when the new war gathered force.

Six months later, my mother came running to the house with a letter she received from Hai. She was very excited because Hai's letters were so rare and she was sure this one contained good news (at least *some* news) about Sau Ban, from whom we had heard little (with the exception of some love letters to Nham), and perhaps some encouraging things she could tell her new daughter-in-law, who continued to live with us and was growing despondent without a husband. Unfortunately, because I was the only one in the family who could read, the task of exploding my mother's hopes fell to me.

As soon as I opened the letter I knew the news would be bad. Hai's handwriting was never good and now it was next to impossible to read, which meant she had probably written the letter in a hurry or in a moment of great strain. All it said was that Sau Ban had lived with her for a few months then "left in a hurry to take a new job with Uncle." Although she didn't specify which uncle it was, we all guessed it was "Uncle Ho"—Ho Chi Minh and the liberation army. Because the mail was sometimes censored even in those days, she couldn't give us any more clues about what this meant. Had Sau Ban joined the local Viet Cong or was he on his way to Hanoi? Would he be a front-line fighter or would he be a scout like Bon Nghe? For that matter, would his special skills keep him occupied safely behind the lines, building bunkers and command posts and infirmaries for our troops? As it had been for Bon Nghe, we assumed, so would it be with Sau Ban. We would probably never learn his exact location, health, or situation, and he would have to dwell only in our memories, hearts, and prayers until the war was over.

My mother received the news with relief: at least her sons would not be fighting each other in the war that, every day, became more violent and struck closer to home. My father, on the other hand, acted as if the letter had been Sau Ban's death notice. He went into private mourning, burned incense at our family altar, and could not eat for several days. We even kept the news from Nham because her family's sympathy for the Viet Cong was uncertain. As far as she was concerned, Sau Ban was simply traveling, as he had traveled before, on his construction jobs— although when my mother finally told her what happened, she reacted indifferently—so used were the people in Man Quang apparently, to seeing families torn up by the war.

For myself, I found I could not be alone without missing my brother terribly. When I sat outside in the evening, his face was in the moon and his voice was in the rustling trees. When I did my chores, I felt his helping hand on my rake and heard his careless laugh in the calling birds. When I closed my eyes to go to sleep, I felt cold where my soul had been warmed by Sau Ban's sunny spirit.

When New Year's, 1963, came and went and we still had heard nothing about him, my mother went to the village shaman with her sons' dried navels—saved in a box since they were born—and asked about their fate. (In the countryside, we believed the navel still connected the child to the mother—even when the two were far apart.) The old man answered that although my mother's oldest son ("Hanoi" Bon Nghe) was strong and healthy, the youngest boy was in a place too gray for him to see. When my mother pressed the psychic to tell her what this meant, the old man answered that such feelings usually meant the person asked about was dead, although it was his practice never to speak with certainty about those things which were still in the hands of god.

My mother rushed home and broke the news to my father, who, weeping openly, began performing funeral rites at our family shrine: gathering some of Ban's things—a couple of his drawings and some coins—and a handful of sweet rice and burning incense on the altar. But my mother snuffed out the candles, overturned the smoking pots, and knocked the souvenirs from the shelf.

"*Ba lam gi vay* (What are you doing)?" my father asked in horror. "You're dishonoring our son!"

"No!" she shouted. "You're dishonoring him! Sau Ban is still alive. I know it. I feel it in my bones. God wouldn't do these things to us without a reason—and we have offended no one. Get up off your knees. Come on! Go back to work—" She spanked him with her hands until he got up and then she turned on me. "You too, Bay Ly!"

She gave me a swat and I scampered, teary and confused, with my father from the house. Outside, he put his arm around me and said, "We'd better do what your mother says, Bay Ly. It's only the word of the shaman, and he's been wrong before." Still, we cried the whole way out to the fields and couldn't work much once we got there.

That evening, when we tried to sleep, I swore I heard my brother's voice—clear as a bell—in a storm that howled around the house. He was cold and wanted to come in. I got off my mat and went to my father, but he was already awake. "I know, Bay Ly," he said, "I heard it too."

The next day, while my mother was out working, my father brought the village shaman to our house. When we got inside, the wizard asked why we had brought him. My father said, "That's *your* job. You tell us!" The shaman sniffed around the house awhile, then stopped at our family shrine.

"You hear funny noises?" he asked as if he already knew the answer. "Maybe voices—last night in the rain?"

We nodded in amazement.

"Well, here's your problem, then. Your spirit house is too small. You have a relative who needs some shelter, that's all. Just build a little alcove outside and things will be fine."

The shaman left and without saying a word, my father got his tools and with loving care added a small altar on the north side of our house. We never spoke again of the shaman's visit—to my mother or to each other. We never heard Sau Ban's voice again either, in the rain or wind or in the calling jungle birds. We didn't weep anymore, for that matter, until Uncle Luc came by a few months later to tell us Sau Ban had been killed by an American-made mine on his way home for a New Year's visit.

As for Nham, the word of Sau Ban's death broke her tenuous links to our family. Being without child, there was no real reason for her to remain in our house and she returned to her relatives in Man Quang— perhaps to find a new husband. But too many young men had been chewed up by the war, and when her father passed away, Nham struck out on her own. We heard stories about her from time to time, but she never took another husband. Like dew on a cool winter morning, Nham eventually disappeared from sight, and, I think, was missed by no one but me.

Past Midnight, April 4, 1986:
Lobby of the Continental Hotel HCMC

Anh has seen his son grow up in my photos and now he sits back in his chair in the lobby of the "new" Continental and we look each other straight in the eye. I am dead tired, but I don't want to say good night and end our reunion. I study his face as he studies mine, the way tenants eye an old house in which they used to live. We have both withstood twenty seasons—twenty winter moonsoons—since we last laid eyes on each other. We must rediscover each other the way one climbs an old staircase—carefully, groping for footholds along the way. I see the light of compassion in his face, though his manner since coming to this state-run hotel has been guarded. Perhaps the Communist clerks make him nervous. Then again, maybe it's me.

"Well," I say, trying to seem relaxed about everything, "you've done okay for yourself, brother Anh." He protests but I continue. "No, no, I mean it. You fit well with the old regime, it's true, but you found your way with the new one, too. Not everybody can say that. You have nothing to be ashamed of. Just be happy, like me, that fate or luck or god has brought you in one piece to enjoy this moment, eh?"

He regards me intently and we both feel a spark pass between us— shall we go up to my room or not?—but it quickly dies, snuffed from both sides. He *has* become my brother—the brother of my soul—and I his soul sister. Knowing it or not, he gave me a son and helped put me on a life course that brought me to America. For that I can't be anything but grateful.

"Well, it's very late—" I stand up and stretch.

He stands up too, looking at his watch, "Oh no it isn't; it's only morning!"

We laugh and take each other's hands. Anh says the next plane to Danang is on Monday, April 7, and he'll make our reservations in the morning. He says he has some errands to run and asks if I would like to pass the time by coming along to see the new Saigon. I tell him I would love to—after he escorts me to "my meeting" with the *Ban Viet Kieu* officials. Neither one of us can refuse such charming invitations. We embrace, patting each other on the back affectionately (one cannot kiss good-bye, even innocently, in front of the prudish party minions) and I watch Anh mount his scooter and disappear into the night.

Daylight comes too soon, announced by the bedside phone. It is Anh, waiting in the lobby. I tell him to go have breakfast—American women need some time in the morning to find their face and put it on.

The day is fresh—puffy, dark-bellied clouds play hopscotch with the sun and keep the city's streets from becoming too hot too soon as we whiz through them on Anh's Vespa. We stop at several places and pick up papers, including the government airline office where we get our tickets for Danang. Again I am amazed at how old Saigon masquerades as a Communist city. It is a typical workday, yet the place is one tenth as busy as the old capital—more like a Mexican village than Paris of the Orient. Aside from asking me casually where my family lives, nobody seems to care what I do or why I'm in the city. They don't want to know. In this new Saigon, it seems, there is no profit in asking too much.

At two o'clock we go to my infamous *meeting* with the Vietnam National Committee in a residential part of town. Their office is in an old, French-style house with a well-trimmed lawn and a broad porch on which several small tables and chairs have been arranged almost like a restaurant. A few Vietnamese locals are sitting there drinking tea and Anh joins them, saying he'll wait until I'm finished. I don't know if he's being courteous or if he has some other reason to avoid the party officials, but I don't press him further. If we Vietnamese have learned anything, it's when not to press our luck.

Inside, what used to be the living room contains three desks occupied by clerks. At the first desk sits the official who picked me up at the airport and for once, I find his craggy face reassuring. I smile at him, remembering his name from the drive into town.

"Hello, brother Quang. It's good to see you this afternoon!"

He nods politely, takes back my invitation (I presume he'll stamp and counterstamp it later), and points me toward the group in what used to be the formal dining room. About fifteen other expatriate Vietnamese— *Viet Kieu*—have already found chairs at a long wooden table. They all look as bewildered and wary as I do. (Our nerves are not helped by the unaccustomed heat, which is beginning to affect even me.) Although nobody chats, I see them holding passports, magazines, and paperback books from places as diverse as Canada, France, Australia, and the United States. The shelves on the painted concrete walls are covered with expensive decorations: porcelain, ivory, tortoise-shell art, lacquerware, and other handicrafts arrayed like displays in a tourist shop. On the wall behind the speaker's dais hangs the inevitable portrait of Uncle Ho, but in this one beams of light radiate from behind his head, like Jesus or Buddha. Although the picture is supposed to convey a sense of Ho's spirituality, I find it triggers old memories and more than a little discomfort. The religious aura of the picture only reminds me of the awesome power of the state compared with puny individuals like me. A look around the room shows that a similar disquiet has settled over the others—they drop their glances, fiddle nervously with their fingers, or just sit like panting dogs, eyes closed, in the heat. As practiced victims, we have learned our roles too well.

* * *

IN KY LA, like the rest of Vietnam, most people were Catholics or Buddhists. Because President Diem and Madame Nhu admired things French and worried constantly about opinions in America (a Christian nation, which they feared would not defend a Buddhist state) they tried very hard to make Vietnam reflect, if not adopt, Christian ways. Diem's brother, Thuc, was Archbishop of Saigon and even in Quang Nam the provincial officials were usually Catholic. This discrimination against Buddhists, who were more numerous as well as more closely linked than Catholics to Vietnam's traditional culture, dismayed many peasants and made them suspicious of anything the government did. This in turn made the Republicans mistrust the peasants and turned even the simplest political dispute into all-out religious war.

For example, in the presidential referendum in 1955, villagers were told to vote—to exercise their rights and responsibilities as citizens. This seemed like a fine idea, so many Buddhists went to the polls in order to show their displeasure with Diem's policies. Unfortunately, the government also used the election to issue identification cards to all citizens—you got your card when you voted, as proof of citizenship and participation. Even this wouldn't have been a bad idea, except the cards were marked with a small cross, which was also the Catholic symbol.

Naturally, the Buddhists in Ky La, including my parents, didn't want to carry around the Christian symbol, so they threw the cards away. This caused them untold grief when they were stopped by the authorities.

"Why don't you have your card?" the police would ask. "Didn't you vote in the elections?"

There was no way Buddhists could successfully answer this question. If they said, "Yes, I voted in the election," they would be accused of lying because everyone who turned in a ballot got a card. If they said, "I voted, but I threw my card away," they would be accused of favoring the Viet Cong, for only enemies of the state would be afraid to participate in the ID system.

Consequently, the weeks after the election were horrible in Ky La. Police and soldiers terrorized anyone who didn't have a card and because most of these people were Buddhists, they bore the brunt of the harassment. Once dissenting families were identified, civilian thugs (many of them Catholics, although some were government agents trying to root out Viet Cong) came into their homes and tore down family shrines, often beating and torturing the family. A few people, the most devout Buddhists and those who resisted with force, were actually killed and their bodies tied up in rice bags and dumped in the nearby river. I even heard one story of a Buddhist holy man being buried alive after one of these raids, but by that time emotions ran so high on both sides that people couldn't believe even half the stories they heard.

For a while, there was almost no distinction between the religious war and the political war. A few Buddhists organized demonstrations against the terror tactics, but they were arrested as subversives. Only in Danang and the bigger cities were the Buddhists organized well enough to resist. But even there, these demonstrations (some of which ended by Buddhist priests setting fire to themselves) were little more than futile gestures. In the countryside, we had to play down our Buddhist heritage and go along with the program. Some of our neighbors even became token Catholics to escape the government's wrath. In private, however, we kept to all our customs and even made up songs to show our contempt for our oppressors. We made up one song because the traditional leap day in one month out of four on the Buddhist calendar had been prohibited:

> La-la la-la la—catch Diem like a cicada!
> When Diem disappears it will be time
> To dare to go to temple!
> When Diem's around, everything's turned upside down.
> The pagoda's destroyed and the monks all arrested—
> And after the arrest, there's the order to kill!
> We have gone four months without our leap!
> Because Diem is stupid—
> Nhu is a fool—
> Can is crazy—
> And Thuc is cracked!

About this time, in the late fifties, the police began arresting people who had relatives who "went north" after the war with the French. They were herded into pens and interrogated. Most were released after a few days, but some were beaten and tortured and sent on to military prisons in the jungle where they were forced to work on land reclamation projects while attending Republican lectures. These forced labor camps (*di dan,* we called them—"places where nobody lives") were greatly feared because bad water and big insects caused many deaths, and many people who survived the diseases were rumored to have "simply disappeared" in the jungle if they resisted indoctrination. My sister Ba Xuan, who had already lost her husband to Hanoi after the war with the French, experienced new scrutiny—and much terror—for this reason.

It began when one of her husband's cousins developed an eye for her and took advantage of her husband's absence to make himself a nuisance—forcing his attentions on her even when she made it clear his advances were not welcome. He followed her while she ran her errands, sweet-talking her along the way, and hung around the door to her in-law's house (where she lived) or to our house (where she often visited) when she went in or out. He would only leave when my father was around to shake a rake at him and tell him to mind his own business.

During the religious turmoil, the cousin (Chin, the man who later helped me out of jail) enlisted in the Common Guard, the local police force commissioned to help the army keep peace in the villages (although the guardsmen often provoked more trouble than they prevented). Now that he had a policeman's badge, Chin's advances became more than a simple irritant. He would stop Ba in the street and make her talk to him for hours, calling these sessions "interrogation." When she began to avoid him by staying indoors, he sent her love notes and when those didn't work, letters threatening to have her family investigated because of her brother and husband in Hanoi. Since so many people had already been lost to the camps—"gone *di dan*," we would say—my parents took his threat very seriously.

Finally, Ba decided to do something on her own. She sent a note to Chin telling him to meet her at a secluded place after dark. Nobody knows exactly what happened, but afterward Ba appeared more often in his company, compliant and nonresisting. When my father saw them together, he went up to Chin in a rage.

"How can you do this to a married women?" he bellowed. "And to the wife of your cousin as well!"

Because the rest of his squad wasn't around to back him up, Chin cowered before my father and didn't answer back.

"And you, Ba"—my father turned to my sister—"if you keep seeing this man, I'll tie you to a post and whip you like a runaway cow!"

My father took Ba home and when we didn't see Chin for the next two days, we assumed our problems were over. Unfortunately, they were just beginning.

At dusk on the third day, a squad of guardsmen came by with a warrant for my father's arrest. When my father came out of our house, he saw that Ba was already in custody.

The guardsmen took them to a temporary interrogation compound that had been set up beside my school. Although my mother was upset, she was sure they would be released once my father explained the situation to Chin's superiors. Still, I decided to check things out from the school yard—to see if I could spot my father and Ba in the compound.

When school was over, I went with a friend to the fence around the camp. Because the camp was run by local officials, they made no effort to keep people away. In fact, they encouraged visitors because relatives brought food and that meant the government would not have to give prisoners rations.

Because it was getting dark and we couldn't see my father or sister anywhere, we sneaked up to one of the temporary buildings on the perimeter, climbed atop some crates that were stacked against it, and peered through a painted window that was cracked for ventilation. Inside, we saw a naked woman hanging by her feet from a rope and pulley. Her hands were tied behind her back and her head was suspended over a tub that was filled with soapy water. Her wet hair hung down like a mop and there were suds all over the floor and on the pants legs of the soldiers gathered around her.

The soldier holding the rope eased her down and the woman's head went into the bucket. For a moment, her pale body bucked and squirmed like a fish on a line, then went still and the soldier raised her up. She blew soapy water from her mouth and nose and shook her head, flinging water around the room. Although she gasped noisily, she did not scream—air seemed too precious—and the soldiers asked no questions. They simply dunked her again and again—for sport, training, or punishment, we couldn't tell.

"That's not your sister?" my companion whispered hopefully.

"No," I answered. "Ba has short hair." To be truthful, I had never seen my sister without her clothes and the woman's face was so bloated and mottled from hanging upside down that she could have been anyone's sister.

We made our way like mice along the tops of the crates, to the next window of the building taking care to be quiet. This time, the hastily painted window was not open, and I had to work my way along the glass until I found a little place where the brush had missed.

In this room, a shirtless man was tied to a chair in such a way that his shoulders and head fell forward over his lap. Although there seemed to be many soldiers around, I could see clearly only the one who was asking the questions. He cradled a short whip in his hands and when it struck the prisoner, it flayed the skin so badly that I guessed the whip was made of wire. After every few lashes, another soldier stepped forward and threw white powder onto the wounds. From the way the victim twitched and screamed it must have been something that stung a lot—like salt or the quick lime we used to sprinkle into graves that held no coffins. Although the cruel show made me sick, I couldn't turn away and I dropped only when my friend pulled me down by my shirttail.

"Let *me* see—!" She squeezed up to the peek hole. "Ohhh—" she gasped. "Is that your father?"

Without seeing the man's face—seeing only the glinting whip and pink muscle and the puff of white powder—I couldn't say for sure. "No," I answered finally, hoping I was right, "I don't think so—"

"Hey, you!" someone called from the darkness at the end of the building. "What are you doing up there? Come down!"

We clambered as fast as we could in the opposite direction—hearts pounding—sending boxes tumbling behind us. A beam from a flashlight caught us momentarily as we jumped and we hit the ground running like frightened rabbits for the trees behind the schoolhouse. Luckily, the sentries were guardsmen and were too lazy to give chase. "Damned kids stealing equipment!" I heard one shout behind our backs. The next day, we saw the crates had been removed and that the painted windows along the ominous wall had all been boarded up.

When I got home, I told my mother that I had gone to the camp after school but could see neither Ba nor my father in the compound.

"Of course you didn't see them," my mother said. "They were released this afternoon."

"What? You mean Ba and Father are free?"

"Free?" my mother frowned. "No, not exactly. The guardsmen said that if Ba would give up her marriage to the Hanoi traitor—recant her vows—and marry Chin instead, they'd let them go. If she didn't, they said they'd turn them over to the army as Viet Cong spies."

"Oh, Mama *Du*—no!"

"Yes. Fortunately, Chin bragged that he was taking a post with the security police in Danang—him being such a sharp patrolman and all! —and that your sister would lead a better life with him than as a war widow in the village. Phooey! At least it means that if he marries Ba, she won't be around the shame us."

"Is sister Ba going to marry him? Will I ever see her again?" I felt a big lump in my throat.

"Of course you will. You'll see her tomorrow—and your father sooner than that. They're over at Ba's house right now deciding what to do. Anyway, that's not for you to worry about, is it? I ought to whip you for hanging around the camp. That's an evil place, Bay Ly. You're never to go there again—no matter who's been arrested or what kind of noises you hear from the school yard. That place is nothing but trouble. The stories I've heard! Just stay away from it, that's all, and pray the policemen never come for *you!*"

A few days later, Ba came by to tell us that she would be moving to Danang soon to marry Chin. My mother made a farewell dinner for her that night but we all spent most of it crying.

By the end of the year we learned that Ba was pregnant by Chin, but even the news of a prospective grandchild, which should have delighted my father, only made him more unhappy. He told me that although Ba had been with her first husband only a short time before he left, she loved him very much, just as we loved and missed my Hanoi brother, Bon Nghe. I said that my new brother-in-law must be an evil man and that I would hate him forever for doing what he did to Ba.

"No," my father replied sadly, "don't hate Chin—and don't hate Ba for marrying him. Hate the war for doing what it did to them both."

SIX

A Question of Faith

ALTHOUGH A FEW STRAGGLERS enter the dining room of the old colonial house and take seats around the table, we *Viet Kieu* expatriates are, for the most part, assembled. At precisely 2 P.M., brother Quang comes in, stands behind the podium, and opens a folder with his notes. His movements seem full of self-importance—as if he were a priest. If so, he is the perfect acolyte to the Christ-like Uncle Ho bursting from the picture frame behind him: a sturdy peasant, tested by war, given now in victory the task of helping stray sheep return to the flock according to the rules. Everyone at the table looks up at him nervously like kids on the first day of school.

"The Socialist Republic of Vietnam welcomes you," he says in a voice that almost sounds as if it's true. "The purpose of this meeting is *pho bien*—to disseminate information—to let you know the rules that apply to your visit: What you can do, what you must not do, and what you should do to have a pleasant stay. First of all, if you wish to travel outside Ho Chi Minh City, you will need permission from this office. This allows us to issue you a special travel card that will give you priority passage to your destination. If you wish to deviate from the approved itinerary, please inform this office so that you will not be unnecessarily detained. If you wish to visit friends and relatives, you may arrange to have them call on you at your hotel, but you may not share your accommodations without permission from this office. In short, if you keep us informed of your activities and what you wish to do, your trip will be most pleasant, I assure you."

Quang steps from the podium to the items arrayed on the shelves. Like a professor, he points to the things we may take from Vietnam as purchases and what must be left behind. "Any deviations from this list," Quang adds when he is finished, "may be made only by permission from this office. Also, changing money at unapproved places or making undeclared gifts of foreign currency is a serious offense and may cause your visitor's visa to be immediately revoked!"

This last comment brings a flurry of nervous coughs. U.S. dollars are the mainstay of the underground economy and smuggling as many of them as possible to relatives is rumored to be the chief preoccupation of many returning *Viet Kieu*. Although the average expatriate was rumored to bring in over ten thousand dollars apiece, I had decided long ago to avoid any dealings with Vietnam's new black market—even the street-corner money changers, let alone a modestly corrupt official. Once the subject of bribery has been broached, even in an offhand way, you're in their clutches and at their mercy. Offer too little, and you're arrested for attempting to corrupt the people's officer. Offer too much, and you have no money left for the people you're trying to help. Besides, I had discovered from my own experience that there is a kind of "black market of the spirit" that can make left-handed dealing one's preferred way of getting by. I want to help my family as much as anyone, but I know there is a better way to do it than playing the old game that helped bring down the old regime.

After his speech, Quang fields a few questions: What happens if we want to stay longer? (Real question: What happens if our relatives are worse off than we thought and need our help?) What happens if we lose our travel card? (Real question: How much will you punish us for selling it on the black market?) The official answer is always the same: *Just keep us informed. Don't do anything without permission and you'll get along fine.* (Real answer: Crimes not committed don't need to be punished. Good visitors, like good citizens, never ask too much.)

The meeting is adjourned and people leave like the room is on fire. Before we get away, though, Quang points to a list of names beside the door. "Our socialist republic is not a rich country," he needlessly reminds us. "The National Committee depends on your contributions to keep our office open—to help tourists and returning *Viet Kieu* like yourselves see their families and stay out of trouble. The names you see on the wall are people who have made donations to the committee. Your dollars will help others who follow in your footsteps."

We all look at the "blackboard of honor" as we file out. I notice he said dollars, not *dong*, with his request, so like everyone else, I drop a couple of small U.S. bills in the money box—but for us it's like a wishing well, not a treasury chest: insurance against future hassles.

For the next several days in Saigon, however, I am a very bad tourist. Anh shows me the sights as he goes about his business, but I can think of little else except seeing Ky La and my mother and Tinh, the niece with whom I grew up, and my sisters Hai and Ba, and if fate or luck or god allows it, my long-lost brother Bon Nghe, who reportedly works for the Communist government in Danang.

On April 7, the day of our flight, I get up at 5 A.M. to pack my things, put on my lucky blue *ao dai,* and make myself up like a Western tourist. When I'm done, I look at the curious woman in the hotel mirror—half Vietnamese, half American, and entirely bewildered—and wonder if I can hold myself together long enough to make it to the lobby, let alone to the airport and Danang. There have already been too many *big days* on this trip and now they are catching up to me just when I need my strength and energy—my higher consciousness—the most.

Anh meets me downstairs and helps me load my suitcases, boxes of presents, and his own slim overnight bag into a taxi. Anh's government-owned firm has a factory in Danang and, because he still visits the place several times a year, he'll have plenty to keep him busy while I see what kind of a reunion fate allows me. The drive to the airport is solemn and I don't talk much to anyone. Memories come quickly, stack up, and begin to weigh me down. At Tan Son Nhut check-in, fortunately, my *Ban Viet Kieu* travel card whisks us through and we board the dirty, unkept twin-propeller airplane only a few moments before its scheduled takeoff.

Because flights to Danang run only once a week, the state-owned plane is crowded and Anh and I can't find seats together. The flight attendant —suitably proletarian in manners and dress (she wears black peasant pants and a simple white work shirt)—reminds us that such "special arrangements" should have been made at the National Committee office and are not her problem. Consequently, we find seats at opposite ends of the plane and wave to each other down the littered aisle. The experience with the surly attendant confirms one lesson I had learned so far from my travels in this new Vietnam: Because nobody is special, nobody cares especially what happens to anyone else—whether he is properly served or if the product he buys works the way it should. It makes me wonder how Ho's fledgling nation will ever earn the Japanese yen or U.S. dollars it needs to get back on its feet. But I am a tourist, not a politician. I can vote only with my money, so I decide to reward good service anywhere I can find it.

After an uncomfortable ride, the old plane crosses the coast and begins to descend. It suddenly occurs to me that Ky La—or Binh Ky, as it was known during the American war—might be visible through the window. I unbuckle my seatbelt and lean rudely over the passenger next to me, hoping my explanation—a desire to see my old village—makes up for my bad manners; but all I can make out through the watercolor haze is a tangle of narrow highways, buff plains, sawtooth mountains, and a sprinkling of thatch roofs amid the quilt of paddies and jungle. Unfortunately, as soon as I'm out of my seat, the frowning flight attendant comes down the aisle and commands everyone to buckle up. Because she has identified me as a backslider who lacks proper communal discipline, she stands over me until I'm safely strapped in place. Ky La, if it's out there, glides by without my seeing it.

* * *

THE FLIGHT to Danang after my expulsion from Anh and Lien's house was decidedly different from the one that had brought my mother and me to Saigon over a year before. Then, what I lacked in faith I made up for in hope. Now, what seedling hopes I nourished had been crushed by the human seedling I carried in my body. And the dangers of Quang Nam province were well known and immediate. The best we could do was *get by*. I vowed to shun the Republic and its wheels of corruption just as I knew I must elude the Viet Cong if my child was to be born and have a mother after that. As for my own mother, she was still so disgusted that she didn't speak to me the entire flight, preferring instead the company of the well-dressed, empathetic lady who sat beside her. As it turned out, I was lucky to be ignored.

The woman had a prosperous husband and a comfortable house with room for a pair of Saigon refugees. When we arrived, we followed her to a nice residential area where many Americans and Vietnamese officials made their homes. In her cozy house, my mother explained how I was the bride of a Republican soldier who had just been sent to his unit and so needed "a quiet place" to start my family. My wedding had been beautiful (of course) and when my mother began embellishing the virtues of my nonexistent husband and well-to-do in-laws—wishful thinking about the kind of life she desperately wanted me to have—my heart became so heavy I could no longer sit still and hold my grief. I excused myself and went for a walk around the neighborhood.

While I walked, I thought about the things I heard my mother telling the woman on the plane. It seems my father spent much of his time sitting in our doorway pining for his family. Every time he saw someone new approach Ky La—even a vagabond or orphan—he would jump up and shout my name, or even worse, the name of Bon Nghe or Sau Ban, whom he knew would never answer. Our neighbors said he was drinking heavily, whiskey from Danang and bad beer thrown out by the soldiers. He often had hallucinations: dead people like Aunt Thu and Sau Ban, missing relatives like me and my mother, and even Phung family ancestors from a thousand years ago. Because the villagers didn't know how to respond to someone with this problem, they laughed when he wandered down the road, drunk and depressed, and called him a coward for sending away the wife and child whom he was supposed to protect from harm. With no compassion from his friends, my father retreated further into himself, even though that private world was becoming a living hell. Finally, unable to cope with his loneliness, he went to Danang to visit my sister Lan—a woman in her twenties who had already seen much of life.

Lan had gone to Saigon in 1960 and moved back to Danang in '64 when the American buildup made that city a more profitable place to work. She rented a studio apartment paid for by her income as hostess in a Danang bar. Her job was to entice the patrons—mostly U.S. servicemen—to buy her drinks. Although these drinks were just iced tea (hence the catch name of her profession: *Saigon tea girl*), the proprietor charged the servicemen for whiskey and split the difference with the hostess. Although they made their living in the company of men, these bar girls usually weren't prostitutes. If a soldier wanted to take a girl home, he would have to ask her for a date, like any other woman, and could always be refused. But many of these hostesses had American boyfriends whom they saw both at and away from work, and Lan was no exception.

When my father got off the bus from Marble Mountain and found his way to Lan's apartment, he was greeted by a big American wearing just a towel. The American told him Lan was working and wouldn't return for hours, but my father decided he would wait. This infuriated the GI, who shouted one of the few Vietnamese phrases he knew, "Papa-san: *Di di mau!*" (Old man, stupid farmer—get out of here quick!) and shoved my father into the stairwell at the center of the building. Because this common area contained the toilets and showers for the six units on each floor, my father quickly had company and he passed the afternoon chatting with strangers as they relieved themselves, showered, or cleaned fish in the communal basin.

At a little past five, he heard Lan come home and went in through the kitchen door. Rather than being pleased, my sister was distressed to see him and felt torn between honoring her father, as she had been raised to do, and pleasing "her man," which was what the Americans expected. In the end, she told my father to wait and took her American into the bedroom—which was actually no more than a small area of the studio bounded by a curtain—and did what she had to do to please him. According to my mother's story, my father sat on the couch and cried.

After an hour, when my sister had not come out, my father went back to Ky La, where he found some villagers waiting in our house. They accused him of going to Danang to consort with Americans and questioned him angrily. They mocked him for his "American daughter" and criticized him for not bringing back the whiskey, cigarettes, and medicine they asked for. For several days he was so terrified he wouldn't leave his home except to get food and water. Eventually, he became ill and when Republican soldiers came through the village and discovered his emaciated condition, they evacuated him with their wounded to Giai Phau hospital in Danang.

Fortunately, Lan heard about this and, having been freed of her American boyfriend, visited him immediately—even though it was after hours and she was forced to climb over the security fence to do so. She apologized for her previous behavior but insisted she had no choice. There were too many differences, she said, between the ways of the city and our father's to uphold the traditions.

Hearing this, my father decided that a life without his family was not worth living. When he was finally released, he bought a box of rat poison in Danang and consumed it with a final meal at our house. Fortunately, his hereditary "warrior physique" was stronger than his spirit and the poison only sickened him. He spent the next day doubled up in agonizing pain, vomiting and voiding his bowels in the bushes across from our house. Apparently this lesson in the futility of self-destruction was well timed. It was shortly after this that my mother visited him and returned with the letter that cured me of my ulcer and self-pity and put me back on my own path toward life. She also convinced Hai that my father would surely die without somebody to look after him; so Hai quit her job in Saigon and returned with Tinh to Ky La to help out as best she could.

While these thoughts preoccupied me, it began to get dark and I discovered I had wandered down a block where the high walls around the houses ran close up to the street. Over the walls, I could see the branches of well-trimmed trees and lights in the upper floors of the homes and thought again of Anh. I began to sob not only for my father and Lan, but for my mother—who was also beginning to prefer a dream world to reality—as well as for myself and my unborn child, whose future looked anything but bright.

After a few moments I stopped and wiped my nose but my sniffling had been replaced by the sound of shuffling feet. I turned and saw three young men—not soldiers, they were too young—following me down the otherwise deserted street. At first I was not alarmed; they were smiling and had combed hair like city boys going out on the town. But they weren't talking either—and smiles without talk meant trouble. I continued to walk—faster and faster—and heard their footsteps speed up behind me.

"Hey, beautiful! What's the hurry?" one of them shouted.

I broke into a trot and looked for an alley or street or house to duck into, but the only things around were faceless walls too high to climb and iron gates designed to lock people out. Before I could reach the intersection, a strong hand caught my elbow and jerked me back. My head cracked against the wall and three leering teenage faces blotted out the branches overhead.

"You're not very friendly, sweetheart!" the center face said. His breath reeked of garlic and beer.

"Please—let me go!" I said, heart pounding. I instinctively put a hand over my jutting belly but the first boy slapped it away.

"Well, well," another said, "let's see what she's got to hide!"

While one boy pulled up my blouse, another forced down my pants and I yelled and tried to cover myself and protect my baby but more hands pushed back my arms and pinned my shoulders against the wall. My pants were almost to my knees and I shrieked as loud as I could and wondered why nobody was on the street—I *hated* this street as much as I hated these punks!—when the wall began to vibrate and air began to churn and *thunka-thunka-thunka* filled our ears. A cold white light, bright as angel fire, fell over us. A second later, a windstorm of dust and leaves almost swept us from the street.

The three punks bent down—one fumbling to raise his pants—and scrambled away in different directions. The searchlight stayed on me while I sank to the pavement and straightened my clothes, then it retreated down the street in pursuit of the boys. An instant later the whining and thunking were an echo on the walls and the police or army helicopter was gone. For the first time in my life I thanked fate or luck or god for the American *may bay chuon-chuon*—dragonflies that had previously brought so much terror into my life—and ran as fast as I could for our hostess's home.

When I got back, my mother gave me a disapproving look for my mussed-up hair and the missing button on my blouse and spanked my head when our hostess wasn't looking. Again I said nothing—what's the point of cursing rocks that bruise you when you're tumbling down a river?—and went to bed. As I waited for sleep, I wished I had at least waved *thank you* to the crew of the helicopter. It seemed a curious quirk of nature that the same machine—the same men—could act as tormentors in one instance and saviors in another. It occurred to me then that many things I had previously seen from one side might, in fact, have other perspectives. All I knew for sure was that I would never see or hear a helicopter in quite the same way again.

The next morning we went to visit my uncle Nhu—my mother's oldest brother, who lived in Danang. Nhu was surprised to see us and even more surprised by my swollen belly. "Why didn't you invite us to your wedding?" he asked, recalling that we had gone to Saigon many months before. "Why did you suddenly come back to Quang Nam?"

My mother went through her litany of lies again, but this time added my story about a visitation from my paternal grandmother, who beckoned us north with glowing, ghostly arms. She also said she had received a letter from Lan saying my father was in bad shape and needed help—so here we were. "And by the way," she added, almost as an afterthought, "Bay Le Ly shouldn't suffer the hardships of Ky La in her condition. Perhaps she can stay here and work for you while she waits for her baby?"

Uncle Nhu, unfortunately, had other ideas. His family was too close to the Republicans to risk discovery of a "Viet Cong sympathizer" in his household. So, after a trip to the market to give Ky La neighbors a message telling my father of our return, we went to Lan's apartment and caught her just as she was dressing for work.

"You want to stay here?" Lan's voice, encumbered by a toothbrush and foamy paste, was amazed. "But where? Look—there's barely enough room for me!"

My mother poked around her little studio. In one corner, by the window, was a table and four chairs, and in the other a cabinet for her clothes, which were the fanciest I'd seen for anyone in our family. I flinched when my mother drew back the curtain around her tiny bed, half expecting to see Americans come running out in a flurry of towels, ammunition belts, and beer cans. Lan finally called us over to the kitchen, which was little more than an alcove halfway out to the stairwell behind the apartment. She pointed to a tiny space between the stove and the well from which she pumped her water.

"I suppose Bay Ly can sleep here," Lan said, zipping up her satin dress. Commas of black hair dangled by her cheeks while she put on her high heels, reminding me of the pictures I had seen of oriental girls drinking Coca-Cola and snapping pictures with Kodak film on Saigon billboards. I couldn't imagine that I was related to anyone so beautiful. "But she'll have to work and pay her way," Lan continued. "I can't pay a housekeeper and feed a pregnant sister at the same time."

"Of course," my mother said, relieved to be spared an argument with my strong-willed sister. "She'll be quiet as a mouse and work like a horse."

After my mother had gone back to Uncle Nhu's, I told Lan the truth about my predicament—partly because I was sick of hearing and telling lies, and partly because I thought Lan would be impressed by the attention shown to me by a handsome and wealthy man. In some small way, it made me seem more like her, and I assumed that similarity would please her. In that I was completely wrong.

"What?" Lan barked, snatching up her purse. "You seduce your employer's husband, then come brag about it to me? You little slut! Why didn't you follow Mama *Du*'s advice and keep your big mouth shut? Well, I hope you're not going to try any of your stunts around here! I have a boyfriend—I have *lots* of boyfriends—and I'm not about to give one of them to you! Just mind your own business and do what you're told or I'll toss you out on the sidewalk—baby or no baby, sister or no sister. Do you understand?"

I nodded yes and Lan put on her sunglasses, even though it was almost dark outside, and left. I still thought she looked like a queen and I hated myself for upsetting her. I vowed to be a good sister and good housekeeper; but as things turned out, those would be very hard promises to keep.

At first, my duties were simple: bring in water from the well for cooking and cleaning, keep the apartment swept and scrubbed, and go to market with the allowance Lan gave me. After a few weeks, however, Lan began to insist that I tend to her personal needs as well, such as preparing and throwing out the wash water and rinsing her soiled underwear. Eventually I had to serve food and liquor during the parties she had almost every weekend and act like a servant, and not a sister, when strangers were around.

Of all these distasteful duties, the parties were the worst. Usually two or three Americans would show up in the afternoon and Lan's girlfriends would come by soon after. They were cheap girls—not classy like Lan

—with foul mouths and bad habits like smoking cigarettes and drinking real whiskey. When people arrived, Lan would turn on the radio and make me prepare some food and walk around with a tray of soda and ice, then sit in the kitchen until I was called to bring in something else or clean up the floor where someone had spilled something or thrown up. Almost always the girls and men joked about my belly and pinched me when I passed by. After an hour or so the girls would sometimes take off their tops and dance or sit on the GIs' laps. I used to hide in the bathroom until things settled down.

But as bad as the parties were, they didn't scare me half as much as when Lan's boyfriends came over alone—especially when Lan wasn't home. I didn't speak English and what Vietnamese words they knew were usually sex words or commands to "stop," "get out of here," or "drop your weapon." The older men (mostly civilians with balding heads and lots of money), sailors, and soldiers in clean uniforms weren't so bad; what I feared most were the marines in fatigues who sometimes stopped by on their way back from the field—smelling like water buffalo, unshaven, with weapons and the reflection of death in their eyes. To me they were as terrible as the "slash-faced" Moroccans who loomed out of the trees like giants thirteen years before.

One rainy day, one of these smelly, wild-eyed giants came to Lan's apartment while she was out having her hair done. He wore a pancho over his field gear, which made him look as big as a tank. I peeked through the door after his full-fisted knock and he asked a question which I couldn't understand. I assumed he asked "Where's Lan?" because when I didn't respond he simply forced the door and looked around the room himself. When he was satisfied she wasn't home, he crashed down on the sofa, wet slicker, backpack, and all, and made it clear he intended to wait. I knew from the neighbors there was a military curfew and that American soldiers violating it could be arrested by their own MPs. Perhaps that's why the soldier barked at me when I started to sneak out and signaled for me to close the door. When I had done so, he asked for something else in English, and when I showed him I didn't understand, he cupped two fingers near his thumb and made a drinking motion toward his mouth. Unmistakably, he wanted whiskey, not a beer, but I was not about to be stuck alone in Lan's house with a drunken marine who was desperate enough for sex to risk his own commander's wrath. I went to the kitchen, but instead of getting the whiskey, I ducked out into the stairwell and hid inside the showers until he decided to go.

After he had gone, I crept back into the room and noticed he'd left a large package on Lan's table—something he'd obviously kept hidden under his raincoat. From the label I could see it contained an American-made appliance—probably a fan (of more use to Americans unaccustomed to the heat than to native Vietnamese), which had been purchased at the post exchange.

When Lan got home, I told her what had happened. "Here," I said, "he left this package for you."

"What?" Lan blinked in anger, "you just let him leave without saying anything?"

"I don't speak English," I reminded her in a tiny voice.

"Well, did you serve him a drink—make him feel at home?"

"I was too frightened. He was awful-looking—big and tough and he carried a rifle—"

Lan's stinging slap cut short my explanation.

"You little fool!" she shouted. "Do you know what you've done? No! You don't know, do you? You're just too stupid! A stupid little girl who got herself knocked up because she doesn't know any better! I don't know why I let Mother talk me into taking you. Pregnant women are bad luck and you've caused more trouble than you're worth. The house looks like a rat's nest and your cooking tastes worse than *tam* rice—not fit for beggars in the street!"

"That's not fair!" I protested. "You don't give me enough money to buy decent food! How can you expect good meals from bad vegetables and old fish?"

"That's enough!" Lan batted me again, this time like my mother: absently, on the head. "You've worn out your welcome here, young lady! No more charity for you! Get out—right now! Go on! What are you waiting for?"

A few moments later I found myself on the sidewalk in front of the building, rain pouring down on my head, hands clasped on my swollen belly. Although I was mad at Lan, I also felt sorry about disappointing her and knew how crushed my mother would be when she heard that I was once more in need of help. I began to walk aimlessly, tears mingling with the warm rain on my cheeks. After half an hour, the rain stopped and people came out of their houses. I felt better having company and eventually wandered down Phan Dinh Phung Street toward the river and the new American bridge—a place I used to walk when Lan's visitors got me down.

Finally, I sat on a concrete abutment and began singing a little song to my unborn baby. After a moment, I became aware of another person standing beside me.

"What's wrong with you, child?" It was another woman, also pregnant, but considerably older. I must have been quite a sight with my wet hair, rain-soaked clothes, and big belly.

I told her I had just been thrown out of my apartment and had no money, no husband, no job, and no place to live. She patted her own big belly and said. "We pregnant ladies have to stick together, don't we?" and took my hand. She led me up the riverbank to a nearby house which had a storefront laundry by the street. "You're welcome to stay here while you make your plans," the woman said. "I'll give you a job in my laundry in exchange for your room and board, so my offer isn't charity. You look like a good, strong girl so I'll expect you to put in a good day's work."

Of course, I was overjoyed that this kind woman would take me in, charity or hard work or not. Her small house was clean and crowded with relatives and employees (ten of them—half men and half women), some of whom lived as well as worked on the premises. After I dried off and shared their evening meal, I went to sleep on a mat in the corner and prepared myself for a workday that would begin before sunrise the next morning.

From five until eight, I hauled water from the well down the street to the big basin the women used to wash clothes. After that, I went with the woman to a nearby market and helped her do the day's shopping— which was considerable for so many people. After that, I cleaned the house and watched her children while she supervised the ironing (strictly a man's profession) or ran errands, then began cooking the daily meal, which was served to the entire crew.

After three days of this schedule, which never varied and was enforced like rules in a military camp, I decided my own clothes needed a wash. I asked permission to go back to my old apartment where I would try to talk Lan into giving me my things or, if she were gone, sneaking in and getting them myself.

When I got there, Lan herself answered the door. I steeled myself for another dressing down and another blow to the cheek—but her attitude, this time, was different. It seems our father had finally gotten word of my return and had gone up to Uncle Nhu's to find our mother. After learning from her about my pregnancy (the first he'd heard of it), our father was surprised when Lan arrived at Uncle Nhu's looking for me.

"I told him what happened," Lan said. "I explained to him that I didn't know why you ran away. It was just a joke. I didn't think you'd take me seriously—honestly. I was only mad for what you did to my boy-friend!"

Apparently my father liked her explanation even less than my mother's and exploded at them both: at my mother for letting me get pregnant in the first place, and at Lan for mistreating me later.

"Who do you think you are?" he demanded of Lan. "The government? Do you think you can throw a relative out of your house just like that?" She said he tried to snap his fingers but couldn't, he was so angry. "That's not how we do things in my family! In my family, the good leaves cover up the bad!" She said his face was purple and spittle flew out of his mouth and then he turned his anger on me, even though I wasn't there. "I want you to find your sister," he said to Lan, "and when you do, take her back into your house and apologize for abusing her. Give her back her job as your housekeeper and let her live her life in her own way until the baby is born! As for little Miss Ly, tell her that I never want to see her again! She is *chua hoan*—an unwed mother! She has disgraced me and my family and I never want to look at her insolent face again!" With that, she said, he left Uncle Nhu's and went straight back to the village, weeping and arguing with himself as he went.

By now, Lan and I were weeping too, and we embraced as we had not done since I saw her off for Saigon. That afternoon, I went back to the laundry and told my benefactor that I would not be returning to my job.

For the next few days, things went well enough. I resumed my housekeeping chores and Lan gave me a little more money for fresh food at the market—although most of her handsome earnings still went into the lockbox in her cabinet or for fancier clothes and better liquor for her guests. Unfortunately, old habits die hard and because I no longer felt like I had to wait on her guests, Lan gave me the choice of staying or wandering around the streets until her friends departed—which usually wasn't until the next morning. Even worse were the times when her regular boyfriends came to town on leave and stayed for days at a time —even though Lan kept her usual hours at the bar. It made me nervous to be alone with them, especially when I saw how they jumped into bed with Lan every time she came home and seldom got up for anything, even to fix a meal. It seemed as if the Americans thought of nothing but sex. We Vietnamese women talked about this often and felt sorry for them. We wondered what kind of lives their wives must have lived in the States.

At these times, I would just take my blanket and move onto the street, checking back every day or so to see if the coast was clear. Because there were lots of homeless people everywhere, these outings weren't too bad; and even when company was scarce and the weather was bad, I looked forward to the rainy nights because the rapists, punks, and randy servicemen usually stayed indoors.

After a few months though, my baby was riding low and I knew my time was near. I found the cool nights on the street harder to take and I forced myself to put up with Lan's parties just to stay warm and dry. Unfortunately, her favorite American boyfriend—the one who had chased my father away—came back on leave and lived with us for a week. Although he was big (over six feet tall, which is huge compared to a Vietnamese man) and had a bad temper when he drank—which was most of the time—he was in the American Navy, which meant he could probably be trusted. He had a brown, round face which looked almost oriental (another reason I didn't mind being around him), a black crew cut, and a perpetual smile, which, unfortunately, was not always a good indicator of his mood.

One night he and Lan were in the bedroom behind the curtain, drinking and laughing, when Lan screamed and they began thrashing around on the floor. Stupidly (but dutifully!), I ran in and tried to pull him off my sister. He was wearing only his undershorts and was sitting on top of her, pounding her with his fists. Of course, I was too puny to do anything, and he swatted me away like a bug. I ran out through the kitchen and into the stairwell (there were always a few people around the toilets) and asked them to call the MPs. Just as I did this, the big GI appeared behind me and grabbed my neck. He was so drunk he could hardly stand up, and with his great size could easily have killed me just by falling down on top of me. Without regard for my baby, he hit me twice—really hard—and threw me to the floor. He tried to grab me again but I darted down the stairwell crying, "Bloody murder! MPs! MPs!" and out onto Phan Thanh Gian Street where I knew I would attract a crowd, and maybe some police.

Fortunately, the GI's head was clear enough to realize this commotion was putting him in danger and he didn't try to follow. Instead he went inside, put on his clothes, and left by the side door to the building. When I returned to the studio, Lan was cleaning up the mess and I thought she was going to curse me for causing the ruckus but instead she just hugged me, trembling like a leaf, and asked if I was hurt.

A few days later, the big American came back to apologize and gave gifts to us both. He hung around quite often until the end of his tour, and I treated him nicely although I kept my distance. When it was time for him to go, Lan gave him some souvenirs to take to America, and the GI gave Lan a present she would not discover for several weeks: a son, who would be born in the spring.

* * *

From time to time my mother came to check on me from her residence at Uncle Nhu's. I asked her what had happened to the monthly payments Anh was supposed to send for our care and feeding and she said that, although she had been instructed to call for them at Anh's sister's house, the woman kept putting her off. First the sister claimed she knew nothing of the agreement; then that the payments had been delayed and would be available shortly—but weeks turned into months. Now it was time to make arrangements for my baby's delivery and we could no longer afford to wait for Anh's sense of guilt or charity to help us. Reluctantly, Lan agreed to pay my hospital bills—partly because she felt grateful to me for saving her life; and partly because she knew I had seen the big stash of money she kept in her strongbox and realized a plea of poverty wouldn't carry much weight with our mother.

A few days after my mother's visit, after Lan had gone to work and I was finishing my lunch, my sister Ba (who had recently delivered a baby of her own) came by to tell me that my father was on his way to the apartment. I gave her a bowl of soup and asked her what I should do when he got here.

"Don't talk to him at all," Ba said. "Mother says he's still very angry and unbalanced. Nobody knows what he might do in his condition. My advice is to—"

At that moment we heard a loud knock on the door and had no doubt who it was.

"Quick," Ba said. "Go hide in the latrine!"

Once again I sought refuge in the communal bathroom, but Ba left the back door cracked so that I could at least hear what was going on.

"Where is your sister?" I heard my father ask. It had been almost a year since I luxuriated in his deep and wonderful voice and my whole body melted closer to the narrow opening.

"Oh, Lan's already gone to work," Ba said. "She left about an hour ago. I was just on my way out myself."

I heard my father shuffle around the apartment—the footsteps of an old and tired man. I crammed myself further into the crack to get at least a glimpse of him before he went away.

"I don't care about Lan," he snapped. "I'm looking for Bay Ly. Why are there two bowls of soup on the table?"

"Oh," Ba mumbled, "that's just dinner. I—uh—I had soup with Lan's maid before she left. She's such a nice girl. Lan's so generous for giving her a meal on top of wages."

My father only grunted. I could hear him poking around the tiny apartment, as if he thought I might be hiding in the cabinet or behind the curtain on the bed. "Well," he said finally, "when you see Bay Ly, tell her I stopped in to see her. Tell her I miss her very much and she shouldn't worry about being punished for her mistake. Will you tell her that for me?"

"Of course," Ba said softly, and I heard their clothing rustle and their hands pat each other's backs as they embraced. I wanted so badly to be in Ba's place that my heart and body almost split in two: half of me running to join them; the other cringing cowardly in the lavatory, still too ashamed of what I had done to face my father. In the end, I decided it would be better if he didn't see me until my pregnant belly was back to its normal size and I was once again the daughter he remembered with love.

I heard Ba rinse the dishes, then they went to the front door together. When my father asked Ba why she didn't close the kitchen door—wasn't Lan worried about burglars?—Ba only laughed and said Lan wanted to air the place out, even though the kitchen opened onto toilets and washtubs that smelled of gutted fish.

After they left, I waited a few minutes, then followed what I presumed was my father's path to the Song Hang River ferry and the bus that would take him to Ba's house and then to Marble Mountain. I took care to remain out of sight, but by the time I was near the boat landing, lots of passengers had gathered and I had to hug the buildings (as if my nine-month pregnant belly could be hidden like a dirty chin!) to get a really close view.

At last, just as the ferryboat pulled up and lowered its gangway, I saw my father climb aboard—a pathetic old peasant in a bustling crowd of city mothers, squawking children, government clerks, and young soldiers going home on leave. As the boat pulled away, I felt a hand on my arm. It was the owner of the shop into which I had ducked to spy him out.

"You okay, little miss?" A fatherly face looked down on my own. "Oh, pardon me"—he noticed my big belly—"little missus! Here now, don't cry. You can still catch the ferry. Look, people are still waiting. Another will be along soon."

"That's all right. Thank you—" I felt sheepish as well as ashamed and wiped my eyes with my sleeve. I trudged back to Lan's but felt miserable trying to sleep in a room which still held my father's scent. I felt like a coward for not showing myself and giving peace to a poor old man. I went out and wandered around the neighborhood, eventually crossing, without aim or destination, into another part of town. By the time it was dark, the air smelled of rain and my legs were too tired to take me home. My drooping belly was beginning to ache and since I was very near my cousin's house, Uncle Nhu's son Nhut, I thought I would drop in and see if I could stay the night. As it turned out, my mother was visiting and Nu's family gave me a kind reception. We talked quietly after dinner about my father and I secretly made up my mind to go see him in the village, regardless of the risk. As the rain began outside, my mother and I curled up on Nu's guest bed and I fell asleep in her arms, resting more soundly and comfortably than I ever had in Lan's kitchen.

About four in the morning I got up to go to the bathroom, which had become my habit in recent weeks, and noticed that my pants legs and all the bedding were sopping wet. Embarrassed that I had wet myself in my sleep, I roused my mother to change the blanket, but she just stared at me in horror.

"My God, Bay Ly—" she said hoarsely, "it's *loi oi!* Your bag of waters has broken!"

We gathered our things quickly, informed cousin Nu of the big event, and—covering our heads with a blanket—scuttled through the rain in the direction of the clinic, only a few blocks away. I wasn't sure why my mother was so concerned about my water breaking; I didn't feel any pain, and the cramps called labor, which I had been warned about, had yet to appear. If I felt anything at all it was confusion—joy and worry all mixed—in anticipation of bringing another living soul into the world.

The birthing clinic was really a one-room house with shabby gray walls and five pipe-frame beds with plywood boards instead of mattresses. We woke the midwife on duty and told her that I had neither water nor cramps and her eyes widened and she wasted no time helping me onto a bed board and gave me a shot to begin my labor. Within moments my baby-big stomach was hard as a basketball and sure hands were lifting my feet into the stirrups at the end of the board. I began to squeeze my stomach and all at once there was a stabbing pain in my navel which crackled around my back like an electric shock, leaving me breathless and scorched inside. The midwife gave me another shot and the contractions began again. Through the cloud of medicine and fear and excitement I heard my mother and the midwife call, "Okay, bear down!" and "No, don't push!" although by this time I felt like little more than a machine of meat and blood totally in the grip of something else. On the tenth contraction I felt a bulbous little head and human elbows and hips and knees slide effortlessly from my vagina. The fullness I had lived with for months gave way to a second of empty calm which ended abruptly when the midwife put the syrupy baby on my belly. I raised my head in time to see her cut the cord that connected me to my child with a pair of blunt-nosed scissors.

"It's a boy—thank god!" I heard my mother say, as if the war did not exist, and I felt happy too.

Before I could touch my baby the midwife snatched him away, dangled him by the feet to clear his nose and throat, and the latest Phung spirit entered the world with a cry like crumpling rice paper. While my mother cleaned up my son, the midwife delivered me of the placenta, then ordered: "Put the baby up to feed, eh?—and quickly. We've got a bleeder!"

My mother unbuttoned my blouse and put my baby at my tender breast. Like magic, my contractions began again, but milder, and the midwife seemed satisfied that the spasms were shutting off the blood that flowed from my torn bottom. "Don't worry," the midwife said, "the doctor will be here soon to sew you up."

But soon was not within the hour or even the hour after that. For the rest of the morning and into the early afternoon I lay on the board— unable to get up—while my mother shooed flies from my torn bottom and other pregnant ladies came in to be checked and collect their vitamins. Despite my discomfort and inactivity, though, I was anything but idle. While my hours-old son napped and sucked, I thought about where we would go and what we would do to live. Lan's hospitality—her promise to help out—ended when my baby was born. If there was little room in her life for a pregnant sister, there would be none for an unwed, nursing mother.

Finally, the resident physician made his rounds and my poor ripped tissues, having congealed on their own, were ripped again for a "nice, tight repair," as the doctor called it. I suppose he thought my nonexistent husband would be grateful. Although I appreciated his attention, I could not force myself to reply to his pleasantries or even to answer his simple questions. Instead, for some reason, tears filled my eyes and I began to cry and refused the dinner of brown rice and salty cow viscera—food for health—my mother brought as a gift from cousin Nu. Even my baby on my breast would not console me and it wasn't until noon the next day that the strange, dark cloud that sometimes overtakes new mothers lifted from my heart.

For the next twenty-one days, that plywood clinic bed was my home. My mother often slept on a neighboring bed, when one was free; or on the visitors' bench, when no one was there; or on the floor when the house was full. She did my laundry, brought my food, and kept me and my baby clean, although she sometimes lost her temper for lack of sleep and treated me like a little kid myself instead of another mother. For the first few days, I felt pretty weak and it was all I could do simply to walk to the toilet. During this time, I daydreamed a lot about how my little boy—Hung, we now called him—would go to school or work with his grandfather in the paddies or drive our water buffalo to and from the fields, even though our buffalo had been killed and half our property had been bombed to rubble. Whatever anger I felt for the war and Viet Cong and the government and the invading Americans now rattled outside my consciousness like wind around a house. With Hung in my arms, I simply could not hold onto hateful feelings. I knew Anh would love this tiny baby—all mottled and puking and noisy as an air-raid siren—as much as he loved the babies he made with Lien. I knew, too, that my father would love his grandson as soon as he laid eyes on him, as did my mother—although she still advised me against a visit until my father had gained "a steadier grip on the plow."

After three weeks I left the clinic and went with my mother to sister Ba's. Ba had always been nicer to me than Lan, but her policeman husband, Chin, still refused to call me friend. I suspect my mother had to promise him something to buy his sufferance, especially for a month-long visit, but at least I had a place to stay and my baby and I were off the streets.

A day or so after our arrival, my father came to Ba's with the traditional offering of fresh brown rice—given to new babies as an expression of love, good health, and good luck, the way Westerners give flowers. From the amount he brought, it was obvious he spent a couple of days husking the rice, which was a sign of his generosity and forgiveness. Still, my mother and Ba forbade me to see him, and I again waited in another room and listened while his sad and tired voice rose with joy at the sight of his grandson's bead-black eyes and wobbly head.

A day after that, my sister Hai came up to see the baby. By tradition, a newly birthed mother isolates herself from everyone but her closest relatives during a period of *buon de*—a time of spiritual renewal and physical rejuvenation. (My mother told me, "Before one baby, a man can't keep his eyes off you. After two, he has to close his eyes to pass." The *buon de* rituals, she said, were designed to keep a husband looking at you after many more children than that.) So Hai, like other visitors, chose not to break my isolation, but talked to me from behind a half-closed door. Her advice on what I should do from here, however, seemed anything but sisterly.

"Chop up your baby in three pieces," she said sternly. "Commit *chat lam ba* the way the elders say," which meant to wrap the head, stomach, and legs in a blanket and throw each piece into a flowing river so that my mistake would be washed away. Even though I knew she didn't mean this literally, the thought of giving my baby to an orphanage or to a family I didn't know seemed so criminal that my heart broke as I heard her speak. For an instant, I wondered if my mother had put her up to it, but I knew it could not be so. The love my mother had showed me and my son through her own sleepless nights proved that her grandson meant no less to her now than he did to me. We had already gone too far down the path of life, my mother, my son, and me, to think of anything else.

After a month of *buon de*, I took my baby back to cousin Nu's and paid for my room and board by caring for his family of eleven. His wife sold souvenirs to Americans and whenever I could, I accompanied her to the swap meets where she purchased the Vietnamese handicrafts she needed for admittance to the American base. Her method of doing business was simple but ingenious and the more I helped her, the more I learned about how to survive without a fishing pole, a hoe, or a man to pay my way.

Once we had access to an American facility, it was a simple matter to sell our souvenirs (*ao dai* or marble jewelry, the trademark of the region) and give the cash to GIs who were willing to purchase cigarettes, liquor, soap, or gum—the four staples of the black market economy—on our behalf. When we were off the base, South Vietnamese of all classes were willing to pay big money for these things—in Republican *piasters*, red military currency, or, most valuable of all, in U.S. greenbacks themselves. This wealth, in turn, allowed us to buy more merchandise from the craftsmen, and repeat the cycle with ever-increasing profits.

Eventually, I asked my mother to baby-sit with Hung and the other children so that I could have a few hours each day to prospect for business by myself. Although I had learned enough English to make these transactions ("You buy smokes?" "You buy whiskey?" "How much?" "Too much!") I did not know enough to discriminate between products and sometimes these differences were important. Once, a Republican neighbor placed an order with me for laundry detergent and I asked a friendly GI (once I had gained admittance to the base with my bucket of bracelets), "You buy soap?" and the GI returned with a bar of Palmolive.

After a few weeks of trading, I began to notice a half-dozen other Vietnamese girls—tough-looking teenage city girls—who worked at the same business. We would show up at the swap meet at about the same time and often found ourselves hustling the same friendly GI in front of the same post exchange. Although we were wary of one another at first, we soon learned that what we might lose on one sale, we more than made up for by bringing customers to the girl who had exactly what our buyer wanted and splitting the profit. Eventually these girls taught me many new tricks of the souvenir/black market trade. Instead of taking orders for American merchandise and selling only to Vietnamese, for example, they showed me how I could make even more money selling American goods to Americans simply by taking goods from the post exchange to GIs who were unable to go there themselves. Soldiers waiting in a convoy, for example, would pay big money for cold soda, sunglasses, newspapers, or magazines with dirty pictures—so we carried our "store" in our buckets and hustled all over town to find GIs who were too busy or too isolated to buy these things themselves.

After a month or so of this, I discovered that I, too, had something to teach my partners. Because most of my new friends were city girls and uncomfortable away from Danang, they were amazed when I told them I could make even more money by taking my goods to the American firebases out in the countryside. Here, GIs had been on duty for days or weeks "in the bush" and loved shopping through my bucket and buying things for their wives or girlfriends, whom they missed and feared they'd never see again. Sometimes they bought things just out of boredom, even though they didn't want the item and had no idea what they'd do with it when they had it.

Each morning, a girlfriend and I (or, more often, I alone) would take the bus up Highway 101, get off at some little village, then hike into the countryside wherever the local people said Americans had been operating. My girlfriends, of course, were terrified to follow me too far, but because I knew the signs of war—which situations were dangerous and which looked worse than they were—I was able to sell most of my merchandise and come home in the evening with my undershirt full of cash. My biggest problem, in fact, was not avoiding combat and booby traps but convincing the GIs that this little Vietnamese girl who appeared mysteriously by their bunkers out of nowhere—in places where their own supplies could get in only by helicopter—was neither Viet Cong nor a prostitute: for both had short lifespans in the jungle. After that, my next biggest worry was that the soldiers would just hang around and talk—want to flirt instead of buy things—which made the effort of reaching them not only dangerous but a waste of time as well. Still, they liked female company and after a half-day's bus ride, cross-country walk, and hard climb to a hilltop fort, I too sometimes appreciated a few quiet minutes with these poor young men who were hot and sweaty and scared and missed their homes as much as I missed mine.

One of my partners actually took an American-Indian boyfriend during these trips and made love in a bunker whenever we visited—but even then, her love was not for the American, but for the child she hoped he'd sire. For her own husband was sterile and she hoped the Indian, who looked a little oriental, would help her start the family she would otherwise be denied. It was a plan that would have shocked me only a few months before, but the war and my own baby had caused me to see many things differently.

After a few months in this business, I was able to save enough money to ask cousin Nu (who needed a housekeeper more than another black marketeer) to find a house for me, my mother, and son. The next day he reported that one of his Republican friends—the manager of a U.S. Navy mess hall near the base—owned a small house that had just been built for him by the Americans as part of his salary. He didn't want to live in the place (he had a nice house already) but would consider selling it to a person who could get along with his employers. After another day of bargaining (I let cousin Nu handle all this himself) my mother and I took Hung, a few utensils, and some bedding to our new home and spent our first night since leaving Ky La in a place not owned by someone else. I expected my mother to quiz me about where I got the money or what I did on those days when I was gone so long from home, but she remained silent. Perhaps she was just happy to be rid of our Republican relatives, whom she never really liked, or perhaps she believed my girlfriends and I simply bought and sold souvenirs like Nu's wife and was content to leave it at that. As it turned out, it might have been better if she had taken more interest in her teenage daughter's new career.

One day after I had made a particularly big sale to a Republican bureaucrat in Danang, my girlfriend said, "You should stop worrying so much about soapflakes and chewing gum, eh? Here—look at this!"

She showed me a plastic bag full of green leaves that had been chopped up like spices. "What's that?" I asked innocently.

"Boy—you really are a country girl, aren't you?" she answered. "It's *ma tuy*—marijuana, pot, grass—*Mary Jane* is what the GIs call it."

"What do they do with it?" I took a smell and wrinkled my nose.

"They roll it up in paper and smoke it like a cigarette," she replied, "but some of them put it into pipes or mix it with their food. Anyway, who cares? They pay even more for this than whiskey!"

"Have you ever tried it yourself?" I asked.

"Are you kidding?" she put her hand on her chest as if she were having a heart attack. "No way—and you won't either, if you're smart. You never know if the dealer's giving you bad shit or not and bad dope makes you sicker than bad food. Let the invaders take the risk—if you kill a few, so what? Who'll miss them? Just be sure you get the hell out of

camp before they smoke it. If it's bad shit, they'll come after you with
knives, especially the black ones. Let me tell you, I've seen it happen to
other girls!"

Although I didn't care particularly for the risks my friend described,
the thought of carting a few little bags of pot into the bush and returning
with enough cash to buy a case of American scotch overwhelmed my
better judgment.

"Sure," I said finally, wrapping a magazine around the plastic bag.
"Let's go!"

The trip to the firebase was long and dusty and, although I did not
sell out, profitable as well. On the way back our bus stopped at a checkpoint
run by Republican soldiers and, as usual, we were all ordered to get out
and put our belongings on the ground. The soldiers snooped through the
crowd and a few of us with possessions were called into the office, a little
hut by the side of the road. This was nothing new: it was where the
wheel of corruption in Vietnam really began to turn—where the army
encountered the people—and it continued up the spokes of authority from
sergeants and officers to provincial officials and finally bureaucrats at the
hub of government. Besides, I had been through all this before. Inside
the hut, an officer would take anything that could be resold. If the citizen
complained about this legalized theft, the officer would arrest him, charge
him with black marketeering, and still confiscate the goods, claiming it
to be evidence for the trial. Of course, the evidence would vanish before
the defendant had spent the night in jail, and the citizen would be released,
grateful that the officer had "decided not to press charges."

When a soldier noticed I had some goods in my bucket (I was in double
jeopardy, since my girlfriend had given me her supplies as well before
she got off at the previous stop), I was escorted to the hut.

"What's all this stuff, little miss?" the officer said as he laid my merchandise out on his desk.

"Just my things." I tried to sound innocent, but I knew I couldn't
outfox a fox. "I've been shopping for a lot of friends!"

We smiled at each other, but my smile went away when he discovered
an unsold bag of marjijuana inside a rolled-up magazine.

"Well now, what's this?" The officer's face lit up. Not only had he
stumbled onto a more than usually lucrative cache, but he might even be
able to turn in a "drug-dealer" and gain a few extra points with his boss.

"I don't know," I lied. "That magazine belongs to my girlfriend."

"Well, it belongs to the public prosecutor now. Take her away."

I was handcuffed and led to the jail; but instead of taking me to the
holding cell where most "suspects" were kept overnight—chatting and

smoking and dozing on the concrete floor until their automatic release —I was taken to a separate cell used for more serious offenders. This startled me and I began to wonder if selling *Mary Jane* was something more serious than my partner had let on.

After a while, a second "criminal"—an older man close in age to my father—was admitted to my cell. He had shifty eyes and broken capillaries in his face and my first thought was that putting him in here with a helpless teenage girl must have been the guards' idea of a joke. At first, the newcomer was friendly: he kept his distance and asked why I was there. When he surmised I was a street girl, he moved closer and said, "We shouldn't waste any more time" and promised that after I did what he asked—which turned my stomach just hearing it—he would pay me when both of us were released. Although I tried to convince him I was not a streetwalker, he kept forcing himself on me—grabbing my head and pushing it down toward his pants—but I batted his hands away, screamed, and ran around the cell. After a while, he got tired of chasing me and rested in a corner. I went to the opposite corner and we sat there for several minutes, eyeing each other like wrestlers. Finally, the guard came back, opened the door, and ordered me out. I was happy to leave, of course, but experience had also taught me that being taken from a cell often led to worse things. While we walked down the corridor, my ears strained to hear muffled cries, the slap of rubber hoses on bare skin, or the characteristic hum and snap of the hand-powered generators, but if any of this went on, it was not going on today. Instead, the guard took me to the desk where I had been booked and told me to go home.

"The charges against you are dropped, young lady," he said, returning my bucket. The magazines and gum were still there, but not my money, the liquor, or marijuana. "And, between you and me, you should learn to be more careful."

"What do you mean?" I thought he meant I should get off the bus before the checkpoint as my friend had done.

"We tested your bag of pot—it's fake. That's why we're letting you go. Just be glad we discovered it and not your stupid American customers. Now get going. And if we see you come through here again with a bag of phony shit, we won't take you out of the tank so fast. Just give us something to make it worth our while and we'll get along just fine."

I caught another bus outside the jail, but didn't have enough cash for the fare. When we got to Danang, I had to "dump" my merchandise on the corner for whatever it would bring, pay the driver, and walk home. After my release, I felt dirtier than ever before. The guard had talked to me as if I was *one of them*—a corrupt official, a running dog—the very people the Viet Cong had trained me to fight against: the ultimate traitors to our people. And I was not even a decent criminal at that, but a dumb little girl who had not yet learned to play the game of greed in the same league as the pros. Little by little, I realized I had come to worship at the shrine of the street-smart and shrewd, the tough and canny, and not at the altar of my ancestors. I had become my own worst enemy.

This arrest also opened my eyes to other things that had been happening all around me. Too often, some of the happy-faced GIs we picked out to go shopping with our cash at the PX simply took our money and ran. We could not file a complaint with their MPs for two reasons. First, the soldiers were supposed to shop in the exchange only for themselves. Turning them in for theft would be admitting we broke the law ourselves. Second, even if we could report the case, we wouldn't be able to identify the offenders—all Americans looked alike to us, and who could remember their strange-sounding names? It was only after several such losses that I began to see the value of looking into the face of another race the same way I studied the faces of my own. At first, I would pick out distinguishing traits and give little nicknames to my American contacts: a thin man with a scrawny mustache might be "little caterpillar"; a big-chested American with bushy hair would be "buffalo boy," and so on. One American I did lots of business with was a short, fat fellow with glasses whom I named "four eyes" because that's what his buddies called him. The reason I liked working with this man is because every other Vietnamese girl avoided him. We had a proverb: *Tranh nha nguoi le dung get nha nguoi lun*, which meant Don't sign contracts with the cross-eyed; don't get short-changed by a short man. Because he was bad luck for everyone else, he was very grateful for the attention I would show him.

There were other Americans we avoided—but usually for better reasons. Well-educated men (officers and well-dressed civilians) were off-limits because they were more likely to turn us in and tended to be unkind—telling us brusquely to "Scat!" as if we were pesky children or beggars. Also, because the black American soldiers ripped us off the most and were dangerous when cheated, the other girls avoided them completely, but it only made me more determined to really look for character in their faces and see where charity, honesty, and good nature really lay. Eventually, some of these GIs became good friends to me as well as good customers, and some of my best protectors turned out to be Americans, like the "honcho" who commanded a convoy and one time kept me from getting raped inside a tank. On the other hand, some of my worst antagonists were Vietnamese: bureacrats as well as soldiers. The dividing line between friends and enemies—spiritual kinsmen and barbarian disruptors—gradually became a blur.

Not long after we moved into our new house, Lan came over to see us. I took this as a high compliment from my sister. When I saw her, she was a couple of months' pregnant with the child of her American boyfriend. She tried to convince me to take an American boyfriend, too, and earn gifts for myself and my son just from lying on my back. But I told her no. For the first time in my life I was truly independent—of the Viet Cong and the village and the government and even our mother and father—and I liked that feeling very much. Why should I sacrifice my freedom to invite a male dictator into my life? Half joking, I told Lan that I would settle down with a foreigner only if he was the kindest, handsomest, highest-ranking, wealthiest man around. She said I could look a long time to find a man like that who was willing to marry a pipsqueak from the country with a bastard child. I replied that if that was the case, I would rather buy happiness with hard work than from selling myself too cheap. For once, Lan looked as if I had done the face-slapping. We changed the subject and Lan left shortly thereafter. It wasn't exactly a fight we had, but Lan never brought up the subject again and it was quite a while before her next visit. I think she needed time to mourn the passing of the little sister she used to know.

MIDMORNING, APRIL 7, 1986:
DANANG, SOCIALIST REPUBLIC OF VIETNAM

Our approach and landing at the great Danang airport is smooth and uneventful, but the calm of the cabin belies the anxiety in my heart. I wonder about the reception I'll receive from my Hanoi brother, Bon Nghe. Will he remember me fondly or with the narrow eye of a party official looking down on a fallen hero? And above my brother looms the figure of my mother, now almost eighty. Will she greet me as the long-lost daughter of her womb—the unlikely child she bore in middle age and nurtured with buffalo milk and songs? Or will time and the ocean that came between us—the events that separated her daughter from a daughter's duty—diminish me to a shadow: a Westernized ghost whose eyes have become "too round" to see the spirits of the past that still inhabit Ky La?

As we step from the plane to the passenger stair, the moist, earthy air of the Central Coast wraps me like a familiar old blanket and I feel the

same surge of joy that gripped me days ago in Saigon. Only this time
"home" is truly *home*—Ky La is no more than a few hours' walk or a
short half-hour ride by car. The coconut and palm trees sigh in the wind
and the sweet smell of fertile sod—that delicate mix of decayed vegetation
and fresh new growth that is the bouquet of the jungle, as much its
signature as the salt air at China Beach—embraces me like a perfumed
aunt. The biggest change is on the airport tarmac: it is almost bare of
planes and ours is the only airliner on the base. In its heyday, when
American bombers struck targets all over the North and South almost
twenty-four hours a day, Danang was one of the busiest airports in the
world.

We go into the terminal to claim our luggage and while we wait for
the handlers to sort things out, I am scanned by one of the many *bo
doi*—the uniformed soldiers—who wander aimlessly around the building.
By accident, our eyes meet and I give him a friendly smile. It's enough
to make him amble over and begin a conversation.

He gives my Western-style hair and makeup the once-over and says,
"You are *Viet Kieu*?"

I nod and smile some more.

"*Cho toi coi thong hanh*" (Show me your passport), he says abruptly.

I hand him my travel card, which is supposed to take care of such
things, but he still holds out his hand expectantly. *So much for brother
Quang and his National Committee!* I find my passport at the bottom of
my purse and reluctantly hand it over.

"Please step over here." The soldier walks a few paces away from the
passengers. I give Anh a concerned look but he signals for me to follow.

"It says here you're from Quang Nam—" the soldier asks. I can tell
from his accent that he's from the Central Coast as well.

"Yes—I was born in Ky La, called Binh Ky during the war," I reply,
suggesting by my friendly tone that such a soldier should not give too
much trouble to his provincial sister. To my mild surprise, the soldier
smiles back and returns my passport.

"I fought a big battle there in 1963!" he grins. "Of course, the village,
like everyplace else, was renamed after the war. It's called Xa Hoa
Qui, now."

"No kidding!" I stow my passport quickly and we chat for a while
about the old days. I am tempted to reveal my brief career with the Viet
Cong but think better of it. It's quite likely that I was near this man at
one time or another, and his recollection of "Miss Ly's" fall from grace,
if he knows of it at all, is probably not the same as mine. Fortunately,
all he asks are questions about America. Like most Vietnamese I have

met on the trip, he is more fascinated by, than hateful of, his former enemy.

The baggage arrives and I buy a basket of mangoes to present as an offering to my father's spirit at our family's shrine. I take them into the women's lavatory and sitting in one of the doorless stalls, slip a half-million *dong*—about five hundred dollars—out of my purse and under the basket's paper lining. Everyone has said that the provinces are rougher than the capital. It stands to reason that my purse would be a more likely target for thieves than a box of fruit.

Outside, pedicab drivers mob us like hungry fish. Although there is more than enough business to go around, it is strictly dog-eat-dog as big drivers shove back small ones and young drivers squeeze out the elderly. I am shocked that the youth in this new Vietnam have so little respect for their elders until I remember what they have been through. From the looks of the drivers, half of them belonged at home (if not the hospital) in the care of their grown children; and the other half, in school. But the Central Coast's thin economy cannot support such luxuries as a peaceful old age and secondary education. The population has increased dramatically since the end of the war and everyone must work just to get by—from sunup to sundown, from the cradle to the grave.

Because of this, we worm our way through the commotion to the outlying *siclos* and hire an old man and a skinny boy—probably his teenage nephew or grandson—to take us to my hotel: the old man's cab for Anh, the young man's cab for me, my boxes, and mangoes.

The ride through Danang's dusty, tree-lined streets—filled with pedestrians and bicyclists and workmen harnessed like mules to pull-barrows filled with lumber—is a bittersweet homecoming. We pass a few blocks from my sister Lan's old building—apartments stacked like crates three and four stories high—and instantaneously I relive my many nights on the street, shedding one by one my girlhood dreams while waiting for Anh's son to be born.

When we arrive at the Pacific Hotel (its name is curiously unchanged from the glory days of the American war) I find myself again suspended between two worlds and am grateful for the warm reception we are given. Although it is less well kept than Saigon's new Continental, it is rustically charming the way a country cousin should be. If the desk clerks have caught the "Saigon sickness" and are less than anxious to serve us, they are also less officious than the bureaucrats of the bigger state-run facility, and their lazy, pleasant welcome puts me further at my ease. After checking in, I trudge to my second-floor room (the elevator has long been out of service) and discover that, although the bathroom lacks hot water (and what cold water there is runs all night!), a mosquito net instead of nauseating insecticide protects the single bed. At least nothing will come between my nose and the sweet smell of the ocean!

While I wash and unpack, Anh goes back into the heat to let Tinh, my niece—Hai's daughter, now a grown woman with a family of her own in China Beach—know I'm here. At first I try to be energetic and happy as I go about my chores. *I am home.* I'll soon be seeing Tinh and my mother and Hai and maybe even Bon Nghe and everyone else who's survived those awful years! I imagine their expressions of delight when they see me—of my own joyful tears as I hug them to my soul and squeeze away all the years and bad news that have come between us.

But the afternoon wears on and when Anh does not come back, the butterflies return to my stomach.

I lie down in my suitably shabby Communist bed and think seriously about how the years may have changed them. I had assumed my American "health and wealth" would impress my relatives, but maybe I'm just kidding myself. The longer I am in Vietnam, the less these material things seem to matter. Yet never have I seen—even in time of war—a place more in need of the things that money can buy: food, medicine, warm clothes, and shelter. Am I right to expect my mother and sister and niece, let alone my Communist brother Bon Nghe, to feel as good as I do about my well-fed, healthy, stereo-playing American boys? Do I deserve envy for my painted fingernails and hygienist-cleaned teeth and four-bedroom home in California, or pity for the spiritual things—a life with my family in the land of my ancestors—I gave up to obtain them? For that matter, what if my poor old mother has died since Anh last heard from Tinh? Or worse, what if the shock of seeing me kills her?

There—I'm doing it again: Letting my imagination run wild! I thought I'd gotten over that in Saigon, but I guess not! Shame on you, Le Ly! Shame, shame, shame!

I kick my shoes off, stretch out, and try to relax. The moist coastal air sighs through the window and stirs the mosquito net. I close my eyes. It's already been a long day since my wakeup call in Saigon. Perhaps a little rest will put an end to these stupid fears.

Bay Ly, Bay Ly—another, deeper voice murmurs in the wind, tickling my cheeks with feathery fingers. *My little peach blossom—haven't you learned yet that fate or luck or god works in its own way, and reveals its secrets in its own time? When has it ever paid you to turn your face from life? Keep your faith, Bay Ly: Look those deepest, darkest, most terrible fears in the face and learn the lessons they've come to teach—*

SEVEN

A Different View

MY WARTIME "souvenir" business lasted almost two years. During this time, my mother tried to look after Hung while she fretted over her two other Danang daughters, our various aunts and uncles who lived in the area, and, whenever possible, my father in Ky La. Because I was preoccupied with my business—making money to pay for our needs, saving for emergencies and for better times—I spent very little time at home. Because of our joint neglect, little Hung came to look like a typical Danang street urchin. His skin always suffered from one rash or another and his belly ballooned like a pregnant woman's from eating sand to comfort his feelings. I felt bad for my baby but I didn't know what to do. If I stayed home, we would lose our house and be forced to live again on the street or on the charity of others. Besides, my mother had raised six strong children already. If she couldn't keep Hung healthy, how could I do any better?

There seemed no solution until one day I learned from a girlfriend that a new American firebase had been set up outside Ky La. Because I now felt safer around Americans than ever before, this seemed an ideal time to go back to the village, visit my father—as I had longed to do for years—and see if it might be possible for Hung to live and grow up in the house where I myself had been raised. Failing that, of course, I could always make some sales.

I left my mother at sunrise praying for my safety. Both she and Ba had tried to discourage me from making the trip—saying there were rumors that my father had been beaten and that danger was everywhere—but they understood neither the risks I had already taken in my business nor the fact that I now knew Americans to be a bit less brutal and more trustworthy than either the Vietnamese or Viet Cong forces. To avoid combatants on either side, I traced the route I had taken in the storm almost three years before, through the swamps, jungle, hills, and brush country from Danang to Marble Mountain to Ky La but this time the weather was fine and I had plenty of time to think about my father and what to do when I got home. When I arrived, however, the village I remembered no longer existed.

Half of Ky La had been leveled to give the Americans a better "killing zone" when defending the village. Their camp, which was a complex of bunkers and trenches with tin roofs, sandbags, radio antennas, and tents, lorded over the village from a hilltop outside of town. Around its slopes, homeless peasants and little kids poked through the American garbage in hopes of finding food or something to sell. In the distance, through a screen of withered trees (which had been defoliated now by chemicals as well as bombs), I could see that Bai Gian had not been rebuilt, and that the few remaining temples, pagodas, and wayside shrines—even my old schoolhouse and the guardsmen's awful prison—had been wiped away by the hand of war. Beautiful tropical forests had been turned into a bomb-cratered desert. It was as if the American giant, who had for so long been taunted and annoyed by the Viet Cong ants, had finally come to stamp its feet—to drive the painted, smiling Buddha from his house and substitute instead the khaki, glowering God of Abraham.

With the sickening feeling that I was now a stranger in my own homeland, I crossed the last few yards to my house with a lump in my throat and a growing sense of dread. Houses could be rebuilt and damaged dikes repaired—but the loss of our temples and shrines meant the death of our culture itself. It meant that a generation of children would grow up without fathers to teach them about their ancestors or the rituals of worship. Families would lose records of their lineage and with them the umbilicals to the very root of our society—not just old buildings and books, but *people* who once lived and loved like them. Our ties to our past were being severed, setting us adrift on a sea of borrowed Western materialism, disrespect for the elderly, and selfishness. The war no longer seemed like a fight to see which view would prevail. Instead, it had become a fight to see just how much and how far the Vietnam of my ancestors would be transformed. It was as if I was standing by the cradle of a dying child and speculating with its aunts and uncles on what the doomed baby would have looked like had it grown up. By tugging on their baby so brutally, both parents had wound up killing it. Even worse, the war now attacked Mother Earth—the seedbed of us all. This, to me, was the highest crime—the frenzied suicide of cannibals. How shall one mourn a lifeless planet?

Inside, the neat, clean home of my childhood was a hovel. What few furnishings and tools were left after the battles had been looted or burned for fuel. Our household shrine, which always greeted new arrivals as the centerpiece of our family's pride, was in shambles. Immediately I saw the bag of bones and torn sinew that was my father lying in his bed. Our eyes met briefly but there was no sign of recognition in his dull face. Instead, he rolled away from me and asked:

"Where is your son?"

I crossed the room and knelt by his bed. I was afraid to touch him for fear of disturbing his wounds or tormenting his aching soul even more. He clutched his side as if his ribs hurt badly and I could see that his face was bruised and swollen.

"I am alone," I answered, swallowing back my tears. "Who did this to you?"

"*Dich.*" (The enemy.) It was a peasant's standard answer.

I went to the kitchen and made some tea from a few dried leaves. It was as if my father knew he was dying and did not wish the house or its stores to survive him. If one must die alone, it should be in an empty place without wasting a thing.

When I returned, he was on his back. I held his poor, scabbed head and helped him drink some tea. I could see he was dehydrated, being unable to draw water from the well or get up to drink it even when neighbors brought some to the house.

"Where were you taken? What was the charge?" I asked.

"It doesn't matter." My father drank gratefully and lay back on the bed. "The Americans came to examine our family bunker. Because it was so big, they thought Viet Cong might be hiding inside and ordered me to go in first. When I came out and told them no one was there, they didn't believe me and threw in some grenades. One of them didn't go off right away and the two Americans who went in afterward were killed. They were just boys—" My father coughed up blood. "I don't blame them for being angry. That's what war is all about, isn't it? Bad luck. Bad karma."

"So they beat you up?"

"They pinned a paper on my back that said 'VC' and took me to Hoa Cam District for interrogation. I don't have to tell you what happened after that. I'm just lucky to be alive."

As sad as I felt about my father's misfortune, growing fury now burned inside me. There was no reason to beat this poor man almost to death because of a soldier's tragic mistake.

I made my father as comfortable as possible and climbed the hill to the American fortress with my bucket of merchandise, intent on making a different kind of sale.

"Honcho?" I asked the first soldier I saw on the trail. I didn't understand his answer, but eventually I made myself understood well enough to impress him with my harmlessness: "You buy? Very nice? No *bum-bum*! See captain. Where honcho?"

Eventually I made my way to an officer who poked around my bucket, which by now had been searched four or five times by Americans for explosives. When he finally understood I wanted to talk to him about more than the price of bracelets, he called for the camp's Vietnamese translator.

"Thank god!" I said, bowing politely to the frowning Republican soldier who was not from the Central Coast. I explained the situation quickly to him in Vietnamese. I told him there had been a terrible mistake and that my father lay badly wounded in our house down the hill. I told him I wanted the Americans to take him to a hospital where he would be cared for and to help repair his house when he came back. I told him I knew the Americans were required to do all these things by their own regulations.

The Republican translator only laughed at me. "Look, missy," he said, "the Americans do what they damn well please around here. They don't take orders from anybody, especially little Vietnamese girls. Now, if you're smart, you'll take your father and get the hell out of here!"

"But you didn't even translate what I said to the captain!" I protested. "Come on—give the American a chance to speak for himself!"

"Look—" the translator exploded. "You'd better get out of here now or I'll denounce you as VC! If you have a complaint, go to district headquarters like everyone else! Put your request through channels— and be prepared to spend some money. Now run along before I get mad!"

I gathered my things and went back down the hill. Although some

GIs tried to wave me over, I was too upset to make a sale. I just wanted to help my father and keep things from getting worse.

Because the Americans so dominated the area, I felt comparatively safe staying near my house and tending to my father. Unlike the Republicans, who commandeered civilian houses for their quarters, the Americans kept their distance and so managed to avoid a lot of friction with the peasants. I no longer tried to sell anything (the villagers still hated anyone who dealt with the invaders) and pretended I didn't speak English when their troops stopped me from time to time. Although people going to the toilet or gathering firewood were still shot occasionally by jumpy soldiers, things remained blessedly quiet. It had been months since a major Viet Cong attack and a new, if smaller, generation of children now played in Ky La's streets. More dangerous were the Koreans who now patrolled the American sector. Because a child from our village once walked into their camp and exploded a Viet Cong bomb wired to his body, the Koreans took terrible retribution against the children themselves (whom they saw simply as little Viet Cong). After the incident, some Korean soldiers went to a school, snatched up some boys, threw them into a well, and tossed a grenade in afterward as an example to the others. To the villagers, these Koreans were like the Moroccans—tougher and meaner than the white soldiers they supported. Like the Japanese of World War II, they seemed to have no conscience and went about their duties as ruthless killing machines. No wonder they found my country a perfect place to ply their terrible trade.

I discovered that most of the kids I grew up with (those who had not been killed in the fighting) had married or moved away. Girls my age, if they had not yet married, were considered burdens on their family— old maids who consumed food without producing children. They also attracted the unsavory attention of soldiers, which always led to trouble. One reason so many of our young women wound up in the cities was because the shortage of available men made them liabilities to their families. At least a dutiful grown-up daughter could work as a housekeeper, nanny, hostess, or prostitute and send back money to the family who no longer wanted her. Many families, too, had been uprooted—like the refugees from Bai Gian or those who had been moved so that their houses could be bulldozed to provide a better fire zone for the Americans. For every soldier who went to battle, a hundred civilians moved ahead of him—to get out of the way; or behind him—following in his wake the way leaves are pulled along in a cyclone, hoping to live off his garbage, his money, and when all else failed, his mercy.

This is not to say that rubble and refugees were the only by-products of our war. Hundreds of thousands of tons of rice and countless motor-bikes, luxury cars, TVs, stereos, refrigerators, air conditioners, and crates of cigarettes, liquor, and cosmetics were imported for the Vietnamese elite and the Americans who supported them. This created a new class of privileged people—wealthy young officers, officials, and war profiteers—who supplanted the elderly as objects of veneration. Consequently, displaced farmers—old people, now, as well as young—became their servants, working as maids to the madams or bootblacks for fuzz-cheeked GIs. It was a common sight to see old people prostrate themselves before these young demigods, crying *lay ong*—I beg you, sir!—where before such elderly people paid homage to no one but their ancestors. It was a world turned on its head.

Of those villagers who remained in Ky La, many were disfigured from the war, suffering amputated limbs, jagged scars, or the diseases that followed malnutrition or took over a body no longer inhabited by a happy human spirit.

Saddest of all these, perhaps, was Ong Xa Quang, a once-wealthy man who had been like a second father to me in the village. Quang was a handsome, good-natured man who sent two sons north in 1954. Of his two remaining sons, one was drafted by the Republican army and the other, much later, joined the Viet Cong. His two daughters married men who also went north, and so were left widows for at least the duration of the war. When I went to visit Quang I found his home and his life in ruins. He had lost both legs to an American mine, and every last son had been killed in battle. His wife now neglected him (she wasn't home when I called) because he was so much trouble to care for and he looked malnourished and on the verge of starvation. Still, he counted himself lucky. Fate had spared his life while it took the lives of so many others around him. All his suffering was part of his life's education—but for what purpose, he admitted he was still not wise enough to know. Nonetheless, Quang said I should remember everything he told me, and to forget none of the details of the tragedies I myself had seen and was yet to see. I gave him a daughter's tearful hug and left, knowing I would probably never see him alive again.

I walked to the hill behind my house where my father had taken me when I was a little girl—the hill where he told me about my destiny and duty as a Phung Thi woman. I surveyed the broken dikes and battered crops and empty animal pens of my once flourishing village. I saw the ghosts of my friends and relatives going about their work and a generation of children who would never be born playing in the muddy fields and dusty streets. I wondered about the martyrs and heroes of our ancient legends—shouldn't they be here to throw back the invaders and punish the Vietnamese on both sides who were making our country not just a graveyard, but a sewer of corruption and prison of fear? Could a god who made such saints as well as ordinary people truly be a god if he couldn't feel our suffering with us? For that matter, what use was god at all when people, not deities, seemed to cause our problems on earth?

I shut my eyes and called on my spirit sense to answer but I heard no reply. It was as if life's cycle was no longer birth, growth, and death but only endless dying brought about by endless war. I realized that I, along with so many of my countrymen, had been born into war and that my soul knew nothing else. I tried to imagine people somewhere who knew only peace—what a paradise! How many souls in that world were blessed with the simple privilege of saying good-bye to their loved ones before they died? And how many of those loved ones died with the smile of a life well lived on their lips—knowing that their existence added up to something more than a number in a "body count" or another human brick on a towering wall of corpses? Perhaps such a place was America, although American wives and mothers, too, were losing husbands and sons every day in the evil vortex between heaven and hell that my country had become.

I sat on the hill for a very long time, like a vessel waiting to be filled up with rain—soft wisdom from heaven—but the sun simply drifted lower in the west and the insects buzzed and the tin roofs of the American camp shimmered in the heat and my village and the war sat heavily— unmoved and unmovable like an oppressive gravestone—on my land and in my heart. I got up and dusted off my pants. It was time to feed my father.

Back home, I told him about my visit to "our hilltop." I said I now regretted fleeing Ky La. Perhaps it would have been better to stay and fight—to fight the Americans with the Viet Cong or the Viet Cong with the Republicans or to fight both together by myself and with anyone else who would join me.

My father stopped eating and looked at me intently. "Bay Ly, you were born to be a wife and mother, not a killer. That is your duty. For as long as you live, you must remember what I say. You and me—we weren't born to make enemies. Don't make vengeance your god, because such gods are satisfied only by human sacrifice."

"But there has been so much suffering—so much destruction!" I replied, again on the verge of tears, "Shouldn't someone be punished?"

"Are you so smart that you truly know who's to blame? If you ask the Viet Cong, they'll blame the Americans. If you ask the Americans, they'll blame the North. If you ask the North, they'll blame the South. If you ask the South, they'll blame the Viet Cong. If you ask the monks, they'll blame the Catholics, or tell you our ancestors did something terrible and so brought this endless suffering on our heads. So tell me, who would you punish? The common soldier on both sides who's only doing his duty? Would you ask the French or Americans to repay our Vietnamese debt?"

"But generals and politicians give orders—orders to kill and destroy. And our own people cheat each other as if there's nothing to it. I know—I've seen it! And nobody has the right to destroy Mother Earth!"

"Well then, Bay Ly, go out and do the same, eh? Kill the killers and cheat the cheaters. That will certainly stop the war, won't it? Perhaps that's been our problem all along—not enough profiteers and soldiers!"

Despite my father's reasoning, my anger and confusion were so full-up that they burst forth, not with new arguments, but tears. He took me in his arms. "Shhh—listen, little peach blossom, when you see all those young Americans out there being killed and wounded in our war—in a war that fate or luck or god has commanded us to wage for our redemption and education—you must thank them, at least in your heart, for helping to put us back on our life's course. Don't wonder about right and wrong. Those are weapons as deadly as bombs and bullets. Right is the goodness you carry in your heart—love for your ancestors and your baby and your family and for everything that lives. Wrong is anything that comes between you and that love. Go back to your little son. Raise him the best way you can. That is the battle you were born to fight. That is the victory you must win."

When I got back to Danang, I found my sister Hai had come up to sell snails at the market and had dropped in to visit my mother. It was the first time we had talked like equals—I was no longer a puny, stomach-sick little girl, but a self-supporting woman and mother who was beginning to think and feel for herself. I was in a sober mood, and we talked a long time about the people we had known and what happened to them and if it all made any sense. I told her about Cuu Loi, our refugee neighbor from Bai Gian, and she told me that Mrs. Loi, too, had been killed and that Thien had been released from My Thi, near death and deranged, and was living a shadow life in another village. My mother, eavesdropping on our conversation, only grunted. "They were too rich for too long," she said. "Maybe they finally got what they deserved." Hai and I said nothing to this, but looked at each other and felt sad for our poor mother—hammered and forged by so many years of deprivation and Viet

Cong propaganda. Certainly, she was among a growing number of Vietnamese who could find solace only by blaming the victims themselves for their otherwise senseless deaths.

Over the next few weeks, I made several trips to see my father. The relative peace around Ky La, brought about by the strong American presence, allowed village life to regain a kind of normalcy. Relieved of their daily patrols and the threat of imminent attack, the GIs began to make some friends among the villagers—their natural preference for peace, poor attitude about the war, and longing for their own families finding many spiritual and emotional allies among the people—and especially the children. We began to notice a number of Amerasian babies —children with Vietnamese mothers and GI fathers—around Ky La and in other villages. Although most of these kids were looked down upon as the product of unnatural and ill-fated matings, my sister and I always viewed them as unlucky rather than bad. From the midst of war had come new life, and however inconvenient that life might be from one viewpoint or another, it seemed much better to make babies than to kill them, no matter if their eyes were rounder and noses longer than their neighbors.

When he was fit to travel, my father made several visits to see Hung, my mother, and me in our house in Danang. Although Hai sometimes took Hung to see his grandfather in Ky La, my father discouraged this, fearing the fragile peace that had descended on the area might collapse. When they were together, my father would sing to my little boy—some of the songs being the same ones I learned as a child—and go fishing and chase ducks and play with the piglets in the street.

On his last visit, when my mother and Hung had gone to the market to get something for lunch, my father told me that, since our communications were now so frequent and I was accepted by the Americans, the Viet Cong ("they" is how he referred to them) had given him a note to deliver to me.

"What does it say?" I asked, concerned that the cadremen had come back, like a lingering disease, to disturb the inner peace my father was beginning to find.

"The details don't matter," he said. "You can imagine the kind of mission they have in mind. They want you to smuggle explosives onto the base—to blow up people. I just wanted you to know what they asked, so you'd understand—in case anything happened to me."

"What are you saying?" I asked, alarmed.

"It doesn't matter. Don't worry. I'm just fed up."

I could see him sinking deeper into the same black mood that had almost cost him his life when I was in Saigon. I was afraid he might be thinking of harming himself again and did not want him to descend into that pit this time without having a human hand to grasp at. Wisely or foolishly, I opened a bottle of black-market whiskey and poured him a drink—to loosen his tongue and see if he would talk more about what was bothering him and what we might do about it. Instead, he gave me another sort of message.

"After New Year's, I went to the village psychic for a reading. You remember the fellow—the one who came to our house after poor Sau Ban went missing. Anyway, he asked if I was going to continue living in Ky La. 'Of course,' I said. 'This is my home. This is my farm. This is where my ancestors' bones are buried.' 'Well then,' he says, 'I have nothing to tell you.' Just like that—he says I have no future."

"Oh no, that can't be what he meant!"

"Of course, it's as plain as day. If I stay in the village, I will die—he saw it. But you know those wizards. They hate to give people bad news."

"You're just imagining things. There's nothing to worry about—"

"Who's worried? What's wrong with dwelling forever with your ancestors? I'm only worried about you, Bay Ly—and little Hung, and your sisters, and your mother—and dear Bon Nghe, if he's still alive."

My mother and son came back and we ate an uneasy lunch. When my father was ready to go, I gave him whatever I had in my trove of merchandise for that day: some canned food, a tin of New Year's cookies, the bottle of whiskey, and a pair of white pajamas which are a peasant's formal dress. He left with a careless wave of the hand, telling me not to forget what he had said, and went down the street toward the bus stop, singing the way Sau Ban used to sing when he was off on an adventure.

Afterward, I told my mother that I was worried about my father.

"He's acting strange," I said. "He doesn't care anymore what happens to him. He talks like he's angry—bitter about things—and that's not like him."

"Don't worry about *Ong*—the mister," my mother said solidly. "He's been through a lot. He's a strong man—stronger than you think. Unlike us, his strength comes from another world. He's stronger than the Viet Cong—stronger even than the Americans. He's stronger than the whole damn war!"

It was the first time I could remember hearing my mother curse. Perhaps she had been hanging around Danang too long and was becoming a tough city girl like me. Nonetheless, I had a very sad feeling that it would be a long, long time before I would see my father again.

Three days later, I was visiting Lan when Ba's policeman husband,

Chin, arrived on his bicycle. His uniform was sweaty, as if he had been pedaling fast, but his face was pale. For a moment, he just stood in front of us, as if his horrible message would deliver itself through his watery eyes and gaping lips and so save him the agony of expressing it. Finally he said:

"*Cau chet roi.* (Our father is dead.) He was found this morning on the ground outside his house. He tried to kill himself by drinking acid. They called the army medics who took him to Giai Phau Hospital in Danang, but it was too late—the stuff had already eaten through his body. By the time I got there, he was already gone."

The policeman's eyes—this man who had badgered poor Ba out of one marriage and into another, whom my beloved father once threatened with a rake and who had refused to help me when my life was endangered at My Thi, this man who represented in his sweat-soaked uniform everything we had come to hate about the war—now broke down and cried with me and my sister. Together, we felt like babies who were suddenly alone in the world. Only little Hung, being too small to know what was going on, stood by, his face as tearless as the hopeful future for which my father had given up his life.

EARLY AFTERNOON, APRIL 7, 1986:
THE PACIFIC HOTEL, DANANG

I awake with a start. The sun is on my face and the sea air is perfectly still. I am bathed in perspiration, but it is my nightmare—and not the heat of the day—that caused it. I get up and splash water on my face, hoping the image of my dying father—of the dying village and dying earth around him—will somehow disappear with the swirling water.

I glance at my watch on the dresser. Although my nap was short, the dream has left me drained. The small room closes in on me and I decide to stretch my legs. Perhaps Anh has left a message at the reception desk. Something tells me, anyway, that I should check.

From the top of the stairs I see a woman in black hand a note to the clerk. The clerk looks up and points in my direction and the woman's eyes follow his finger. An instant later I am looking at my niece—Hai's daughter, Tinh—in the face.

"*Di Bay!*" (Aunt Bay Ly!) she calls, running forward.

We both fly to the middle of the room and embrace. We pull back and through teary eyes examine how time has turned us both from young girls into women. I see in her my elder sister and through that face, my mother, and hug her again. But Tinh has seen an American in my face and her embrace is now stiff and formal. The Vietnamese in the lobby shake their heads at our breach of etiquette (even long-lost sisters are supposed to show passionless calm in public), go back to their newspapers and conversations.

"Where are your mother and grandmother?" I ask, glancing around behind her. "Sister Hai and my mother?"

"My second son Cu went to fetch them," the pretty face says.

Little Tinh has sons! I knew about her family from the letters I had received as early as 1982—but letters are not the same as the person who can laugh with you and share your tears. Apparently she feels the same, despite my American look, for her hand now gropes my arm from wrist to shoulder.

"My god, Bay Ly—you're really here!" Tears well in her eyes again.

We embrace a third time and, feeling the disapproving glance again, I ask the desk clerk if it's permitted for us to go out.

"Of course," he answers, "but your passport must stay here."

I try not to show the clerk how bad an idea I think that is. In the old days, going anywhere without your ID card or pass was an invitation to arrest.

"But don't worry," the clerk adds quickly, as if reading my mind, "you can keep your *Ban Viet Kieu* travel card. It tells officials where to find your papers. It's really much safer that way. You'd be surprised how many people would like to steal an American passport."

Although his explanation makes sense, it is not reassuring. I find more comfort in the fact that he takes the trouble to explain his demands at all. Still, rules are rules. While I go upstairs to get my mangoes, Tinh goes outside to hire a *siclo* for our brief ride to her house near China Beach.

Away from the hotel's eyes and ears, Tinh talks more freely. She tells me what happened to people we knew since the Communist takeover in 1975, and the kind of reception she thinks I'll receive from my family. Chin was sent to a Communist reeducation camp after the war and now works quietly as a peasant farmer, content to be left alone by wary neighbors. She says my sister Ba kept most of the presents I had sent to the family for herself—at first because she was afraid to be seen handling U.S. goods, but later because she felt entitled to them as compensation for her suffering, which, she believed, had been worse than everyone else's. Fortunately, some of my gifts—mostly good American clothing and vitamins—got through and Tinh was able to sell them to pay for needed improvements to her house; but that alone was not enough to erase the stain on Ba's reputation with the family. When Anh wrote to them about my visit, they agreed to keep Ba away—I cannot see her without their blessing—and, as a penalty for her selfishness, to keep for themselves whatever money or gifts I would have given her. Although Tinh explained these things calmly, my heart sank at this example of peasant justice—at how grasping and vindictive my family seems to have become since liberation. During the war, we stuck together as best we could. Even when we didn't get along, we at least did our duty to one another. Now, after more than a decade of Communist rule—of wartime during peace—it seems we have become the very thing the war was fought to prevent: a nation that puts *things* above people, vengeance before love, and greed before god. Whether this was by government decree, postwar necessity, or my family's own karma, I have no idea. I only hope, before the week is over, to find out.

If Tinh's story depresses me, the streets around us do little to restore my spirits. The endless gray blocks are dirty and poor—the urban "houses" no more than shanties with chicken coops and storefronts populated by half-naked kids, nursing mothers, and thin, unemployed young men. Although traffic is heavy, there are no cars or buses in sight, but thousands of bicycles and an army of pedestrians—some drawing carts or leading dung-laying animals through the street. We ascend the highway to Da Lach bridge built over the Danang River by Americans in 1966. The wide new structure replaced the worn-out French trestle that still stands like a rusty monument to that gone-but-not-forgotten imperial age. I feel a tickle of pleasure at seeing the sturdy American bridge still standing—a healthy, healing gift from my new country to my old one —now bearing goods and produce and people instead of tanks and cannons and convoys.

A few minutes later we arrive at Tinh's house. I renew my acquaintance with Tinh's husband, Bien, an older man I met just before coming to America in 1970. I am saddened to see him bent beyond his years from malnutrition and a barber's life in service to other men, though Tinh's own joy-of-living shines from his face and warms the hand he offers gladly. His shop, furnished with a hard wooden chair for customers and a banged-up metal desk for his implements, opens onto the street from his house. The front of the house itself (in fact, every house on the block) looks to my American eyes more like a packing crate than a home, with flat, gray-washed shutters that open like barn doors. Only inside aren't barnyard animals, but Tinh's five children and a gaggle of neighborhood kids.

Tinh directs me to their dining area—a well-worn pair of benches by a table and the wrought-iron door that marks the real entrance to the house. The only decoration on the unpainted concrete wall is a pasted-down map of Vietnam showing no North and no South, but a continuous patchwork of provinces—one state for one nation; one homeland for one people. Although the significance of that simple fact has probably long ago escaped my niece and her husband, it now hits me like a truck as I sit with them toasting our family with tea. That single, simple map was what the war—our decades of suffering—was all about: one people; one family. Despite the desperately poor surroundings (the shock of which is still seeping into my brain), I feel warmed—not only by the tea, but by a blossoming sense of belonging that unfolds like the petals of a flower. The more I think about it, the harder I find it to concentrate on Bien's second toast: to the luck of our reunion. I feel Tinh's hand on my shoulder and suppose she wonders when her silly American aunt will stop weeping.

We finish our tea and Bien asks questions about America, but my answers all seem to end with counterquestions about my mother, sisters, and brother. When Anh announced my arrival, Bien says, he dispatched their eight-year-old son to Ky La (about three miles away) to fetch my mother and Hai. They've had plenty of time to return, however, and Tinh is now getting worried.

"You shouldn't have sent a small boy on such an errand," she says. "You should have sent little Bien—at least he's ten and has a head on his shoulders."

"Stop worrying," Bien replies, but he directs his reassuring glance at me. "The boy's been there dozens of times. Besides, Bien had to get soup. What sort of visit would it be if we couldn't offer Bay Ly a helping of *mi quang* noodles, eh?"

Bien was right. Like America's Idaho potatoes, Central noodles are famous throughout the country—not just because they are good, but because they are simply *more* of what homemade noodles should be. As if on cue, the oldest boy appears with a steaming pot and Tinh splashes the noodles and broth in our bowls. Although they seem to think I would no longer relish such rustic fare after sixteen years of hamburgers, chocolate, and Coca-Cola, I wolf down two bowls and don't decline their offer of a third. This would normally be too much—too expensive—even for an honored guest, but Bien is so amused by my appetite that he ladles the extra serving himself. Although the soup is only a nickel a bowl, I know it's a lavish gesture of love and I don't deny them the pleasure of making it. Besides, the gifts in my hotel room—bolts of cloth, vitamins, and more—will make up for the expense.

After we eat, I lay on a bamboo mat while Tinh works in the kitchen and we wait for my mother and sister Hai to come. Bien excuses himself to keep a vigil by the entrance, but after he shoos away some customers, I know it is not because he is tending shop. He's worried that some nosy gossip will spot his American guest and spread word around the neighborhood. Just as it was in the war, special attention breeds special trouble.

I ask Tinh for more news about my two brothers, Sau Ban and Bon Nghe. Of course, everyone knew Sau Ban had been killed in 1963, but a sister's hope springs eternal. Perhaps there had been a mistake. Perhaps he was found wasting among the crippled and mindless in a government veterans' hospital—but Tinh refuses to feed my fantasy.

"Sau Ban is long gone," she says. "The government pays Grandma Phung seven hundred *dong* a month as his pension, and they wouldn't let go of that if they thought he might still be around." My heart sinks even further. Seven hundred *dong* is about thirty U.S. pennies each month—small compensation for the loss of such a magnificent human spirit.

"Of course, Uncle Bon Nghe is another matter," she continues. "Every time I got your letters, I'd show him and tell him you'd be coming home someday for a visit. He'd just laugh and call me a dreamer—that there was no way your country would let you out and no way our country would let you in. If he could see you sitting here now, he'd fall over in a faint, you can believe it!"

It is now after 3 P.M. and Tinh's eight-year-old still isn't back. Bien attributes the delay to a small boy's wandering mind, but dispatches the ten-year-old on a bike nonetheless to find out what's wrong. In the meantime, Tinh invites me to go with her to the Cho An Thuong market near China Beach—not far from the one used by the villagers from Ky La—to pick up tonight's dinner. "Of course," she adds, "you'll have to slip out of that *ao dai* and put on some peasant's pants. We can't have you looking like an American tourist, eh? Danang isn't quite ready for that!"

I change clothes eagerly, happy to be doing something that will keep my mind occupied. Because my American makeup would quickly mark me as a foreigner, I also put on Tinh's sun hat and try to walk with the kind of gliding shuffle that is the hallmark of overworked, underfed women everywhere in the Orient.

Tinh's neighborhood, China Beach—once home to a large military population—now shows little evidence that the Americans were ever here, save for a few permanent buildings, power poles with too-few electric wires, big intersections with podiums long abandoned by traffic cops, and shacks made from scavenged war materials—some still marked with GI stencils. The market itself, though, is just as I remember—a long line of peasants squatting by their baskets with produce arrayed by type and quality—from fresh mangoes, oranges, and bananas, to peas, potatoes, live chickens in wire cages, and ungutted, silver-skinned fish resting in flies and stink. While shoppers meander back and forth like suitors, the vendors rest on their haunches, straw hats angled like parasols. The people who bargain, if not well fed, are certainly far from starvation and as many wear Western-style clothes as they do black pajamas. Most unusual to me is the quarrelsome way in which they bargain—not buyer and seller, as I remember, but predator and victim. It is as if, now that the war is behind them, the marketplace has become their battleground, and to lose a few *dong* in a transaction is, perhaps literally, like taking a wound in the belly. I watch Tinh tear into a woman vendor she's known all her life, arguing about this and that—bruised fruit, dried-out vegetables, undersized berries—like snipers trading potshots in the jungle, and I wonder how fast simple scarcity would bring me, too, down from my lofty American high horse. I suppose it was not for nothing that my mother used to call mean-spirited people "fish-sellers in the market."

Still, the longer I watch the more I sense another force at work—something I had forgotten about in the supermarkets of America: the power of community. In the United States, I had learned to bargain only for luxuries—a car or a house. Here, people bargain from one meal to the next—consumer and producer looking each other in the eye and taking nothing for granted. The contract they arrive at—the "price" of a mango or a fig—is really an affirmation of their need for one another; a pledge of trust in the midst of suspicion; a lesson in how to survive as a community when that sense of community itself has been shattered.

* * *

MY FATHER'S DEATH caused special problems for me, my mother, and my sisters. In addition to being on our own, with no male head of the house to guide us, we wanted to give my father a traditional funeral—despite great odds against it.

First, we had to gain approval from the Republican district officials who regulated activities in the village. Then, we had to secure permission from the Americans, who oversaw all comings and goings in the local area. Finally, we had to submit our plan through Uncle Luc to the Viet Cong, who viewed themselves as the rightful peasant government and who could easily disrupt any gathering and cause great loss of life. We also needed their permission if my mother and myself were to return to Ky La openly without fear of reprisals.

An hour after Chin arrived with word of my father's death, I went to claim my father's body at the Nha Xac morgue. It was a long, low concrete building of such dispiriting coldness that even trees and grass refused to grow outside. Inside, the unmarked bodies were arrayed on stretchers and covered with sheets and flies, bestowing on the place the hellish perfume of rotting flesh that gagged me as I went in.

Gathering all my strength, I made my way down row after row of the dead, uncovering old women and girls and boys and farmers with their heads and arms blown off and vitals blown out but tossed back in with the body so that the victims, so much as possible, would appear to go whole to their graves. After a survey of twenty such corpses I finally found him.

My father's brown face was unnaturally blanched and his purple lips were drawn back from his toothless gums by muscles contracted in death. His eyes were tear-swollen blue slits—as if his soul was still trapped inside and crying for release. I kissed his waxy, stubbly cheek and repeated his name, telling him, "Don't worry; I'm taking you home."

Because I had seen plenty of death in my time, my father's mortality —his change from man to corpse—did not affect me as much as his new inaccessibility. He was now in a place I could not reach and from which he could not visit, except by the weird and tortuous ways of spirits. I regretted I did not know more about how such connections were made and vowed to make it my job to find out.

Because everybody thought I had a head for business, I was chosen to buy the coffin. However, I was in no mood to bargain and going to the first mortician I found, bought the best casket I could afford without questioning the price. I next had to bribe our local policeman, the one we "tipped" sometimes to get extra protection, to deliver me with the funeral clothes and casket to the morgue after curfew so that my father would not have to lie naked on a stretcher.

The next day, Uncle Nhu's son, Nu, the Republican officer who helped me when Hung was born, requisitioned a truck to transport my father and the rest of us from Danang to the village. And so we went: my father's casket on a wooden pallet between us with his wife and daughters and assorted aunts and uncles on troop seats along the sides.

Compared with our usual, secretive way of coming and going, the dusty drive on the rutted, shell-pocked dirt road seemed almost like a royal return. The spring air was full of blossoms and a sizable crowd had gathered when we finally parked and transferred the coffin into our house. As it was with so many wartime funerals, we had not had the luxury of consulting a wizard for the correct astrological time for transferring my father's body to the coffin or for putting him into the ground. We only knew that we must not bury him under his own or his eldest son's (Bon Nghe's) astrological sign, which would result in the family's destruction within three years or within three generations. We had come close enough to that without the curse of heaven.

The pallbearers conveyed my father's casket, feet first, through our home's middle door (which was used only for festivals and funerals), to his bed, which had been covered with white cloth. Each of its four legs had been placed in china dishes which were filled with water and kerosene to keep crawling bugs away. As many of his worldly goods as we could find were lined up between the bed and the wall. Through my father's clenched teeth my mother put the traditional ball of sweet rice (mixed with three coins and a hard-cooked egg—no one wants his beloved to depart for the spirit world poor and hungry), as well as a little sandalwood to keep the body from smelling. With the assistance of my uncles, she wrapped him in the red and white monk's robe that would be his gown for eternity. They also wrapped his hands and feet with cloth so that his bones would stay together in case his body was moved to another cemetery. In this manner he lay in state for two days and one night, so that relatives and friends could come for his funeral.

On April 7, Hai, Ba, Lan, and I, dressed correctly in white clothes and no jewelry, put three sticks of incense and two white candles above his pillowed head, then chanted sutras with the Buddhist priest who had been summoned for the occasion. In strict accordance with custom, my mother and sisters and I sat on the floor while the male relatives stood. First we prayed for the Buddha, and then for my father's departed soul —that it should not grieve for us or for leaving its worldly possessions behind. Because we did not have *Cao Vong* silk to catch his spirit while he was dying, we went straight to the *Cao To* ceremony, which informs the soul that the body will be buried properly and that it should not worry. Part of this meant writing my father's name on a scroll with our other ancestors and departed relatives, which included my brother Sau Ban.

When all this was done, it was time to carry my father's coffin to the graveyard. First went the scroll carriers, the youngest children in the family who were capable of that task, and relatives who threw *giay tien dang bac*—paper money—side to side to pay the old ghosts to look after their newest member. Then came the bearers (in this case, my aunts) of sweet rice and cooked pork and tea. After them came the altar carriers and drum players—village men who gave up a morning's labor to help us out—followed by the catafalque, which bore my father, feet first, in the direction of his grave. At the end of the procession came the women—my mother and sisters and me, bowed in homage, shuffling and crying in the dust of all the rest.

At the gravesite, our wailing became more formal. From now on, our mourning was solely to show *song goi thac ve*—that we recognized the new spirit life of Phung Trong, husband and father, as he would come to occupy our home. My sisters and I got down on the ground to bring our mourning closer to the earth which held his bones, for we knew his spirit would be pleased by this sign of love and attention to ceremonial detail. As was the custom, all the guests clasped their hands together like Chinese and gave three bows.

For the next hundred days, while my father was being judged in the spirit world for taking his own life, we followed the norms of public mourning. Three days after the funeral, we held the "open grave" ceremony (although the grave is still closed) wherein all the family members who could be reached brought incense and flowers to decorate his grave. For the next forty-nine days, we put an extra serving of food at our table and every seventh night prayed with the Buddhist priests that my father's soul should find the nearest temple.

On the hundredth day itself, we held the "stop crying" ceremony, which would be followed, on the first anniversary of my father's death, by a memorial service in which we would burn a paper bed, paper clothing, and special funeral money printed for this purpose. Those in my father's immediate family wore the *ao tang* made of linen: a smock with three fringes in the back and an emblem showing our position in the family— in my case, the device of a sixth child who was an unmarried, natural daughter. My mother continuously wore a linen scarf on her head; and I did, too, until it became too cumbersome for business. Life went on, and I knew my father's spirit would not be pleased if my son and mother went hungry because a customer refused to deal with a mourning daughter. No matter how we mourned, though, we made it clear in our hearts (and to others when we helped them) that each charitable act we did was in the name of Phung Trong, so that his passage from hell to heaven would be hastened.

In all of these things, my duty was to lead my mother and sisters. When my father was alive, my mother and Ba and Hai and Lan were content (indeed, they were required) to leave such rituals to him. When Bon Nghe went north, my father's remaining son, Sau Ban, received his instructions in spiritual matters to ensure that the worship of our ancestors and the proper ceremonies of daily life could continue should something happen to our father. Still, my father worried that without his sons around, he would lack a proper funeral, so he gave his eldest daugher, Hai, some training too. When sister Hai went to Saigon and Sau Ban was killed, these duties naturally fell to me—a puny, sixth-born girl—simply because

I was at hand. As things turned out, I was a better student in these matters than anyone expected.

At the end of the hundred days, five Buddhist monks performed a three-day mass to celebrate my father's release from fear and want, and to entice his soul back to our house through continuous chanting. (I learned from my father that if a person dies away from home, his spirit will roam the countryside until prayers can guide it back.) We knew these prayers were working because on the second night, a neighbor woman (the widow of Manh, my old teacher) reported that my father's ghost had entered her house to tell her about the money and gold he left buried around our farm. We chanted louder and on the third morning, the monks were satisfied that my father's spirit had found its way home.

Later that day, a wizard called Thay Dong, a spirit teacher from another village, offered himself as a vessel for my father's spirit. This was necessary because my father died without leaving a will and only a stranger could act as a medium for the distribution of his property.

To give the wizard privacy while this channeling took place, he was put into a bamboo cage, which we covered with a blanket. To see if his trance had been successful, some of us walked by and asked if he could identify us correctly. When he did, we knew his spirit eyes were working and the ceremony could go forward. We let the wizard out and followed him to our rice paddies, and our sweet potato and cinnamon fields. With a long stick, he marked the ground into segments of nearly equal size for my father's surviving relatives. He also spoke in spirit language of places where my father had hidden gold and money, but because nobody could translate this clearly into Vietnamese, most of his savings, what little of it there had been, were never found.

Finally, the wizard led us to my father's gravesite (this was really spooky, because the stranger had no idea where my father was buried) and spoke to each relative in turn. Because she was the eldest offspring present, my father (using the medium's voice) commanded my sister Hai to occupy the family house and tend his shrine and see to the worship of our ancestors. Although Hai knew she couldn't decline my father's last request, she begged his forgiveness because she could not correctly identify all the family graves or remember all the rituals. My father, through Thay, told her not to worry, and recommended my assistance when it was necessary. "In any case," the wizard said, "those duties will pass to your brother Bon Nghe when he returns from the war. Till then, just do the best you can."

This last seemed to exhaust the medium and we knew the time of my father's possession was near an end. The stranger hugged everyone tear-fully while thanking them for coming to his funeral, and then bowed politely to the monks. When the man stood up again, my father's spirit had rejoined his ancestors at our family shrine.

Hai returned to our house at once and continued working the land in our father's place. Within a week, a neighbor asked Hai if he could purchase a fruit tree that was on our land. Hai said yes, and sold him the tree for a small sum of money, which she needed badly to repair the house. The next day, however, the man came back and said he had fallen down every time he tried to pick some fruit. He asked if Hai had *xin keo*—consulted our father on the matter—and she replied that she had not—and could not—because he was deceased. The man laughed and showed her how to make requests of the dead by using two coins painted white on one side. If the coins land with one white side showing, the answer is "yes." If both coins land with the same side up, the answer is no." When the two coins showed her father was in favor of the sale, the man said that was all the answer she needed. He returned to the tree and filled his basket without incident and Hai went on with her work. After that, Hai consulted our father frequently on matters of our family's wel-fare, for—dead or alive, and certainly for as long as she lived or until Bon Nghe came back—he would still be head of the house.

Once my father was properly buried and his soul dwelled comfortably in our spirit house, I discovered that a good many things had been buried with him. I was no longer confused about where my duty lay—with the Viet Cong? With the legal government and its allies? With the peasants in the countryside? No—my duty lay with my son, and with nurturing life, period. My father taught me this on our hilltop years before as the night of war was falling, but only now was this duty as clear as the morning sun. I no longer had to struggle with myself to achieve it day by day. I had only to live and love and act in concert with those feelings. My father himself had demonstrated this principle many times in his life, most recently when he forgave me for my sin of *chua hoam*—becoming an unwed mother—and embraced my little child to his heart. He had not been angry at me for bringing new life into the world—far from it! He was angry that I did it in such a way that my child was denied a father. After all, where would I myself be—how long would I have survived a war that claimed so many others—without Phung Trong to guide me? Through him, I learned that although great love alone cannot remove all obstacles, it certainly puts no new ones in the path toward peace: between soldiers, civilians, and between a woman and herself. I saw that a determination to live, no matter what, was more powerful than a willingness to die. Just as the Christians believed Jesus gave his life so that they might live forever, I believed my father's death was his way of giving me eternal peace—not in the hereafter, but for every instant of every day I was alive. Vietnam already had too many people who were ready to die for their beliefs. What it needed was men and women— brothers and sisters—who refused to accept either death or death-dealing as a solution to their problems. If you keep compassion in your heart, I discovered, you never long for death yourself. Death and suffering, not people, become your enemy; and anything that lives is your ally. It was as if, by realizing this, an enormous burden had been lifted from my young shoulders. From my father's death, I had finally learned how to live.

EIGHT

Sisters and Brothers

Late Afternoon, April 7, 1986:
In the Marketplace near China Beach, Danang

TINH HAS FINISHED BARGAINING for fish and vegetables and now looks for a firewood seller to buy fuel to cook the evening meal. I have not been everywhere in the market yet but I have seen enough to stir old memories. I turn to follow Tinh when her eight-year-old son, Cu—the one Bien sent to find my mother and sister Hai in Ky La and bring them here—appears from nowhere and grabs his mother's arm. Tinh points to me and Cu runs up and shakes my hand like a little gentleman.

"I'm pleased to meet you, little Cu," I say and look around for my mother. "Where is your great-grandmother?"

"She couldn't come," he answers matter-of-factly. "She had to stay home."

"Why can't she come? Is she sick?"

"No. She said someone had to stay and take care of the farm. She said she'd try to find Grandma Hai, though, then told me to go home."

All of a sudden I am very alarmed. "Well, how did she act when you told her I was here? Was she happy I came back?"

Already the little boy's attention is wandering. He looks down the line of peasant vendors. "Aunti Ly," he says, "do you want to see Grandma Hai?"

"Of course! Is she back at your house?"

"No." He tugs my arm and draws me forward. "She's right here— on the other side of the market!"

Excitement and fear grip me like two hands around the throat. *Hai— my eldest sister—here? Now?* Suddenly I realize I am not yet prepared to meet her—to see anyone from my family. I want to look nice, to wear some nice American clothes or *ao dai*, and put on new makeup and brush my hair and look better than I know I do. I pull back from the straining little fingers and scan the line of peddlers. "Where is she?"

"There!" Cu points again, happy to be so important. "Selling snails! Come on!"

The boy pulls my hand and we run through the crowd. As we draw nearer, I can see the object of his excitement: an old lady hunched over two flat baskets of water snails. She's drawn a big crowd and business is brisk. I see that one basket contains *oc buu*, large-shelled snails; and the other, *oc ra*, smaller snails that are tasty but less expensive. So many snails of each kind meant a long day wading in the marshes—pulling off one leech for every snail that went into the basket. Perhaps that's what detained my mother; she had gone looking for Hai in the swamp, to tell her the news, but Hai had already left for the market. Perhaps my mother is out there still—wandering around in the twilight, getting chewed up by mosquitoes and leeches because of me. I feel terrible!

"Aren't you going to say hello?" the boy asks, wondering why I've stopped.

For several minutes, I can only stare with the crowd at my sister. I am afraid even to position myself to get a clear look at Hai's face. The hands that sort the shells and scoop the money are little more than bird claws —thin with long, dirty nails. The bare feet that hug the ground beneath her haunches are muddy and splayed like a duck's. Her peasant's black pajamas look at least as old as Tinh and the face beneath the tattered sun hat is lined and crusty as dried sod.

I feel the boy's fingers give my hand an urgent squeeze. I shuffle next to Hai and squat down. Her ancient face is totally absorbed in business —the leathery lips purse and quiver while she works.

"Chi Hai" (sister Hai), I say softly, and put one arm around her.

The crone's face looks at me in annoyance for having broken her concentration, then fills with terror.

I pull back and put my own hands over my mouth to hide my shock. Hai's eyes go blank—as if the recognition behind them has been purposefully switched off—then go immediately back to work. When the crowd of buyers has thinned, and still without looking at me, she says, "Please—for the love of god—go home!"

"I—I can't!" Tears are streaming down my face.

"Where are you staying?" She sorts her snails with a vengeance.

"I am at Tinh's—"

"Good. Go back to Tinh's and wait. But for god's sake—get out of here! Take pity on us—please! Let us live a little longer!"

I get up and stagger back, holding my cheeks with my hands. Just when I thought I had mastered myself—conquered my own foolish fears—these poor people confirm my worst suspicions. For them, the war has not ended.

Instantly, the market becomes an evil place. Reflexes I have not used for sixteen years now take control. In seconds my eyes absorb the crowd: searching too-big jackets for concealed weapons and sagging pockets for grenades; suspicious faces for policemen's eyes; and gutters and alleys and doorways for shelter that will deflect a spray of bullets or passing cloud of shrapnel.

Without thinking, I snatch the boy's arm and set off after Tinh. He must think I am angry because he drags his feet and whines until we are clear of the market—of the battle zone—where I release him and he scampers, wide-eyed and teary, ahead to join his mother.

I trail them all the way back to Tinh's house, confused and miserable. Around us shops close in the dusk and families settle into their dimly lit homes. Every once in a while, Tinh looks over her shoulder to see if I'm still there, but, because of instincts of her own, she leaves me alone. I have never before in my life felt out of place and unwelcome. Because of my own selfish desire to see my mother and brother and sisters, I've crushed their lives like a falling comet—a flashy American meteor who's smashed into their homes and disrupted their quiet routine and set loose a regiment of zombies—dead memories and mortal fears—to terrorize their world. Even worse, some of those zombies are not so dead; they still wear the long faces of the cadre leaders and can command their fellow citizens to *come to a meeting.*

My god—by coming here I've endangered them all! They're afraid of Communist informers—of their neighbors as well as the government! By appearing here unexpectedly, I threaten to associate Hai and my entire family again with the *De Quoc My*—the hated enemy. As much as everyone wants the wounds of war to heal, they are reopened whenever a farmer steps on a forgotten mine or burns incense to a victim of war. Was this the purpose of my return after all these years—to bring more terror to the people I love?

By the time we get home, I have so many confusing thoughts that thinking itself is a nightmare. Once I'm inside, Bien begins closing the doors and shuttering the windows, making me feel more than ever like contraband or a spy or a dirty old lady peddling the worst kind of American smut: freedom from want and worry.

Fortunately, Anh arrived while we were gone and I rush to his arms, weeping, and he comforts me like a husband. Over Anh's shoulder, I see Tinh motioning her children to be quiet and she and Bien exchange knowing glances. *Yes, poor Bay Ly*, they seem to be saying. *Now she understands what's going on. Poor girl. Give her a while to adjust. Thank god Anh's here to take care of her. And make sure those windows are bolted!*

I pull back from Anh and see that his face is full of understanding.

"I—I saw Hai—" I can hardly hear my own voice through my sobs.

"I know. Don't feel too bad," he says softly. "Things are different than you remember them. She just needs time. Everyone needs a little time."

"Yes, the more things change, the more they stay the same!" I wipe my eyes and try to give him a smile.

The change, of course, is that the machinery of wartime control has turned back upon the Communists. The fear and violence it created have now become the people's property; and even if the government wants to change it, it's had two generations to imbed itself. In a way, it's a kind of awful, practical joke. To create the perfect prison, the Communists have turned the prisoners into wardens: the whips and chains carried in their hearts.

I sit for a while on a bamboo bed in the kitchen and watch Tinh cook while the men talk in the other room. The children run through the house, shouting and playing, ignoring Tinh's command to be quiet, but I ask her to leave them alone. Warm laughter makes a better first course than cold worry.

Just as we are about to eat, the front door opens and a tallish peasant woman with a sun hat, black pajamas, and two empty baskets comes in. When the sun hat comes off, the tight bunned hair and long "Buddha" ears and proud, upturned face remind me instantly of my mother and my hearts jumps—but my brain reminds me it cannot be so. Despite the harshness of the years, the woman before me is no more than fifty-five (my mother's age when Ban died in 1963)—and not the mother god has preserved for seventy-eight years. However my mind's eye sees her, sister Hai is an eerie double vision from the past.

I get up cautiously and smooth my clothes. Now I will see how much of Hai's fear and mistrust is for the government and neighbors and how much is reserved for me!

Hai bows in greeting to Anh—he is regarded as a son-in-law now by everyone, as I am considered his second wife. He turns her toward the kitchen and points silently to me. I see Hai's eyes sparkle when she beholds me in the lamplight.

"Oh—Bay Ly!" She extends her arms and runs forward.

My broad smile almost splits my face and we embrace. She smells bad—worse than the buffalo pens! (which is where she probably found some snails)—but none of that matters. We pull back and stare at each other a long moment. The warm lamplight is kinder to her time-worn face than the sunlight at the market and I can see the womanly softness beneath her farmer's hard exterior.

"Oh!" I say, remembering the mangoes and cash I had hidden at the airport. "I brought something for you to take home—to put on our father's altar." I fetch the fruit, which is none the worse for wear, and present it to her with a bow. "And be sure to look under the paper—there's something for you and Mama *Du* as well." She accepts the basket graciously, and Bien goes to burn some incense in honor of our reunion. While he does this, Hai goes to Tinh's cupboard and fills a plate with New Year's cookies left over from Tet.

"Our mother made these to honor our father," Hai says, laying the cookies on the plate like coins. "She told me to give them to all our relatives. Now that you're here, Bay Ly, this share is for you."

"And did you save some snails for me too?" I ask, kidding her about her good luck in the market.

Hai doesn't get the joke. She looks around with a fallen face. "I didn't think you'd eat those filthy things anymore, so I threw them in a pond! I didn't want you to have to see them!"

I hug her again and tell her that, except maybe for *mi quang* noodles, I can't think of anything more delicious.

We sit at Tinh's table and Hai asks about Hung. I tell her, "We call him *Jimmy* now in the States," although that name sounds funny after a week in Vietnam. Anh shows her my photographs like the proud father he is and Hai laughs and claps her hands to see this handsome young man with his bike, buddies, and girlfriends on the modern college campus, which must have looked to her like a city on another planet.

"I remember carrying little Hung back and forth from Ky La on my shoulders," Hai says. "What an active boy he was—always getting into mischief with our father! Of course, our father was like a boy himself sometimes—do you remember, Bay Ly?"

I say, yes, I remember my father.

"I remember," she continues, "he used to tell Hung: 'If anybody asks, *Where's your mother?*, you should answer, *She is selling noodle soup!* If anyone asks, *Where's your father?* tell them, *He is selling soup noodles!* That way nobody will get too curious about your parents!' "

Hai looks between Anh and me and realizes she may have said something impolite, then tears come again to her eyes. "Oh—Bay Ly! Anh Hai! It's so wonderful to see you both together!"

I can tell Anh regrets not having been a father to Hung when he had the opportunity, but the past for everyone is full of missed chances. Surviving to understand them, if not to set them straight, is one of the hings that makes the next breath worth taking.

* * *

DURING THE FIRST FEW MONTHS after my father's funeral, I stuck close to home to make my sales. I wanted to spend more time with Hung, who grew more curious about the world each day, and with my mother, who missed my father so much she allowed me to hold her in my arms, which she seldom did before. I think she envied my inner calm—my father, after all, was always with me, while she just felt cold and alone. For her, my father was as distant as Sau Ban or Grandpa Phung or a thousand other ancestors. She was in limbo between this world, of which she despaired, and the next, which she did not understand. I tried to surround her with love, but even the richest soil needs fertile seeds to bring new life—and it was as yet too soon for a new understanding of these things to take root within her heart.

Because I now dealt more frequently with strange GIs and local officials, I was cheated more often; but miraculously, this no longer upset me. Why should it? Everything in the commissary was the Americans' to begin with! The other girls used to yell: "Le Ly—you're so stupid! Hire a punk to go after them!" But I saw no point. How would I be better off by sponsoring such vengeance? *Remember, my little peach blossom*, my father had said, *revenge is a god that demands human sacrifice!* By blackening my own soul to avenge a crime, I told them, would I bring more or less darkness into the world? My friends always went away shaking their heads, but I don't think they really listened to what I was saying.

By now I knew lots of Vietnamese in our neighborhood, especially refugees who had come to Danang and worked in the menial jobs around the base. They supported themselves and their families as housekeepers, truck drivers, or day laborers in the many construction projects that seemed to pop up wherever Americans went. Although these people depended on the invaders for their livelihood, their hearts remained with Ho Chi Minh, and most of them could be counted on by the Viet Cong to smuggle weapons or supplies from place to place. There was hardly a truckload of garbage or building materials that did not have hidden within it Viet Cong material. This was important to the Viet Cong's strategy, too, because it was easier to position fighters when their equipment was already in place—as they demonstrated to horrible effect in the '68 Tet Offensive. Here was where the corruption culture really backfired on the Republicans. Often, whenever one of these partisans was stopped at a checkpoint and a government soldier prepared to search his cargo, the driver simply bribed the local officer with cash, some whiskey or commissary goods, and a knowing wink, and the officer would let them pass, believing that the trash cans or rice sacks or lumber contained contraband, not weapons. Because these corrupt officials had long ago stopped fighting for a cause and cared only for themselves, it was as if the Republican army, which still contained many loyal patriots, had been cut by half. No wonder the Americans came to feel more and more isolated in our war! As their strength increased, more and more South Vietnamese were content to let them shoulder the load. These corrupt Vietnamese then felt free to concentrate on their own private welfare, evade serious duty or danger, and profit when the chance occurred. By the late 1960s, the Americans had indeed become (at least to us peasants) the French—but without the French colonial machinery or a hundred years of familiarity with our people. Given the strong antiwar feeling in the U.S. and among many GIs themselves, lots of Vietnamese concluded about this time that the American effort was doomed, despite its successes in the field. For myself, I recalled my father saying that god's creatures had two basic ways to survive: either by great speed and power, like antelope and tigers; or by the strength of numbers, like insects. Indeed, we Vietnamese had a saying: *Con kien cong con vua*—by sticking together, the tiny ants can carry the elephant. By 1968, the American elephant could rage and stomp on the Vietnamese anthill, but time and the weight of numbers guaranteed that it would eventually be the ants, not the elephant, who danced on the bones of the victims.

The most amazing example I knew of the Viet Cong's growing ability to penetrate Danang's defenses was the infiltration of two North Vietnamese agents who were trained to know about airplanes. According to an acquaintance, who helped the agents get into the area, these men were light-skinned, disciplined, self-confident, and a little bit jaunty—just like the South Vietnamese Air Force pilots they had been assigned to impersonate. To get into the city and onto the base was no problem—their forged papers, stolen uniforms, and security badges were never questioned by those officials who had been paid to "streamline their paperwork." For weeks they lived in the area, on and off the base, enjoying the life of elite Air Force fliers while they reconnoitered the right places to plant explosives. Some of my city friends who supported the Viet Cong asked me to help when it was time to bring in the explosives (I was often able to pass the corrupt officials with just a wave and a nod because of prior bribes), but I refused, telling them that as far as I was concerned, my father was, or should have been, the last casualty of the war. They let me alone after that, partly because they thought I was unreliable but also because my new attitude was, for them, simply too weird to comprehend. I never found out what happened to the agents—some of their bombs were discovered and others went off as planned—but they were just two of dozens of such people who roamed almost at will throughout the American facilities.

About this time, I also became aware of a new industry—slave traffic in Vietnamese girls—that was flourishing right under my nose. These girls weren't prostitutes but young women—some not even in puberty— who came into the city on buses to escape the war in the countryside. Like me, these girls were peasants, ignorant of anything but life on the farm, who had been sent by relatives to find a safer, better life in the city. When a refugee bus arrived, an older woman (accompanied by a couple of handsome young men) would ask if anyone aboard needed a job as housekeeper or nanny. Because these were jobs the girls had been told to look for, and because the handsome young men paid attention to them, the winsome young girls quickly gathered around. The woman then promised them housemaid jobs with good families for good pay, and then took them to her home where they worked a few days "just to show what they could do." The young men stayed nearby, "to help guard you from the riffraff," the woman would say, but they also flirted with the girls and so kept them interested in hanging around without having to be coerced. While the new batch of girls was thus occupied, the woman would visit her contacts and describe the new "merchandise"—sometimes complete with Polaroid pictures she took after the girls had been cleaned up. Her customers were usually corrupt officials or wealthy individuals with bizarre sexual tastes, although some of the customers exported these girls to similar clientele in other countries: to Thailand, Singapore, and even as far away as Europe and the United States. The virgins went for the highest prices, but all the girls were expensive because of their youth.

When a girl was sold, the woman and one of her boys would take her to the customer's house, where she would be impressed with the wealth of her new "master" and convinced that she was lucky. It wasn't long, however, before the real purpose of her job was made clear. Strangely enough, most of these poor, ignorant girls made little fuss about being raped and brutalized by their masters—they were used to taking orders from older people and thought that this was just what housekeepers and nannies had to put up with to earn a living. If relatives got suspicious, the master or the slave trader merely made the girl write a letter saying everything was fine. For these girls, innocence was not a virtue, but a prison.

Some, however, rebelled and ran away. When they did, the customer exercised his "warranty" and the girl was either replaced or tracked down by the woman's guards. These goons then beat up and tortured the young girl (experienced interrogators, trained by the army, were always in ready supply) and either returned her to her master or put her "back into inventory" for another deal. Even when girls didn't run away, some customers returned them after a weekend, a week, or a month, after which the woman would ship them out to another client. When these girls had been through a few such transactions, they looked pretty bad and the connoisseurs no longer wanted them. That's when they were sold to foreigners, and when the complaints from even these second-class customers got too numerous, the girls simply disappeared—victims of "the enemy" that claimed many such lives each day.

The regular prostitutes, by comparison, had a much better life. The cheapest whorehouses, those located near the military installations, were often no more than shacks whose owners rented a room (or even single beds that were lined up like those in a hospital—only a curtain shielding them from the bed next door) to local girls who plied their trade with the resident servicemen. Many of these girls were widowed by the war or were rape victims like me who despaired of a proper marriage. They would catch the soldiers near the bases and "do their thing" in bushes, in trucks, in tanks, or in alleys—no matter how hot and sweaty and smelly their customers might be. Some of these girls had their boyfriends or male relatives dress up like policemen or QCs and escort them onto the base using stolen ID cards or by pretending they had been arrested. Inside, the phony officer would solicit GIs, and protect the girl if her customers got rough. Once, when I was on the Bong Son military post outside Danang, I observed a line of GIs standing by an open trench. When I went over to sell some merchandise, I looked down into the trench and saw a naked girl taking on the servicemen one at a time. Her husband, dressed as a Republican "secret" policeman (they all wore white shirts and black pants like a uniform), stood at the far end taking cash as the soldiers descended. I even heard stories of prostitutes who took money for having sex with dogs to amuse the GIs, but I never saw any of this myself.

The better hookers had a madam (an older woman—often married to a corrupt official) who organized the girls, looked after their health, and maintained the whorehouse where they worked. Sometimes these houses employed young men to act as barkers at the door, calling "Hey, Joe— you want *bum-bum?*" as the GIs passed by outside. Others had squads of men and boys called *dan My* who scoured the neighborhood bars, cafés, and street corners looking for likely customers to lead back to the establishment. *Dan anh* were pimps who protected their territory from rivals, and their girls from the police. Lowest on this scale of outcasts were the *so khanh* con men, who promised customers everything for a down payment, then ran off with the money; and *di duc*, the boy prostitutes who catered to homosexuals.

If the madam or her husband was highly placed, they had real policemen (also called *dan anh*) to protect them. These girls charged more for their services, but both the madam and the policemen took a cut of what they earned. This caused some of them to steal money from their tricks in a variety of ways. If they had a young brother or boyfriend, the youth would sometimes stay under the bed or behind a curtain while the couple made love. When the GI was preoccupied, the youth would take his wallet, remove some—but not all—of the money, and return it to the GI's pants. Taking all the money, of course, or the whole wallet, would cause the soldier to make a scene, which nobody—especially the hooker—wanted. In such circumstances, the policemen in attendance quickly became enforcers of the madam's business rules.

More common was the risk girls took of contracting serious venereal disease or experiencing brutality at the hands of those GIs who behaved more like gangsters than soldiers. One girl I knew had been eaten up so badly by infections inside that she could no longer tolerate the pain of normal intercourse—let alone the acrobatics most American servicemen enjoyed. (She used to wonder how the little bamboo beds didn't break, designed as they were for smaller Asian couples.) Still, she had to support her fatherless children, so she became an expert in oral sex until the venereal disease left her face disfigured and unappealing to her customers.

Much worse was a practice I witnessed coming back after a day of selling in the country. At a crossroads ahead of our bus, a GI truck stopped briefly and threw out some garbage: big sacks and a couple of boxes. As usual, our driver stopped to allow the passengers to inspect the American trash—too many edible or resalable things were thrown away to be left to birds and insects. When we opened the largest box, however, everyone stepped back in horror. Inside was a young woman, naked and mutilated—but not from war. From the look of her (makeup streaked by her final tears, tight mini-skirt pulled up around her waist, etc.) she was a hooker who had been "trashed"—used, abused, and dumped—by the servicemen. After making sure all the body parts were in the box (it would have made the tragedy worse to let her be buried with pieces missing), we sealed it to protect her from animals, marked the box for the authorities, and got back on the bus. It wasn't much, but it was all we could do; and I'm sure the poor girl's spirit appreciated it.

For myself, I never minded the flesh peddling as long as the women were of age, did it voluntarily, and understood the risks they were taking. And, of course, I could hardly fault the GIs for acting like men—especially when they faced death every day three thousand miles from home. What disturbed me most—aside from the girl slavers and murderers who would be criminals in any society, war or no war—were the madams who sold others' flesh for profit and the corrupt policemen who used their badges to intimidate the customers. I also felt shame for those madams who had wealthy husbands—bureaucrats or high-ranking officers—and used their connections to drive competition, usually poor city girls who were too dumb to survive any other way, from the neighborhood. Were they worried the supply of horny servicemen would run out? No way! Here was another case of privileged people using their power to harm the people they should be helping.

It also distressed me to see the young boys—the girl's brothers or boyfriends—working as pimps for their sisters and sweethearts. Blood ties and the duty to protect a loved one are sacred. To prostitute your own body is one thing. To prostitute your relative's or lover's or wife's is something else. It was, for me, like selling out one's ancestors. If blood relations meant so little, why were we all so busy killing each other for the country of our blood?

Another sort of maggot rooted up by the war were the gigolos who chased married women whose husbands were missing or in the service. Some of these women were widows who inherited money, heiresses with French estates, or women whose husbands' had businesses or investments.

To make matters worse, the war created a very lopsided ratio of women to men. Even well-bred girls had trouble finding mates, which meant the others—those not so attractive or those disqualified by fate, like me, had virtually no chance of getting married. This made Vietnamese women very possessive of men, and so these poor rich women were easily duped by slimy males.

There were also those who committed crimes for big institutions—as volunteers or as a sideline to their regular jobs. Some of the black market items wound up in the coffers of the Catholic Church (which was favored by the government, and so was seldom hassled) or were sold by zealous Catholics who donated the cash they made. But this really harmed no one and to the extent the Church helped my people and didn't persecute the Buddhists, I never considered it a crime. Much worse were some army commanders who altered the casualty lists to keep dead soldiers on the payroll. Of course, it was said that certain Vietnamese lawmakers encouraged this practice, too, because it allowed them to withhold pensions (some of it paid by the U.S.) from the dependents and line their own pockets. This kind of corruption really infuriated me, because those illegal profits were really food stolen from the mouths of poor people who had sacrificed sons and fathers—their own future security—to the war.

Throughout all this, these were the people I admired most: those who kept up their spirits and did their best for themselves and their loved ones, no matter what happened. I patterned my life on what they taught me. I learned that you were only a victim—truly a victim—when you felt like one: when you got knocked down and didn't even try to get up. The victims were women who let themselves be sold into prostitution when they had another way to live, or men who earned a good living as officials and still had to steal. GIs who began to hate themselves for simply answering their country's call were also victims. In a world where most people were victims, we all had something in common—including the power to liberate ourselves. When the worst around you are only victims, forgiveness and compassion come much easier.

EVENING, APRIL 7, 1986:
TINH'S HOUSE, DANANG

We sit around Tinh's table and she serves *ca thu* fish and shrimp she bought at the market, salty *mon man* pork to clear the palate, followed by a main course of *xoa*, or chow mein vegetables.

While we eat, I expect to learn what will happen when and if I meet my brother Bon Nghe. Sadly, my four companions seem to have grave doubts that such a meeting should take place at all.

Tinh says to her mother, Hai (who was against the idea from the start), "Bon Nghe will faint when he sees Bay Ly. He never believed she would be allowed to come home. He called me a dreamer for even suggesting it. I say: Let him see her for himself."

"Oh." Hai turns pale and shakes her head. "He'll think she's a spy or saboteur! Maybe even a party agent assigned to ferret out defectors!"

"Bon Nghe can't believe Bay Ly even *wants* to return," Anh says. "Why would an American come back to Vietnam? People pay pirates and profiteers to take them out and the orderly departure program has been logjammed for years. It just doesn't make sense to him."

Logical or not, it makes perfect sense to me. I have not seen my older brother—keeper of my father's and my family's name—for over thirty-two years. When he left, I was a worshipful sister of five. As a teenager, Bon Nghe was more like another father than a brother. Where Sau Ban had my father's easygoing nature, Bon Nghe was more like my mother: serious, filled with duty, less partial to the spiritual world than to the world of day and night, a person singled out in youth to show courage and independence. From what little I know about Communists, I'm sure he makes a good one—and is probably better than most, since it's unlikely his Phung nature has been soiled by abuse of power.

Hai looks at me while she picks through her mint salad, served by Tinh as a final treat.

"Besides, Bay Ly," she says, "Bon Nghe's a different man from the boy you kissed good-bye back in 1954. He's a dedicated party man. He studied accounting as well as war in Hanoi. Uncle Ho's government trusted him to deliver payrolls to the south for many years—and they don't trust Southerners easily. If you really want to see him, you must be willing to risk disappointment."

"I haven't come this far to back out now," I reply. "And Bon Nghe is not the only person who's changed. Maybe we'll both be pleased by what we see."

Bien leaves for Bon's house on Anh's motorbike and I help Tinh wash the dishes. He's gone a long time—over an hour—and I begin to feel nervous. Perhaps Bon's out of town and I'll miss him altogether. Or worse, perhaps he's home but doesn't want to see me, despite Bien's pleading. Gradually, I notice Anh and Hai sitting like baby-sitters on either side of me. I laugh and take their hands and they take mine, and so we sit and wait.

Around eight we hear the Honda sputter outside and the kickstand snap into place. Male voices speak but I can't make out a thing, although I grasp for clues. Is the other voice Bon Nghe's? If it is, does it sound happy, sad, or cross?

"Well—it's about time!" Tinh says, and all of us get up. Our eyes are riveted on the space on the door where we know Bon Nghe's face will appear. An instant later, a boy-man who looks exactly like the dog-eared photo I have carried from America comes in. Bon's chestnut face is better preserved than Hai's, although care lines crease the mouth and eyes and the boyish mop of hair shows streaks of gray. He shakes hands cordially with Anh, bowing slightly in the manner of close-but-not-too-close relations, then turns toward me. Like Hai's, his initial expression is one of shock, not pleasure.

"*Co Bay!*" (Miss Number-Six "Aunt"!) He uses the ceremonial form of greeting—one reserved for distant relatives—rather than the familiar *em bay* for number-six sister. It almost breaks my heart. Before this greeting, I thought about throwing myself in his arms. Now I know that although the gulf between us has been narrowed greatly, these last few feet may be the hardest of all to cross.

"How did you get here?" His voice is barely a whisper.

Obviously, he thinks I landed with a CIA parachute or bribed my way past Vietnam's stolid watchmen. Had I been wearing designer jeans, high heels, and a Disneyland sweatshirt, I could not have felt more conspicuously American.

"Like any other tourist," I answer with a smile, longing to hug him, "on an airplane at the airport. You look wonderful, Bon Nghe!"

"Airport? You mean Ton San Nhut—Ho Chi Minh City? Or Hanoi?"

These are a policeman's, not a brother's, questions and I feel tears come again to my eyes. Bien, now inside the door, also senses the tension and hovers close to Bon, perhaps to restrain him if he becomes enraged. Yet it is essential that I keep my composure. East is meeting West. Despite my warmest feelings, an epoch of war and politics has come between us. I must play the game on dear Bon's terms until he feels comfortable enough to play on mine.

"Tan Son Nhut," I answer, "with lots of other people—UN workers, some French and Russians—lots of people. But you took so long getting here. I hope my visit didn't take you away from important business."

Bon Nghe relaxes a little and Bien laughs.

"As a matter of fact," Bien says, "Bon Nghe wasn't home when I called. I sent his son looking for him with a message: 'You must come to Tinh's at once,' and he thought something had happened to his mother. So when he rushed home and learned it was you, Bay Ly, who wanted to see him, he was relieved and shocked at the same time. You should have seen his face!"

Bon steps closer, but his manner is still guarded. "So, you're here on an American passport and everything's okay?"

He is still worried that I sneaked into the country! *How can I convince you, brother Bon!* "Yes," I laugh as carelessly as I am able. "Everything's okay! My passport is safe at my hotel. But I have a *Ban Viet Kieu* travel card and a letter from the Vietnamese mission at the United Nations, if you'd like to see those—"

I begin to fish in my purse and Bon Nghe, perhaps feeling a little sheepish for doubting me, reaches out to stop me. The Phung male hand on my arm almost turns me to butter, but I hang tough.

"Oh no, that's not necessary," he says, then withdraws the hand quickly. "So—how are you getting along in the United States?" At least he tries to smile. "How's your family? Do they get enough to eat?"

"I'm doing okay," I say firmly, genuinely touched by his concern. "We're doing just fine. And your family? Can you provide for them okay?"

I sense that Bon's waiting for me to ask him about his politics—is he really a Communist or not? Perhaps he's waiting for me to ask him for a favor, as most bureaucrats expect—especially from relatives. I had learned already that most Vietnamese officials feel defensive about their poverty-stricken country. Instead, we talk about our families, and I hear in his voice an earnest desire to push governments and politics aside. The problem is—after all those years of discipline and training—he doesn't quite know how.

Tinh invites us to tea and the last of the New Year's cookies. Anh and Hai and Bien try to break the tension by crowding in their own light questions: *Wasn't today a scorcher? Bon Nghe—how's that new accountant working out at the office? Do you think they'll end rice rationing soon? You should've seen all the snails Hai sold today!* But Bon Nghe and I just sit there looking at each other, and after everyone has had enough cookies and tea to be polite, Anh and Bien go outside and Tinh and Hai play busy in the kitchen. I am left alone with my brother to talk.

"You know, Bon Nghe," I begin, "I had this terrible fear you would despise me."

"Oh no—!" He tosses the idea off politely.

"Well, you know, I married one of your enemies—an American civilian worker—and left the country while you were still fighting. That doesn't bother you now?"

"Well, it's been so many years—" Bon's voice trails away and he changes the topic. "I just can't believe you're really here. You just got your visa and flew in?"

"No," I smile, "I had to write some letters first. And boy, did I talk to a lot of people! Some said go and some said stay, so I finally had to follow my heart. But if my earlier gifts could make the journey, why not me?"

"I wouldn't know about those," Bon Nghe says quickly. "I never touched them. Not that I didn't appreciate your thoughtfulness, *Co Bay*, but it wouldn't have been right. I am a member of the party, after all. But for Tinh and Ba and the others—that's all right. They needed all the help they could get. Things have been very hard for them."

"And for you?"

Bon smiles his *old soldier* smile—almost every veteran has one. "Well, I had been through the war, you know? For us, it was a seven-days-a-week, twenty-four-hour-a-day job. We used our own excrement to grow vegetables, eh? Rice was a luxury. I ate enough *cu san cu mi*—coarse yams—to last a lifetime! And of course, we never had a full night's sleep. Half my life in those years was spent underground—to walk around on a sunny day was high holiday, I'll tell you! Once, I was wounded by a fragment from a mortar round. I woke up in a coffin and escaped being buried only by pounding on the lid! I tell you, *Co Bay*, our life was so lousy, all we had to hold onto was the future. And because we knew that future wouldn't arrive unless we won, we kept fighting no matter what. It wasn't so much because we were brave but because we just didn't have the option of quitting."

"Like the Americans?"

"Yes, like the Americans. If the situation had been reversed, I'd have quit too—wouldn't you, Bay Ly?"

My familiar name on my brother's lips is music to my ears. I wriggle closer to him in my chair.

"But you missed out on so much!" I say, touching his arm for emphasis. "You never knew about Sau Ban or Father, or how Lan and I went to America, until after the war!"

"I never heard anything from anyone. You know, in 1971, I was trapped on a mountainside by an enemy bombardment. In the foxhole next to me was another Regular—but from a different unit. We started talking to pass the time and I noticed he had a Central accent. 'What village are you from?' I asked. He answered, 'From Ky La.' I couldn't believe it! So I asked, 'What's your father's name?' And you know what? He was Aunt Lien's son—my own cousin! So we sort of hung around together after that. He didn't know much about the village, except that it had suffered a lot of damage. I didn't know about you and Lan until much later. Nineteen seventy-five was a bad year for us, despite liberation. In some ways, for those of us who fought for the North, it was worse than the war. When we came south on furlough to find our families or to take posts with the new government, we saw that everything was different from what we had been told. We believed the South was poor—but look at the wealth of Saigon! We thought Southerners would welcome us as liberators, but everyone was suspicious. Our mother was even afraid to tell me that you and Lan had gone to America until she was certain there would be no retribution. She just said something must have happened to you in the city—can you believe it? So for a couple of years, I thought more than half my family was dead! I even asked her for a recent picture so I could look for you, but she refused—worried that someone who knew you would tell me the truth. When your letters and presents started coming, of course, she couldn't deny you were alive in America."

"What did you think when you found out?"

Bon Nghe laughed, "I couldn't believe it! At first I was offended— that any relative of mine could live with the enemy. Then, I didn't care so much, as long as my sisters were alive. *Cuc mau cat lam doi*, eh?— How can you divide a pool of blood? I thought you must be living in prison or in a reeducation camp. I couldn't believe Vietnamese could just walk into the United States and start a new life."

"What did you think of my letters?" I asked.

Bon Nghe looked down at the table. "Somehow it didn't seem right to read them. We were still brother and sister—we shared the same mother—but we have different hearts and minds. I respect you for coming back, Bay Ly—for taking the risks, whatever they were. But I must ask you now to do something else."

"What's that?"

"Leave Mama *Du* alone. Don't go to the village, whatever you do. If she wants to come and visit, she will—but let her do it in her own way."

For an instant I think Bon Nghe is telling me that my mother no longer loves me and tears fill my eyes. Certainly, she had a chance to come and see me this afternoon, but sent little Cu back to Tinh's with the flimsy story that she had to stay and feed the chickens. "I don't understand—"

"You must understand, Bay Ly: the war is still going on for us. We can't turn trust on and off like a light switch—"

"I have come here only to make my heart and soul happy, Bon Nghe," I sob. "I don't want to harm anyone. I don't want to open any wounds. You see, I waited all those years in America, just like you waited in the jungle, to see my family again. That's what kept me going. I came back to see you and Mother and everyone else—to see if I still had a family."

"Good. Then don't spoil things for them. If the officials think your mother is receiving money from the capitalists, she may lose her pension. And there are still certain villagers—you know the ones I mean—who haven't forgotten the war: the things our mother was accused of. She must still be very careful. *You* must be very careful."

I take out a handkerchief and blow my nose. Tinh and Hai take it as a signal to come to my rescue with happy talk. As I put my hankie back in my purse, I notice I still have an American-made chocolate left over from the flight from the United States. Having nothing else with me to offer, and being unsure that I will ever see Bon Nghe again after tonight, I take the candy out and hold it up as a pathetic gift.

"Moi Anh an?" (Would you like a candy?) I smile through my tears as I did when I was five years old offering my brother sweet rice on the day he left for Hanoi. "They're pretty good!"

Bon Nghe refuses to take it—to even touch the wrapper. "No, no thanks," he says, holding up his hands.

"Oh, come on! When's the last time you ate good chocolate?"

"I couldn't really. You see, a lot of the American food was booby-trapped after liberation. Even the grocers didn't know about it. I wouldn't feel right, honestly—"

Honestly, my brother thinks I might—just *might*—offer him food tainted on purpose in America! A weight so heavy I can't breathe pushes me into my seat. I turn immediately to Tinh.

"Tinh—may I give some candy to your son?" The oldest boy was still awake and doing homework in the other room.

She answers yes and the ten-year-old is beside me before I can call his name. He unwraps the candy the way a groom unveils his bride and slips it into his mouth, intent, apparently, on making it last the whole night. Before he leaves, Tinh barks another order.

"Oh no, you don't, young man!" She snaps her finger at the fire under the stove. "The wrapper—into the fire with it! Right now, before you forget!"

I sag deeper into my chair. Even Tinh must be careful not to let so dangerous a thing as a capitalist candy wrapper incriminate her family! All evidence must be eaten or burned! The long day and the weight of the war and all the years in between bear down on me like the planet itself. My feelings must have shown on my face.

"Look, it's getting late," Bon Nghe says. He reaches into his shirt pocket and brings out a piece of paper and pencil. "I want you to meet my family, Bay Ly—and I don't want to have to lie to my superiors to arrange it. Please write down what I tell you, eh? Go ahead—'I, Phung Thi Le Ly Hayslip, ask permission to visit with my brother, Phung Nghe, and his wife and son, at two o'clock on April 9, at—' Where are you staying?"

"At the old Pacific Hotel—"

"Oh, that's a nice place—kept up well for important visitors! '. . . at the Pacific Hotel, Danang City.' Now sign your name—right there below it—and I'll take it to the office. This first visit, the one tonight—we'll agree didn't happen, okay? It's just for you and me. For the record, we'll meet for the first time on Wednesday. I hope that's okay?"

I tell him I would be happy to see him again anyway I could, and would love to meet his pretty wife and fine son. I again resist the urge to give him a hug and kiss—it would not be proper and even if it was, he would likely worry that I was wearing poisoned lipstick, compliments of the CIA!

I say good night to Tinh and her son and after Bien runs Bon Nghe back to his house, Anh takes me to the hotel on his Honda. Despite the barriers between us, I cannot say that I have ever loved my older brother more than I do right now. No matter how many men you love, or how many men love you, no bond is thicker than the blood which passes through the umbilicus to brothers and sisters—*Mau dam hon nuoc la*, blood *is* thicker than water—and Bon and I, through our poor old mother, can never lose that connection.

I get off at the hotel's front entrance and before leaving for his sister's house—Anh's residence in Danang—he says over the noise of the motor, "Don't worry, Bay Ly. Bon Nghe knows why you came back. He admires you very much, though it will be difficult for him to say so. He even knows you're writing a book. He told me he wants to write one too, when he retires. It's true! He's very proud of you for telling your family's story, even to the Americans."

"Maybe our relatives should read it too, eh?" I pat Anh's shoulder. "Then maybe everyone can stop refighting the war!"

"Don't hold your breath, Bay Ly," Anh smiles bravely, waves, and drives away.

In my room, I take a tepid shower (the best my hot-water faucet will do) and am amazed at how kind to me my life has been. Even if my visit ended now, I have at least had the satisfaction of seeing my sister Hai— the next best thing to my mother—and my long-lost brother Bon Nghe, who now heads my father's family. As I pull my fingers through my wet hair, I can feel the tendrils of my life forming a circle before my eyes—but in such colors and such rich textures as I could scarcely have imagined.

I climb into bed, rejoicing at the roar of surf. Tomorrow, if fate or luck or god is willing, maybe I'll see my mother and smell the perfume of her leather skin and brittle hair and feel those ancient arms wrap around me and make me, for an instant at least, as contented as the newborn infant they once held.

But fate is sometimes fickle; luck is not always good; and god, in his heaven, sometimes turns his face from life. What if my poor old mother still refuses to see me or is destined to breathe her last tonight? There are more than enough things for which I can be punished—and what jungle justice it would be for me to come all this way after all these years just to walk in my mother's funeral!

Bay Ly, Bay Ly, the whispering ocean says, *My little peach blossom . . . !*

NINE

Daughters and Sons

WITH MY FATHER GONE and Ky La and the neighboring villages left in shambles by the war, there was nothing much any of us could do but take care of ourselves and each other.

Uncle Luc's wife (*Bac Luc* we called her—"Auntie Luc") was a good woman who had always been kind to me when I visited their fine home in Bai Gian. She was a talkative, affectionate person who always had a joke or some gossip and because I sometimes wished my mother would be more like that—more demonstrative with her love and less serious about the world—I occasionally fantasized that I was Bac Luc's daughter.

One day, she was out in the fields with her adult second son when the village dogs begin to bark—our usual "early warning" of intruders. Sure enough, a moment later they heard a helicopter's flapping blades and the whine of engines and a moment after that, a parade of American helicopter gunships appeared above the trees.

Despite his own experience and all warnings to the contrary, including the screams of his mother, Bac Luc's son panicked and ran for cover. Although he wasn't a fighter (or even a member of the Secret Self-Defense Force as I had been), he favored the Viet Cong and thought their victory was inevitable. Perhaps with those "guilty thoughts" in the back of his mind, he feared the Americans more than he should. Without changing its course, the lead gunship fired a short burst and Bac Luc's son crumpled amid the broken stalks of rice.

Shocked out of her own good sense, Bac Luc dropped her hoe and ran after him—to save his life if she could, or at least shelter him with her body. In seconds, however, she too was cut down in the same mechanical way—as if the Americans and their machines were merely chopping back deadwood from the edge of the paddies. As the helicopters droned off in single file, she clawed her way through the mud until she reached her son's body. In horror, she saw he had been killed instantly—cut in half by the bullets. She let out a long, mournful cry, which her neighbors heard. When they arrived, she was unconscious.

When Bac Luc came to, she was lying in a charity hospital ship run by West Germans in Danang harbor. She had lost her vision in one eye and had only partial use of her arms. Everything below her shoulders had been paralyzed.

When Uncle Luc took her home, he told her that all their remaining children and grandchildren, except one—the twelve-year-old boy of another of Bac Luc's sons (who had gone to Hanoi in 1954)—had fled to the swamps. Beyond himself and this boy (who already lived in their house), Uncle Luc said solemnly, there would be no one around to take care of her. To make matters worse, Uncle Luc himself had to spend more time with the Viet Cong, who now called him away with other village men to build defenses in the local area.

At first, Bac Luc and the boy got by okay. The boy kept house and brought her the things she needed and helped her to the toilet and, after cooking dinner, took rations to his relatives in the jungle.

One day, however, he went into the swamp to take his young cousin fishing. This cousin was a much smaller boy who had no father to teach him things, so the twelve-year-old carried him around on his shoulders —just as Sau Ban used to carry me—and told him stories and taught him songs while he set their poles and nets around the pond. When they had caught enough fish for everyone's dinner, he picked up his cousin and headed back to the encampment where his relatives lived. Unfortunately, the path took him past an American ambush which had been set a few hours earlier. When he appeared in his black pajamas, long-barreled fishing pole on his arm, and the younger boy riding hunched on his shoulders like a backpack, the Americans opened fire and both children died instantly. That afternoon, their bodies turned up at the American base outside Ky La with the rest of the day's "kills"—a paper with the hastily written letters "VC" pinned to their tiny chests. Neighbors said Bac Luc was so shocked, all she could say for days was, *"Chau toi My ban chet roi!"* (The Americans shot my little boys!)

When I heard about this, I made it my business to visit Bac Luc as often as possible. This woman, who in many ways had been my surrogate mother, had gradually lost everything to the war. She used to live in a beautiful house in Bai Gian with all her loved ones around her. Now, the old house was in ashes, the forest around it defoliated, and her new house was nothing more than a shack—like the huts the duck-watchers use—with a sand floor, drafty bamboo walls, *ra* (thatched rice stalks) overhead for a roof, and straw for a bed. Whenever I called, therefore, I brought spare food and sat with her on the straw and talked about events in the village and Danang (she couldn't get out of the house without being carried) and brushed her hair and helped her to the toilet and did whatever I could to make her life more bearable. In every way, I tried to be the good daughter that fate or luck or god had somehow seen fit to deny her.

Finally, after events had kept me away for several weeks, I returned to her shack for a visit only to make a shocking discovery. The door banged up and down with the wind and appeared to have been open for days. Rain had come in and soaked everything. Wild birds sat on the shelves and floor pecking away at whatever food the stray dogs, lizards, and insects hadn't taken. The whole place smelled like a latrine and when I spotted Bac Luc, she had somehow rolled over and was pinned on her stomach. When I turned her over, a cloud of flies swarmed from her mouth, which was smeared with human feces.

"Bac Luc—!" I cried. "What happened!" I rolled her back onto her bed of straw, half expecting her to tell me that enemy troops or brigands had ransacked the place and tortured her. She was badly dehydrated and barely able to speak.

"Is it Bay Ly—?" Her good eye rolled feebly in its socket trying to identify the soft blur that held her. "Please—I'm so cold and hungry!"

"Yes—I'll get some water and clean you up!" I shooed away the flies and birds and came back with a bucket of well water. "Who did this to you?"

"No one. Everyone."

"I don't understand." I sponged the mess from her face and helped her take a long drink.

"Luc has been gone for weeks. A grandchild stopped in a while back to pick up some things, but she didn't have time to fix my food. My water ran out days ago and I was too weak to crawl to the toilet or even to cry for help. My bowels moved where I lay and I was so thirsty and my stomach so empty that I had to eat something—!" She began to cry. They were racking, tearless sobs with little breath and no moisture to back them up.

I finished cleaning her and changed her urine-soaked bedding. I dressed her in fresh clothes and got what food we could spare from our house and made sure she had something to eat. She was now almost totally blind and her good arm worked spasmodically at best. She could no longer manage a spoon, let alone chopsticks, and had to feed herself with shoveling fingers like a monkey. In the space of a few months, she had gone from a strong, handsome woman of fifty-five to a white-haired, hollow-eyed ghoul who looked to be more than one hundred. I tried to boost her spirits by singing and telling her jokes and gossip—as she had done for me when I was little—but secretly I knew she wanted to die, to spare herself and everyone else the anguish of watching her lose her humanity as well as her life. When the end finally came, I marched behind her coffin like a daughter.

Gradually, Ky La became a village filled with such ghosts—both living and dead. Census takers could only come, take a look at the number of orphans, beggars, bastard Amerasian kids, and "hump-backed" (freshly dug) graves that had increased since their last visit, and know that the village—and the way of life it once knew—was dying. In a way, Ky La had spawned its own "lost generation": brothers and sisters who had never known love, family rituals, and peace—only terror, starvation, and war. I wondered how many would know how to survive when the shooting finally stopped.

It seemed as if the more we prayed for peace, the more vicious the war became. Like many others in the South, my gradual belief in the inevitability of the North's victory was matched by the certainty that our country's past, like the Republican cause, was on the verge of being lost forever.

But with a two-year-old son on my knee, a depressed and increasingly disconsolate mother by my hearth, and a Phung Thi woman's heart in my chest, I concluded that such idle mourning must be left to other people. If baby Hung and I and my father's spirit were to survive the death of Vietnam, we would have to turn our eyes elsewhere—to the West—to the direction of the rising, not setting, sun; and pray that sun would one day shine again on our country.

MORNING, APRIL 8, 1986:
PACIFIC HOTEL, DANANG

The morning is bright and prematurely hot. I start the *punkah* ceiling fan and jump into the shower, dressing afterward in the clothes I borrowed from Tinh. If I have learned one thing from my encounter with Hai at the marketplace, it's better to blend in than stick out in this new Vietnam.

After breakfast with Anh, during which he reassures me that my mother still loves me and probably did have to stay with the chickens overnight—to prevent pilferage by her neighbors!—we go to the local *Ban Viet Kieu* office and confirm arrangements for the remainder of my stay. After another day in the area around China Beach, I am scheduled for a government-sponsored tour of the countryside—to Marble Mountain and beyond. But "Xa Hoa Qui"—Ky La—I am told, is off-limits. I ask the official (using the intimate voice of a Central Coast sister, which I hope will bring a candid answer) if that means the village is suffering unusual hardships which tourists should not see. The fellow only smiles and waves my concerns away.

"Oh, don't worry about your relatives," he says, lighting another pungent Vietnamese-made cigarette. "It's your own welfare you should be concerned about, not theirs. You know these peasants. Sometimes the law extends only as far as our policemen. A stranger in a village is like a drop of honey on an anthill, eh? And some of these ants have pretty sharp pinchers—especially the old Republican bandits who take what they want and terrorize their neighbors."

"Yes, I know about ants and anthills."

"Good. Then you'll realize our rules are only for your protection."

I'm sure the rules are designed to protect something but I don't press the point. After reviewing the rest of my itinerary—a dinner tonight with Anh and some party officials; a luncheon tomorrow with workers at Anh's factory and a government-sponsored car tour of the countryside; a final day with my Tinh and my Friday departure for Saigon—I am told everything's in order. I fish through my purse for the obligatory pack of Marlboros.

"I hope you will accept this small gift for your kind service," I say as we stand up. The official takes the pack, looks pleased, and bows.

"That's why this office is here"—he offers his hand politely—"to help make your stay more pleasant."

"Good—" I take his hand and pause, looking him straight in the eye. "Because there is one more thing—a very small thing, but it would mean a great deal to me. I hope to see my mother while I am here. If I can't visit her in Xa Hoa Qui, may I have permission to invite her to the hotel one evening—to spend the night?"

The warm handshake turns cool; but I don't let go.

"Well," my official *helper* squirms, "that's a most unusual request. We have very strict rules about—"

"I know," I smile my most charming smile, "but she's a very old lady. Who knows when I'll have the chance to do something nice for her again?"

I let his hand drop and he slides the Marlboros into his pocket. "Well," he says, "we'll see. Perhaps something can be worked out. You've been very cooperative so far. I'll speak with the *can bo* at your hotel. Perhaps, in a day or two, I can arrange a pass."

"That would be wonderful!" I bow again, but lower to show my true gratitude, and we depart. On the street, Anh takes my elbow.

"You must be more careful, Bay Ly. By requesting a visitor's pass, you've suggested to them that your mother has asked to come—that she wants to consort with an American."

"To visit her long-lost daughter!" I correct him. "What's wrong with that?"

"That's not how some people will see it. Even if they don't think you're a spy, they'll acuse you both of setting up some black market deal in private. The officials are terrified of Western visitors. If it was just a matter of sending in toothpaste and family clothes from America—that's all right. But they say some *Viet Kieu* have sent in money and guns for an insurrection."

"Phooey! I'm not a counterrevolutionary!"

"I know. And neither is your family. I just think you should let your mother decide for herself. Remember, when I came to look for her in '82, after receiving your letter with Ba's address, I saw how much your mother had suffered. She and Hai weren't starving, but their clothes were in rags and their farm tools were lost or stolen. The house needed repair and most of their animals had been sold or slaughtered. Nobody in the village cared about them, so they were just two old ladies scavenging and growing vegetables to stay alive. Now, if you turn the village against them—well, I'm sure you can see what might happen."

"No, I don't see at all. How can I prove to people I just want to see my mother unless I go to Ky La or she comes to Danang? Anyway, you were a wealthy man in the old days. She wasn't afraid to see you!"

Anh laughs. "No. In fact, she treated me like an honored guest—a long-lost son-in-law when she saw me. She begged me to take some rice home to my family, can you believe it? She thought I must have been totally ruined by the Communists, so she gave me what she and Hai could hardly spare. Even though I was in a big hurry to get back to the factory, Hai butchered their last skinny chicken so we could have a feast. Your mother even gave me the gifts you sent from America. She said she'd only have to bury them if I didn't take them with me. All she cared about was you and Lan and your children in the States. Were you okay? Did you get enough to eat? She was afraid you'd forgotten what your father taught you and that you had become a capitalist."

"He taught me that material things are just a vehicle to help me get through life. Lots of Americans feel that way—why should my mother worry about that?" I climb on behind him.

"Well," Anh laughs again, "everyone knows how you Americans love your vehicles! Just don't be surprised if it takes her a few days to make up her mind. When she's ready to see you, she'll let you know."

Anh parks in front of Tinh's house and Bien, snipping away at an elderly customer, waves us in with his scissors. Even though he greets us cordially, I know he is touchy about my being here with his neighbors around, so I ignore him and scuttle right past, head tucked low so that even my modest American makeup won't give me away.

Past the outer shop, I untie the scarf that has shielded my hair from the wind (and my face from prying eyes) and pass through the dining room for the kitchen, calling for Tinh. I notice she has a neighbor lady, perhaps the customer's wife, sitting with her son at the table. It occurs to me that maybe this is not the best time to visit, but she did say to return about lunchtime. I turn the corner and see Tinh looking up from a bubbling pot of rice soup. Her eyes are as big as the ladle.

"Bay Ly! You're here!"

"Of course." I'm surprised she seems surprised. "You said to come back about noon."

"Then you've seen her—!"

"What are you talking about?"

Tinh walks around me and points the spoon like a wand at the little old lady sitting in a black kerchief at the dining table.

"There!" she says. "Grandma Phung—your mother!"

The tiny figure—a pillow of blue and black cloth—twists her chair and gets up. Even standing, she is only a little taller than before. She wears a bulky blue sweater over a turquoise peasant's top. The shirttails overhang some baggy pants from which her brown, bare feet stick out like old ginger. Like Hai's, her hands are skin on bone as they pull the kerchief from her brittle gray hair. The eyes under the weedy hairline, however, are black marbles and they transifx me with a look of surprise and hurt and hunger all mixed. If this person is truly my mother, the down-turned, betel-black lips stay mysteriously sealed over the greeting I have waited so long to hear.

"Mother—?" I move past Tinh's spoon. "Mama *Du*—?" I call her my *mother of the breast* so she will know this strange woman is her natural daughter. As the distance between us narrows, the years melt away. The closer I get, the more the shriveled features begin to look like Hai; then like the mother I remember the last time I saw her; then—mostly the earlobes, eyes, and chin—the mother's face I remember floating above my crib.

"Mama *Du!*" I jump forward but the old lady flinches and pulls Tinh's boy—who is absently eating an orange—between us like a bulletproof vest. I stop in my tracks.

"Mama *Du*—"

Tinh calls her son and the youth scampers into the kitchen, exposing my cringing mother. I freeze so as not to frighten this timid deer. While all this is happening, I become aware that the canny old eyes have scanned me from top to bottom, side to side—like a mother's and a soldier's—taking me in and checking me out.

"Bay Ly," the old voice croaks. It's less a greeting than a statement. Perhaps she needs to convince herself that we both are here. I inch closer toward the embrace my body longs to give her. "You look healthy," the voice continues. "How is baby Hung? How is your sister Lan?"

I let out a short sigh and feel dizzy. Slowly, still afraid of scaring this shy creature off, I circle to one of the chairs and sit down.

"They're fine," I say, finding a smile inside the turmoil of my heart. "And Hung's not such a baby anymore. I'll show you his picture. He's a big man now—and college-educated, too—would you believe it?"

The brier face softens. The tiny body settles back onto its chair the way a dry leaf kisses a pond.

"A smart boy, eh?" My mother cackles. "Just like his uncle, Bon Nghe!"

Hearing her chuckle makes it easier to smile. "I saw brother Bon last night, Mama *Du*. He's a bookkeeper for the government!"

"Yes—Bon Nghe. He went to school in Hanoi. How do you suppose he got to be so smart? He hated school when he was little. I had to carry him to the schoolhouse on my back! Now he's doing paperwork for the government. Our government has lots and lots of paperwork! I asked Bon Nghe how he managed it—how he got so smart all of a sudden. Do you know what he said?"

I shake my head *no* because my throat is too lumpy to speak.

"He said, 'Well, I don't have you to carry me anymore, do I?' " My mother gives a wheezy laugh, rolls a tired hand at the wrist, and gazes at the map on Tinh's wall. "Anyway, Hanoi's a strange place. He said all there was to do was work and study. You know, he carried the Northern soldiers' pay from Hanoi to the South along the Ho Chi Minh Trail. He had the bills sewn into his shirt like feathers in a vest. It saved his life more than once, he says—all that money. Never took any for himself, though, Bon Nghe."

She runs out of breath and stares back at me. I lean forward in my chair, aching to take her hands, her arms—to hug her as close as can be—but she leans away from me and goes on.

"When news came the war was over in 1975, I dropped the big basket of rice I was carrying—two day's work!—and ran home yelling *'Con toi ve!"* [My son has come home!] It was like the day the French surrendered in '54, only better. But Bon wasn't there. 'What did you expect?' Hai said. 'You wouldn't recognize him anyway, and neither would I.' So we waited and wondered if Bon would remember how to find the village. Finally, we got a message from a neighbor: 'Bon Nghe will be standing in front of the old district building on Bach Dang Street at noon on such and such a day. If anyone from his family is still living—please come.' Sure enough, a handsome man in a soldier's cap was waiting and greeted Hai politely, even though she couldn't see any family resemblance in the fellow's face. Of course, there were lots of strangers hanging around Danang in those days, with and without caps, trying to find their families. He asked for some money to come to the village and Hai gave him what she had and the man left. We never saw him or the money again. Then Bon Nghe sends another message. He says, 'Sorry I couldn't make it— I was delayed. Please meet me again on such and such a day on the Danang side of the Da Lach bridge.' This time Bon Nghe spotted Hai because she looks so much like me and they had a real reunion. After that, my son came home—but not to Ky La. That was too dangerous. There were Republican partisans and counterrevolutionaries all over the place. We met at Tinh's house—right here—that's where I had my reunion with my son! Right in this very room!"

Tears glisten in my mother's eyes as they now pour from mine. Still, I do not yet have her permission to hug her and hold her and cry out all the tears I've been saving for all these years.

"Okay—time to eat!" Tinh breezes into the room with the soup and her middle son follows with a stack of ceramic bowls. Moments later we are smacking our lips and blowing on our hot soup and my mother spanks the little boy's hand for picking his nose and it seems for an instant I am a girl again in my mother's house.

"Bon Nghe says he's married now and has a son," I say.

"Yes," my mother answers. "His wife's name is Nhi. He met her in Hanoi while he was going to school."

I can tell by my mother's tone that she does not entirely approve of Nhi. Northerners are regarded in the South the way Carpetbaggers were regarded by the Confederates after the U.S. Civil War. They have a reputation for smooth talk, light fingers, and fast feet. To marry one is like marrying a foreign Oriental—Cambodian or Chinese—you'd better have a good reason for doing it or your family may disown you. Whether these cool feelings spring from Nhi's Hanoi origins or the simple fact that she was now the "other woman" in my brother's life, I cannot tell. But my mother's brow wrinkles when she talks of Nhi and her voice goes flat. *What politeness won't reveal always comes out some other way,* my mother taught me.

"What's she like?" I ask, trying to keep a happy curl in my voice. "You know, I'm going to meet Bon Nghe's family tomorrow."

"Oh, I suppose she's a good enough wife." My mother is having trouble being charitable. Perhaps this interloper would score higher marks if she had been trained in her wifely duties by my mother. "As I said, she has the Northern way—stubborn; too smart to want much education; too busy working hard to get things done—you know. Their boy, Nam, on the other hand, is a perfect son. *Chau noi cua me!* [The son of my firstborn son!] How could he be anything but perfect? Very polite—and smart as a whip! Bon Nghe insists on observing all the old traditions. He's a very good father. But here now"—my mother poked at me with her chopsticks—"you never told me about Lan. How are those two boys of hers—the ones with those funny American names? I do so hope I can see them again before I join your father."

My heart aches that my mother has still not inquired about me, or taken much interest in how I got here, or what I plan to do now that I'm here, or anything else. Perhaps she intends to talk family according to protocol—from eldest son to youngest daughter. If so, that's fine. I'll have a long wait for my turn, but it will be worth it just to hear my mother's voice talking about our family. After all, grandchildren by sons have always been more important to Vietnamese grandmas than their grandsons by daughters. With a boy sharing your blood son's place in the "upper house", you know that someone correctly trained in religious ritual will be around to bury you properly and walk *cha don me dua*—as a second generation before your coffin. For my elderly mother, I could see these were not small concerns.

"Eddie and Robert are fine. They're living in Southern California and doing okay. It's funny though—Lan doesn't take much to the Americans. She likes to hang around with her Vietnamese friends—just the opposite of when she lived in Danang. She has some money but I don't think she's particularly well off."

"Hmph!" my mother grunts. "That sounds like your sister. You know, just before liberation, Lan started sending her money to me for safekeeping. Only it wasn't red and green currency, but twenty-four-karat gold leaf—almost two dozen of them!—and some nice jewelry, too. I told Lan, 'I can't be responsible for all this!' but she kept sending it anyway. Finally, I decided to take it all back to her. I got out my old money belt and rolled up the leaf and sewed the jewelry into my clothes—into the sleeve joints and collar so it would be harder to find, and took a plane to Nha Trang—that's where Lan was living then, with an American named Bill. Well, Lan and her husband were too busy to worry about my problems. I stayed for several weeks but couldn't convince her to take her money back. You see, I was worried I'd die and leave nobody to take care of her wealth."

"What about the gold and the jewelry?" I ask.

My mother shrugs. "I didn't want the stuff. It was *lam cuc kho*—bad luck with the sweat of someone else's labor all over it. So I gave most of it to Uncle Nhu's son, who gambled it away. The rest I buried in the yard, to let god protect it. He was bound to have better luck than my nephew! As far as I know, it's still there. Maybe I'll have Hai dig it up and you can take it back to Lan in America."

Take money *out* of Vietnam? Take gold *into* America? I can't believe what I'm hearing! *Dem vang ve my! Dem cui ve rung!*—why not take firewood into the forest? My mother has several thousand U.S. dollars' worth of gold just lying around in the ground while everyone else is starving?

I try to hide my shock from my mother. Tinh grins at me over her bowl. For her, my mother's stories are old hat. Maybe the money didn't exist at all. Maybe it was my mother's way of explaining her disappointment with her number-four daughter. After all, a close relative "on the outs" is really like buried gold. You know her heart still holds a luster if you can only dig it out.

"I hear everyone thinks it's better if I don't see Ba——" I say, hoping the warm soup and Lan's story will have mellowed my mother's attitude.

She slurps her soup noisily. "I don't know what to say about Ba. Did you know that her first husband, Moi, came back to Quang Nam after you left? Can you believe it? After Ba and Chin had produced all these beautiful babies! I think that was in 1972. Yes—I'm sure of it. Anyway, Moi disguised himself so that Ba wouldn't recognize him. When he learned she had remarried, he was very hurt, but very brave. He revealed himself and said the thought of her was all that kept him going during the war. Of course, the wheel turned again in '75. Moi came back to Danang as a party official and Chin got five years in a reeducation camp. That's a long sentence for an ordinary policeman. Anyway, Moi went back to Hanoi and Ba never heard from him again. As far as she knows, he never remarried."

"How did Chin take life in the camps?"

My mother scowled and shook her head. "Not well. He was not too strong to begin with and I think the experience broke him. Of course, having served the old Republic, he'll never get a decent job. He and Ba get by on what they grow, which isn't much. But Chin's turned out to be a good man. He still tries very hard for his family."

"Maybe that's why Ba felt she had a right to take the things I sent over." Now it's my turn to be charitable. "When the Americans left, lots of people lost their way to earn a living—"

"No!" My mother's voice was final. "What you sent was for the family! When Ba kept those things and didn't share them, it was like taking food from our mouths. Things were bad for everyone after liberation, not just the ex-Republicans. *Troi dat doi thay*—heaven and earth changed places! I was near death twice, did you know that? Once from a dog bite! Yes! Packs of stray dogs ran everywhere in those days. You weren't safe outside your home. And there was Hai and me—two old women trying to run a farm! It was impossible! So you see, everyone was suffering. Ba wasn't alone. But by keeping for herself what rightfully belonged to everyone, she set herself above the rest. Well, that's where she'll stay as far as the family's concerned—all alone and forgotten—until she changes her ways. Your father would've understood that. Bon Nghe agrees with me, too."

We don't say much more while we finish eating. I help Tinh clear the table while my mother sits like a forlorn rag heap in her chair. In the kitchen, Tinh says, "Don't worry about Grandma. She won't stay mad forever. This is all old family business—and family's all she's got. One day Grandma will go see Aunt Ba and say 'Let's have a talk,' and Ba will be back in the family like before. You wait and see."

I hope Tinh's right, although she may not realize that I have less than a week to see this miracle happen. I hear shuffling steps behind me and as I turn, some gnarled fingers catch my elbow.

"Come on," my mother says, gesturing to the sleeping mat against the opposite wall, "let's go sit and have a talk, eh? *Doan tu gia dinh*—a family meeting, like the old days!"

I cover the bony hand with my own and snuggle as close as my mother permits. This poor woman seems so feeble; I can't imagine her pulling weeds or harvesting yams or carrying shoulder poles with water, let alone making the long walk from the village to the bus stop for Danang. But working and walking is the way of life in Vietnam. You retire when your heart stops beating. Then, you have an eternity to take things easy.

I help my mother onto the kitchen mat and sit down beside her, our legs stretched in front of us like little kids'. I transfer the old fingers from my elbow to my hand and my mother doesn't object. I realize now that just as it took some time last night to transform myself from capitalist stranger to Bon Nghe's baby sister, so it may take even more time to go from black sheep relative to my mother's beloved daughter. At least the journey now has been narrowed to the width of an old woman's hand.

"Hai brought your mangoes to the house last night," my mother says. "We put them on the altar and lit some candles. We didn't have any incense—we ran out after Tet. The government discourages such things. Maybe you can pick some up for us in the city?"

"I'll get you a big supply before I go," I respond, rubbing her arm for encouragement. "You know, I'll feel bad if I don't see Ba on this trip. At least I know she's alive and her family's okay. If only brother Sau Ban could be here, things would be perfect."

"Oh, he's closer than you think!"

I did not expect this comment from my mother. Not only was Ban's death an unmentionable subject with her for many years, but she never felt much kinship with the spirit world. It was one thing that made my father's death, like Sau Ban's, so hard for her to accept.

"What do you mean?" I ask hopefully.

"Years ago, when Hai and I repaired the house, we had to move the family shrine outside. When we moved it back, a large black watersnake followed us inside."

"You must have been scared! Did you throw it out?"

"Hai started to beat it with a broom, but I stopped her. 'What's unusual about this snake?' I asked her. She said, 'I don't know—it's a snake, and a big one! Come on, let's knock it out!' Then I said, 'No—look. See how long it is? It must be over two meters—just as long as your brother Ban was tall!' 'So what?' Hai says. 'A snake is a snake! Come on—get a broom!' 'No wait,' I tell her. 'Look at the snake closely. It's in pretty bad shape. This is a sick snake!' 'Big deal,' Hai says, and she's ready to bop it with the broomstick. 'Back up or it's going to bite you!' she says. 'Remember how you almost died from that mad dog bite? *Cho dien can!* Do you want that to happen again?' 'Maybe that was because I didn't listen to what Mr. Dog was trying to tell me,' I said. 'Did you ever think of that?' So Hai got down from the chair she was standing on and we both squatted low and gave Mr. Snake a good look. He had very sad eyes and his skin was beginning to fall off. It was cool outside and very unusual to see a snake aboveground."

"So what did you finally do?"

"Well, I crept very close to the snake on all fours and said, 'Hey! Mr. Snake! If you're who I think you are, follow me!' So Hai helped me up and I went out the door and sure enough, the snake followed. 'Come on, Hai,' I called, 'and bring the cutter and a shovel!' I walked very slow so the snake could keep up and encouraged him by saying, 'Come on! It's just a bit farther!' and 'We're almost there. Don't worry, your new home will be very nice!' When we got to the Phung family graveyard, I had Hai cut down a big bamboo shoot whose hollow core was just right for our snake. 'Now we dig!' I told Hai. 'Right here, next to your father.' She said, 'This is crazy!' but we dug anyway. It took us an hour to dig a decent grave that was as long as the pole, and when we were finished, Hai looked up and said, 'So much for your idea, Mother—the snake is gone.' I dusted my hands and walked over to where the bamboo trunk was lying and said, 'Oh yes? Well come here and have a look!' Inside the bamboo were two beady eyes and a black snout. The forked tongue hissed 'Thank you, Mother,' in snake talk, so even Hai was convinced. We grabbed the ends of the pole and lowered it into the ground and pushed the earth in after it. Later on, I went to see the village psychic and he concurred with my opinion. 'The snake held Sau Ban's spirit,' he said. 'No doubt about it. Ban's bones must lie buried in the mud someplace and are cold, so his soul decided to come home in the body of the snake. You did the right thing.' So when I say your brother is closer than you think, Bay Ly, that's why. What should've happened twenty-three years ago was put right on that winter afternoon. So don't worry any more about your brother. His spirit is finally at rest. He's come back to lie in peace beside your father."

I put my arm around my mother and give her a squeeze. Whether the snake had brought Ban's spirit home or not, it has at least brought my mother closer to me.

There is a noise at the door to Bien's barbershop. One of Tinh's boys comes running back yelling, "Uncle Bon is here! Bon Nghe's come back to visit!"

This is really unexpected and my first thought is that something's wrong. Our "official" visit isn't supposed to happen until tomorrow and I can't imagine my straight-arrow brother taking the risk of crossing his superiors twice. I think about getting up to greet him, but decide it's better to let him find me sitting here with our mother, holding her hand—and she holding mine—like beloved mother and daughter.

Bon Nghe comes in wearing a raincoat and cap, even though it's mostly sunny outside. He says something I can't understand to Bien, who goes back to a customer, then comes into the kitchen. He takes off his cap and I see his face is beaming—all smiles. I release my mother's hand and get up. Without hestiation, Bon takes me around the waist and gives me a brotherly hug that lifts me off the floor. When my feet find the ground again, we're turned to my mother, whose betel-black lips are stretched into the widest grin I'd seen on her face all day. Her eyes are moist and she's trying to stand up.

Bon Nghe grabs one arm and I take the other and we ease her up from the mat. Her brown feet—long nails curling over her toes like hooves—flatten out on Tinh's floor, working hard to support her flyspeck weight.

"Come to the table," Tinh says. "This is quite a reunion—we have to celebrate! Close up the shop, Bien! Boys—come to the table!"

While Bon Nghe and I help our mother shuffle back to the dining table, I say, "Well, Bon Nghe, I'm happy to see you—but surprised. I thought our next visit wouldn't be until tomorrow."

"It's not. But when Hai came by to tell me that Mama *Du* had come into town this morning, well—I don't know. I just had to see you two together."

"You won't get in trouble with your boss?" I ask.

"Bon's a good boy," our mother interjects, reaching up to pat his chest, "and a hard worker. Nobody gives him any trouble!"

"I told them I had received a message that my mother needs me," Bon Nghe says, "so I left the office for a few hours." He laughs, "Well—it's mostly the truth!" I laugh with him, but the hokey, last-minute disguise shows that Bon is not as careless of outside opinions as he would like us to think.

From my stock of gifts at the hotel room, I have brought some chewing gum—the kind of sticky sweet terrible bubble gum all American kids seem to love—and give each of Tinh's boys a pack. Their eyes almost fall out of their heads, but Tinh confiscates the forbidden fruit almost as soon as it touches their hands.

"Oh no!" she says. "One stick each and that's all for now! And you have to stay here to chew it at the table—don't even go into Dad's shop. I don't want snoopy people seeing my sons having American treats in the window. I'm sorry, Bay Ly—but you understand."

"Oh yes, I understand."

The boys fold the sticks into their mouths and sit at the table like perfect angels: swinging their legs wildly under their chairs; rocking back and forth with energy they can barely contain; smacking their gum loudly in each other's faces. I assume they will sit there until all the flavor is gone or their jaws get too tired to move, then spit the remains into Tinh's waiting palm for a proper, traceless disposal. I have never before seen a bubble gum feast, but with the extra packs I brought with me, this certainly won't be the last.

I distribute the other goodies I was going to hand out before I left, when, without hesitation, my mother picks up a chocolate and pops it into her mouth. Tinh follows, cooing with gratitude, and consumes her treasure one nibble at a time. I smile at them both and offer a candy to Bon Nghe, who again refuses.

"Bon Nghe"—my mother gives his arm a gentle shove while she chews—"what's wrong with you, eh? Bay Ly is being polite. Be polite yourself and take a candy!"

"I'm sorry, Mother, I can't."

"What? I never heard of such a thing!" Lumps of nougat cling to our mother's toothless gums. "Don't spoil the party, eh? I have my oldest son and youngest daughter back with me"—she holds her arms out like a Buddha—"my two halves on either side!"

Bon's face turns serious, "Two halves, maybe, Mother—but from two different worlds. You mustn't forget, Bay Ly's a capitalist. I'm a Communist."

"Well," my mother persisted, "you've found common ground at this table, haven't you? On either side of your poor old mother—the place where you both came from! Come on, have a chocolate!"

"We share the same mother, I agree," Bon Nghe says, "but, as I told Bay Ly yesterday, we have different hearts and minds. I love her as my sister—no matter how she got here or what she's here to do—but I cannot accept her gifts. You shouldn't ask me to do what I cannot do. Is this what Father would have wanted?"

"Your father would have wanted you to do your duty to your sister!" our mother said. "I am convinced she did not come here to poison anybody or anything—with food or with big talk about America. She's here to find love and compassion and what better place to do it than her homeland, eh? Central Vietnam—*Trung* land—the land in the middle," my mother says. "So come on and do what your father wants and have a candy—"

"No. I am the eldest son and head of the family. I must stand by my decision. That's what Father would want me to do. That's the way it has always been."

"Well now"—my mother took a second candy—"maybe there's another way—a better way—when good sweets are at stake. Better hurry up and decide or we'll finish them all ourselves!"

Bon smiles, "Go ahead. Enjoy the candy. I thank Bay Ly for bringing you such happiness—truly. That's exactly what I hoped to see by coming here."

"Stubborn you are—just like your father!" Our mother pushes the remaining candies toward Tinh, as if she has suddenly lost her appetite. My niece quickly hides them on a high shelf in the kitchen. "All right then," our mother commands, "Bay Ly: have some more tea and tell us about America."

She refills my cup, which I hold to my lips a long time. What can I say? After all those years of imagining this moment—dreaming of a time when I could see my mother and brother together and tell them about the wonders of America—I am strangely tongue-tied. What can I say that won't come out like boasting? What story can I tell that won't sound like science fiction? All I want to do right now is take my mother back to San Diego—to take her to a shopping mall and buy her some pretty clothes and take her to a beauty salon and have her sun-brittle hair washed and set, her poor farmer's hands massaged with lotion, and her earth-blackened nails cleaned and painted like a noble lady—like tens of thousands of noble California grandmothers! My poor mother has no idea of the marvels that I, as an American, take for granted: ten different brands of peanut butter in our stores; electricity to heat and light our homes; TVs to watch and stereos to play and telephones for talking to people we miss, anytime we want, before it's too late for them to hear us say how much we love them. Maybe ignorance of such things is what keeps people sane in the world of privation she's inherited. If so, every fiber of my being wants to take her—to take all of them—away from it; that, or remake that depressing, fearful world into the beautiful place Vietnam used to be.

I see my mother's ancient eyes and my brother's curious, critical face waiting for my reply, but all I can do—this ambassador for America— is break quietly into tears.

* * *

"So you want to write a book?" I ask my brother Bon as we watch our mother play with her great-grandson, Tinh's youngest boy. We are sitting on the mat in the kitchen the way my mother and I sat when he arrived.

"Who told you that?" Bon Nghe smiles.

"Anh. He says you're going to write one when you retire. He says you want to share what you learned in the war. In the meantime, he says you're working hard to take care of Mother and Hai—that you check on them every week and bring them what they need from the city."

"Well, it's tough for two old ladies to get by in the countryside. I've asked them more than once to give up the old house and come live with me in Danang, but they won't hear of it. The funny thing is: not only are they too old to work the paddies anymore, but they don't even own the land. Mother gave it to the state after liberation. Of course, that's what everybody did at the time, even Anh. The government expropriated his five factories, did he tell you?—including the one in Danang. So he donated his personal wealth, what was left of it after his divorce, before it became an embarrassment. Mother says she thought about contacting him from time to time, but she didn't want to be a bother. Of course, she was still afraid of Lien. Yes—she told me all about what happened with you and Anh. All mother had was her pension—the *liet si* the government gave her when Sau Ban didn't turn up after the war."

"Do you think Sau Ban's really dead?" I ask him.

Bon Nghe shrugs. "Whether he is or isn't, I think it's foolish to hope for his return. I believe his remains are resting somewhere. If he was killed on duty, his unit or the peasants took care of him, you can count on that. Did Mother tell you the snake story?"

"Yes—"

"Good. Well, that's put Sau Ban to rest for her, and if she's happy, the rest of us should accept it too. That's what Father would have wanted."

"What do you think about the way our father died? He killed himself, you know, rather than get me involved again with the Viet Cong."

Bon Nghe takes a deep breath and, for the first time, looks fully his age. "I suppose that's why I want to write a book—like you—to tell our family's story. I want to learn how he felt about the war—what enabled him to do such a thing. It's quite different from the way I was taught to think in Hanoi. I admire the strength of his feelings, but I just don't understand them. How could somebody work so hard to survive—to take care of his family—then throw it all away, leaving them alone when they needed him most? After all, when you're dead, you're dead—aren't you?"

I put a sister's hand on Bon's strong shoulder. "Don't feel bad. You want to learn so you can teach. That's good. If you understand that much, you already know most of what our father was about."

An hour later Bon Nghe decides it's time to go back to work. He embraces me and my mother, politely refuses her offer of a final candy, and departs with his raincoat and hat pulled down over his eyes. Bien opens up his shop again and my mother and I return to our mat in the kitchen.

"Bon's turned out to be quite a man, hasn't he?" I say to her. "You must be very proud of your son!"

My mother's brown face glows. "He was worried you'd turn out to be a capitalist tea girl, Bay Ly. Now he sees you're not like that. He has to change his thinking. That takes a little time, especially for someone like Bon Nghe. But he's a good boy. He believes in himself and his principles. He always has—just like Sau Ban, but in a different way."

"I'm sorry he never got to know his little brother the way we did."

"That was Bon Nghe's karma, eh? And Sau Ban's."

Tears well in my eyes but I notice my mother's eyes are dry. "I'm sorry. I can't talk about Sau Ban without crying." I sniff. "My god— how much I miss him, even today! Especially today!"

My mother waved her old hand carelessly, "That's one benefit of living to be an old woman, Bay Ly. The longer you live, the more time you've had to use up your tears. You come into this life happy and the rest of the world tries to take that happiness away from you. Tears are god's way of paying you back for what he's taken. You feel better after you cry, don't you? Okay—you're young. Go ahead and cry for Sau Ban if you feel like it. My tears for my sons and daughters are all used up. I've cried them to all points of the compass; north for Bon Nghe, south for Sau Ban, east for your father, and west for you and Lan—my American daughters."

I hold my mother tightly and, for the first time since our reunion— for the first time in sixteen years—she hugs me back. I feel her warm breath on my neck and hear it ragged in my ear, but I can't tell if she's crying. Of course, it doesn't matter. I am young. I have enough tears for us both.

TEN

Power on Earth

I CANNOT REMEMBER the exact moment I decided to leave Vietnam. But one day I became aware that everything I had done for the past few months had been a preparation for departure—a ritual leave-taking that meant little when those acts were considered by themselves but, when viewed together, were much like my father's own preparations in anticipation of his death. I found I was spending more time with my family (especially Lan, who had just given birth to her first American son, Eddie) and was neglecting my black market business. I traveled less far to make sales; partly because something inside told me not to take risks, and partly to stay close to my mother and son. I was cheated more often by GIs and Republican officials, but I felt almost glad because of it—as if I was returning soiled merchandise and tainted money to the awful system that produced it, purifying myself in the process for the new life that awaited me.

Once this idea came into focus and my recent acts took the shape of a conscious plan, it was much easier to confront the realities that faced me. Although I would have been satisfied to escape anywhere—to just get the hell out and as far away as I could!—the choices were pretty limited.

For young Vietnamese women, the options were a foreign education (if you had a wealthy family); a foreign husband (if you had the looks and skills to land a good candidate, especially an American); or an "exporter," someone who could get you out legally (usually by paying a foreign man for a phony marriage) or illegally (via a network of military contacts, ordinary criminals, and government graft takers). Any of these options, of course, involved a high degree of *hy sinh*—personal sacrifice—regardless of the hoped-for benefits. The sacrifice was conscience, honor, and money, but what else were we to do?

Although the safety and future of my son were, of course, uppermost in my mind, so was the well-being of my mother. Because my mother had other daughters to care for her in old age, I didn't feel so bad about putting my son's and my own interests first, although I was not sure how she would take my "defection" to the land of the invaders. I also knew that buying my way out of the country would take more cash than I had seen in a lifetime—especially with the losses I had recently incurred from faithless buyers. The lower my money supply ran, in fact, the more urgent my departure seemed to be. This sense of necessity led to one rash act that, looking back, was to change my life tremendously.

When Lan's baby was born and she could no longer work because of her period of *buon de,* I divided my time equally between my house, her house, and my souvenir business. First thing in the morning, I would stop by Lan's and see if there was anything I could do, such as going to the market or cleaning the place up, then I would stop by again on the way home and prepare her evening meal. When I was satisfied that my sister and her baby were all right, I would go and repeat those chores in my own house, giving my mother any extra cash from my dwindling daily profits. With the expense of two households and less money from my sales, I could see the day would come when we would all be back out on the street. With the memory of our homeless days in Saigon still fresh in my mind, I determined I would do anything before I let that happen again.

One day when I was hanging around the "Freedom Mill" post exchange waiting for a likely looking GI to solicit with my shopping list, I was approached by an American MP everybody called Big Mike. Normally, this would have been my signal to move on, but this particular MP, a sergeant who came in a jeep periodically to check on the sentries, was an old acquaintance and we both winked at the rules when I needed to conduct some business or he needed something special—like good marijuana or Chinese jade—through my connections. This time, he had something very special—something very different—on his mind.

"Le Ly!" he called me impolitely, although I had never instructed him in the proper salutation for an unmarried Vietnamese woman. "These grunts over here"—he pointed to two clean-faced marines in fresh fatigues by the guard shack, "they're short-timers, you understand?"

"Sure," I replied, giving them a smile. "They want souvenirs? I got plenty. Big Mike friends get good price!"

Big Mike laughed. "Yeah, they want a souvenir, all right! They want boom-boom before they go back to the States!"

This caught me by surprise. Big Mike knew as well as anyone that there were plenty of prostitutes just outside the gate—the *Hoa Phat* or *Nui Phuoc Tuong* bar girls were the best for miles around. Asking me about *bum-bum* was like asking for joints at a cigarette stand: I knew exactly what he wanted, but it wasn't what I sold.

"Okay," I answered, pointing to the row of houses outside the base, "they got plenty *bum-bum* out there!"

"They get plenty crabs out there, too!" Big Mike said. "Look, Le Ly —these guys are figmo, you understand? They're getting on the fucking plane in half an hour and they haven't been laid in the Nam. Now that's not right, is it?"

"Horny GI go see *siclo* girl." I threw up my hands, still wondering why Big Mike was bringing me this particular problem. "Bye, bye. I go do business!"

I started to walk away but Big Mike caught me by the arm. "Listen—you still don't get it, do you? These pencil dicks are clean, right? They've been in the bush since they got here. Not even a fucking knob job in twelve months! Hell, one guy's going back to his wife, for Chrissakes! You want him to go *bum-bum* with some scuzz bag and take home a dose of clap? No way, sunshine! They want somebody clean—clean as they are. No shit! And they're willing to pay twenty dollars a head!"

"Le Ly *good* girl!" I pulled my arm away, genuinely shocked.

"Hey, that's a lot of bread, baby doll! Those scum bags out there go for five bucks a pop! I'm offering you twenty!"

"Then GIs pop scum bag. Fuck off, Big Mike!"

"Okay, Okay." Big Mike took something from his shirt pocket. "Look at this, eh?" He unfurled five *American flags*—twenty-dollar bills—not red military currency, which was worth only half as much—but U.S. greenbacks. "And this is just for one of them," the MP added. "I got another roll just like it from the second. I told 'em clean poon would be expensive. They even paid me in advance!"

I couldn't take my eyes off the roll of cash—big as a cabbage! One

hundred dollars green money would support my family for two months, even at Danang's inflated prices. Two hundred, with a little nursing, could get us through half a year—and all the money I made from my business could go to my escape fund! Still, he was talking about selling my body. I didn't know what a Phung Thi woman was worth, but it had to be more than that.

"No deal, Big Mike. No *choi boi!* Le Ly not that kind of girl!" I turned away again.

"Okay—Jesus Christ, you drive a hard bargain!" He pulled me toward the guard shack. "Here it is—" He pulled another wad from his pocket. "Four hundred fucking dollars! And that's it, man! That cleans me out. That's all they gave me."

I stared at the cash the way a thirsty prisoner stares at water. Four hundred dollars would support my mother, me, and Hung for over a year—a year I could use finding a better job and making connections or, as a last resort, greasing palms for a paid escape. And to make it, I wouldn't even have to work up a sweat or risk going to jail or getting blown up by a mine or blown away in an ambush. Just lie down and let these two American boys be men. What could they do to me that hadn't been done already? Maybe it was time some men paid me back for what other men had taken—

"Hey, come on, sweetheart! I ain't got all day!" Big Mike demanded. "These swingin' dicks go back to the world in half an hour. Take the fucking money and give 'em a story to take home, what the hell? Don't tell me you're cherry?"

"Le Ly no cherry girl," I said in a small voice, still eyeing the money. "But Le Ly no whore."

"Okay then! Fine! Great! Do it for fucking world peace! Do it for better U.S.-Vietnamese relations!" He shoved both rolls of cash in my hand—a big risk for any American to take with any Vietnamese: in a second I could've been outside the gate and lost in the maze of "slants and slopes" inside the slums. It was an impulsive gesture of frustration and trust that made me instantly believe everything he said: that these GIs were clean, on their way home, and that was all the money there was to be had.

I looked over at the two marines. One was standing with his hands on his hips, cap back on his forehead, grinning the way a young father grins when he watches a baby daughter at play. The shorter one wore black-rimmed glasses and actually held his hat in his hands. He had the timid look of a teenager—as if he feared me more than the combat that had just claimed twelve months of his life.

"Go on," Big Mike coaxed. "Get your little ass over there and send those poor bastards home with a smile!"

Without thinking, I tucked the cash into my bucket of merchandise. The short walk across the stretch of dirt that separated us was one of the longest in my life, during which I forced myself to disregard everything I had learned from my family about honor, self-respect, VD, pregnancy, rape, making love for love, and even the ever-present risk that the money—a lot of cash even for Americans—would be taken back as soon as the GIs were finished. If that happened, of course, it would be my karma—just as karma, a smothering sense of *hy sinh,* seemed to propel my feet across the ground.

I approached the towering Americans and looked up into their faces.

"Okay, you good boys, right?" I asked, giving them a stern motherly look, as if interviewing them for a job. For an amateur hooker I don't think I was very sexy.

The tallest one smiled crookedly. "Why, yes, ma'am! Good as you'll ever get!"

I dropped my eyes to the second GI, whose cap was trembling in his hands. "Okay," I said. "Shorty first!"

The tall marine laughed heartily while I led the shorter man by the wrist to the only private place in the area: the sand-bag bunker the MPs used when the base was under attack. Inside, despite the gun ports on three sides which gave some ventilation, the air was thick and dusty; but at least there was a cot with blankets and I would not have to further degrade Mother Earth by pressing my naked backside against her while I took seed from the invaders.

I rolled onto the cot and quickly pulled my pants down to my ankles. I lay there for a moment, staring up at the corrugated steel ceiling, legs angled out like a pregnant lady awaiting to deliver. The GI stood beside me, unbuckling his belt and lowering his pants. After he stood there a minute, I looked up at him, wondering what was wrong.

"I'm—I'm sorry, miss," he said, pointing at the crumpled pants that held my ankles together. "I think you're going to have to take those off or something."

Irritably, I slipped one foot free of my pants and planted my heels on the edge of the cot. Carefully, as if the bed and I might break from his weight, he crept around and embraced me with his body. As he did so, I found myself fighting a sudden urge to scream. The weight of his body and the sudden fullness in mine and the heaviness of the air in the tiny bunker made me feel like I was suffocating—buried alive! The cot began creaking rhythmically and his sweaty huffing in my ear was like shovels of dirt on my face, on the corpse of my father's daughter.

After another minute he was finished and pulled back. His red face was covered with perspiration and he quickly pulled up his pants. Strangely, I felt in no hurry to do the same, despite my shame; partly because I knew I had another "customer" to satisfy, and partly because I could not take my eyes off this young man—this American, this invader, this pink beast who had come with his ravenous pack to devour my country; this poor, sad little fellow who missed his family as much as I missed mine and who was just so grateful that he had beaten the odds and finished his tour and had now left his seed in a final, nonlethal explosion: a gift to a local girl not much younger than himself as a remembrance that their paths, like it or not, had crossed and changed them both forever.

"Um, thanks—" The red-faced boy smiled sheepishly while he tucked in his shirttail. He put his cap on squarely, military style, and went out.

As soon as he was gone, I heard a male voice call out, but I couldn't understand what was said. I lay on the cot for several more minutes, frozen in this silly position: knees bent, arms cocked as if embracing a ghost, like a machine—a receptacle—a strong box waiting for the next deposit. The next person I saw, however, was Big Mike, whose face appeared through the door.

"Okay, prom queen," he said, "the coast is clear. Get your little butt outta here!"

Startled, I folded up like a butterfly and pulled up my pants. I grabbed my bucket of loot and ran out the door. When I got out, I saw that both the marines had gone.

"What happen to tall guy?" I asked.

"You timed it just right, sweetheart," Big Mike said, putting a cigarette to his lips. "The shuttle bus just took 'em to the flight line. Guess that jughead was more anxious to get home than get laid."

"But he pay money!" I now thought I would get beaten up for sure. I had cheated him, even though I didn't intend it.

"Aw, hell," Big Mike drawled, "hang on to it. You earned it! He ain't never coming back. Just look at it this way: you now got the highest-priced pussy in Danang! You oughta go pro, little lady! We'd make a bundle!"

"No, no!" I fished among my trinkets to make sure my money was still there. "I quit. No more *bum-bum*. I quit souvenir business. You good guy, Big Mike. Here—" I stuffed the greenbacks into my waistband and gave him the bucket. "You make present all you buddies, eh? Tell them Le Ly go home!"

Big Mike laughed and put one of the marble bracelets on his muscled wrist. "Okay, Le Ly. You're a good girl. You go home. But I bet a quart of Jack Daniel's I see you shakin' your booties up here next week. Papa-san gonna drink up that cash chop-chop!" His big American hand pinched my drippy bottom and he walked away toward his jeep. Still, I knew I should run through the gate before he or anyone else could decide they'd rather have four hundred dollars than a good laugh at this little "gook" girl.

When I got home, I was faced with the immediate problem of telling my mother how and where I had gotten so much money all at once. To tell her what actually happened was unthinkable. Even if I hadn't been too ashamed to do so, the mere suggestion that her baby daughter had sold herself as a prostitute would have killed her—or at least the part of her that loved me, and that's something I would never risk. Love, like money, was in too short a supply just now to risk on peacetime honesty.

Consequently, I changed only one hundred dollars (a magnificent enough amount!) into Vietnamese *piasters* and told her I had an exceptional day selling bracelets. While she busied herself hiding the cash in various places around the house and wondering aloud about gullible, too-rich Americans, I buried the rest of the greenbacks in the yard—hoping, I suppose, that the fertile earth would make them sprout into the kind of cash I would need to take me and my son to a place where Vietnamese and Americans could face each other over something more civilized than guns or hooker's cots.

While my mother was thus occupied, I douched myself and began counting the days to my next period, which, thanks to fate or luck or god, occurred on time. When I failed to break out in rashes or sores or diseases of any kind, I thanked god, too, for the favor of honest men— as few and far between as they seemed to be. To explain the increase in cash from my shorter working hours, I explained to my mother that Lan had agreed to pay me from her savings for my help around the house. So, little by little, my big cache of U.S. dollars found its way into my mother's hiding places around the house. At times it seemed like a silly game, but if it would eventually lead me to a better life and my mother's peace of mind, it was a game that was well worth playing.

When Lan recovered from childbirth and resumed her job at the bar, she began to bring men home again, as she had done in the past. This time, however, I was no pesky teenage mother, but a young companion who knew her way around the block. My English was now pretty good, although I understood far more than I could speak. Languages came easily to me and the more I dealt with Americans, I discovered, the more I learned to think like them as well. As a result, I had an instant rapport with many of Lan's friends, even though I could express only a fraction of what was on my mind. I had no desire to be a bar girl, but I knew that I would have to make the acquaintance of many people in high places—Americans included—if I was ever to emigrate from Vietnam. Consequently, I told Lan she could count on me to help entertain the soldiers and civilian contractors on whom her livelihood depended, and after a while these visitors began bringing friends of their own for me to "date." Although I still drew the line at going to bed with these guests, my instinctive fear of Americans—and especially GIs in fatigues —had somehow gone away after that brief interlude in Big Mike's bunker.

Because I was friendly, understood English, and always tried to act like a lady, I eventually drew respect, rather than passes, from Lan's guests. A few months after my "big score" in Danang, one of Lan's friends introduced me to a nice-looking American named Steve, who had big blue eyes and a handsome American nose. It was obvious Steve was interested in me, and although I let him kiss me (in fact, I found it enjoyable), I told him I would only go to bed with my husband. He accepted this limitation graciously, but didn't come back for several weeks, so I assumed he had found another, more willing Vietnamese girl. I was startled, then, when Steve came back and, instead of trying to talk me into bed again, offered me my first real job—with so much regular pay it amazed me—working as a nurse's aide at the Nha Thuong Vietnamese Hospital in Danang.

SUNDOWN, APRIL 8, 1986:
THE PACIFIC HOTEL, DANANG

My mother was anxious to get back to Ky La before nightfall, so our first reunion ended only an hour after Bon's departure. On top of seeing my mother unexpectedly, the joy of seeing her and Bon together made the visit sweeter than the sweets poor Bon refused. If my trip ended now, I couldn't regret it—except for not seeing Ba and wanting more and more of the same, like a glutton at a feast: more time to find myself in my mother; more time to discover my father through Bon Nghe; more time to see my future through the eyes of my family's past.

Still, as I freshen up at the hotel—change out of my borrowed peasant's clothes and into my lucky blue *ao dai*—I can't shake the feeling that some important discoveries of my trip still lie ahead. In fact, the first of them may be as near as the next ring of my phone: Anh's call from the lobby telling me our dinner hosts have arrived.

As recently as yesterday, I would have dreaded this conference with the unspecified "party officials" *(can bo* is the only way Anh refers to them) Anh said he wanted to meet when we got to Danang. At first I couldn't imagine why this should be. Certainly, Anh depends on the bureaucrats for many things and can scarcely ignore their opinions about his activities with foreign visitors. Yet I had a feeling from the way he talked that our dinner meeting would be something more than an excuse for a nice meal at government expense. Perhaps these men are kindred spirits: people looking for a way to heal their country's wounds while putting food in its belly and the fire of life back into its war-weary heart. Then again, they may only be bureaucrats; suspicious paper-shufflers Anh feels he must satisfy with a firsthand look at this undesirable alien. Either way, I hope Anh is not entrusting me with a task that lies beyond my puny powers to explain or persuade.

The room phone finally rings. Anh says our hosts have arrived and that he'll wait with them in the restaurant (also called the Pacific) next door to the hotel. I finish putting on my evening face (the new Vietnam looks down on any sign of personal vanity—proper women no longer take time to fuss with their hair or make sure they're dressed just right before going out—but it's a habit I have trouble giving up!) and descend the creaky stairs.

The Pacific Restaurant is clean and filled with appetizing aromas. Although only a couple of tables are occupied, the staff looks busy—perhaps because they know party officials are in attendance and it wouldn't pay to goof off. With white tablecloths, soy bottles, lacquered hardwood and mother-of-pearl decorations on the wall, the establishment could have been one of a thousand Vietnamese restaurants anywhere in the world.

Anh catches my eye and waves me over to the table. The three men stand up together, abandoning for the moment their unfinished beers. The two officials are about Anh's age and are conspicuously well dressed. They look healthy and fit—not just from the comparatively good life such officials usually lead, but from a lifetime of honest labor which reveals itself in an upright posture, level gaze, and firm hand-shake.

Anh introduces the first man as Long and I guess from this sequence that he is the senior of the pair. Long is very tall and looks like he's lived a hard life which, for a Vietnamese his age, usually meant front-line duty during the war. His associate, named Xa, is of average height but has big "warrior bones" like my father—but with little meat on them. He, too, has a time-scarred face, though it is the round face of a worldly uncle rather than a fighter and I find him instantly likable. Although neither specifies his job, there is something about the factory or machine shop in their manner and, given the nature of Anh's business, I assume they work somewhere in the industrial ministry.

As soon as we sit down, however, the official barriers go up. Xa sits across the table from me, stops smiling, and tents his fingers like a judge. Long, sitting at my elbow, moves his beer glass a little further out of reach, as if to discourage himself from drinking too much during my "interrogation." He takes a thoughtful drag on the cigarette he's been smoking and the awkward silence is broken only by the waiter.

"Welcome to the Pacific, miss." He bows politely. "May I get you something to drink?"

"An orange soda would be nice!" I smile back. "Judge" Xa looks surprised.

"Only soda pop?" he smiles quizzically. "The Americans I remember prefer whiskey!"

"Is that right?" I grin. "Most of my friends in the States don't drink at all—except for a little beer or wine. I don't smoke either—"

Mr. Long hastily tamps out his half-smoked cigarette, which I notice from the brand-mark was made in the West. Whether this means he favors reconciliation or simply accepts high-priced gratuities I don't know; but it is a fact I file for later.

"But it doesn't bother me if you smoke," I tell him, "so please, don't let me interrupt you."

"My goodness," Xa says, relaxing a little, "a *Viet Kieu* who has lived so long in the States and doesn't smoke or drink and acts like a lady! We are very impressed. That's not how we remember most Americans."

I laugh, "Well, flowers grow in the mud without getting muddy, don't they? Don't forget, I'm a daughter of Vietnam, too, and Buddhist. I was taught by my father to live in the world but not be swallowed by it. Anyway, there are certainly as many different kinds of Americans as there are Vietnamese. More, I think—because the Americans, for better or worse, open their borders to everyone."

"Including many Vietnamese," Xa says, but his smile is narrower. "Tell me, Miss Ly, do you live in the Vietnamese ghetto?"

"No," I reply. "I live in a middle-class suburb outside of San Diego in a nice four-bedroom home. If the Vietnamese live together in America, and some of them do, it's because that's their choice. Nobody makes them do it. And there are no ghettos—no government camps—at least none that I have heard about, even in rumors. Of course, I don't go out of my way to listen to people with complaints and resentments. I bring only my own opinions which I am happy to share with anyone."

Mr. Xa is obviously concerned about the ex-Republicans living in the United States—especially the ones with infiltration, invasion, counter-revolution, and vengeance on their minds. He seems to want information—perhaps intelligence—from one of their own. On that score, I'm afraid I'm going to be a very disappointing guest.

Mr. Long lights another cigarette, but courteously blows his smoke away from the table. "From your experience then, how do you think your Vietnamese friends in the States feel about our socialist republic?"

"Most of them are still hurt and angry," I tell him truthfully. "They are *ho khong chap nhan che do cong san*—they cannot accept their country under communism. Not everyone who served in the army or the government or worked for the Americans was corrupt. Many were and still are fine patriots who will always love their country. Most of them have relatives in Vietnam whom they're worried about. In '75, remember, even the honest ones lost everything. Because of this, they seldom smile. It's hard for them to start over—to make the most of American life. Even now, they refer to liberation, your *chao mung* victory holiday, as *mat nuoc* [the day we lost the country]—a day of mourning and resentment. And that's how many of them act: like children who are still grieving for lost parents."

"Of course," Xa says, "we understand why they are bitter. Bitterness is the harvest of defeat. But don't they realize they always had a choice —to change sides or sue for peace—to see the inevitable coming?"

"Perhaps," I respond, "but fear and loyalty prevented many from acting until the last minute. Besides, most people I know don't want to reopen old wounds. Like me, they want to make the most of peace and get on with their lives. The *Viet Kieu* in the United States—at least a sizable number of them—have done pretty well for themselves. They've learned how Americans do things and have managed to get by without corruption, crime, or harming anyone else. They want to see their countrymen in Vietnam do as well, that's all. From what I've seen here, though, the Vietnamese government is afraid to give its people the same chance."

I feel a flush on my cheeks and glance at Anh—to apologize silently for getting on my soapbox—and expect him to look mortified. Instead, his eyes are twinkling. Even stranger, Xa and Long are smiling too.

"I'm sorry," I tell them. "I'm making speeches, eh? And I don't sound very modest. I apologize sincerely for being a bad guest."

"Oh no!" Xa shakes his head, "we want to hear your candid views. That's why we're here."

The waiter returns now with our meal—several courses served all at once, Vietnamese style: shrimp, rice, *xao,* and *mi quang* noodles, of course, but also big servings of crab and lobster. Whoever arranged for the meal has spared no expense to make this a feast and I am impressed, but a little nervous, too. It is grand enough to make me suspect this is, indeed, more than the Vietnamese equivalent of an expense-account lunch. It seems like a *gesture*—but for what?

"Please—" I continue, "I have talked too much. I would like to know your opinions of America, and what you see as the future relationship between our two countries."

Xa answers first. "You are right about one thing, Miss Ly. Much of what our two peoples know about each other comes only from the war, and that is most sad. I would be discouraged to think Americans believe we are a country full of terror squads, secret police, death camps, and starving peasants."

"Most Americans and *Viet Kieu* believe that, I think—yes," I tell him, looking him straight in the eye. "It's hard to doubt the horror stories when one sees how afraid your people seem to be of their government."

Xa seems more hurt than angered by this. "I'm sorry to hear that. Of course, there have been excesses in our reconstruction efforts, but I assure you, excess is not our policy. We have made mistakes and we honestly regret them. But you must remember, Miss Ly, our government was formed in time of terrible, all-out war—"

"I know. Remember, my family fought for Uncle Ho! Now I've come back and seen what the Communists have done with their victory, and I'm not sure it was what we were fighting for. The banners over the streets say 'Victory and Freedom' but I don't see those things on people's faces or hear it when they speak."

Xa still looks unperturbed, "I understand your feelings, Miss Ly, but please—try to look at things a little further through your Vietnamese eyes. For us, it was a war for survival. Unlike the Americans, we simply could not declare victory and go home. If you take men who learned to govern during twenty years of total war—of terrible *civil* war, as well as a war against invaders—and put them in charge of a country that's suddenly at peace, yet full of old memories, hate, and suspicion, what do you think will happen?"

"Well, I don't know—"

"I'll tell you: Some will try to run things the way they did before the war because that's their only idea of peace; the others will try to run things as if the war was still going on. They'll watch for enemies everywhere and take no chances because they're afraid of losing everything they've gained. Of course, that won't work either. So gradually, we are discovering that a new approach is needed to make socialism work in Vietnam. Don't forget, we faced terrible problems after liberation. We had to reclaim defoliated forests and croplands, and detect and defuse old bombs and mines that studded the ground like stones! Do you know that a tenth of all the ordnance expended in the war didn't explode on contact? Yes—and most of that's still out there! We had to care for the casualties of *both* sides as well as their civilian victims. We had to find land and housing and jobs for an army of refugees. What is surprising is not that mistakes were made, but that we didn't make more of them. Lots of people wanted to continue the war—to take revenge even after the Americans had gone. But that wasn't our goal in fighting the war. Our goal was to make Vietnam a sovereign nation and leave it better off than before. We succeeded in the first. Our task now is to succeed at the second. To do that, we'll need the help of every Vietnamese, wherever in the world they live. And yes—even the Americans."

I stare at Xa. This is something new. This is something even the *Ban Viet Kieu* had not talked about.

"You see, Miss Ly," Long picks up where Xa left off, "our task now is to ensure our nation's safety and rebuild our society into something better than it was under the Americans and French. More war and more hatred won't do it. Our action in Kampuchea—which you call Cambodia—is strictly defensive and necessary to secure our southern borders; and it will end by 1990. Our skirmishes with China, too, must eventually stop. Socialist peoples should march together, shoulder to shoulder, not against each other like feudal kings. In the long run, these things only threaten our independence and don't make us more secure."

"I don't mean to be impolite," I answer, "but some *Viet Kieu*—and many Americans—say you have already sold the country to the Russians. There is a song they sing—you know how the Viet Cong taught us to sing songs when we're in trouble!—which goes like this:

> Sitting in the doorway,
> Cool breeze passing over me,
> I look for my family
> In a sad and empty house.
> With tears, I miss my father,

> With anger, I hate the Viet Cong.
> You brought the elephant home
> To walk upon our graves.
> You took our pretty country,
> And sold it to the Soviets.

"The people who sing this ask themselves: 'Did I fight so long and hard to get rid of the French and the Americans just to hand everything over to the Russians?' "

Strangely enough, rather than being insulted by my question, Xa and Long—and even Anh—only smile more broadly.

"Tell me, Miss Ly," Xa asks, "how many Russians have you seen on your trip?"

I shrug and honestly try to remember. "I don't know. Maybe a couple on the airliner to Saigon—I'm sorry!" I put my fingers in front of my mouth. "I mean, Ho Chi Minh City!"

The officials laugh. "Don't worry," Xa says. "I make the same mistake myself. Everyone does. We have more important tasks before us than slapping everyone's wrists when they give in to old habits."

This is certainly a different view from the one Per had told me to expect from Communist officials. Perhaps Per, too, had some useless fears packed in his suitcase.

"But to answer your question about the Russians," Xa continues. "They are present, even to the small extent you saw, because they were the only nation that stood by us throughout the war and continues to help us as we rebuild. We believe that when America's President Nixon visited Beijing, he secretly promised Chairman Mao that if China would help the U.S. withdraw from the war, the U.S. wouldn't oppose them if they invaded Vietnam to install their own puppet government. Naturally, we had to turn to China's rivals, the Russians, to protect our independence. Even so, we have made it clear to the Soviets that Vietnam is nobody's lapdog. Our great, mutual task now is to create a better life for our peoples."

"Besides," Long adds, chewing noisily, "nobody listens to Russian music on the radio or buys Russian clothes on the back-door markets. When people think of a better life, they still think of America and Japan and Europe, not the Soviet Union. We want trade and foreign exchange with many nations, just like the Russians. Isn't that how things should be among independent states?"

"Of course," I answer quickly, "but countries that love independence should respect the independence of others, isn't that also true? You fought

America because it invaded our country; yet you invade Cambodia and say it's okay just because 'it's necessary' for your security. Isn't that just what the Americans told you?"

"But, Miss Ly," Xa says earnestly, "Vietnam never threatened America's sovereignty! Look at it this way: if Canada threatened American borders, wouldn't the U.S. feel justified in 'invading' if that was necessary to keep their nation safe? Isn't that, in fact, what America did to its neighbor to the south, Mexico—not once, but *twice,* in its history?"

Xa takes out his pen and draws a crude map of Indochina on the tablecloth. "See here—the Khmer Rouge, an aggressive, warlike government in Kampuchea, is backed by China. If they become strong enough, we'd have hostile forces on two of our three sides, with our third side to the sea, which is controlled by China's ally, the U.S. Navy. Now, see how simple it would be for our old Chinese enemy to divide our country again—to take the North while we defend the South, or to let the Khmer invade the South while we fight China in the North! And if we are defeated then, there will be no 'orderly exit program' or 'boat people' paddling to freedom! There would be a massacre the likes of which the world has never seen—even the Nazi Holocaust and Khmer Killing Fields would seem tame by comparison!"

Xa puts away his pen and shakes his head sadly, "No, Miss Ly, we take no joy from our task in Kampuchea. Nobody longs for peace like old soldiers, and our armies have been in the field since 1946. But our peace must be the peace of a strong and independent nation—not the peace of a slave camp or a graveyard."

My hosts talk awhile longer about Vietnam's seemingly unquenchable thirst for security and when they are finished, I push my plate back and ask, "So, when you feel safe enough to open yourselves to the outside world, what are the first things you would ask for?"

Long laughs. "It's a very long list, and the meal is almost over! Our first concerns are humanitarian. We have lots of people who are old or sick and not enough health workers or hospitals to take care of them. Similarly, we have many orphans and children who were born with maladies caused by the war—birth defects from Agent Orange and babies who suffer from venereal disease and drug addiction received through their mothers. And we need enough artificial limbs to literally equip an army! We also need foodstuffs and textiles and spare parts for our trucks and factories so that our economy can become self-sufficient. Most of all, I think, we need to be accepted back into the community of nations—to have trading partners and tourists that will give us the foreign exchange we need to buy the things we can't make ourselves. It means everyone in the world must agree that the Vietnam war, finally and forever, is over."

"Well, I can't speak for the whole world," I say, "but I can speak for some people in the United States. A lot of GIs and their families, and some politicians, say the war won't be over until the MIAs—America's missing-in-action—are accounted for. They think your government is holding onto them, or at least information about them, as a bargaining chip to get American aid that was promised to you in the peace treaty. I don't know about such things myself, but I certainly understand their feelings." I tell them about my family's frustration concerning Sau Ban.

Xa sighs and sits back in his chair. "I can't say what was true in the past; I can only tell you the way things are today. If the government could magically produce every American MIA—or their dogtags or burial records or remains or *anything*—and make them appear on the White House steps tomorrow, they'd do it. The problem is, there's nothing more they can do. When the government exhausted its official channels of inquiry, it turned to the people. We promised rewards for uniforms, name tags, ID cards, photographs, skeletons—anything that would satisfy the Americans. You know what we got? Dog bones, surplus insignia, old photographs of GI boyfriends who returned to the States, and wild stories.

"As far as I can see," he continued, "many missing Americans will never be found. Some of our people I regret to say—people whose hatred for the Americans is as great as those Americans' hatred for them—would rather die than tell anyone what they know. They want to go on punishing America forever, and that's exactly what they're doing. Until those most injured by the war in both countries can put their pain aside, the war will go on and on. How much wiser it would be for officials on both sides to simply comfort those pitiful souls and tell them the truth: The war is over. Stop your mourning and enjoy what's left of your life. Your son or husband or brother has not disappeared into a void. His spirit is alive in both countries, building a bridge between our peoples. What war took away from you, only peace can restore. Your loved one was fighting to preserve your happiness. Don't let his sacrifice be wasted."

While we finish dessert, Xa and Long fill my head with statistics. In Vietnam, only one person in ten holds a job that pays a living wage. Some are simply unemployable—the sick, the aged, and the crippled; others are incapable of work through lack of skills or education. Still others can't work because the raw materials for their jobs are lacking: spare parts, tools, facilities, and equipment. Less sympathetically, I hear Long talk about the Vietnamese who have been declared administratively "unfit" for paid labor because of their ideological mistakes in the past: they held positions of authority in the Republican army or with the government, or made money from serving the Americans. From my hosts' perspective, it would be obscene to give these people work while "honest citizens"— Viet Cong and North Vietnamese Army veterans and their supporters and relatives—are still waiting for work themselves. Unfortunately, because of their ties with the West, a good many of the nation's health care workers, technicians, and managers—the people that made the old Republic function as a modern society—either fled the country or were broken in the reeducation camps. But my hosts can't see this paradox. As Xa said, old prejudices die hard, even if one's people must pay the price.

It is eight o'clock when Anh and I finally say our farewells and I make the only promise to Xa and Long I know I can deliver: to tell as many Americans as I can about what I have seen and heard in Vietnam and encourage them to investigate things for themselves—to prove me wrong; to see if I'm right; to end the war that may still be raging in their hearts.

For their part, Xa and Long thank me for giving them my honest impressions of their country, for telling them about my experiences in America, and for being willing to leave hurt and vengeance outside the door. All these things, they say, will find their way into the written report they must file with their superiors after meeting with a foreigner. They get onto almost-new motorbikes, (a badge of their status, Anh says) and disappear in curls of blue smoke.

Because the night is so pretty and my energy is still high from our discussion, I ask Anh if he wants to go for a walk while I calm down.

"Better than that," he says, eyes twinkling, "let's go for a ride."

Feeling like a privileged official myself, I climb onto the back of Anh's motorbike and we sputter off in the direction of the Song Han waterfront. A few minutes later, the bike is parked along Bach Den Street in an area known as White Elephant Front. During the war, it was a pleasant, tree-lined neighborhood where U.S. servicemen and merchant seamen used to share picnics with the middle-class Vietnamese families who worked in the city. The street behind the park was lined with classy establishments: a U.S. military officers' club, bank branches, and jewelry stores. Now, the O-club has been replaced by a war museum and a *cong ty du lich*— a shabby bureau for foreign visitors. All around us on the sidewalk and on the grassy slope that descends to the river, young couples stroll and look at the stars—it's one of the few acceptable places where such lovers can be together without layers of unwanted chaperones.

Anh pays a bike-watcher for an hour's worth of security and we walk out to a stone bench and sit down. The air is cool and the drifting river glows with city lights. I pull off my shoes and dig my toes in the moist grass—for an international diplomat, I will always make a better farm girl! Anh beams at me like the moon.

"You didn't talk much tonight." I give him a lazy smile. "I hope I didn't embarrass you too much!"

Anh laughs. "On the contrary—I enjoyed myself thoroughly. You're a rare person, Bay Ly: someone who doesn't bear a grudge. You're no official, either, so Xa and Long didn't need to toe the party line. You're one of us; yet you're an American. Besides, it's the first time on this trip I've seen you speak out as well as listen. To tell you the truth, that's one reason I arranged the meeting. Xa and Long want more than anything to help our people. They don't want our sacrifices to be wasted. That's why I wanted them to meet you."

"Why me? I'm just a tourist—and a capitalist tourist at that! What can I do for them? What can I do for Vietnam? Anh Hai, your troubles are just too big!"

"I'm not so sure." Anh's face changes subtly as if he is now talking business at one of his factories. "I'm beginning to see you differently since those first few days in Saigon, Bay Ly. Before, you *were* a tourist—a dear little ghost from my past whom I wronged very badly. Now, after seeing you with the *Ban Viet Kieu* and with your family and with these officials—well, I don't know. You have a talent for helping people look past their pain and into their hearts—to see the things that really matter."

"I'm glad to hear that. I only want my family to be happy. But what has that to do with Mr. Xa and Mr. Long?"

Anh shrugs. "Maybe nothing. All three of you want to make things better but the system keeps working against you. The people who make our policies and plans are all much better at following orders and staying out of trouble than taking risks to make things better. Because everyone's afraid to say 'yes,' we've become far too good at saying 'no.' That's why Xa and Long are so important. They're willing to take a chance—to try new ideas. And more people like them are stepping forward each year into positions of responsibility. The Sixth Party Congress is coming up in December. I think we'll see some changes—or at least a beginning of change to more contact with the West and more public debate about our problems. The point is, Bay Ly, these people need allies: in Saigon, in Danang, in Hanoi, in the villages—even in the United States."

"But I'm not a politician. I'm not a banker. I'm just what I've always been: a person who's trying to get by. I was willing to talk to Xa and Long about our two countries, yes—but as brothers and sister. I don't want to hear a knock on my hotel room door at two in the morning and be told to come to a meeting! What do I know about those men? For that matter, Anh Hai, what do *you* know about them—I mean, really and truly, what do you know? Maybe they're secret police? Maybe *they're* CIA? How can you be sure?"

Anh smiles his fatherly smile again and gives me a pat on the shoulder. "Bay Ly, Bay Ly! My little mud flower! You see how much you're still like us? That's good. That's how it should be. Don't ever change. Don't ever forget what it feels like to worry about the next knock on the door or what your neighbors may be saying. Always remember how much it hurts to take a risk. Vietnam needs many things—money, machinery, medicine, technicians, and all the rest. And I am convinced we will get them when the time is right. But that time will never come unless a few people on both sides of the ocean are willing to take some risks—including the biggest risk of all."

My goodness—it sounds like dear old Anh is about to propose something big and startling, but I'm just a peasant girl from Ky La! I run a little restaurant in Southern California! I'm not a smuggler or rabble-rouser or politician or anything like that. I am almost afraid to ask him what he means.

"I can't guess what you're talking about," I tell him truthfully.

Anh laughs again, gets up, and dusts the seat of his pants. He offers me a hand and I stand beside him.

"That's easy," he says. "Overcoming our pain from the war. Learning to trust when we're afraid. Learning to honor the past while letting go of it at the same time. These are the things you came to Vietnam to learn, Bay Ly—isn't that so? Perhaps it's your turn now to teach."

ELEVEN
Almost in Paradise

THE FIRST DAY on my new job at the hospital in Danang was like a day in paradise. I reported to my supervisor, a kind, well-educated Vietnamese nurse, who introduced me, over the course of our working day, to the rest of the staff. In contrast to the hustlers I dealt with in the black market, these were educated people dedicated to helping others—not exploiting them. In contrast to the overseers I had worked for as a housekeeper, they were kind and considerate employers. And to be paid a decent, living wage on top of that was too much to believe. Although the patients who came through our doors were often in bad shape—civilians who had stepped on mines or been caught in a crossfire between troops —the cleanliness of our facility and the availability of painkillers, medicine, and doctors saved most of them; a stark contrast to the helplessness I often felt assisting Viet Cong nurses in the jungle trying to save arms, legs, and lives with none of these basic tools. As good as I felt about being able to support my mother and son through honest wages, I felt even better about doing so in a way that helped other people and hurt no one in the process.

After a few days, however, one of the hospital's administrators, an overweight Vietnamese sergeant in his fifties, made it clear he had his eye on me. At first he simply lingered in the area where I worked, drinking coffee and watching me while he chatted with the nurses. Later, he found excuses to talk to me directly, often calling me into his office to help him tidy up. When nobody was around, he frequently bumped into me or touched my hands and body when he gave me things to put away. His conversation, too, turned personal and teasing and he often told me smutty jokes to see how I would react. I realized I was spending less time with the patients and nurses—the work I really enjoyed—and more time as his companion, doing make-work tasks whose only purpose was to keep me within pinching and patting distance. Still, although this was not the first time I had faced this situation, I was too afraid of being fired to complain to anyone about my treatment.

Fortunately, a red-haired, freckled young American—a U.S. Navy medical technician named Greg (although everybody called him "Red") whom I had met on my first day and with whom I had talked briefly during my breaks—became aware of my plight. He occasionally stopped by the sergeant's office to drop off records and always smiled and said hello. On one occasion, he took me to get coffee and asked how I was getting along with "Sergeant Octopus."

I wasn't sure what he meant and said, "Oh, he very friendly."

"You mean he hasn't tried to give you a full pelvic exam yet?"

"I no understand—"

Red laughed. "Don't worry. You're not the first girl Sergeant Fingers has latched onto. His reputation is all over the hospital. He likes young women—especially those from the country who aren't too experienced. If he gives you trouble, let me know and I'll get you another assignment."

This is heaven! I thought. *Strangers come to solve your problems even before you ask for help!*

I explained as best I could what was happening and sure enough, the next morning Sergeant Octopus told me sourly that I had been transferred to the radiology lab. I was not surprised to see that this was the same department where Red worked.

Although helping the technicians with the X-rays and cleaning up after patients was less enjoyable than working with the nurses, I at least spent my day unmolested and I was grateful to Red for that. At the end of my first shift, he offered to drive me home.

Although he had been very kind to me, I did not find Red attractive. He seemed like a loner and was picked on by other sailors who often made him the butt of their jokes. His long American face was covered with freckles—quite strange to Vietnamese eyes—and his buck teeth made him look like the field mice we were always chasing from our rice bin. Besides, I had other reasons to feel uneasy about his invitation. I was ashamed of where I lived—a very poor house in a trashy part of town —and believed no American (or even a Vietnamese man with good manners) would like me after seeing it. There were also lots of prostitutes in our area, and if our neighbors saw me coming and going with strange men—particularly Americans—tongues would wag and my mother would be embarrassed.

Nevertheless, I was indebted to Red for his favors and did not want to hurt his feelings or jeopardize my new assignment. I finally accepted his invitation with thanks.

Outside the long, one-story clinic, I waited about thirty minutes until Red appeared in an American jeep. I did not know until later that he only lived next door to the hospital and had to requisition the jeep especially for "our date." In any event, he drove me to my house, which was not too far away, and took my hand when I started to get out.

"I like you very much, Le Ly," he said. "You're different from the other g . . ."—I thought for a moment he had started to say *gooks,* but he quickly finished—"girls. I want to see you again—you know, after work. Let's go out on the town tomorrow night."

"Oh, I am sorry," I said wishing my English was better—up to the task of telling him how I really felt. "I have a child—a little boy—I take care of. My mother—she live at home too." I pulled my hand away as gently as I could and got out.

"But, Le Ly—we could really have fun together!"

"Maybe other time, eh? You good fellow, Red. I like you. See you tomorrow."

The mouse face looked crushed, but managed a smile. Red waved and put the jeep into gear. "Okay," he said, "we'll go out some other time. But that's a promise, now—you remember!"

For the next few days, contrary to my expectations, Red continued to be a gentleman and respected my wishes. Other men in my life had always used their power to get what they wanted, but Red seemed to add patience and self-restraint to his other virtues and I began to see him in a new light. Although he still took me for coffee and we ate lunch together several times a week, he never pressured me for a date. We talked about all kinds of things—my life in the countryside (although I never mentioned the Viet Cong) and his life in the States. My English improved as did my appreciation of America in general and for American men in particular. One day he asked if he could take me home again and I said yes. When I said good night he took my hand and I did not resist. He kissed me lightly on the lips which, despite my previous bad experiences and lack of attraction for him, sent a shiver down my spine.

"Maybe you're ready now to cash that raincheck?" Red smiled.

"Raincheck?" I didn't understand. For a horrible instant I thought Red was going to ask for money for getting me transferred; or worse, that he was, using some American slang I had not heard before, offering to pay me to go to bed with him.

"You know—our date? Go out? Go to a show? Have some beer and a few laughs? Okay?"

"Okay!" I laughed with relief. I got out of the jeep and waved good-bye enthusiastically.

"We'll go somewhere next week!" Red waved as he drove off. When I got inside, my mother gave me the evil eye.

"Who was that?" she snapped. Baby Hung—not so much a baby anymore—was dangling from her hip eating a rice cracker covered with drool.

"Oh—that's Red. Someone from work. He offered to drive me home. I said yes. I wanted to save bus fare. Wasn't it nice of him to offer?"

"He's an *American!*" Venom dripped from my mother's voice.

"Mama *Du,* I work with Americans all day! So does Lan—"

"Lan is a mature woman. You're a little girl."

"I'm not a little girl, Mama *Du!* If you hadn't noticed, you're holding my baby son in your lap! And who do you think's been supporting us for the last year and a half?"

I walked past her into our kitchen looking for something to eat. All of a sudden it struck me that I had just treated her the way my father felt he had been treated by his daughters shortly before his death. I turned and saw my mother's tear-filled eyes. I ran over and gave her a big hug.

"I'm sorry, Mama *Du,*" I said. "I sincerely apologize. I had no right to talk to you that way. It's—it's the Americans, you're right. It's hard to be around them and not pick up bad habits. But I'm not turning into a Westerner. My eyes aren't getting round."

"Boom!" little Hung suddenly shouted, laughing and pointing his glistening finger at me. "Rat-tat-tat-tat-tat!"

The next day I walked to work on a cloud. I felt so much luckier than Lan, who seemed to meet only greedy, horny, dangerous Americans, whereas I had the good fortune of meeting a kind and decent man— someone even a Vietnamese parent would be proud to call an in-law— my first day on the job. Despite the hectic pace of the hospital, I dreamed all day about "our date," and imagined the jealous looks I'd get from the Vietnamese street girls when we passed—a lady on my gentleman's arm.

So possessed was I by these fantasies that I decided I couldn't wait for Red to approach me again. After all, I had made him suffer enough by acting coy. Although I spent years dreading the touch of a man and still felt bad about being abandoned by Anh and selling myself to start a nest egg, I could no longer look into my heart and say honestly that either men or Americans revulsed me. After all, sex was as much a part of life as being born or dying and I had already experienced the first and seen enough of the latter to last me all my years. Perhaps fate or luck or god had picked this kind, earnest, gentle man to be my guide back to the world of love between men and women. Who was I to turn my back on the will of heaven?

That afternoon, the first sign that I had made the right choice appeared. My supervisor asked if I wished to work overtime at the end of my shift. Without thinking twice, I said yes, then hustled outside to make arrangements. I sent a message boy to my house to tell my mother I'd be working late and would spend the night at Lan's, since her apartment was closer to the hospital than our house. My real plan, of course, was to surprise Red in his little trailer and confess my budding affection—and perhaps true love for him—after which I would simply let nature take its course. I imagined I might very well spend a tender night of bliss nestled in his gentle arms—protected in a way my father could never protect me; loved in a way the father of my child could never love me. From there, my fantasy took me quickly to a hasty wedding and, at the end of Red's tour, passage to America as a Navy wife.

Just in case Lan should, for some reason, come looking for me, I sent her a second note saying that although I had planned to come and visit, I would probably wind up spending the night at home. It seemed like a wonderful, foolproof plan.

When my overtime was finished, I borrowed some perfume from a lady co-worker and freshened up as best I could in the lavatory before I left. Outside, it was quite dark and smelled of rain. Still, the sunshine in my heart seemed to light my path and I hopscotched nimbly through traffic to the line of temporary military houses across the street. There were many vehicles parked out front—jeeps, motorbikes, and even a couple of French-made cars. In the air, thumping rhythmically through the trees and in the very ground I walked on, was the heavy bass of a GI rock station. The vibration and noise increased as I climbed the steps to Red's house, took a breath, and knocked on the door.

It opened onto a blaring radio and Red in his undershorts holding a sudsy beer in his hand. I watched the grin on the mousy face fall flat.

"Le Ly!" Red sputtered. "What are you doing here?"

I peered inside to see a half-dozen GIs in fatigues or underwear sitting on the floor or in the bed with a like number of Vietnamese girls in various stages of undress. All were drinking beer or hard liquor and the pungent smell of pot was as thick as the awful music.

"I'm sorry to bother you," I peeped, a sudden knot in my stomach. "I—I just wanted to ask you something."

"Huh? What do you mean?"

His eyes were bleary from liquor and marijuana and I could tell he was trying to clear his head.

"Hey, Red—bring your little babe inside!" a voice called out. "There's always room for one more!"

"Uh—sure," Red backed up, opening the door. "Come on in, darlin'," He looked down at the beer in his hand and then at his own bloated belly and ducked behind the door. "I'll just put on some pants and—we'll go out. We'll take a walk—"

"No, no." I tried to smile but I was sure he could see my heart breaking. "I don't want to bother you. I'll see you tomorrow. Good night—"

I ran down the steps just as the rain began to fall.

"Wait—" Red shouted from the door. "Le Ly!"

I ran back to the hospital, oblivious of the cars and mopeds that honked and rang their bells and skidded on the rain-slick street. I was confused and hurt and angry but when I tried to get back in the lab, I found the door was locked.

Now I had done it. I told my mother I would be at Lan's and Lan that I would be at my mother's and now I couldn't go to either place without arousing suspicion. To make matters worse, the hospital was locked for the night and although the emergency room was open, it was right next to Sergeant Octopus' quarters, and going there for the night would be worse than sleeping on the street.

Finally, I remembered the only other building in the complex that never closed: the morgue. I clutched my blouse tight against the rain and ran head-long down the sidewalk. Sure enough, the "body shop" was open, tended by a married couple who lived in rooms at the back of the building. Although I had never met them before, they looked up from their work and smiled pleasantly as I came in. Both of them had lumpy faces, as if they had been wounded or burned in the war; although their little girl was fine, lively, and healthy.

"Excuse me," I said, shaking off the rain on their nicely swept floor, "I work at Nha Thuong next door—"

"Yes, I know," the woman said cordially. "I've seen you around. What can we do for you?"

I made up some story about how I couldn't go home because of family problems and asked if I could stay the night with them. I said I would sleep anywhere: a vacant bed, an unused cot by the body bags, on the floor—anywhere out of the rain.

"Certainly, child," the woman said with an understanding smile. She came over and put her arm around me. When she got closer, I could see she was in pretty bad shape—one scarry lump on her face weeped fluid in the light. "Why don't you have a little tea to warm you up? You know, we don't get many visitors here—just police and QCs and the poor souls they bring in from the street. Perhaps that's why God found this job for us, eh? Where else can poor lepers go?"

Although I tried to be still, I tossed and turned all night trying to be small in my borrowed bed. Although I had been taught that leprosy was much less contagious than everyone supposed, it was one of the few jungle diseases we peasants really dreaded and my heart was not about to let my body rest despite reassurances from my brain. Besides, that brain was still too shaken by my experience with Red—too shocked and over-whelmed from gaining, then losing, the American knight I thought would rescue me and my son from our predicament.

The next morning, I went back to the hospital, washed my face in the same lavatory where I had prepared myself for my date, and went to work as usual. Red came in late and although he tried to catch my eye all morning, I always looked away. As soon as we got our break, however, Red pulled me into a linen closet and apologized earnestly for the previous night.

"That whole thing was my roommate's idea, Le Ly—you've got to believe me! I just went along with the guys. Those girls—those sluts— what are they to me? Nothing! I feel sorry for 'em. You're the only girl I'm interested in."

"Really?" I sniffed, trying not to cry. "I think maybe I make you wait too long for me—"

"Oh no, baby," he held me close. "I'd wait for you forever, darlin'. You know that! For the whole damn war, if I had to!"

He kissed me tenderly and hugged me again the way I had imagined he would the night before—the way I'd hoped Anh would have held me years before. Only this time the man who held me was unmarried, about my age, and—beyond the barrier of race, which was growing smaller every day—bore with him no obstacles to our happiness. I forgave him instantly and agreed to start our relationship over with a clean slate.

For the first week or so, everything was as blissful as I had imagined.

I saw no more of his rowdy American companions and we spent our evenings wandering the crowded shops, cafés, and waterfront of Danang. After our third night out, we went back to Red's house and made love. It was at this point that I became starkly aware, despite my other experiences in life, how unprepared I was to be a wife. Because I came to sex with the feelings of a victim, I responded to him, at best, like a little girl and not a woman. He had to teach me how to kiss a man correctly and how to use my hands to stimulate him and to show my own attraction. To make matters worse, Red in bed was like many of the Americans I head heard my girlfriends talk about. Where Vietnamese men were satisfied with passive acceptance, American men demanded acrobatics. It was as if all these Americans, in the way they used their women, were trying to find something in the act of sex that escaped them elsewhere in their lives. With Red, I could not guess what that missing thing could be. I only knew that what we made was more lust than love, and that whatever I did to please him never seemed to be enough.

One day after making love in his room, I asked Red why we never socialized with his friends.

"Why do you think?" His answer was almost surly.

"Well, I don't know," I replied, buttoning my blouse. "That's why I asked."

"Well—look at you!" Red held out his hand as if he were gesturing to a pile of dung or an old workshed that needed painting. "You look like you just came off the farm!"

"Of course that's how I look—I'm a farm girl! I thought you liked the way I look!"

"Le Ly—you're a pretty girl, but you can't go through life looking like you just stepped out from behind a plow! You look like—well, like a damned Viet Cong or something!"

I tugged at my shirttail and looked at the black slacks I had worn like a uniform since my first day at the hospital. As poor as they were, they were almost new and much better than anything I had ever had in Ky La. I really didn't think I looked all that different from the other Vietnamese women who worked in and around the clinic. That, apparently, was the problem. American men, it seemed, liked their lovers to be special; to look different from other women.

That evening I went to Lan's and tried painting my fingernails the way I had so often watched her paint her own. I also took part of my paycheck, which I had intended to give my mother, and got my hair done in a fancy beehive like the tea girls Red always noticed when we were out. From a girlfriend at work, I borrowed some eye shadow and tried to paste on some false lashes I had purchased in a store to make my narrow Vietnamese eyes look bigger, rounder, and more American.

When I knocked on the door to Red's house for our next date, rouged and teased in my red *ao dai,* I could see the new Le Ly was much closer to what he wanted.

"All right!" Red grinned. "Come in, darlin'! Hey, Miller!" He called to another GI who was sitting in a chair, drinking a beer and smoking a cigarette. "Take a look at my girl!"

"Hey, man," the GI said, "Where you been hiding this one? She's too much, man!"

I felt like too much of something, that was for sure, but I was so happy to finally please my man in front of his friend that I forgot all the worry and labor and money it took to put on this painted face and the hurt looks my mother gave me on those few occasions when I stayed home to care for my growing boy. It was, after all, *hy sinh*—the things you must sacrifice for your man.

Because Red was now more anxious to have me around, he gave me money and told me to locate an apartment for us to share—away from his roommates and all the bustle and traffic near the hospital. Having never picked a place for an American to live before, I hardly knew where to start. Everywhere seemed too expensive or too dirty or too dangerous for a lone GI. Finally, I settled on a place on Gia Long Street right across from a Republican police station—a place that was bound to be safe, no matter what.

Unfortunately, it turned out to be a very bad idea. The local policemen resented Vietnamese women who fraternized with other races. Koreans or Japanese or Thais could be accepted with some grumbling—at least they were oriental; but Americans were out of the question. They began to harass us (stopping to question us, giving us dirty looks, shaking us down for various "fines," and all the rest), so we wound up spending as much time away from the apartment—at clubs and restaurants outside the neighborhood—as we did inside of it.

Now that my appearance had changed, Red began taking me to night-clubs where we had never gone before but where everyone seemed to know him and he knew everyone else. I learned to drink—or at least to pretend to drink, alcohol still upset my tender stomach—and dance the jerky-quick and dreamy-slow dances the Americans seemed to like. Some of these clubs were pretty bad places where the women danced without tops and there were lots of fights among patrons. One day, we went to one of these bars during our lunch hour and Red introduced me to its Korean proprietor.

"Lee, here's the little darlin' I was telling you about!" Red said, putting his arm around me proudly.

The Korean smiled and gave me a clammy handshake. "Excellent!" he said, looking me up and down. "Please—walk over to the bar." I did as I was told. "Excellent! Now be so kind as to turn around. Yes—that's it! Just spin around on your toes."

I felt completely foolish—like a skinny chicken in the market rather than Red's girlfriend.

"Can you dance?" Lee asked.

"What?" I responded, confused. "No, I don't care to dance, thank you." There wasn't even any music playing!

"Charming!" Lee clapped his hands.

"Hell, she dances like a firecracker!" Red clapped the Korean on the shoulder. I looked at him uneasily as I walked back.

"Red," I said, clutching his arm, "I don't understand—"

Lee clarified things immediately. He said he would pay me a week's hospital wages for a single night's work as a go-go dancer in his club, which he said was very high-class and visited by lots of Americans, most of whom tipped extra money to the girls that put on the best show. I don't remember saying yes, but the sound of all that money—a month's wages for a week of doing what Red and I did anyway—prevented me from saying no.

In the jeep driving back to the hospital, Red said, "Hell, you made a smart decision, Le Ly. Didn't I say I'd take care of you? You'll make more money than your mama-san can spend and have enough left over for new clothes, new jewelry—everything!"

"I don't know," I said. "I promised my mother—my father—I would not be a bar girl. I—"

"You aren't gonna disappoint me, now, are you?" Red really sounded angry. "I already told everybody my girl's a classy dancer at Dai Hang's! They're all going to stop by and see you."

"You wouldn't be ashamed if your friends saw me doing all that?"

"Hell no! I'd be proud of you! When we get back to the lab, I want you to march right over to administration and tell 'em they can go to hell—get another girl to empty their damn bedpans! You got better things to do now, don't you? Come on, you sexy thing—what do you say?"

What I said was, "I quit!" to the clinic director who had so kindly given me a job on Steve's recommendation. After that, Red and I went back to the apartment where we made rough love after which he went to work and I waited alone, confused and uncertain, until he came home.

After making love again, we got dressed and went back to Lee's club.

It was now packed with servicemen and the first pair of girls were beginning to dance. To my horror, this too was a topless club.

"No!" I said, averting my eyes. "I'm not going to do that!"

"Now, Le Ly, darlin' "—Red moved his chair closer—"don't disappoint me. I really want to see you up there. These guys—" his voice dropped to a whisper, his eyes were wide and his upper lip was sweaty —"see, they think I'm just a runt, a pisshole—some swabbie med tech they can shit on whenever they want! Shit—it's *always* been that way for me! But with you—with you up there on that stage—I'll *be* somebody! *You'll* be somebody! Now come on, be cool, darlin'. Here comes Lee. Just tell him you take the fuckin' job and that's that!"

But Mr. Lee and I did not have that conversation. Instead, I took my purse and left the table, music blaring in my ears the way it had when I ran from Red's house on that awful, rainy night.

"Le Ly—you come back here!" Red shouted. "Where do you think you're going? Damn you, woman! You aren't the only gook girl in the world! You hear me—!"

Out on the street, the air was cool and blessedly free of smoke and music. I smelled the dinners cooking in the apartments above the shops and heard the familiar buzz of motorbikes and the cries of vendors hawking food from pushcarts in the street. Some children brushed by me, running home for supper, and I unpinned my hair and shook out the rat's nest as best I could. It would take awhile to walk home without Red's jeep, and, dressed as I was, I would have to endure wolf whistles and propositions of the servicemen the whole way, but it was worth it to be free—to be back in a world I understood.

LATE MORNING, APRIL 9, 1986:
ON HIGHWAY 1 OUTSIDE DANANG

We are on our way to a luncheon Anh has arranged at one of his state-owned weaving factories, the QN-DN Compound, two miles outside the city. I don't know if this is another of his curious "tests" of my acceptability to Vietnam's new dreamers or simply an opportunity to break his workers' unrelenting routine with a glimpse of an exotic visitor from the United States—rarer in these parts than cheap gasoline and good beer.

As we buzz down the potholed highway, I get my first real look at the countryside since I arrived: farmers threshing rice with wooden flails; children riding water buffalos like pets (just as I did mine a generation before); old men driving ducks along narrow, crumbly dikes; gristled grandmothers carrying buckets of gravel on shoulder poles like oxen laboring in a yoke; underfed road crews handmaking a highway; bicycles being walked by their handlebars, the seats piled high with rice bags, coal sacks, and bananas.

Before long we bounce down a short gravel road to the compound gate. I can tell it's nearly lunchtime because the farmers are beginning to cluster around the many charcoal braziers stuck like smudge pots under trees along the road. While the mothers and grandmothers cook, the fathers, road crews, and red-kerchiefed schoolkids stream in like ants for their first—and perhaps only—hot meal of the day.

Anh parks the motorbike beside a weathered brick building. I try unsuccessfully to brush the red dirt from my tailored black slacks and white blouse, but it is as tenacious as the Viet Cong fighters its tunnels once protected. Happily, I have found a way to dress "American"—with stylish clothes—but in subdued Vietnamese colors that will not startle my hosts. As the people on whom his livelihood depends, Anh's employees are like an extended family. Meeting them will be a different kind of test from my dinner with the officials—they are less well-informed, less comfortable with their lives, and, perhaps, less tolerant of foreign visitors from the land that caused them so much trouble.

Inside the factory, the textile machinery is clattering and I am introduced as Anh's "second wife" to the general director, Ho Van Thuong, and his assistant, a mature woman named Tam who wears a nondescript gray suit and kindly smile. We greet each other politely and exchange pleasantries about how wonderful it is to be host and visitor at this "reunion" between our two nations. Thuong takes me on a brief tour of the factory floor and I am struck at once by the equality of jobs between young men and women. Poverty is a great equalizer and I wonder in passing how long Communist egalitarianism, a close cousin to communal village life anyway, would survive if everyone was suddenly bitten by the capitalist bug.

As we are about to leave, I notice a young woman staring at me intently. She labors at a loom with practiced efficiency, as if her arm were but an extension of the lever she operates. I walk over and give her my best tourist smile.

"How do you do? How are you?" I say, and watch her face light up. Like the rest of the hard-worked machinery, she looks older than she is, although the amazed, curious eyes can't have seen more than twenty summers.

"May I ask you a question?" the girl asks shyly, not missing a beat with her machine.

"Of course!"

"Your face—" she stutters, hunting for words the way I would stumble if I had to adddress the captain of a flying saucer, "it—it *glows!*"

I laugh, knowing she's referring to the faint mascara, eye shadow, and lipstick on my face. Very likely, this young girl—born in the countryside and raised in an era of postwar austerity—has never seen a woman in makeup. Like a mother showing a daughter her unborn sister in the mother's pregnant belly, I take the girl's hand from her machine and trace it lightly over my cheeks and eyes. She draws it back and looks in amazement at the pale rainbow on her fingertips.

"See?" I say. "It's nothing. Just makeup!"

"Is everyone in America as beautiful as you?" she asks in a reverent, totally unself-conscious voice.

I laugh again. "Compared to some, I'm ugly; compared to others, I'm pretty—just like in Vietnam."

"Do you think I will ever be able to go to America and look like you?"

I am suddenly aware of the director general's eyes drilling holes in my back. He seems a nice fellow, and knowing Anh, he probably is; but I have no way of telling if he is amused or irritated by this exchange. In a voice slightly louder than necessary, I say, "No—you don't have to go to America. If you work hard enough right here, you and your friends can look any way you want without having to go anywhere!"

The girl smiles, nods a muted *thank you,* and embraces her machine while I fish around in my purse. The little tube of lipstick is almost empty, but when I set it on the counter next to her, the girl stares at it as if it were a bar of gold. "Here," I say, "this will last you until you all get rich enough to buy your own!"

Inside the adjoining office building, the clerks are busy transcribing records with fountain pens. If there is a typewriter in the place, it has probably died of old age. The papers on their desks look like hand towels from a gas station lavatory—coarse, brown, and wrinkly from too much recycling. I am greeted with a disquieting mixture of cold glances and forced smiles.

We enter a large conference room which has been converted to a dining area set for fourteen people—all the factory's supervisors. Besides myself, Tam, and a couple of waitresses, there are no women in the room. I sense that here, where real decisions are made, sexual equality probably ends —as it does too often in America. Certainly, so many male and so few women managers can't be the result of Vietnam's legendary shortage of men! Nonetheless, I am greeted cordially by everyone and seated in the place of honor, with Anh at my right and Tam on my left. While people settle in and the food service begins, the lack of women in authority seems like an appropriate place to begin a conversation with my hostess.

"You must feel lucky," I say, trying to feel out her opinions on the subject, "one woman working with so many men!"

Tam smiles wearily. "I feel a little lonely, too! But these are hard times. Everyone knows it's pointless to bicker about who does what. As you've seen, our country is very poor. The economy's so bad because our boys went to Hanoi and became soldiers and politicians instead of managers and technicians. Even now, eleven years after liberation, we're still skimping along on wartime shortages. Most of our engineers and professional people—Southerners like us—left the country in '75. Those who stayed aren't stupid, of course, but nobody's been trained in business and technology. We had to learn everything for ourselves and, believe me, we still make plenty of mistakes."

"I wish there were some way we Americans could help you," I say, surprised at the edge on my voice. "We have everything you need. More than everything. We *waste* the things you need and think nothing about it—paper, material, smart college kids—you name it! I wish there was something I could do about it!"

Tam shrugs philosophically and sips her rice soup. "The world is always out of balance, eh?" she says. "Unfortunately, it's the young people, like that girl you talked to on the line, who are suffering the most. They had nothing to do with the war, but they're still paying its price."

My hostess asks about my life in the United States and what I think of her new country. After giving what has now become my standard answer to such questions ("What can I say?"), I find it's easier to talk about such things in pairs, such as "California has pretty beaches, like Quang Nam," or "Yes, our food is fairly cheap and plentiful, but there are more brands than anyone needs and most have too many chemicals," and so on. It does not seem appropriate to point out that many Americans spend more money than she makes in a year simply to lose the weight they gained by eating food they didn't want.

When the meal is over, General Director Thuong makes a short, lively speech expressing everyone's desire to improve relations with the U.S. For entertainment, a couple of workers stand up and sing some folk tunes, and I return the compliment by singing a little song my father taught me from the time of the French called "Vietnam Uses Both Ends of Its Chopsticks"—a thinly veiled jibe at the colonialists who "grew fat" skimming away the resources Vietnam needed to feed herself.

They all laugh when after the song I say, "I notice nobody's using the other end of your chopsticks today!"

After our luncheon at the factory, Anh and I return to the *Ban Viet Kieu* office in Danang where we set off on our tour of the countryside, beginning with Marble Mountain. The "official" touring car is a rickety 1950s four-door sedan (a Mercedes, I am told, despite the missing hood ornament), painted gray one time too many to postpone its demise from the salty air. Like a chauffeur-driven queen, I sit in the back with Anh, my bored-looking consort, to whom travels with chauffeurs are nothing new. But to me, this is a big change from the last time I covered this stretch of road as a black-marketeering teenage mother in the back of a ramshackle bus.

Our driver's name is Tuan, a talkative ex-Viet Cong who has already told me the adventure of his life, and has now begun retelling it, with embellishments, like a musician repeating a favorite tune with ornaments. In the right-front passenger seat is our *Ban Viet Kieu* escort: a state-sponsored tour guide who is more concerned about keeping to our itinerary and not violating rules (such as where not to take pictures or mingle with people) than pointing out landmarks that I probably know better than him.

After a visit to China Beach and the Soviet-sponsored hotel (built with the sweat of Vietnamese peasants), which our guide hopes will soon be full of tourists, we rattle south on Highway 538, a stone's throw from the ocean. The almost-island of Monkey Mountain dwindles behind us while the sugarloaf peaks of Marble Mountain—square-topped and flat-sided like a row of sand-pail castles—loom in the windshield. The driver reminds us of the district's colorful and ironic history.

"You know, this is the whole war, missy—right here at Marble Mountain!" Tuan says over his shoulder as the steering wheel shimmies in his hands. "Everybody knows about the marble-cutters who live around the mountain, right? Every marine at China Beach came up to buy trinkets at one time or another, right? The GIs even had a lookout station on the summit—to keep an eye on us, right? Ha! They never suspected we had the biggest Viet Cong hospital in the province right under their noses—in caves inside the mountain!"

It was true. For years the Americans on China Beach—a whole Marine Corps regiment including a hospital and an airport—virtually lived on top of one of the Viet Cong's showcase facilities. Because the base of the mountain was riddled with caves, many of them converted to Buddhist shrines, the Americans declared them off-limits—not only for the obvious dangers involved in exploring them, but in a laudable attempt to respect our Buddhist religion. The fact that the Viet Cong wasted no time putting the Americans' scruples to work against them was also symptomatic of a war in which soldiers on opposite sides often patrolled and slept and fornicated and daydreamed within an arm's length of each other—and never knew it.

Tuan parks the car next to a Russian tour bus and we climb the broad steps to the nearest temple. The artisans and stone-cutters are still here, of course, but the little marble Buddhas have been joined now by busts of Ho Chi Minh. Children are everywhere, clamoring for our attention: to have their picture taken, to sell us something, to touch our clothing. I notice that many of the teenagers have round eyes and long noses— more legacies of the Americans at China Beach. If I were Caucasian, I'm sure my pockets would already be stuffed with unsolicited letters "to whom it may concern" asking for information about fathers in the United States. It's faint hope that keeps these children going, but faint hope is better than none at all.

Behind the first pagoda is a modest little hollow that leads to the main underground facility. Light filters through an opening in the cavernous ceiling, but it's enough to see the enormous Buddhas carved from living rock and their companion holy warriors: statues painted in bold colors which, having been sheltered from the sun, are as bright today as when the ancient artists created them. With scarcely a nod for these wonderful artifacts, the escort leads us to a small memorial plaque against one wall recounting the history of Marble Mountain Field Hospital.

"Now," our *Ban Viet Kieu* guide tells us, beaming, "you can take all the pictures you want!"

We return to the car, which Tuan has trouble starting, and pick up the highway going south. After a mile or so, the road bends inland and I feel a lump form in my throat. We are now so close to Ky La—to Xa Hoa Qui, as it's now called—that I can almost smell the jungle flowers, the boiling lunch pots, the humid air on the flooded paddies, and my own perspiration as I hoe the muddy earth. I roll the window down and let the air rush over my face, happy as a puppy drinking wind on a California freeway.

"I don't suppose we could stop for a moment—" I finally ask our tour guide.

He looks surprised. "Why? What's wrong? Are you feeling ill? A little carsick?"

"Ah—yes." I quickly weigh my alternatives and decide that a little lie now is better than the big lie it would take to get back to this spot before my trip is over.

"Go ahead"—the escort nudges the driver—"pull over anywhere. Hurry up, eh?"

I glance at Anh and see he is watching me carefully. He has zoomed me around on his motorbike too often during the last few days to think I might vomit from this gentle ride in the Mercedes. As the old car slows down, my heart races faster.

We stop on the narrow shoulder and when the cloud of dust has passed, all four doors open at once. I climb out and sniff the air. A girlish giggle wells up inside of me that I can hardly contain. The *Ban Viet Kieu* guide gets out and stares at me nervously over the roof of the car, convinced I am about to throw up. Tuan stays at the wheel, nursing the sputtering engine. Anh walks around the car and joins me.

"Are you okay?" he asks. "Do you need anything?"

"Yes," I say, "a pair of wings. You know, Ky La is less than a mile away—down that little trail over there. This is where we used to catch the bus to Danang."

I point to Quang Cai, the little hamlet to the right of the highway, where a raised road edged with red dirt—just wide enough for a single vehicle—cuts through the fields and into a line of trees that thickens until everything is lost in haze. It was a place where the Viet Cong regularly ambushed American and Republican forces—the proverbial trail into the valley of death—now trafficked by peaceful water buffalo and old ladies taking vegetables to market. To the right is the lake formed by the Vinn Dien River, and beyond that, the swamp with the little island which was supposed to have contained my grave. If Tuan could be talked into taking that road, I could be back in the village of my birth in five minutes. In six, I could be hugging my mother inside the house my father built.

"Don't even *think* about it, Bay Ly," Anh whispers behind my ear.

"But it's so close—!" Tears burn in my eyes.

"I know. But think about your mother. Think of Hai. If they wanted you to come they'd've asked you. But it's just too dangerous—for you and for them."

"Hello over there!" The escort shades his eyes and raps his knuckles on the metal roof. "Are you all right, Miss Ly?"

I turn around and I'm sure my suddenly pale face and miserable expression convince him I'm sick. Certainly, the pain in my heart is real enough.

"What? Yes. I'm fine." I wipe my tears with the flat of my hand. "I just needed a little air, that's all. It's okay. We can go now."

"You're sure?"

"Miss Ly is fine," Anh says with finality as he helps me into the car. The door slams like the barred door of a prison.

When everyone's inside, the driver spins the wheel and the laboring engine pulls us slowly onto the asphalt. My head is full of visions—of ten thousand GIs who crowded this place during the war and the thousands of ghosts they left behind—when a blast on the old car's horn brings me back to the here and now.

"Damned farmers!" Tuan leans on the horn again. On the road ahead of us, an old man is prodding a water buffalo with a stick. As the mud-slick animal finally turns and ambles into the field, we all notice at once that it's pink-eyed and stark white—an albino—and very rare.

"Well, looky there!" Tuan says as we swing around the farmer. "A white buffalo! Must've had an American father!"

Everybody laughs, but I'm not sure the Amerasian kids who crowded around us at Marble Mountain would have understood his humor.

"This is our lucky day," the *Ban Viet Kieu* man says despite his party's official policy discouraging superstition. "Did everyone make a wish?"

I look out the window as the car accelerates and the countryside flashes past like pages in a family album. A roadside vendor stands at a cart peddling cheap Vietnamese cigarettes, packets of green tea, and a few bottles of warm soda. The headstones of a cemetery for war victims—Republican soldiers, Viet Cong, and peasants alike—flicker by like slats in a picket fence. Somehow, it seems to confirm that this was, after all, one war for one country. Past differences in politics, religion, status, physical beauty and prowess—even race—are now dust like the victims themselves. If war produces one thing, it's fine cemeteries; and in cemeteries, at least, there are no enemies. Perhaps one day in the far future, a child on her mother's arm will ask who these people were—why they died and why they are buried all together. I find myself praying most fervently that the mother, having known war only from distant legends, will be unable to answer. On that day, at last, the spirit of war will no longer hang over my village.

"Yes," I answer my tour guide, managing a smile. "I've made my wish."

TWELVE

Finding a Family

AFTERNOON, APRIL 9, 1986:
ON HIGHWAY 540
CROSSING THE CAU DO RIVER

OUR TOUR CONTINUES as our dusty gray sedan chugs northward on the winding road toward the bridge across the Cau Do River, downstream from the Tuy Loan fork. Our driver gears down and we coast toward a small house just short of the river. It used to be owned by Nguyen Van Troi, a Viet Cong hero well known for wrecking Republican bridges—blowing himself up, poetically, with the last one he destroyed. His house is now a tourist shrine, where admirers can ponder his adventures in the shadow of the very structure that made him famous. Because we fought the war in our own laps, Vietnam is full of such ironic places.

Even so, there seems little to showcase in the country except the vestiges of war: graveyards both well kept (military) and weedy (civilian), monuments, orphanages, and the tiny Tram Y Te health clinic—a shell of a building with no permanent staff—for the maimed, diseased, and broken. On each Viet Cong or North Vietnamese soldier's grave is carved the words *Ghi on Liet Si* (In Memory of a Hero)—not because every soldier was heroic, but because Uncle Ho promised the dead that their sacrifice would make them so. Even in Nga Ba Cai Lan, outside Danang, there is a monumental statue honoring a Vietnamese mother who hid seven Viet Cong in her house. When the Republicans came and asked, "Where is the enemy?" she pointed away from her house and at their own troops. For this her children became instant orphans. The monument, made entirely from U.S. cannon shells salvaged after the war, shows her pointing nobly toward her destiny. This, to me, may be the cruelest sight of all. It is a mother's first duty to protect her family, not give it up to the machines of war. Such monuments as this seem aimed more at recruiting new victims than at honoring the dead.

I turned away from it with a sickened stomach which my *Ban Viet Kieu* guide misinterpreted as patriotic fervor. "I know," he said proudly, "I weep for joy, too, whenever I see it!"

Walking back to the car, our driver, Tuan, said in a low voice, "Don't be upset, missy. These monuments are for visitors, not the peasants. Don't think we enjoy remembering the war. We just don't want outsiders to forget it." After saying that, Tuan seemed less the cocky veteran than the old man the war had made him.

The old Mercedes pulls up at a country store just short of the Van Troi house. I decide to turn the tables and make this a stop these poor men will remember.

Tuan shuts down the rattling motor and we all get out. Under an awning beside the store, a side of beef is hanging in flies and heat. But it is not just any beef, it is *bo thui va mam cai*—barbecued beef of the Central Coast—a treasure as rare to me as *mi quang* noodles!

The proprietor, a smiling bald man with a bloody butcher's apron, comes out and welcomes us like family. His well-fed wife shows us the contents of an old, unplugged refrigerator but instead of choosing Indonesian Coca-Cola or flat Vietnamese beer, I spring my surprise on them.

"Your *bo thui* beef," I ask, throwing a thumb over my shoulder, "is it for sale?"

"Of course." The proprietor's smile brightens, "Do you want to take it with you?"

"No, no! I want you to prepare a nice meal for my companions—beef and steak sauce with rice noodles and *Rau Hung*. And serve them some good beer, too. Something imported, eh? No local stuff. From what the men don't eat, put half into a bag for me to take to my family. The other half you can keep for yourself and enjoy with my compliments."

For a few precious *dong,* the proprietor and his wife set a spectacular table for my companions, who, when they overcome their initial shock and I foil their polite refusals, sit down and eat with gusto. Even Anh. who already had soup at noon with his workers, attacks the roast like a hungry laborer. They wash it all down with Singapore beer, which puts even our rule-quoting escort in a mellow mood.

While they eat, Tuan's conversation turns from his war adventures ("Tales for the Russian tourists!" he claims) to stories of his home, his relatives, and the hard life they're still living so long after their costly victory. "It's as if everyone's forgotten how to lead a normal life," the driver says. "At least the war gave you something to look forward to: the day the fighting would be over. Now, who cares about tomorrow when the best that can happen is more of the same?"

Surprisingly, the official escort chimes in with his own complaints, "You think you've got it bad?" Sauce sticks to his cheeks like a clown's grin. "The power goes out at the office twice a day—you can almost set your watch by it! At least you're outdoors, Tuan, driving big shots to appointments. It's easier for you to get what you need—to get a little something extra for your ration tickets. I've had to take a second job clerking in the Industrial Department just to feed my family!"

We had started out as a very unlikely ensemble: the one-time millionaire; the peasant girl turned American tourist; the cocky, sad-eyed veteran; and the anxious bureaucrat. Now, after nothing more than a good meal and a little kindness, we were almost talking like family.

* * *

WITHOUT A JOB, an inventory for my business—or now, even a boyfriend—my situation was much more serious than it seemed when I left Red at the Korean nightclub. I felt free of a terrible burden and still had lots of cash from my windfall with Big Mike, but I didn't want to spend my escape money for daily expenses. I had to find a new job—a new way of getting by—and find it fast.

If nothing else, my experience with Red had given me a more presentable image—at least to Western eyes. Before, I was basically a farm girl living in the city. Although my manners became more refined and my awareness of hygiene improved a lot after working at the hospital, I still looked and dressed like a peasant from Ky La. After Red, I at least knew how to fix myself up and act the way Americans expected. It was now within my power to find a really good-paying job that could bring me into contact with people who could help me find a better life.

I believed I found this opportunity in one of the tamer clubs that Red and I had visited—a place called the Kim Chee House on Phan Dinh Phung Street. It was advertised as a "casino" but was really just a large house trailer with a bar, a few gaming tables, and slot machines. The club was owned by a Korean and I was impressed with his honesty when he told me that although the space below the trailer (small rooms built into the concrete foundation) was leased to prostitutes who supplemented his income, none of "his" girls were required to solicit customers, most of whom were ROKs—soldiers from the Republic of Korea, allies of the Americans.

Because the owner made his money from gambling, not liquor or prostitution, his main interest was in keeping the slots and gaming tables busy. As a waitress, I made sure his customers played continuously and so was spared much of the tedious conversation and unwanted passes Lan and the other tea girls endured at the regular GI bars. I was also allowed to dress simply and wore a minimum of makeup. My pay was nearly as good as what I had been promised for dancing almost naked and the hours were better. The only problem was my mother.

At first she was suspicious when I began leaving home in the morning dressed for a night on the town. To her, all women who didn't look like farmers were hookers and I did nothing to diminish her suspicions by the large amounts of cash I brought home at the end of every shift. Eventually she accepted my assurances that I was not disgracing our family name and appreciated the extra time I was able to spend with Hung.

At work, however, things didn't turn out quite so well. During my first few weeks, about half of my customers had been Americans. They appreciated my fresh appearance, passable English, and pleasant manner and we got along just fine. During the second month, however, more and more Korean soldiers began to frequent the place, driving the Americans away. Because I couldn't speak Korean and their English was worse than mine, I couldn't communicate with these new customers and was frequently taken for a prostitute. Some Koreans were not used to being refused by women, let alone those in an "occupied" country, and became angry when I foiled their advances. Because my boss was seldom around to enforce his rules and his Korean employees were hesitant to intervene with their countrymen, this harassment went quickly from bad to worse.

One Sunday, on my way to work, a masculine voice called out in heavily accented Vietnamese, *"Chao Mung Nam Moi!"* (Happy New Year!) Because I was used to getting wolf whistles and cat-calls while I was on the streets in my casino "uniform," I ignored the call and kept on walking. The masculine voice called again.

"Miss—please! I just want to ask you something, all right?" The voice had an odd accent and I couldn't help turning to look. It belonged to a handsome young man in civilian clothes riding a motorbike. He was certainly not Vietnamese, but neither did he look quite American with his dark skin, broad forehead, and the vaguely Asian features around his aviator sunglasses. I slowed down to get a better look.

"What do you want?" I asked, trying not to appear too interested.

While he coasted along on his idling motorbike, he told me his name was Jim. He said he was a civilian contractor who had just gotten into town and didn't know anyone and was looking for a nice Vietnamese girl to show him the sights.

I answered that any bar girl would be happy to accommodate him and that the *siclo* drivers knew all the whorehouses in town. "You don't need me for anything," I said, sounding pretty snobby. "Besides, I'm late for work."

"Then show me where you work!" He gave me a handsome grin and gunned the motorbike's engine.

There was something about the man—not just his persistence, but his dark skin and handsome, almost-oriental features, perhaps, that made it difficult for me to shake him off.

"Okay, Okay," I said. "The Kim Chee casino. It's just ahead. Do you see it?"

"No—why don't you show me? Hop on!" He patted the seat behind him. Although it was not particularly wise, I was still a young girl and enjoyed having a handsome young man's attention again, so I got on and held myself against his strong body. He rang his motorbike's bell and we zipped off into traffic so fast it tickled my stomach.

We arrived at the casino a few minutes before my shift so my new acquaintance and I had a little time to talk. It turned out he was himself an Amerasian (his mother was Chinese, his father Irish) who worked as a civilian helicopter mechanic on contract to the U.S. Army. He had been in Vietnam a long time—almost two years—but this was the first time he had been assigned to Quang Nam. He had learned to shun the hookers and con artists in a new town and looked instead for sweet, attractive, local girls as his companions. I replied that I didn't know how sweet or attractive I was, but I certainly knew the local scene! Because Jim was soft-spoken and asked me lots of friendly questions, I soon found myself telling him all about my son and mother and the life I had led since coming to Danang. I told him I had learned, if nothing else, that a "regular life"—one with work and wages and self-respect—if not very glamorous, was for me.

For the rest of the afternoon, Jim watched me serve our mostly Korean customers and I rejoined him at his table to talk whenever I could. Because he was experienced—a "Cheap Charlie" who nursed his watered drinks and did not gamble—the pit boss began to pressure me to "get this asshole to spend some money or turn the table!" and get him to leave. I replied that Jim was a nice fellow on his first trip to Danang, but the pit boss didn't care. "Hunt for boyfriends on your own time!" he barked, and began to be rude to Jim as well as to me. Finally, Jim simply got up, took me by the arm, and hauled me into the street.

"What are you doing—?" I cried, startled. "I work here! You're going to get me fired!"

It was already dark and the prostitutes who worked "below decks" were ascending the stairs and giving Jim a good look.

"Good!" Jim said. He was a little high from his drinks, but his voice was firm and clear. "Look, I won't play games with you, Le Ly. I'm going to be in Danang a long time and want a woman to take care of me."

"Well, you better get busy looking!" I said, trying to pull away.

"Don't you get it?" he held me fast. "That woman is you. It's as simple as that."

I laughed at such a stupid idea, "You're a fast worker, aren't you? I mean—I just met you today, for goodness' sake!"

"Okay—" He let go. "If you want to spend the rest of your life serving cheap hooch to a bunch of ROKs who treat you like shit, that's your business. But if you come and live with me, I'll take care of you. You'll have a nice place to live and plenty of money for your family. You'll never have to work in a craphouse like this again. All you have to do is be my woman for as long as I'm here. If you don't like it, you can always move out—no big thing."

Although I was flattered by this bold American's interest in me, I was also disturbed. Things moved fast in wartime, it was true, but he was already talking to me like a husband or boyfriend, not a casual acquaintance or even a horny American pickup. Besides, I was still unsettled by my experience with Red. What if all American men turned out to be like him? What if I went home with this big handsome man and could not please him—in bed or out of it—and be the person he wanted? On the other hand, the situation at the casino was getting worse by the day. Could I afford to pass up such an easy way out?

"But I don't know anything about you!" I protested.

"Hey—what's to know?" He grinned like a wolf in the forest. "What you see is what you get!"

"Come on, Joe," one prostitute said, grabbing playfully at Jim's bottom as she went down the stairs, "I got hot pants for you, Joe! Come on—we party!"

"See?" Jim laughed. "What do you say?"

I couldn't help laughing too. "Okay," I said finally. "But we go slow—"

"Slow as you want—"

"And I don't want to be *left for laundry!*"

"You mean 'left high and dry'?" Jim laughed again. "Never! Here—" He thrust two hundred dollars into my hand. "You quit your job right now and use this money to find us a place to live—someplace sunny and nice where you'll be happy. Okay? Do you believe me now?"

The next day, I rented a two-bedroom house a block away from my old apartment on Gia Long Street. Our new landlord was a college professor who lived nearby, and both he and his wife welcomed us warmly when we moved in. Our first night together, in fact, was just like the honeymoon I had hoped for with Red—not an athletic contest, but a night of passion and caressing, tenderness and sighs. I sensed that what Jim wanted even more than sex was some kindness and gentleness in his life, and that all he said about wanting a woman to cherish was not just talk. In Jim, to my great and wonderful surprise, I had finally found a man who was as happy to simply hug a woman as make love to her.

A day or two later, Jim said he wanted to meet my son and mother, and again I could tell it was more than talk. Of course, I was thrilled that any man would take an interest in my poor fatherless baby, but, given my mother's attitude toward the invaders, I had never dreamed of actually introducing her to an American. However, Jim looked and acted differently from most GIs. Because he was half Chinese, his appearance was much like us, and I knew that would comfort my mother. Because he had been raised by an Asian mother, he knew how to act shy and humble when it was necessary—always good manners for a young man courting an oriental daughter. It was with great relief, then, when we finally spent an afternoon together with my family on the White Elephant Front, picnicking with other mixed couples on the sloping lawn. My mother not only seemed to tolerate my big American, but she actually let herself be seen in our company by the other Vietnamese. It gave me a feeling of such satisfaction and warmth that I couldn't express it to her, although I'm sure she could see how much better I felt not having to sneak around to see my man.

Over the next few weeks, Jim helped me buy some things for my mother's house and engaged a housekeeper at his own expense so that she would be relieved of all tasks except looking after my growing boy, whom he treated as kindly as his own son. He even purchased a "Fifty CC" Honda for me and taught me how to ride it. In return, I cared for him like a wife.

Quite often, I brought little Hung to our house for a day, a night, or a weekend. Jim paid to have his picture taken, played boy games with him, bought him American kid's clothes at the base exchange, carried him around on his shoulders, taught him words in English and in Chinese, and at bedtime told him stories about cowboys and Indians.

Because "Phung Quoc Hung" was difficult to pronounce and did not come easily to American lips, we began calling my little boy "Jimmy." It was a good American name, borrowed from a fine American man.

For a few months, my life with Jim was idyllic—or as near to that blessed state as I could imagine in a nation beginning its long slide into the abyss of a losing war. Then, all of a sudden, a sign that our life together—as well as the world around us—might be changing for the worse, came to me in a dream; one that repeated itself several nights, and sometimes even during the day as a startling vision:

I am a small girl lost on a busy street in a nameless city. Cars and buses and bicycles are everywhere, and people—lots of people—hurry to and fro but they have no faces. I am walking, quickly but not urgently, down the sidewalk. I stop and look in a store window. There is lots of merchandise in the shop—electrical, metal things that whirr and blink and buzz. I step back to see where I am—to see if this is where I am supposed to be going—and the reflection in the window is Lan. I know I am still Le Ly, but for some reason I look like Lan—complete with fancy hairdo and bug-eyed dark glasses and lipstick. I start walking again, only faster, and I gradually notice the crowd is moving with me. They are shouting—some people are crying—and everyone's excited, but I can't tell what it's about. Their featureless faces hide their true emotions. For a while, I am swept along with the crowd. It's moving so fast—like a river—I suddenly become worried that I will drown. Just as I am about to be swept with them off the curb into a dangerous intersection, a strong hand clamps down on my arm and pulls me back. It is a big hand—not chocolate brown like my father's, but pink and old with white hairs on the back. I feel grateful that this person, whoever he is, has saved me, but I still feel frightened and cautious. Because I am a little girl, my head only comes up to my benefactor's belt buckle. Strain as I might, I cannot see his face. The man's other hand points to a newspaper rack on the corner.

He says with a deep, garbled, dreamy voice, "See, Bay Ly? There it is! That's why everyone is shouting!"

I squint at the newspaper and try to read the headlines. The print is in Vietnamese, but the words keep changing as I read them—fading in and out like pictures on television, saying one thing then another. The harder I try, in fact, the harder it is to make sense of the paper. The big hand tightens on my arm and gives me a little shake.

"Come on now—you can read it!" the deep voice says sternly.

Although I still cannot read it, I gradually begin to sense the newspaper's meaning: The war is over! Wonderful news! The fighting has stopped!

"That's wonderful!" I say, and find that I can now see my benefactor's face. It isn't an old man, but my brother Sau Ban. He looks happy and rested, but a little out of breath. His eyes are mischievous and playful.

"Come on, Bay Ly—" He begins pulling me into the crowd. "We've got to go!"

Faster and faster, we move with the throng. Everyone's running now—top speed—and some people fall and roll along the sidewalk, but I still can't tell if they're laughing with joy or crying with pain. My brother finally scoops me off the sidewalk and onto his shoulders and we outdistance everyone on the street. I hear an airplane roaring overhead, then helicopter rotors, then car engines racing down the street. The car noise envelops me and I find myself sitting in a GI jeep, bumping along the dirt road going into Ky La. I look over to Sau Ban in the driver's seat, but it's no longer Ban, but Jim—big hands wrapped around the steering wheel, twisting it furiously, dodging potholes. Ahead by the side of the road, in front of misty village houses, I see my brother Bon Nghe, who looks just like my father; and Sau Ban again, waving us forward with a grin. My mother and sisters are there too, all clapping, as they would a racer approaching the finish line. "Look!" I cry out to them, standing and holding onto the jeep's windshield for dear life, "See what I've brought you—a father for Jimmy!" and I clutch the top of the windshield even tighter as we bounce and shake. I yell to Jim to slow down, but he just keeps driving like a mad man, faster and faster, bouncing and shaking and I wake up clenching my fists and grinding my teeth with my body sweating and trembling.

I looked down at the big hand wrapped around my arm and it wasn't white and old or brown, but young and strong—so I jerked away and sat up in bed fighting to catch my breath.

Jim sat beside me, hair mussed from sleep. Outside, the morning sky—orange and yellow and blue—gave a cry like a tropical bird: delivery truck horns and convoy motors and tug whistles from the river. It was half an hour before Jim's alarm clock was set to go off.

"What is it?" Jim asked. "That stupid dream again?"

"Yes." I felt embarrassed.

"Sure like to know who that white guy is you dream about! Sounds like you like him better than me!"

Jim got out of bed, slipped on his shorts, and began to dress for work.

It was March 1968. New Year's—the holiday of Tet—had just ended and the Americans in Danang were still celebrating the defeat of the terrifying Viet Cong offensive. Like many Americans in Vietnam, Jim had become a heavy drinker, and the surprise attacks throughout the country that winter had given them all the more reason to drown their fears in alcohol. Although Jim had often come home tipsy before the offensive, he now staggered back to the house barely able to find the bed. At these times I remembered my mother saying: "Talk to a wall before you talk to a man who's been drinking!" Little things set him off—made him lose his temper—and my suggestion that he cut down or stop drinking was always met with either sullen silence or wild accusations about my seeing other men. Of course, I was sure his problem was my fault. A Vietnamese wife, even an unmarried one, was always responsible for the happiness of her man.

One time, during an argument over a house key I had lost, Jim accused me of giving it to "a boyfriend." He got out the automatic pistol he always carried for protection and fired a couple of shots into the ceiling. Our landlord, the college professor who often looked in on us, rushed over and saw the damage, but decided not to make an issue while Jim was standing there with a gun. The next day, after Jim had gone to work, he came back and told me I should leave—that Irish-Americans were notoriously bad drunks and very dangerous. I replied that I loved Jim and could handle things all right. Nonetheless, the landlord must have complained to the police because I noticed their patrols came around our house more often.

One night late in March, after I had gone to bed, Jim came home from another drinking party. I woke up long enough to hear the door open and close and recognize his footsteps; but because I was exhausted from a long and busy day, I didn't get up and went right back to sleep.

The next thing I knew, I was fighting for air. Jim's big hands were wrapped around my throat—crushing my windpipe.

I thrashed my arms and legs, dug at his hands with my fingers, but could do nothing. My puny feet jabbed at his chest and belly and testicles, but his body was like concrete. All I could think of was my sister Lan and the close call we had suffered from another drunken, enraged American. Through my ringing ears, I could hear Jim shouting about the key and how unfaithful I had been. I don't know if it was because I was still half-drugged by sleep and had been dreaming again about the end of the war and the resurrection of my dead brother, Sau Ban, but I believed— while Jim was choking me—that I died. His enraged face dwindled down a long, dark tunnel and his shouts dissolved into the hum of a Buddhist mantra. I saw my soul slip through the tunnel toward a blip of light that grew more intense as I approached. All of a sudden, my rocketing ascent slowed, stopped, and I felt myself fall back. The warmth of the white light receded and gave way to coolness as my soul and body spread out together like a sheet on a shady bed. As I came to, Jim was splashing cold water on my face.

"Oh—thank God!" I heard him say. "I thought I had killed you!"

He caressed my face, then clutched my ragdoll body to his chest. He then made drunken love to me—although I could only lie there, dazed and exhausted, unresponding—then he passed out.

The next morning, as soon as Jim had gone, I stopped the first MP jeep I saw and told them what had happened. They drove me to a nearby station where I was examined by an American doctor and questioned by a dependent's counselor. He said very little but took lots of notes. When I had finished, he shook my hand and told me not to worry. Although American civilians generally did not come under the jurisdiction of the military police, he said that now, after Tet, a lot of rules had changed. He said the MPs would take care of everything.

That evening, while I was fixing dinner, Jim came home from work. As he approached the door to our house, two MPs stepped out from a jeep which was parked nearby and took him into custody. I ran out shouting, "No! Stop!" and begged them to let him go. I tried to assure them that I had talked to the counselor who told me everything would be all right. They told me they were only following orders. Jim didn't resist nor did he speak to me or look at me while I struggled vainly to pull him free.

The next day, I rode my motorbike to the MP station and asked to see "my husband," although I had no papers to show that Jim and I were married. All they would do was confirm that they had my man in custody. If I wanted more information, they said, I would have to come back later when the provost officer was in.

Returning that afternoon, the officer received me courteously and informed me that Jim was about to be deported to the United States.

"This isn't the first complaint we've had about him in-country," the officer said. "Not even the first by a Vietnamese woman. He's been examined by the post psychologist. I'm afraid he's just one of those people who can't handle himself in a war zone. I'm sorry."

"Well—" I asked, dazed, "can you give me his new address? Where are you going to send him?"

"I'm sorry, ma'am. I can only release that information to the next of kin. Do you have any proof that you're his wife?"

I returned to our suddenly empty house and tried to figure things out. While I was gone, the MPs had come and removed Jim's belongings and the rooms seemed barer and sadder than ever. The landlord was sympathetic and said I could stay until he found new tenants, but the memories were just too strong. I packed my few things, returned to my mother's house, and fired our new maid whom we could no longer afford without Jim's help. Within a week I was back in my old place, paying more rent than before I had moved.

Although returning to my family after previous bad experiences had always restored my spirits, this time I couldn't shake the blues. I don't know if I really *loved* Jim (at least the way I believed I had loved Anh), I certainly loved the way he treated me when he was not drinking: like a wife—with respect and affection for me and my family. I vowed I would never get involved with another man—American, Vietnamese, or anyone else—unless marriage was part of the plan. These fruitless affairs were bruising me inside and out and turning me into an old woman. Because marriageable men were so few and far between—especially those who were willing to love a fatherless stepson—I gave up any hope of having a soulmate in my life. Marriage, for me, was simply one more thing on the long list of things I would never have. Besides, with Jim suddenly gone, I had more pressing things to worry about—like finding a job and keeping my family off the streets.

MID-AFTERNOON, APRIL 9, 1986:
THE PACIFIC HOTEL, DANANG

It is close to three o'clock—forty-five minutes past the time I was supposed to meet my brother Bon Nghe and his wife for our first "official" reunion—when we finally return to the hotel. Despite the good vibrations after our happy, even tipsy barbecue feast, the old Mercedes refused to start and Tuan, the village-boy-turned-jungle-fighter-turned-mechanic was obliged to raise the hood and coax the rusty jumble of hoses and wires back to life. Tuan blamed corrosion and the *Ban Viet Kieu* guide blamed Tuan, but it seemed to me just another case of the physical world showing its indifference to Uncle Ho's totally planned society.

In front of the hotel, Anh and I get out, but Tuan stays behind the wheel nursing the engine, determined to avoid further embarrassment from his mechanical partner. I say good-bye to our guide, walk around the car, and lean into the driver's window.

"Good-bye, brother Tuan." I shake his hand warmly, giving him my biggest grin. "You'll get a new car to drive one day, I'm sure of it!

Someday you'll have a long line of Yankee tourists waiting to hear your stories!"

"I hope so, Miss Ly." He gives my hand an extra shake. "This really is a pretty place—a wonderful country. Maybe that's why the Americans hung around so long, eh? Anyway, you tell them we make better hosts than enemies. Tell them there are pretty dreams in Vietnam for everybody. Most important, when they come, tell them to ask for Tuan!"

I squeeze his hand and give him a pack of American cigarettes from my dwindling supply.

Inside the hotel, Anh goes to the lobby to wait and I am directed to a conference room for my reunion. The door opens onto a startling picture. A table has been arranged as if for a press conference—with a white tablecloth and chairs lined up along one side but not the other. The chair at the head of the table is conspicuously empty (apparently my place as the guest of honor) next to which Bon Nghe sits with his chin on his hands. A long-faced woman sits next to him; I assume it's Nhi, his wife. Whether her sad expression is habitual or just because of my tardiness is hard to tell. Next to her is a man in his twenties who looks strikingly familiar, and a younger woman sits next to him. There are other people in the room, too: a few waiters and men in suits, but they hover around the door and talk softly among themselves, going out of their way to appear uninterested in this strangely formalistic "reunion." As soon as Bon sees me, though, he stands up, as does everyone else at the table. I try to hide my surprise and confusion with a happy grin.

"Brother Bon! I'm so sorry! Our car broke down on the Cau Do bridge—" I cut my eyes to the party men superintending our reunion. I cross the floor quickly, then remember—despite the expected emotion of the occasion—that this is the reunion of a Vietnamese, not an American, family. I fight the urge to hug my brother, as I fought it originally, and stop to face him across the narrow table.

"I am your little sister, Le Ly—though not such a baby anymore!" I offer him my hand.

Bon Nghe glances at the approving smiles on the men behind me and shakes my hand like a salesman. "Bay Ly—you look wonderful. I am so pleased to see you after all these years. May I introduce my wife, Nhi?"

He passes my hand down the reception line to his Hanoi bride. I see now that the long face is just her usual look—serious, most of the time—though she seems to have found a weak smile for me. Standing, she is taller than I am, which makes her a good match for Bon. Her long hair is drawn tight into a bun above her fiftyish face and there seems to be not an ounce of fat on her body, even in places where it might be becoming. She wears a purple shirt and black pants which are nice enough to let me know she thinks our meeting is a special occasion.

"I'm so pleased to meet you," I tell her truthfully, and give her hand a special squeeze. Has Bon Nghe told her about our earlier meetings? I think so, for her eyes and hand reveal a warmth her face and voice reluctantly deny.

"This is a great occasion," she says diplomatically, if without much conviction. "We have so few visitors from the West. May I introduce you to our son, Nam, and his wife?"

She passes my hand to the image of my father in his twenties—a youthful, masculine face I never saw, but one that must surely stir my mother in her old age. No wonder she is so charmed by her grandson! And this handsome fellow with his firm handshake is certainly no boy, as my mother suggested. He confesses to be a recent college graduate, just married to the plain-faced girl in a white blouse and dark pants who bows at me from his elbow. Before we can really talk about anything, my brother interrupts us.

"Please, have a seat, Bay Ly." Bon points to the chair at the head of the table. We sit together and I look down the rank of anxious faces all staring at me expectantly. For an instant, I feel like I am presiding over the meeting of a family business that has had a very bad year.

"Oh—I almost forgot, I brought you a present!" I put the sack of leftover beef on the table. "It's good *bo thui* beef, eh? Just carved this afternoon. I thought your family would enjoy it."

"Oh"—Bon Nghe looks at the sack nervously, the way a guilty child eyes a switch—"that's very kind, but no thank you. Perhaps your niece, Chau Tinh, can use it."

I think of asking Bon Nghe if he would prefer a chocolate instead, but decide from the real discomfort on his face that it would be a very bad joke. From the expression on the other faces, however, I see Nam and his wife labor under no such inhibitions. I will offer it to them before I go.

"Well, now, you have to tell me all about your life, brother Bon," I say brightly. "You know, the last time I saw you, I was a very little girl and you were a very young man. Our mother cried enough tears to fill the whole Pacific Ocean during the years you were away."

"I know. It was a great relief to see her after liberation. Did she tell you the story of our reunion? It's really quite comical—"

And so my brother and I stage our reunion for the benefit of the officials who become increasingly less engaged by our conversation and more interested in the refreshments the waiters produce as we talk. Perhaps they are tape recording the event anyway to review at their leisure. In any case, the room quickly divides into two camps: the cluster of "escorts" who sit together by the door telling jokes, complaining, and talking shop; and this brand-new family which draws closer over the table with each minute.

"So tell me," I ask Bon and Nhi, "why don't you have a bigger family? Nam is a fine young fellow—but just one son? Is this the way of the new Vietnam too?"

"Children are very expensive," Bon says. "And the government discourages them. We already have more mouths than we can feed. When our country gets back on its feet—then, perhaps, people can think about big families. Until then, we'll all do the best we can with what we have. And Nam is as fine a son as anyone could want. You should be proud of him as your nephew."

I look the young fellow in the eye, "You know, you look a lot like your grandfather. Has anyone told you that?"

"Mostly Grandma Phung," Nam replies with a long-suffering smile. I suspect he hears that every time she sees him.

"I would like to get to know you," I tell him. "There are lots of stories about your family you should hear. Perhaps one day, you can take me to visit your grandfather's grave."

"One day, perhaps," Bon interjects. "Right now, Nam is interested in helping our people who were harmed by the war; to educate the peasants and get medical treatment for those in need."

"Is that so? That's a very big job. I've thought a lot about the same thing over the last few days."

"May I ask you a question, Aunt Ly?" Nam says.

Bon looks concerned but says nothing. This does not sound like part of the script they have rehearsed and I am pleased Nam is enough of a man to think and speak for himself.

"Of course!" I respond cheerily.

"We were all surprised to hear you had arrived. I mean—everyone knows you have a good life in America and Vietnam has pitifully little to show its visitors. Why would a rich *Viet Kieu* like you ever want to come back?"

I am not puzzled at all by Nam's question and, although a thousand answers leap to my brain at once, I am curiously tongue-tied. Has Vietnam gone so far down the road toward materialism—the very thing Bon Nghe and everyone else fought against for twenty years—that the magnet of simple family love has lost its power to attract even the most opposite of relatives? I cannot—will not—believe it has. In truth, it was the lack of that family bond in America, despite my three good sons—that put me onto that airliner in L.A. Jimmy and Tommy and Alan are all Americans—thank god—but I am something else: not quite Vietnamese anymore, but not so American as they. How can I find a way to tell this wonderful young man, this college-educated product of the new Vietnam and heir to my own Phung name, that my spirit, too, dwells inside him—and in the rocks and trees and paddies and summer rain outside? His question should not have been, "Why did you come back?" but "How could you stay away so long?"

"My—my family is here," I tell him with a sudden crack in my voice. "I have lived in America—and it's a wonderful place—but I could have lived on the moon and still been drawn back to the land of my father. I am not a spy or a politician, Chau Nam. I am not even a very good tourist. If anything, I am a pilgrim. Like everyone, I must come back to start again. Does that make any sense to you?"

Around the table, all the women's eyes are glistening. Bon Nghe shields his face so nobody can tell if he's overcome or not—that would be unbecoming. Only Nam seems composed, perhaps because his keen mind is absorbed by the puzzle this crazy foreign lady represents.

"Om bung ma khoc," Nhi says, smiling with a quivering lip, and covers my hand with her own. *Hold your stomach and grit your teeth,* she says —that's how Vietnamese women have dealt with such things from the dawn of time.

I can see now why my brother finds so many admirable qualities in this woman and why my mother sees Nhi as a threat to her privileged position with Bon Nghe. Nhi may be from the North, but she is Vietnamese through and through. Perhaps there has been another, hidden purpose for this odd, manufactured reunion. Perhaps the family being born today will wind up much closer than any of us suspect.

* * *

FORTUNATELY, one of the places I learned about while living with Jim was the American employment office in Danang. This bureau brokered the best wartime jobs in Danang—many of them for the military and the dozens of civilian contractors who supported them in the area. Although very few Vietnamese were allowed to apply for these jobs, even the lowest positions were safe, respectable, and well paid. As soon as I was able, I made an appointment, using Jim's name as a reference, with one of the job counselors.

The morning of my meeting, I fixed myself up in my best cocktail waitress dress and reported for my interview half an hour early. The American counselor assigned to see me was a young man, prematurely bald, who wore thick black-rimmed eyeglasses and a trim mustache—as if he hoped to regain by his stodgy appearance the air of authority his youth might otherwise deny him. He was very busy and gave me some forms to fill out, telling me to come back at noon, when he would have more time to talk. This seemed odd, since noon was the traditional American lunch hour and I could not recall a U.S. organization in Danang that did not honor it religiously—often stretching that one hour into two or three or a whole afternoon.

Nonetheless, I completed the forms as best I could (I read very little English—mostly street signs and stencils on vehicles, buildings, and crates—and had to ask a girlfriend for help) and returned at the appointed hour. When I arrived, most of the employees were out, except a couple of men playing cards at a corner desk. They gave me funny looks when I came in and told me to go directly to the counselor's office. Once there, the counselor acted completely different. He welcomed me warmly and took my hand in both of his and held it for a long time as he spoke. He offered me a seat on his couch (not the metal chair beside his desk which I had seen the other people using for interviews), closed the frosted glass door to his office, and sat down beside me.

"You're a very lucky girl to have been referred to this office," he began, removing his glasses and sticking them in his shirt pocket. The flesh around his small eyes looked soft and waxy. "And you're especially lucky to have come to me."

"Yes, that's what I understand." I tried to sound positive and enthusiastic despite the fishy way things were beginning.

"You know, you're a very beautiful girl. I don't think I'll have much trouble placing you at all. No trouble, that is, provided you play ball. You understand that American expression: play ball?"

"Oh yes," I laughed pleasantly, "play softball—like the GIs all the time! I don't know how, but I'm willing to learn!"

He gave me a sickly smile. "No, not baseball. What I mean is, ah"— he glanced at my name on the paperwork—"Le Ly—what a pretty name! What I mean, Le Ly, is that you scratch my back and I'll scratch yours. You're a big girl. I think you know what that means."

"No, I don't know," I said rather sharply. "If you want your back scratched, there are plenty of *siclo* girls for that! I came here for job. I'm a hard worker. And you said yourself, I look just fine. I'll do a good job for anyone!"

"Well, Le Ly," the counselor persisted, looking at his watch, "you'd better start by doing a good job on me. No big deal"—he began to unzip his pants—"we'll do it any way you want. You do your best; and I'll do my best. What could be fairer than that?"

I got up from the couch and went quickly to the door. At least there were other people in the office and I would be safe outside. Unfortunately, the doorknob simply rattled in my hand.

I turned and faced him, trying not to show how startled and frightened I was. "Okay, mister whoever-you-are—open this door right now! Right now, or I scream and you'll be looking for a new job too!"

The pink, smug face only laughed. "Hell, I don't have the key! Somebody must've locked us in! Go ahead, baby. Scream your head off. Maybe they'll come and rescue us!"

So that was it. The door *was* locked from the outside. The men at the table were in league with this nasty little man—all buddies helping each other to get their "rocks off" over lunch—to get a "nooner," a "quickie" from the stupid gook girl! That's why I was told to come back when everyone would be out of the office. He probably made bets with his buddies on how fast he would get under my skirt!

"Oh, come on, Le Ly." The counselor got up lazily, his penis peeking from his fly like a timid pig's nose through a barn door. "Don't make such a damn big deal about it! Just a little suck, eh? Who the fuck cares if—"

I had the back of the metal chair in my hands, pointing its four legs at him like a battery of guns.

"Now what the hell are you going to do with that!"

Instead of braining him, which is what I wanted to do, I swung the chair full force into the glass window on the door—shattering it to pieces. The chair swung back and I flung it at him, catching him off-guard. By the time he could deflect it and leap around his desk, I had opened the door from the other side and was running down the hall. In the main office area, the counselor's buddies were standing white-faced by their table, cards scattered all over the floor. Through the front entrance, the first wave of workers—including several women—were coming back from lunch.

"You hold it right there!" I shouted at the cardplayers. *"You"*—I pointed to the first woman in the room, stopping her in her tracks— "you call the MPs! Right now! That man tried to rape me!" I turned and pointed down the hall to the counselor, who was fumbling with his glasses in the doorway. He would have been wiser to have zipped up his pants. *"Move!"* I shouted.

The woman turned and ran out, calling for the police. The other new arrivals—all Americans—confronted my tormentor and asked what was going on. Within minutes, a pair of MPs and a Republican policeman were inside, along with the office manager. My fury now gave way to terror and despair. What chance did I have now of getting any sort of job with the Americans? And who would the authorities believe: an American in a responsible position or a little "zipper head" girl who broke their window and threw a chair at their counselor and was probably Viet Cong anyway?

I collapsed into a chair and started to cry, trembling all over. Some of the women in the office tried to comfort me—they must've thought I was a very delicate girl to come unglued over a mere close call when so many others were losing their lives in horrible ways every hour outside the city. Nevertheless, something inside me had snapped when I saw that little man come at me with his open fly and smug face. I just could not let him—let any of them—get away with it anymore. I would not be their victim, nor—if I had anything to say about it—would any other innocent girl. Too many nice Vietnamese ladies went looking for jobs to support their families while their husbands were away at war. Too many fell victim to slimy operators like this.

To my astonishment, the MPs did not just wink at the incident or arrest me instead of the man, but took my statement, name, and address, and led my assailant out of the building in handcuffs. I will never forget the look on that little man's face as he filed past, manacled like a criminal in front of his friends! As an even bigger and better surprise, the office manager apologized personally and promised to handle my placement himself. Within the hour, I was walking back to my apartment, still dizzy from my victory. That Americans could take the side of a poor Vietnamese girl over one of their own made that curious nation of barbarian-saints even more wondrous in my eyes. Perhaps, someplace in this cruel and dangerous world, justice *was* the order of the day, and not just the exception.

Evening, April 9, 1986:
On the Road to China Beach

My "reunion" with Bon Nghe went overtime, like my tour, and we are now late for dinner at Tinh's house; so Anh twists a few more rpms from the motorbike's straining engine and we zip faster through the balmy, darkening streets.

On parting, I offered Nhi some nice material for making clothes—part of the cache I had brought into the country as gifts. She declined it politely, on the model of her husband, and said Tinh, who had small children, probably needed it more. She said that, before Bon Nghe had confided about his wayward American sisters, she had been amazed at the sumptuous gifts my mother produced for her son—clothing and school supplies that had been made in the United States. Nhi supposed her mother-in-law had spent a lot on the black market for such things, but now she understood their source. "In no small measure," she said in a quiet voice, "you are partly responsible for Nam's fine education!" I shake her hand again, longing secretly to hug her tight and welcome her to the family. I thought again how proud of her my father would have been.

When it was time to take Bon's hand, I asked him if I would see him again on this trip. His eyes jumped to the officials who were rising from the table by the door.

"Who can say?" he answered with the hint of a smile. "Danang is not such a big city. People run into each other all the time." I thought I saw a wink in his blinking eyes.

"Very good," I smiled. "If not, I'll certainly see you on my next trip, only then I hope to be accompanied by lots of Americans."

"Veterans coming back as tourists?"

"Some. And others who simply want to see things for themselves—to make a difference—people who want to end the war and make a fresh start; people who want to make things better than they are. There is so much America can do to help Vietnam, Bon Nghe. I can't imagine that among our two hundred and fifty million people, we can't find a few who want to rekindle a forgotten friendship. Perhaps we'll build a clinic for the poor people of Danang. I used to work in a hospital—did you know that? A hospital would be a fitting place to start. Of course, we'll need some land—"

"If you can bring the Americans," Bon Nghe said, "we'll find a place to build their clinic!"

"And workmen to construct the building?"

Nam smiled with his father. "Look around you, Aunt Ly. If Vietnam has one thing, it's ready hands looking for a good day's work!"

"And a good day's pay," I added, smiling with them. "Don't forget, we capitalists expect to pay for what we get. Good wages for good labor, eh?"

It was all very brave and heady talk and I half believed it was going to happen. Of course, speaking positively of such things is the first step toward making them real. I still remember when it first dawned on me that I was actually going to America; and the day I told my boys—in no uncertain terms—that I was coming back to Vietnam. Nothing happens that is not imagined first.

After our farewells, I went to my room for a quick wash and change of clothes and now I am once again zipping down the street on the back of Anh's motorbike—sea breeze in my face like a mother gull returning to her nest. We pull up in front of Tinh's house, which is now so familiar it is beginning to feel like home, and her sons go screeching into the kitchen: "Bay Ly is here! Anh Hai is here! Come on, everybody—they're back!" It is a decidedly warmer reception than when I first arrived. Perhaps the neighbors have nothing more to suspect. Or, perhaps, we have all finally convinced ourselves that we have nothing in particular to hide.

Inside, my mother and Hai greet us and we sit down to Tinh's long-delayed supper of *mi quang,* chop suey, rice soup, spiced beef, boned chicken, and slivered pork. We have been gabbing for half an hour about our tour of the countryside (I don't mention the "carsickness" that almost made me a fugitive to Ky La) and my meeting with Bon's family when Anh reaches into his pocket and produces a little piece of paper.

"Oh, Bay Ly, I almost forgot. A *Ban Viet Kieu* messenger brought this to the hotel while you were having your reunion. I didn't want him to disturb you, but you'd better take it now."

Despite a shadow of worry that flits across my mind—an old reflex I must practice to unlearn—I accept the folded paper and open it quickly. Even if it is a command to *come to a meeting,* I now know I will now have plenty of allies around me.

"Permission is granted herewith," the little paper says, "for Miss Phung Thi Le Ly Hayslip to entertain her mother, Tran Thi Huyen, in her room at the Pacific Hotel, Danang, QN, on the night of 9 April 1986." It is signed, countersigned, and stamped by the appropriate functionaries and bears instructions for processing my mother at the front desk when we arrive.

"Mama *Du.*" I show her the note with trembling hands, tears of joy running down my cheeks. "I hope you brought your toothbrush!"

The purple lips widen over her toothless grin and everyone in my family laughs and embraces everyone else around the table.

The hotel room door opens onto Disneyland.

My mother, tired from the ride on Binh's bicycle, the bewildering paperwork at the front desk, and the short climb up the stairs, enters what is probably the first Western-style room she has visited since Lien kicked us out of Anh's house some twenty years before.

"Very nice!" she muses. "It still pays to be a foreigner in Vietnam."

"Look—over here." I guide my mother to the gift boxes I had arranged along the wall. "This is all for you—to keep or distribute as you see fit."

We squat down to examine the goods. Our hearts race like American kids on Christmas morning.

"Coffee!" I hold up a can of Folger's. "See? Smell!" I puncture the seal and the rich aroma fills the room like perfume. I imagine the housekeeper tomorrow calling maids from other floors to come in and take a whiff.

In other boxes I show her the rest of my gifts—lugged through the lobby at LAX, customs at Bangkok, and two disrepaired airports in Vietnam. Like us, they are veterans of a long and circular path to arrive at this moment. Material of different types and patterns; useful hardware like tacks and scissors; vitamins and aspirin and more, even a little lipstick and perfume. Except for a small sewing machine, there was nothing big or glamorous—just things Americans would use in the course of a normal day and any one of which, in Vietnam, would make a normal day exceptional.

"It's too much," my mother declares. "You must give these things to Anh. He has lost more than the rest of us, and has many more responsibilities. He deserves them more than we do."

I sit back on my haunches and regard my mother closely. "You care for Anh very much, don't you, Mama *Du?*"

"He risked everything to find me in '82," she replies, fingering the material wistfully. "And do you know what he talked about during the chicken feast Hai made? You. Yes—you and his son in America. Not about his problems under the new regime or the suffering he went through during the war or his divorce or what happened after liberation. His thoughts were with his number-two wife. That's right—*he* started calling you that, not me. Remember when people said I should sue him because he got an underage girl in trouble? They said I should go to a lawyer in Danang and insist on our rights. They said he'd pay twice as much just to keep his name out of the papers—maybe even take you back as a second wife, despite Lien's complaints—just to shut me up. But I told myself at the time: 'This is no way to solve Bay Ly's problem. To begin a vendetta against Anh would be to put a millstone around her neck that would follow her into her next life. If, on the other hand, I forgive Anh for his mistake and just do the best I can, Bay Ly and her boy will learn charity and forgiveness.' So that is what I did."

At this moment, I can almost hear my father's voice coming from my mother's mouth—so similar are her soft words to the last things my father said.

"Remember, Bay Ly," she continues, "it's easy to be charitable when you're powerful and rich; more difficult when you're weak and needy—

but that's just when it counts the most! So instead of sowing bitterness, which is what we would be reaping today, I sowed kindness, and you can see the crop we harvest. Like they say, *Mot cau mhin, chin cau lanh*! [One word of forgiveness brings back nine gentle favors!] Because we accepted Anh's wrong with compassion, his own heart was able to grow and he was here for you—for both of us—when we needed him. Anh *is* the Vietnamese husband you never had. He *is* the son-in-law I always wanted for you. We have nothing to regret."

My mother wobbled and collapsed against the wall.

"Mama *Du!* Are you all right?"

She grunted, "For a seventy-eight-year-old lady? Yes!" She stretched her legs out in front of her like brown twigs. After a moment, she said, "No, Bay Ly, I won't lie to you. Seeing you has been good for my old bones, but I know my time is near." She waved her fingers lazily before her face. "My color is changing. It started last year. I've seen it before in others. It's one of the signs. Look here—"

She bends forward and pulls up her blouse, exposing her back. The last time I had seen my mother's back, it was to scratch it as a little girl, when we would laugh and tickle each other after a hard day's work. Now her skin is paper-thin and has the texture of dried plaster; the farm wife's muscles atrophied over a rheumatoid spine and ribs. Beneath her bulky outer garments, she is halfway in her grave.

"Phong thap," she pronounces like a doctor. "Rheumatism. It's all that holds me together."

She pulls down her shirt and I take her hand and rub it briskly. "But you've got to stay healthy until I come back on my next trip! There's so much I want to do! So much I want you to see!"

The old hand relaxes in mine. She smiles and looks me in the face. "You've come back, Bay Ly, and that's what counts. You've completed your circle of growth—the karma that brought you into the world. If you come back again, it will be part of another, new cycle—not the old one. Your past is now complete. The war for you is over. My destiny as your mother is fulfilled. *Nuoc rong* to *nuoc lon,* eh?—low tide to high tide. Poor to rich, sad to happy, beggar to fine lady—you've closed the circle of your life. You may have a thousand returns and a thousand tasks yet ahead of you, but they will be to fulfill a different destiny. As for me, it will soon be time to rest. You ask what you can bring me on your next visit? Bring cement to line my coffin and good silk for my shroud so I won't get cold when they lay me by your father. I am content with everything else. I have no less now than I ever wanted." She smiles again.

"Who'd have guessed what those flirty glances across the fields to your father sixty years ago would have started, eh?"

"Come——" I pull her to her feet. "Let's rest on the bed. That's what it's for, eh? You've spent too many years sleeping on the ground. I want you to tell me about your life and our family and about me growing up."

I help my mother onto the bed and turn out the lights. We lie with the mosquito net drawn back and watch the wind come through the window. I take out the small, hand-held tape recorder on which I have been making oral notes throughout the trip. I change the cassette and turn it on.

"What's that?" My mother cranes her neck and eyes the machine suspiciously.

"It's a tape recorder, Mama *Du.* It's like writing without paper. I don't want to forget anything you say."

She lies back on the pillow and says nothing. After a while I ask, "Well? Aren't you going to talk?"

"I have gotten by quite well for almost eighty years without putting pen to paper, Bay Ly. I'm not about to start now, even with the help of that crazy writing machine. *Xa hoi van minh,* that's what it is! A devil's machine! If you want to remember something, you use your eyes and ears and nose. That's why god gave them to you!"

"Okay, Mama *Du.* Anything you say." I turn off the devil's machine and leave it for the future.

After a moment, my mother begins to talk and images of sunny paddies, a little girl chasing ducks with a stick, and a happy-go-lucky, artistic, loving brother carrying her on his shoulders fill the room. Old spirits, stiff from their graves, stretch and smile and glide with the living once again. My mother's voice grows softer, like my pillow, and the roar of the distant surf seems to call *Bay Ly, Bay Ly—my little peach blossom— why have you been gone so long?"*

THIRTEEN

Finding Peace

EARLY MORNING, APRIL 10, 1986:
THE PACIFIC HOTEL, DANANG

I AWAKE WITH A CHILL. I had fallen asleep in my clothes outside the covers and the morning sun, shining hot on the buildings across the street, throws a glare through the window onto my face.

I roll over the empty space where my mother had been—telling stories when I went to sleep—get up, and pound on my bare feet across the wooden floor to shut the window.

My mother! Du oi du dau? (Where's Mama Du?)

I run to the bathroom to look for her, but she is not on the toilet or (unlikely as it would be) in the shower. Panic fills me to the eyes! Has she wandered off—tried to walk home—and been mugged or picked up by the police or fallen ill with a stroke or heart attack or god knows what and is now lying dead in a ditch or suffering alone by the side of the road?

I fumble to put on my shoes and skid around the end of the bed on my way to the door, almost stumbling over the sleeping form at my feet.

"Mama *Du!*" Hai I cry, bending over to rouse her. "What are you doing down here? Are you all right?"

The ancient eyes blink and the betel-black lips smack and tremble. With great effort, the pencil-thin arms lift my mother's frail torso against the bedpost.

"Is it morning already?" she says, yawning and stretching like a skinny cat. "Seems I just got to sleep!"

"Mama *Du*—you mean you spent the whole night on the floor?"

"No, of course not!" She scowled at my silly question. "Only when I wanted to sleep! That Western bed is so damn uncomfortable! I don't see how you can stand it!"

I help her up and notice that, despite her spartan habits, she had used a piece of material from my gift box as a pillow. As I ease her toward the bathroom, I see that the contents of the other gift boxes had been opened too, probably in the dead of night, and sorted through, caressed, sniffed, and enjoyed, before being put back in their places. *If you want to remember something, use your eyes, ears, and nose, as god intended.*

My mother completes her brief morning routine—relieving herself awkwardly at the odd European-style toilet—and is ready for breakfast. I, on the other hand, hurry through showering, picking out clothes, brushing my teeth, fixing my hair, and putting on light makeup, all under her amused and watchful eye; feeling more like a little girl than ever. I finish in fifteen minutes—a new record—but I can see her shaking her head as if lamenting how many sweet potatoes I could have picked in the same amount of time. Some things about Westerners, I can tell from her expression, will always remain inscrutable to her oriental mind.

After a quick noodle breakfast, I lug the present boxes and my two main suitcases downstairs and load them, along with my mother, onto a *siclo* and give the driver directions to Tinh's house.

"Okay," I say, rubbing and patting my mother's cool hands to give them warmth, "I'll see you this evening for dinner. Anh has invited me to meet some more people today and I don't want to disappoint him. We go back to Saigon tomorrow."

"This is your farewell dinner, then," my mother says.

I am silent a moment, then answer, "Yes, I suppose it is. It would be nice to see Bon Nghe again; to have my family together one last time before I go."

"I'll see what I can do," she says like a *Ban Viet Kieu* official.

The *siclo* rattles off and I return to my room. For the first time since I arrived, I begin to feel the pangs of parting—worse even than the phantom fears of my arrival. Like any pinnacle of pleasure, this is a place—a feeling—I can enjoy only briefly. A sunset is pretty, but the sun does set. A sunrise may be inspiring, but it gives way to afternoon. Fate or luck or god has delivered me to my relatives safely, closing the first great circle of my life, and I feel an immense mountain of peace rising inside me. But to rise above the surface of my life, that mountain of peace must break ground. The happiness of reunions and comfort of new wisdom must be accompanied by the pain of parting—or rebirth—so that I may begin another cycle of growth. Where that cycle will lead me, god only knows.

Of course, even this most sublime pleasure is not perfect. I did not see my sister Ba, so long out of favor with my mother and the family she nurtured, and was nourished by, during the war. Despite the new tranquillity in my soul, I regret that I must quit a battleground where old wounds still beget new ones. In a field of unfolding flowers, there are buds which are ripening still.

Anh arrives within the hour and soon we are tooling through town on his trusty motorbike. Our first stop is the *Ban Viet Kieu* office to confirm tomorrow's departure for Saigon. Unlike the sunshine of the past few days, however, the morning has turned cloudy; ebony and gray presaging rain. Perhaps the Central Coast itself plans to weep with me at my departure.

After completing our chores downtown, we go to a house where some of Anh's friends have gathered for lunch. It is a big house in the part of Danang where I had been accosted by youths and nearly raped in 1966. What was then a fashionable, isolated neighborhood (Called *bai bien thanh binh*, "peaceful beach" in those days) lived-in by upper-crust Republicans and American civilians, is now weedy, disrepaired, and barren. Our hosts, too, show evidence of their decline. According to Anh, they were once proud landlords renting homes to rich Americans, profiting—at least a little—from the machinery of war. After 1975, when the new Communist government took all they owned, the couple was forced back to "honest labor." Unlike Anh, they became so bitter and full of distrust and misery and unreconcilable hate that after a few short minutes visiting them I find my head is splitting and my stomach is tied in knots. In a wartime Vietnam dominated by profiteers and a bumbling, if well-intended American giant, people like these ruled supreme. They preyed on the hopes and fears of those less fortunate, less cunning, less resourceful, and by doing so only accelerated their country's slide into defeat and despair. When the circle of that old life closed and a new one began under the Communists, they had no ability—or desire, most of them—to cope with their new situation. The ghosts they created in the war came back to haunt them—to join hands and imprison them in their own bad karma. What they harvested from those years now sticks to their plate like bitter fruit. Although I had met none of these people before this afternoon, I—like anyone who lived in those times—already knew them better than I should.

* * *

A DAY OR SO after my unfortunate episode with the employment counselor, I went back for my interview with the office manager and was told I would have to produce something called a "birth certificate" before I could get a job with the Americans. When the nature of this document was finally revealed to me, I went home and asked my mother for a copy of mine.

"A piece of paper to prove that you were born?" my mother responded incredulously. "Don't be absurd! Just tell them to take a look at you— flex your muscles—poke them in the eye if they think you're not alive! Birth certificate! Hah!"

"No, Mama *Du,*" I replied, "you don't understand. They want a paper to know I am a good citizen, and not Viet Cong. Proper citizens are given papers to show when and where they were born, and who their parents are. I have to have a birth certificate if I am ever to work for the Americans!"

Of course, my mother was not sympathetic to this goal. To achieve it, I needed help from someone who understood the government bureaucracy and the way its paper machinery worked. The only person I knew who fit this bill was our landlady, a wealthy Vietnamese woman named Hoa, who had first introduced me to the legalisms of daily life when I signed a lease on the apartment I rented for Red.

When I called on "Sister Hoa" (as she liked to be called), I felt like I was petitioning a great dowager empress or queen of the witches. Her house was large and filled with servants and expensive American goods. She wore elegant clothes and tons of makeup that made her look more embalmed than beautiful. At first, she simply shook her head and said there was very little I could do. She said I would need the help of influential people, and that such help would be expensive. Even the normal processing of paperwork these days had become time consuming and costly; for someone who needed something special—something purchased through the "back door," like replacement of a document which never existed— the price could be enormous.

Still, I realized this costly piece of paper was the cornerstone of my escape. I told her to speak to whomever she had to in order to obtain the certificate—that price, in my case, was no object. At best, it was a promise to spend all my savings if that was necessary—many peasants had caches of gold buried around the countryside and the rich city middlemen were always alert for opportunities to get their hands on some of it. At worst, it was a wonderful bluff; and I hoped Hoa, as a fellow black marketeer, would appreciate it and give me some kind of discount. Nonetheless, I was told to gather what would become the first of several large cash payments and wait at home to be contacted.

A few days later I was surprised by a knock on the door. It was a plainclothes policeman wearing a pirate's black eye patch. Because I still had the habit of giving new people I met nicknames to help me remember them, the image of a "Rogue Elephant" immediately popped into my head. (In Vietnam, a one-eyed man is compared to an elephant with one tusk—he usually lost it in a nasty way and tended to be very mean as a result.) Because the man was overweight, too, I had two folk-reasons to distrust him. Also, he was not the local patrolman whom we had been paying for extra protection, and this made me triply suspicious. Perhaps our policeman had been killed or transferred and this was his replacement, showing up to shake us down. Perhaps our landlady had turned me in, or given my request for back-door documents to the wrong people. In any event, despite my usual contempt for the corrupt civilian police, I knew I must be careful.

"Phung Thi Le Ly?" the officer asked.

"Yes, that's me!" I smiled, putting on my happiest waitress face.

"Come with me—" He turned to leave. I saw he had a motorbike parked outside.

"Wait," I protested. "What's wrong? What's the charge?"

He stopped and smiled. "You need replacement documentation, is that correct?"

I didn't know what story my landlady had given her contact, so I said, "Yes—why do you ask?"

"Well then, you'll need fingerprints and snapshots, won't you? And who takes fingerprints and mug shots? The police department, that's who!" he laughed. "Come on, little lady, shake a leg. I've got other things to do than fuss around with a pipsqueak who can't hold on to her papers! And by the way, I was told you'd have your fee ready for pickup—in small bills."

"Of course!" I grabbed my shoes and paper bag filled with *piasters* and followed him to the street.

Chatting on the back of the motorbike, on our way to Hoi An City, which was where his headquarters was located, I learned the policeman was a senior official with the chief district office and so was in a good position to do favors for important people—and a few not-so-important ones who were prepared to pay the price. He hated the Communists, though, and was quick to point out how many Viet Cong he had caught, tortured, and killed since the war had come to Quang Nam. He was no stranger to the My Thi prisoner camp, either, and boasted that his last victim, a woman prisoner not much older than myself, had hung herself with the drawstring of her pants rather than face another of his sessions. "If it weren't for this bad eye," he said, "I'd be with army intelligence —you can believe it!"

All I wanted to believe, of course, was that my own past connections with the Viet Cong would somehow escape this man's notice, or that he would not suddenly recognize me as one of the girls tied to the antpole at My Thi!

Inside the headquarters I was photographed, fingerprinted, and given a stack of forms to fill out.

"You seem very nervous," the old policeman said. "Don't worry. You're in the safest building in the province. The damn Viet Cong could never get in here. Who knows—you might get to like our little outfit. If you're looking for work, I could put in a word for you myself. We could use a cutie like you to dress up the place!"

"No—no, thank you," I smiled graciously, just wanting to get out of there. "Guns make me nervous!"

I entered my birthdate, December 19, 1949, on the last form and slid the stack of papers in his direction. I thought he was going to make a pass at me or maybe even take me back into a cell and have his way with me, but instead he simply put the material in an envelope and drove me back to my house.

For the next few days, I could hardly eat or sleep out of fear that someone processing my application would recognize my name or picture and remember me from my previous arrests. But such was not the case. Even if it did occur, it may not have mattered. The department's security was as lax as any I'd seen and the cash payment I had already made should have been more than enough to grease the slippery chute of corruption for quick passage of my paperwork. Three days after my trip to Hoi An, the policeman called again.

"Happy birthday," he said, smiling cruelly below his patch. He held up an embossed certificate proving that I had been born on *May* 10, 1950, in the province of Quang Nam. I laughed inwardly at the bureaucrats' imcompetence and thanked them silently for the extra months of youth they gave me. I made my final cash payment—which he would presumably share with Sister Hoa—and tipped him a few bottles of scotch and several cartons of American cigarettes for his trouble. I'm sure he would have stayed and caused me trouble if little Hung hadn't come dashing into the room with a dirty bottom making noises like a tank.

With a new identity to match my new image, I was now able to obtain a job as a cocktail waitress at the U.S. Army Officers' Club near the My Thi camp. Unfortunately, because of the club's location, there were few customers—most of the officers preferring the bigger O-club at Danang. Even worse, what customers there were were usually helicopter pilots and doctors who acted very snobbish: their good educations making little country-girl waitresses the last people in the world they would talk to. When it was apparent that the low volume of business meant the tips as well as the company would be bad, I asked the employment manager for a transfer to the bigger, busier Navy Enlisted Men's Club just across the street.

Because the EM club was in a secure area, all the girls who worked there were brought in by truck in the afternoon and removed the same way at night when their shift was over. Although the place was hopping all the time, with good tips and lots of friendly sailors, it was located right next to the My Thi Hospital and our breaks were spent outside watching helicopters come in with allied casualties—soldiers mangled like hamburger from the front. As if this wasn't bad enough, the bodies of some of those who did not survive (along with the amputated limbs of those who did) were cremated at odd hours during the day and night, and the wrenching black smoke sometimes descended on the club, emptying it of everyone except the staff, who, because we were cleared only for that area, were obliged to stand fast. Still, it was good pay in a safe place, and I had long ago come to realize that death—in all its forms—would be a constant companion as long as I remained in Vietnam.

One day I was early for the bus and stopped for coffee (an American taste I had acquired—my mother and Sister Ba still preferred tea) at a sidewalk café near my apartment. While I was sitting there, a jeep with a single occupant passed along the crowded street, stopped, and reversed in my direction. The driver parked illegally on the street a few feet from my table, and gave me a big, impudent American smile.

When he got out, I saw he was a U.S. Air Force officer—a short, stocky fellow, but very attractive. When he spoke, it was with a broad Texas accent that held a kind of musical humor I never heard in an American voice. He asked what a cute little "thang" like me was doing stopping traffic like that, and I was so charmed I could not refuse when he asked to join me.

We chatted awhile and I learned his name was Paul, a second lieutenant on his first tour in a nice, noncombatant job in Danang. I told him where

I worked and that I would like to talk longer, but the Navy truck had just pulled up and it was time for me to go. He asked when my shift was over and promised to come by and pick me up—sparing me the ride in the "cattle car" with the "ordinary" girls. I was very flattered by his flowery talk and teasing attention and amazed that an American officer (even a junior lieutenant) could be interested in a little ignorant peasant girl from the country.

Over the next few months, I saw Paul often, usually on dates after work or on the afternoons when we were both off duty. Because of my bad experiences with Red and Jim, though, I tried to keep him at a distance; partly to ensure that I would not be taken advantage of or made a pawn in some game I did not understand, but also for fear of losing him. When I finally had the courage to make love with him, I was surprised by his gentleness and by the way he continued to accept me for myself. Perhaps this was because he, too, had been raised close to nature—on a ranch with lots of livestock, open air, and fierce weather that reminded men just who they really were compared with the forces that had made them. Once, after he had received a letter from his parents telling him his favorite horse had been injured and put to sleep, he wept the same way I did when my family's water buffalo had been hurt and butchered before its time. He never said if his family ate the beloved horse, but I assumed they did because I could not believe that, even in America, so much meat would be left to waste. Perhaps the death of his beloved pet, coupled with the loss of friends around him every day, made him look at life a little differently, because not long thereafter, he suggested that we move in together. It was clearly not a proposal of marriage, but by this time I had so completely despaired of finding a husband that the thought of enjoying life with a man who—if not willing to become my husband, would at least allow me to be a wife—was impossible to resist.

By this time, too, my mother had accepted the fact that I, like Lan, was hopelessly involved with Americans and did not fight my decision to take Paul into my apartment on Gia Long Street. I assured her I would continue to pay for her house and food and other needs and would come to see her and my son every day before I went to work.

For several weeks, this new arrangement worked well, though I was surprised at how much time Paul spent at work, or on the road as his duties demanded. He kept very few things at my apartment (which only had cold water and a "walk out" toilet anyway) and preferred to shower and dress and keep most of his belongings at the base where he worked. Nonetheless, we spent most nights together and he would get up and go to work like a regular husband. Although he always treated me with kindness and love, I drew ill-disguised disdain from the neighborhood Vietnamese with whom I came in contact. They were quiet enough when Paul was around, but with another American following so close after Jim, they considered me anything but a lady, regardless of Paul's rank, and snubbed me on the street, in the market, or when I called on tradesmen for this or that.

Still, I felt like a queen—a woman of stature who deserved respect for her officer-consort; a woman who could wake up in the morning and look forward to—and not dread—the day that lay before her, knowing that a kind and caring man would be beside her when she lay down again for sleep.

After a while, though, Paul began complaining about my job. He didn't like my socializing with other Americans "now that I was taken" and grew angry whenever I accepted a ride home from the club, even when it was for my own protection. When I confessed this problem to an older girlfriend at work, she knew right away what was wrong.

"He's a short-timer, child," the waitress said. "He's got all the signs. He's about to ship out for the States and doesn't know what to do with you."

"What do you mean? Do you think he wants to get married? To take me with him to America?"

"Maybe. Or maybe he's just figuring out a way to dump you without getting mud on his pants. Let's face it, to most American men, we're *thay ao,* eh?—shirts they change when it suits them."

"But Paul's been good to me," I protested, "He cares about me, really!"

"That only makes it worse," my girlfriend said. "It's always hardest for the nice ones. That's one time, honey, when you'll wish your guy was a shit. With an asshole, at least you always know where you stand: at the bottom of the heap; with the rest of the dog shit on his shoes!"

That evening, I asked Paul when his tour of duty would be over.

"What kinda question is that?" he replied, looking very hurt. "You gett'n tired of me?"

"Oh no—of course not! It's just that you're acting funny. Everybody says it's because you're about to ship out."

"And who's everybody?"

"Nguyen, at the club. She says she's seen it before."

"Well, y'all tell Nguyen she don't know what she's talkin' about! As a matter of fact, I just re-upped today. That's right! I extended another six months, so nobody's goin' nowhere! I'll be right here till New Year's. Now, how does that sound, baby doll?"

I gave him a big hug and told him he was the most wonderful man I had ever known—American invader or not.

Things couldn't have been going better when one morning, a week or so later, I got up to make Paul's coffee. That day, he had gotten up early and put his clothes on quickly—his dress blues, which he seldom wore —and said he would not have time for breakfast. He came into the kitchen, gave me a long kiss, and held me tight for several minutes—I almost thought he wanted to go back to bed!—then left without saying a word.

When he didn't come home that night, I wasn't especially worried. He sometimes traveled from the local area and if things ran too late, or if the roads were unsafe, he would sleep over at one of the American bases and hitch a ride on a helicopter the next day. When he didn't return the next night or the next, however, and did not send a message to tell me why, I began to worry.

I stopped to sort things out at the base where Paul worked. I asked for Paul's supervisor, an American captain, but the officer was out. Finally, I found a clerk who handled the American payroll.

"Lieutenant Rogers? Don't think he's around anymore but I'll check—" he shuffled through some folders. "Reassigned Stateside. Last duty day was Tuesday—the lucky bastard! Sure as hell wish it was me. Why do you ask?"

I went down the street to meet my bus in a daze. I felt like crying, but could not. First, it would be unseemly; I would look like a refugee, or worse—like a girl with a broken heart—and I was too proud for that. Second, I had decided after Red and Jim that I would not cry for myself as long as I was whole and healthy, let alone over a man. Against my better judgment, but with a heart filled with hope, I had risked my feelings on Paul—staked my happiness on his honesty. Now that it had fallen through, who had I to blame for my disappointment but myself? Certainly, I was not the first Vietnamese girl to be abandoned by her American boyfriend, nor was I likely to be the last. In a way, this idea comforted me greatly. Through love, even for a while, I had found a way to rise above the misery around me. If I could forgive Anh for abandoning me with a baby, Red for changing me around to suit his tastes, and Jim for almost killing me, how could I be less charitable to Paul, who had left me with nothing worse than pretty memories? Perhaps he had a loving wife and kids at home I didn't know about. How could I fault him for going back to his family? And even when I put myself in his wife's position, could I blame him for trying to find peace and comfort in the middle of a war? No—of course not! I decided I should draw the strength of compassion, not the weakness of bitterness, from this most important lesson—from the lessons I had learned from every American that fate or luck or god had sent to be my teacher. Even at their worst, each one had given me something which, to that time, I had lacked in my life. I understood the choices I had made—and the things that resulted from them. What happened had been as much my doing as theirs. For a Vietnamese woman, realizing this was like emancipation to a slave. Hating people who had wronged me only kept me in their power. Forgiving them and thanking them for the lesson they had taught me, on the other hand, set me free to continue on my way.

Over the next few months, I became friends with other American GIs and civilian workers. Although I had many offers to go out, I refused them all, preferring instead to nourish my spirit with my mother and son; and to enjoy family life with my sisters, Ba and Lan, and even Hai on the few times she came up from Ky La.

Of course, Lan pressured me at once to find another American boy-friend. "Don't you remember how happy you were with Paul?" she reminded me, "and all the good things you used to do with Jim? A good woman needs a good man. These days, American men are best!" Although the first part of her argument made sense to my mother (who wanted me to find a Vietnamese stepfather for my son), only the last part made sense to me. The only Vietnamese women leaving the country these days were those with American sponsors, and my policy of keeping the invaders (emotionally, at least) at arm's length seemed only to work against my ultimate goal of finding peace and safety. Still, I had no desire to risk my feelings again, even as bait for someone who could accelerate my escape. It was a riddle that twisted me up inside, so my solution was to put it out of my mind.

On my day off one Sunday in April 1969, while I was driving my Honda down Doc Lap Street on my way home from breakfast, a bar girl whom I had met at Lan's flagged me down. She was an older woman —well past her prime for the kind of work she did—and had lots of children to take care of, including one that stretched her belly below her dress. When I stopped and looked around, I saw she was accompanied by a ruggedly handsome older fellow—an American about fifty or sixty years old wearing a clean white shirt and expensive slacks. They approached me and she introduced the man as "Ed"—a civilian contractor on his first extended holiday after five months in Vietnam. He was tall and white-haired with big hands callused from a life of outdoor work.

"He's a supervisor for RMK," she said in Vietnamese, "you know—the American construction company. He makes a lot of money and is looking for somewhere to spend it. His buddies from work told him to go to Hoang Dieu Street and find a local girl to shack up with, but you know the area—it's full of bums—he wouldn't last an hour! He's really a nice old gentleman. I was just wondering what to do with him when I saw you ride by."

"What do you mean?"

"Look, he wants to meet a nice Vietnamese girl, right? I can't take him home—I mean, look at me! Besides, the last thing I need to worry about now is another man. Just take him out and show him a good time, that's all. He already gave me some money for introducing him to you. I can't afford to give it back. Please help me out, Sister Ly, won't you?"

I looked up into his face. Unlike younger Americans, who would've been impatient with our incomprehensible chatter, Ed simply lit a cigarette—apparently willing to wait us out no matter how long we took. His eyes were kind and wordly—like a village elder—and his voice, when he responded to my friend's request for a smoke, was as soft and deep as music in a Christian church. Still, he was old enough to be my father.

"No!" I replied. "I don't do that kind of thing anymore. I have bad luck with men, you know that. Bad karma!"

"Look, Le Ly—he's already given me the money to fix him up. I can't give it back! I've got nine kids! I need the cash!"

"I'm sorry," I smiled at the man, then revved my motorbike.

"Wait," the woman persisted. "Let me tell him you agreed, okay? He'll give me the rest of the money he promised, then *thoi minh di!*—[We take off!] He can't run after both of us; and if he chases me, so what? I mean—look how old he is! He's deaf in one ear and he smokes all the time. He'll be out of breath by the end of the block. What do you say?"

I had no desire to cheat this nice old man, even if he was a stranger, but I felt sorry for Lan's friend as well. She did have hungry kids to feed and with her fading looks and failing health, her days of earning anything, let alone the good wages of a tea girl, were probably numbered.

"Okay," I said finally. "Tell him I'll go out with him, then get ready to run."

The woman smiled her most innocent smile, said something softly in Ed's ear, and the poor man peeled off a slew of American greenbacks. But when the old eyes fell on me again, they almost broke my heart. Far from containing lust, they showed only loneliness; and endless yearning for something—for companionship, for understanding, for peace of mind—all things I felt myself when Paul walked out the door. When the woman shoved the wad of bills in her purse, I suddenly feared I would not have the courage to twist the throttle.

"Okay," she said in Vietnamese, snapping her purse, "let's go!"

She darted instantly down the street in the direction I had come. Ed looked after her, startled, and called her name with his deep, melodic voice. I wanted to stay, but when I saw the big hands close involuntarily into fists, I took off in the opposite direction.

Although I didn't—dared not—look back, I could hear his shout— more hurt than angry—followed by the slap of his heavy shoes on the pavement. He had chosen to chase me—perhaps because the other woman had already turned a corner; or perhaps, because I was the merchandise he had purchased.

As I buzzed through traffic, nimble as the thief I had become—dodging vehicles and pedestrians and animals—I became aware of everyone staring at me. It then occurred to me that a policeman or MP or QC might be alerted by Ed's shouts—they were all over the place—and that I could not afford to stay on this busy street much longer, even if the old man ran out of air. I also decided I could not return to my apartment; my pursuer must not find out where I lived. So, a few blocks away, I parked my motorbike and ducked into the café where I had met Paul.

A few minutes later, while I pretended to drink coffee from a table that had not been cleared, I saw a *siclo* containing the old American pass slowly down the street. *So that's it—the clever old man hired a pedicab to catch me!* This put a new wrinkle on my problem. Most of the pedicab drivers were street-smart, local boys. They knew the neighborhoods and most of the people in them. I knew lots of drivers myself. If Ed gave the fellow a good description, he might even go directly to my apartment. In any event, given enough money and determination, the old man could hover around for hours. Fortunately, I knew the café's proprietor.

"Do you have a back door?" I asked. "That American outside has been bothering me—following me around all morning. I'm frightened."

"Do you want me to call the police?" the owner asked.

"Oh no. He hasn't tried anything yet. I'm just worried. I want to get home without being seen."

She showed me the kitchen door that opened onto the alley. I made my way past the stinking garbage and rats and cockroaches to a sidestreet and skulked back toward my apartment. When I arrived, the *siclo* with the old gentleman was waiting in front of my building. I stopped, startled at first, then resigned myself to the inevitable. The odds say I should have escaped him easily, but there he was, so I was obviously up against something more formidable than the law of averages. I also had a very guilty conscience. Besides, the police station was right across the street. If he tried anything physical I would have more help than I needed with a single scream. (The local policemen had been looking for an excuse to beat up one of my American boyfriends anyway!) And, if he tried to turn me in himself, what would be the charges? I accepted no money; the other woman, not me, had cheated him—and he had no idea what we talked about. Anyway, there was no place to go, even on my motorbike. Should I lead him to my mother where he could humiliate me in front of my family? No. It would be much wiser and safer to put an end to things now: to march right up and apologize and take whatever lumps I had coming.

To my surprise, Ed only smiled at me—like a father pleased to see a wandering child come home.

"So," I said, "you found me! Good for you!" I tried to make a joke of it. He paid his *siclo* driver and followed me to the door of my building. "I'm sorry we pulled that dirty trick on you. I told my friend I'm not the girl for you, but she wouldn't take no for an answer. She was afraid you'd take back the money you had given her. So you see, it was all just a bad mistake. I'm sorry."

He stood dumbly as I turned the key. I was not about to invite him in. "Yes?" I said, hugging the door. "Is there something else you want?"

"Of course. That's why I'm here." His tone of voice was curiously mellow—not at all like a man who'd been cheated of money and *bum-bum* in a single stroke. I didn't know quite what to make of it.

"Look, I told you," I said, "I'm not interested in being your girlfriend—not for a day, a week, or an hour. If you want a girl, there's lots of hookers around, so don't bother me, okay?"

Ed laughed gently. "I'm a little old for hookers. I just wanted to meet you, to talk to you. I'm not worried about the money. Your friend introduced us and that's all I wanted. She didn't cheat me. Now—since I've gone to all this trouble—may I come in and talk to you for a moment?"

The last thing I wanted on my day off was a pesky visitor, but I had caused him a lot of trouble and he at least was being nice about it. Perhaps he had earned a little kindness.

"Okay, but just for a minute. And I'm going to leave the door open. One funny move and I'll scream for the cops—they're right across the street, you know. I'm a good girl!"

"I know," Ed said, "and a very beautiful one, too!"

Hoa's tenement apartment—at least the one I could afford to rent— was a studio off one of the building's larger units. Except for cold water in the kitchen, I didn't even have my own bathroom. Paul never really liked the place, so I was sure this older American would hate it even more and want to leave as soon as he saw it. I sat down on the edge of the bed and he pulled up a beat-up wicker stool which was the only other place to sit. We stared at each other for about five minutes. I was a terrible hostess and offered him nothing; no conversation—not even tea. After a while I said:

"Okay, thank you for the visit. I have to go see my sister now, so good-bye and I hope you enjoy your stay in Danang."

"I'm quite comfortable, thank you. I'll be happy to wait for you until you come back."

"Oh no. I'll be gone many hours—"

"That's perfectly all right. I have no place to go. Besides, I gave most of my money to your friend. I don't think I could even afford a taxi to get out of here. I could go to a bank and get more money, but to tell you the truth, I'm kind of tired from our little race."

Now I really felt bad—but not bad enough to encourage him.

"Okay. You can rest here for a little while—but then you have to go. Please lock the door behind you when you leave."

"Perhaps we can have dinner tonight—?"

"No. I always have dinner with my sister. I'll be back very late."

"That's no problem—"

"No, really," I was up and almost out the door. "Just lock up when you go. Nice meeting you. Good-bye."

I went directly to Ba's and then to see Jimmy and my mother. It was around eight o'clock in the evening when I finally got back. With great relief, I saw that the front door to my apartment was closed.

I went inside and started to undress. I washed my face in cold water at the sink and snapped on the single bare lightbulb overhead. To my astonishment, a big male figure sat up blinking in my bed.

"Hi!" Ed said casually. His voice was thick with sleep, like a hibernating bear. "I hope you don't mind if I stretched out for a minute. That little stool got kind of uncomfortable."

"What?" I said, almost shouting. "You're still here?"

"Well, you said I could rest. And I do want to take you to dinner, to thank you for your hospitality." He swung his legs over the side of my little bamboo bed, which creaked almost to breaking under his great weight.

"Oh no. You don't understand! I don't want to go to dinner. I already had dinner with my family—"

"Then we'll go for a drink. Or just for a walk, it doesn't matter to me."

"No. I want you to go. You're a nice fellow, Ed, but you can't be my boyfriend. I don't want another boyfriend—"

"Do you have a boyfriend?"

"No—no boyfriend. I already had an American boyfriend and I don't want another!"

"I'm sorry. It sounds like he must have hurt you very much." Ed got up and smoothed the wrinkles in his clothes. If he was going to jump me and pull me into bed, I supposed he would have done it by now, but his old bones creaked almost as loud as the bed frame. It was only then I remembered that I myself was half naked. I put on my blouse quickly and pushed my hair behind my ears. It was late and I was too tired and grumpy to feel sexy or clever or even particularly nice. *What did this old fellow want, anyway?*

"Yes," I answered, going back to the sink to finish my wash.

"I beg your pardon?" Ed said, turning his good ear toward me.

"I said yes—my American boyfriend—he hurt me a lot. But he made me happy, too, so I guess I came out even. Look, do you want me to give you some money for a cab?"

"No, thank you. I'm perfectly content right here."

"I know, you sure seem to be. But this is my house. If you want a woman for the night, I'll have a *siclo* driver fix you up."

"I told you, I'm not interested in prostitutes. I'm interested in you."

I sighed into a towel as I dried my face. What was I going to do with this funny old man? Ed's voice came from the other room.

"Is this your little brother?"

"What?" I peeked around the corner. Ed had picked up a framed photograph of Jimmy—taken by a sidewalk photographer one day on a picnic with Jim.

"I asked if this handsome little boy was a relative. Your brother, maybe?"

"That's a picture of my son."

"Oh—" Ed's face lit up like a grandfather. "Of course—he looks just like you! Lots of spirit in the eyes! He's okay, isn't he?" Ed looked suddenly worried—and for a kid he'd never met! "I mean, he's not—"

"No, he's fine. He lives with his grandmother. I told you, I'm a working girl. I can't stay home and take care of him."

"Oh, I see. Well, I'd like very much to meet them one day!"

Ed put the picture down—carefully, like the treasure it was. I still had no idea what this strange, sad, kind old man was about, but I was beginning to realize he was different from the younger Americans I had met. All of a sudden, an old Vietnamese saying popped unbidden into my mind—one that my mother used whenever a young village girl, usually a widow, took up with an older man: *Chong gia vo tre la tien ba doi* (An old man with a young wife has an angel to warm his bed), meaning that their progeny would be blessed by heaven for three generations.

"Ed—that's your name, isn't it?" I walked into the room slowly, drying my hands. The sad old eyes looked up at me like those of a sleepy hound. "I'm sorry, I haven't been a very good hostess. Would you like to have some tea?"

For the rest of the evening, we talked about my family and his work in Vietnam and how Americans and Vietnamese either got along or didn't and how crazy the whole thing was. It got very late and everything began to blur—my hopes for an escape and all the things I had done to achieve it, some of which I wasn't very proud of, running together with my confusion and reluctance to trust any more American men. In the dim, stark light of my bare little room, this big, kind man stood out like a snow-capped mountain: laughter rumbling like wind in a cave, long arms swaying like branches of a grandfather tree, and I felt as if I had been caught in an avalanche: a flood over which I had no control and no longer had energy left to fight. I said I was tired and wanted to go to sleep, but quickly added that he was welcome to stay the night rather than risk robbery or worse in the street. He got up like a gentleman and looked around for a place to nest.

"Here—I'll sleep here on the floor," he said, and I believe he meant it.

"Don't be silly," I said in small voice. "It would be disrespectful of me to allow that. You may share the bed with me, like a good Vietnamese family, eh? I know there is room for two."

I made love to Ed that night, but not out of passion or of pity. It had been an odd chain of events that had brought us together, and I felt that somehow it would have been disrespectful of fate—maybe even sacrilegious—to further resist the forces that pulled us together. The next morning, however, I dressed quickly, made coffee, and woke him up. He didn't say much—old bears start slowly in the morning!—drank the thick, sweet Vietnamese coffee gratefully, and we went our separate ways. I assumed that, having gotten what he was after, he would never return. Although I certainly didn't love him, or even like him very much, the idea of not seeing him again made me a little sad. I was surprised, therefore, when he knocked on my door the following Sunday—his arms loaded down with bags.

"Ed!" I exclaimed. "What a surprise! What's all this?"

"Just a few things for you and your family," he said. "Come on inside. We'll have Christmas—New Year's—all over again!"

He had purchased expensive packaged food and toys from the PX, but I was not ready to go through all this again. For a Vietnamese woman, having an American boyfriend might be like going on holiday—but all holidays have their end. I grabbed the muscled, hoary arm and turned him around.

"No, Ed—please!" I said. "You musn't do this. You can't—"

He only smiled, "Oh yes, I can and I must. Look, Le Ly, I'm not very good with words. Even if I spoke your language, I don't think I could tell you what I feel. I just want a little peace and happiness, okay? I just want to be with you and help you—and your little boy and your mother, too—as much as I can. Is there anything wrong with that?"

"I'm sorry, Ed," I said, wishing my English was more fluent, too, and up to the task ahead of me. "I don't want to hurt your feelings, but I don't want to be your girlfriend. I don't want to be anybody's girlfriend, okay? Your presents are very nice, but I don't want to be kept. I told you last night, I have bad luck with men—I have bad karma, do you understand?"

Ed laughed, "Bad karma? How much can have happened to a pretty little girl like you?"

"Don't ask!" I tried to push him toward the sidewalk and send him back the way he came. I didn't want things to go any further. "Goodbye, Ed. You're a nice man. You deserve a nicer girl than me!"

"Wait, wait." Ed spun around and planted his feet. "Listen, I know all about karma. Mine has taken me all over the world for most of my life! That's why I'm here, Le Ly—here with you right now. It's time I put my life in order. Do you know I have a son older than you—a navy man—stationed right now in the Mekong Delta? Am I supposed to compete with him for adventures and girls and tall stories to tell my grandkids? It's time for me to settle down, Le Ly—to quit pretending I'm going to live forever. I've got another year in my contract and then I'm going home to San Diego—permanently. I've got a nice house there and I've decided I want a wife to share it with me—a good oriental wife who knows how to take care of her man. Le Ly: I want you to be that woman—to come back with me to the States. If you'll have me, I want you to be my wife!"

EARLY EVENING, April 10, 1986:
AT TINH'S HOUSE IN CHINA BEACH

Tinh and I prepare my farewell dinner while Bien, Anh, and Bon Nghe—who arrived openly this time—chat over beer in the front room. My sister Hai sent her regrets, being unable to leave the farmhouse unguarded for the night (my mother's original excuse was true), sacrificing her own pleasure so my mother can spend this final evening with me. My mother, who had been baby-sitting with Tinh's kids, has gone outside with my oldest nephew. Although I regret to say it, I am glad she has stepped out—at least for a few minutes.

The afternoon with Anh's landowner friends left my stomach tied up in knots. It was as if all the progress I had made over the last few days —mastering baseless fears and finding peace—has threatened to come undone. For several hours, these cynical and unforgiving people served up to me the full harvest of their own bitter lives: jealously of relatives living in America; recriminations over their own past sins and missed chances; anger at the inept revolutionary government which took their property and forces them to live in poverty and isolation. To make matters worse, Anh seemed to prolong our visit, making sure I heard out each complaint and let every sick soul bleed bile over my own freshly healed wounds. It was as if he believed this long, tortuous afternoon was a necessary part of my education about this new Vietnam—that I would somehow come away with false hopes unless I was brought down to earth and shown the worms that linger in the foundation of his new nation. "There are," he seemed to be telling me, "such things as willing victims—people who participate happily in prolonging their own misery. You will have to remember that, Bay Ly, and account for them as well." I was so upset, I did not—could not—speak to him when we left. Only when we arrived at Tinh's and I saw my mother and brother Bon Nghe together did my waking nightmare begin to go away.

But my mother herself was preoccupied. Although, with the sad exception of Ba (and Lan, of course, who is safe in America) all of l her surviving relatives are around her, she still seems uneasy. I flatter myself to think her distraction may be because I'm going, but I doubt that is the trouble. She has lost loved ones before and knows how to handle it better than anyone. Perhaps, we both just need some air—some space.

So I stand in Tinh's kitchen, pulling lettuce heads apart and snapping the tails of scallions, fighting off the blues.

"The kids loved their presents," Tinh says, knowing I don't feel so good. "You were too generous to give us all those things!"

"Oh, you can thank my mother for them," I respond. "I told her to distribute them as she saw fit. She wanted you and Anh to share everything. Bon Nghe gets by okay with his government job and she and Hai need very little. I'm just sorry I'm so small and couldn't carry more!"

I notice that Tinh's final meal for me is quickly shaping up into a banquet. She stirs a cauldron of *ca kho*, salty fish soup filled with *mi quang* noodles; and begins to heat a big bowl of *bun bo* and *pho*—flat noodles and fatty pork, the best Danang can offer outside the black market—prepared Hanoi-style in honor of my brother.

"Okay," Tinh says, "you can call the men. We'll eat in a few minutes. Oh—and why don't you find your mother? The boys should come inside anyway; it looks like it's going to rain."

I tell the men, who are very mellow now from beer, to go to the table. Passing through Bien's darkened barbershop, I open the front door onto the street. A gust of wind blows trash along the gutter and the air feels heavy with moisture. A pair of streetlights, undernourished on their rationed energy—like everyone else in this town—gleam dully over the shanties across the street. The road is almost empty—a cyclist passes and rings his bell at some people crossing the street. There are three children in the group—two big and one small—and three adults: one couple and an old woman. The smallest child scampers ahead, running directly at me. From his voice I recognize Tinh's oldest son.

"Auntie Ly!" he shouts. "We're so lucky! Grandma has brought Auntie Ba for supper! Take a look!"

Sure enough, as the group gets closer, the houselights reveal a fiftyish woman with a delicate chin and long "Buddha" ears leading an older-looking man, thin as a rail, beside my mother. Ba's two children, both teenagers now, walk politely behind the rest.

"Oh—Bay Ly—!" A strangely familiar feminine voice calls out as the woman walks faster and opens up her arms. A moment later I feel Sister Ba's hands in my own.

"Chi Ba Xuan!" I cry, looking into a face that, like Hai's, is but an altered portrait of my mother. Only this time, the lines of wear and care seem harsher, turning the mouth down at the corners and knotting the space between the wide, sad eyes. Where sun and hard labor caused Hai eventually to resemble the land that had nourished her all her life, bad luck and suffering seem to have left their mark on poor Ba: etching deep lines of frustration, anger, and finally subjugation on her face—like a weathered rock worn down by rain and hail.

"Oh, you are so beautiful!" Ba says, turning me to the light. "Like Lan, you were always the pretty one, weren't you!"

"Not so!" I protest, turning to greet her husband. "Here is one person who thought you were too beautiful to live without! How wonderful to see you, brother Chin, after all these years!"

The old policeman extends a feeble hand which I shake warmly. *My god—he's a walking ghost! No wonder the Communists leave him alone: there's nothing left to harrass—or even bury!*

"Baby Bay Ly," Chin smiles politely, although he averts his eyes, "I remember you!"

He says it as if the act of remembering alone is an accomplishment—and I believe him. I hold his hand an extra second. "The farmer's life has been good to you," I lie, not knowing what else to say.

Sister Ba introduces her two youngest children, now both nearly grown. Like Bon Nghe's son, Nam—although not nearly so well educated, well dressed, and polished—they have the sheen of the postwar, post-liberation generation. They are better nourished and keener-eyed than the crop of wartime children and seem wonderfully free of their parents' scars. They have the rangy look of wild ponies who, thank god in his heaven, have yet to be broken, bitted, and ridden down by their fellow men.

"Come in, please!" I say, intoxicated with surprise and sheer joy. "You're just in time. Chau Tinh is putting dinner on the table!"

They file inside and I hear Anh and Bien and Tinh and Bon Nghe give them a cordial family greeting. Because she has lived most of her life as Ba's neighbor, I know Tinh thinks my family's feud with Ba is silly, as does Anh. Brother Bon, of course, follows my mother's lead and has his own reasons for keeping Ba and her ex-Republican husband at arm's length. It is an uneasy reunion, yes—one orchestrated solely for my benefit—but at least it's a reunion. A truce, if not full-scale peace, has finally broken out among these injured spirits. If my trip was the catalyst to make this happen, that alone is enough to call it a success.

My mother is the last one to come in. I stop her and give her a long, tight hug. "This is a wonderful surprise, Mama *Du,*" I whisper in her ear. "Thank you. *Thank* you! Now my visit—that life circle you talked about—is truly complete, eh? What a wonderful present!"

My mother shrugs. "It seemed like the right thing to do, Bay Ly. I got to thinking about it last night. I asked myself, 'What good does it do to teach Bay Ly about charity and forgiveness if you've forgotten those things yourself?' What an old hen I've become, feuding with my number-two daughter while my own life dribbles away—water from a leaky old jug! And what was I teaching Ba in the process, eh? How to hold a grudge? 'No,' I decided, 'that simply won't do.' So here we are. Your family's back together again, what's left of it—except Hai and Lan, but we'll set a place for them anyway, along with your father and Sau Ban. See what you've taught me, Bay Ly? That you're never too old to forgive people; that it's never too late to patch the dike and save a little more of whatever life's left you. Come on now"—she turns me by the arm and shoos me in like a little girl—"your family's waiting!"

FOURTEEN

Letting Go

FOR WHAT MAY BE the last time ever, my family gathers around me. Tinh's dinner covers the table Vietnamese style; and certainly, this gathering of the family I have traveled so far to see is a banquet for my eyes.

To make up for the private reunion we never had, Ba is placed on my right (my mother is on my left) and we begin gossiping like schoolgirls. Because we must get to know each other again, we start with easy topics: my trip into the country; what my sons are like; and what happened to old so-and-so (provided that person did not fall victim to the reeducation camps which claimed so much of Chin's spirit). While Ba goes on about this and that, working up the courage to say what's really on her mind, I study the men at the table. Anh, affable as always, balances the conversation between Bon Nghe, the Communist, and Chin, the Communists' former enemy. Maybe because everyone believes Chin to be a changed man after his imprisonment Bon Nghe doesn't mind being seen with him.

Or, perhaps, Bon's natural compassion has overcome the stigma normally attached to former Republicans.

Ba, however, is another matter. Her spirit is fully intact and, as Chin grew weaker after liberation, her strength increased. The more Ba talks, in fact, the more I get the feeling that her differences between our mother and Bon Nghe run deeper than a few purloined gifts from America.

". . . so you see," Ba is saying, "I can't think of one person who's better off since '75. And I don't mean just Mama *Du* and Hai, or people like me and Chin. Everybody's worse off, including Bon Nghe, if he doesn't mind my speaking for him—"

Ba trails off and cuts a glance at her slightly younger brother. It was the kind of gentle poke made often between children growing up, and I thought it was kind of funny—a triple play on words based on our family's peculiar situation: that a sister could speak in place of her brother, who was now head of the family; that a common citizen might speak instead of a party official; that one feuding family member might break the ice with another. Bon Nghe hears what she says but ignores her.

"Of course," Ba continues, louder than needed, "we were helped by the presents you and Lan sent from America. Chin was still away at camp and because I was related to a Republican, I was denied any state aid at all. I assumed nobody would mind my keeping them."

Bon Nghe gives Ba an irritated smile. "I don't think Bay Ly wants her last evening in Danang spoiled by our quibbling, Ba Xuan. Let's just enjoy Tinh's nice dinner, shall we?"

"Of course I'm enjoying dinner." Ba gives Tinh a lavish smile and shovels a bite into her mouth with her chopsticks. "I just want Bay Ly to understand my feelings, that's all. I haven't had as much time as the rest of you to visit with her, you know—to tell her everything that's happened. I was only invited to see her less than an hour ago! I want sister Ly to know how much we appreciate her presents."

"Well, then," Bon answers, rice sticking to his face the way it did to my father's when he was distracted at dinner, "let's put that issue to rest once and for all. I think Bay Ly's presents should have gone straight to Mama *Du* as soon as they got here. She's the one who should decide who gets what; not the first person who lays hands on them."

"Okay, that's fine. When things are normal, I agree. But those were not normal times, do you remember, Bon Nghe?" Like a fighting fish, Ba is not about to let go of the bait once she's provoked. "Who could count on getting what they deserved in those days? I'm not faulting Mama *Du,* of course, or sister Hai. It's just that everything was such a big mess.

You know I got very sick—I almost died!—while Chin was in prison. The kids did what they could to help, but they were so little. Frankly, Bon Nghe, I'm surprised you didn't take better care of everyone back then. After all, you were the party man. You were in charge of helping the workers—"

"You can't help people if there's nothing to help them with, Ba Xuan," Bon Nghe says.

"Ha ha!" Chin laughs like a half-attentive child just joining the conversation. Perhaps he really thinks Bon made a joke.

"That's just what I mean," Ba persists. "Isn't that the first job of any government—to see that people are okay? And if it can't do that, then shouldn't it just get out of their way and let them take care of themselves?"

"It's not as simple as that," Bon begins. "First, you have to—"

"All right, all right, both of you!" Our mother waves her chopsticks over the communal rice bowl like a conductor fed up with her musicians' squawky notes. "Everybody made mistakes, didn't they? So what's the point of digging up these old bones? Let's eat dinner!"

"Ba Xuan made her first mistake when she forgot which fowler tends the chickens!" Bon Nghe says, referring to sister Ba's divorce from her first husband who went north. It's a cruel thing to say, of course, but who can be crueler than a relative with hurt feelings? Besides, he is right. If Ba hadn't yielded to Chin's pressure in those days and stayed married to Moi, a man on the winning side—on the side her parents and village favored—she would have spared herself lots of trouble. Perhaps she would have, if her family had given her more help and braved Chin's threats. The idea that I, too, might have helped my sister more really hurt me, too—more than Bon's bad manners for bringing it up in the first place, especially with poor Chin present.

"There you go again," Ba says, more indignant than hurt, "talking like Chin wasn't here. I wish you'd be more considerate of his feelings."

"I sincerely apologize, brother Chin," Bon Nghe says, bowing at Chin over his plate. If he noticed that Ba herself impolitely referred to her husband only by his given name, and not with an honorary forename or number-name, such as Cau Chin, he did not point this out. Perhaps he really did mean to honor our mother's request and stop fighting.

"That's all right," Chin says pleasantly. He at least seems to be enjoying my banquet, although my own stomach is now full of knots. Perhaps it would've been wiser not to put Ba and Bon together. Perhaps I was too selfish for wanting it—wishing and praying for it in my hotel room every night; and my mother too indulgent for arranging it against her better judgment. *There goes spoiled baby Bay Ly again—wrecking everyone's evening!*

"Please, everyone," I say, smiling bravely, "it's silly to fight like this—"

"Who's fighting?" Ba gives me a charming smile. "Bon Nghe and I go around like this all the time. Don't worry about it."

"Even when they were children—!" our mother says, rolling her eyes.

"Well, there'd be less to fight about if the government had more co-operation and less criticism from our own people," Bon says. "I don't fault constructive criticism, of course; just all this complaining about how good things were in the old days. Well, they *weren't* so good in the old days! Even brother Chin will tell you that. Building a new nation is hard work—harder even than winning a war!"

"Well, if you ask me," Ba says, staring into her plate, "building a nation after a war like ours is like—like—well, I don't know. It's like trying to start a family by getting raped—"

"Aunt Ba!" Tinh says, gesturing to the children.

"Well—you know what I mean," Ba says.

"Why don't we ask Bay Ly what she thinks," Anh pipes up. Again he seems rather amused by this exchange. I give him a little frown. *Why do you keep doing this to me, Anh Hai?*

"Yes, Bay Ly," Bon Nghe agrees, "let's hear your opinion. You've seen both sides now—what both sides can do. Who do you think is right?"

"Well, if you really want to know," I say, wiping my mouth with a napkin, not really knowing what I can or ought to say, "I think neither side really knows what it's talking about. Even Americans don't really know what freedom means, although they live it every day. You, Bon Nghe, and you, Ba Xuan—you love each other dearly but you talk like you don't know what love is all about. Even me—I left on this trip without really knowing why I was coming back; I only knew I had to. You see? People are so stupid! We take all kinds of risks for good reasons we don't understand! Even Mama *Du,* god love her"—I reach over and squeeze her shoulder—"do you know what she told me to do when I got back to the States?"

"Eat more food?" Bon Nghe jokes. "Put on some weight?"

"No. She said to take care of my children—to educate them. And do you know how? By teaching them to be soldiers or politicians or farmers? No. Teach them how to forgive, Bay Ly,' she said. That's all. And do you think Mama *Du* knew all about forgiveness when she said that? Not on your life! She was still angry with sister Ba." I turn to my sister. "How easy do you think it was for her to ask you to come over tonight and see me?"

Ba shrugs.

"I'll tell you: it was pretty hard! You see, I think we are all used to putting labels on things we don't understand. Communists—capitalists —I don't know what these mean anymore. Are they people? Yes. Are they enemies? Well, yes and no. Bon Nghe, you're a Communist, but you're not my enemy. You might call me a capitalist, but does that make me your enemy? I don't think so. What do I really think? I think too many people in Vietnam and in the United States put labels on things they don't know anything about. You know, if you mix a can of soda made in the United States with a can of soda made in Vietnam, the liquids will blend just fine—they don't care which can they came from. A human soul is a human soul—regardless of the label we put on the bodies."

"But you can't deny people in Vietnam live in a Communist system," Bon Nghe says, "and the people in America live in a capitalist system. Those are important labels for both nations."

"No, brother Bon, if you'll excuse me, I disagree," I reply. "Those are labels we give to the *roof* under which those people live. You'll agree, a house is not the person, isn't that so? A person can leave one house and live in or visit another without cursing either the old house or the new one. The difference, I think, is that in Vietnam, people seem to have no choice about the kind of house they live in. They may want to fix the roof, but they can't do much about it, so they fight each other for a dry spot on the floor away from all the leaks. Should we condemn Ba Xuan for taking the bucket I sent in order to keep herself dry? I don't think so."

"Very well, then," Bon Nghe replies. "You say you want to build a hospital in Quang Nam, to help the poor people and victims of the war. That's all well and good. But how do you expect the Vietnamese in the United States or any other Americans to help you when they label everyone in Vietnam a Communist because of our Communist roof?"

"It's easy. I will simply ask them. You see, Bon Nghe, *they* have a choice about what they do. The people here do not. I will simply tell them: Our brothers and sisters under the Communist roof are in a dark age and need a little light. We in the U.S. can give them the light they need—at least a little more than they have right now. Why do you think the Statue of Liberty holds up a torch and not a moneybag or a pistol? I will tell them: Look, you don't have to make peace with the world if you don't want to, only with yourself; then let them decide."

"Then you have no guarantee things will turn out the way you want!" Bon Nghe says, slapping the table.

"Do you have such a guarantee now?" I ask him. "Do you think your son, Nam, will live his life exactly the way you want, even though you raised him the best you could? No, of course not; and neither will my sons. And, down deep, the Vietnamese in the United States realize the same thing. Even if some of them continue to fight the Communist regime and dedicate their lives to overthrowing it, do they have any guarantee that things would be better if they did? Look at all the Vietnamese who sacrificed their lives to establish an independent Vietnam. Do you think the country you live in today is the country they had in mind?"

After a quiet moment, Bon Nghe replies, "Well, people have to believe in something or they won't sacrifice today for a better world tomorrow."

"But what if that better world never comes, Bon Nghe? What if it only brings more revolutions and counterrevolutions and gulags and gas chambers from the enemies you overthrew? Hasn't that made the world a worse place and not a better one?"

"Then let me ask you a question, Bay Ly." Bon Nghe straightens his chair and leans anxiously over the table. "If neither communism nor capitalism nor any other kind of roof is going to make a perfect shelter for our people, if both have good things to recommend them and bad things to fix and both will always be at odds, then what are we to do? How are we supposed to choose between them?"

"That's easy too: we choose as we go along, little by little, the way our ancestors did living in the fields since creation. We take some of this and leave a little of that, knowing that if we try to make every day a feast, we will eventually starve to death. We compromise. We balance things out just the way nature tries to balance things around us. We take some liberties here and make things more equal there. We are strict about some things and show compassion about others. But most of all, it means letting go of all the labels that got us into trouble in the first place!"

"I suppose all that makes sense, Bay Ly," Bon Nghe says with a sigh, "but it's hard to imagine a nation sacrificing its wealth and its people for such beliefs."

"I know," I smile at my big brother, "that's the beauty of it, don't you think?"

* * *

I FOUND IT VERY HARD to concentrate at work after Ed made his proposal. He said that in return for marrying him and coming to America and taking care of him as his wife, he would see to it that I would never have to work again; that my little boy, Jimmy, would be raised in a nice neighborhood and go to an American school; and that neither of us would have to face the dangers and travails of war again. It was the dream of most Vietnamese women and the answer to my prayers—except—

I was still a young woman. The proper time to care for a sixty-year-old husband is at the end of a long and happy marriage, not the beginning. I knew I was attractive to young men and wanted a husband my own

344 • *When Heaven and Earth Changed Places*

age—as my mother and Ba Xuan and Sister Hai all had. On the other hand, I did not especially want to wind up like my sister Lan, who had many lovers, both Vietnamese and American (and now a child by one of them) and no prospects for marriage and a better life at all. Those friends in whom I confided about this problem weren't much help. Some were jealous of my golden opportunity to flee the war, or at least to enjoy the easy life of an American housewife. Others only riduculed me for even considering a union with someone old enough to be my father. It seemed an unsolvable dilemma.

Of course, Ed was as persistent as he was kind. Because I did not want to be disrespectful, I kept putting him off by saying, "It's too far away," meaning the idea was "so distant" that I didn't even want to think about it, although he took it to mean that I thought America was too far away, so he redoubled his efforts to assure me that it was a wonderful place to live. At the core of my problem, I knew, was the Vietnamese distinction between *duyen* and *no*—the components of marriage that every child learns when he or she becomes engaged. *Duyen no* together denotes a married couple's karma—the destiny they share and what they owe to each other to achieve it. *Duyen* means love—physical attraction and affection; *no* means "debt"—the duty that goes with the office of husband or wife. In a marriage without *no*, the flames of emotion run too high and the couple risks burning up in too much passion or despair. In a marriage without *duyen,* which is the union I would face with Ed, there would be no passion at all—no affection beyond good manners—and nothing to look forward to but the slow chill of a contract played out through all its clauses. Worse, marriages of *no*—quite common in Vietnam—often led to the abuse of one spouse by the other, through extramarital affairs, wife-beating, and the thousand other games perfected by cheated souls.

It took me many months to come to grips with this problem and learn my own mind. Young men, I decided, were for marriageable young women—not unwed mothers, black marketeers, and Viet Cong fugitives. By trying to do my duty to everyone in my life—parents, Communist cadremen, rich employers, corrupt officials—I had wound up failing in my duty to myself and the child of my breast, who depended on me. I decided to read the handwriting on the wall. Younger men valued me as a companion, an ornament, and a plaything—that was true enough; but not as a partner for their lives. And why should they? For any American to want me for a wife, he would have to have an extraordinary need—not for a party girl or bedmate or crutch to support his weaknesses, or for someone to help him pretend the times were normal when they were not—but as a companion for the completion of his own life's circle. For me to trust myself again to an American, that man must be such an extraordinary person. In Ed Munro, who was completely unlike the other men I had met in my life, perhaps I—and my fatherless son—had discovered such a man.

In August 1969, when Ed's contract in Vietnam was into its final year, I agreed to become his wife. It was a decision that turned out to be filled with many unexpected costs.

For example, instead of rejoicing wholeheartedly with me, my friends began to warn me about the many legal and practical roadblocks established to discourage Vietnamese-American marriages and emigration to the United States. To make matters worse, the detailed investigations that went into certifying every applicant for a visa made it almost inevitable that my previous arrests (for everything from aiding the Viet Cong to selling illegal drugs) would be discovered and I would quickly be branded an "undesirable alien." What such revelations might mean to my fiancé, I couldn't even think about.

Fortunately, Ed was a man of the world as well as a man of his word. He didn't ask about my past and said that as far as he was concerned, our new life began on the day we met and I could make of it anything I chose; that nothing in my past should stand between us and our future happiness. He said he would be willing to pay whatever was necessary to ensure that our paperwork was approved. Because he had never before dealt with the corrupt Republican machinery, he had no inkling of how costly this blank check might be. Because I had never tried to pull off anything this big either, I was in no position to tell him.

My first step, then, was to return to the landowner—the "dragon lady," Sister Hoa—who had helped me before. Our first meeting was not too productive because she only wanted to talk about the niceties of marriage and how wonderful life was in America; how happy she was that I had found a nice, mature American and how lucky I would be to live in Southern California. When we finally got around to talking turkey, I discovered this particular goose would take a lot of stuffing!

"What you want is very, very expensive!" she admonished me, as if she found the profit she was going to make distasteful. "You'll need permission from government agencies at the city, district, provincial, and national levels. You'll need a marriage certificate and favorable reports from both the Vietnamese and American counselors you'll have to visit. Do you plan to take your little boy with you?"

"Of course! He's my son!"

"That's too bad," she said, smiling pleasantly. "You'll need a birth certificate stating he's *con hoan*—a child without father—and we'll have to get an exit visa for him as well. Tsk!" She shook her head. "The best way to approach it is to tell me how much you and your man are prepared to spend, and I'll try to negotiate the best deal I can at each step, taking my fee from what's left over. That way, you'll know I'm not trying to cheat you."

"How much do you think all this will cost?" I asked.

"It's hard to say without knowing the problems I'll run into. When the war's going well, everything gets cheaper. When there's bad news from the front, everyone gets worried and wants more money for everything. I'd say the basic package should run about a hundred and fifty thousand *dong*—"

"I'll go to America with the caskets!" I start to get up. She was talking almost *double* the amount Ed and I had discussed. Even with my own savings, it would be impossible to pay what she asked.

"Hold on, take it easy!" She put her long-nailed fingers on my arm. "I said that's how much it *should* cost, not how much you will actually have to pay! Remember, you'll have *me* as your adviser. Now, let's talk things over like businesswomen, shall we? Would you care for some tea?"

By the end of the interview, we had agreed upon thirty to fifty thousand *dong* as a reasonable price—but this was for "guarantees" only, and did not include the official fees or gratuities (such as whiskey and cigarettes) that customarily went to decision makers at each level. Despite my earlier remark, I was glad I did not have to buy my way into the illegal transportation network out of the country, such as the occasional Vietnamese who, as rumors had it, rode empty American caskets to Guam or to the Philippines or Honolulu. Even an American's resources would be hard-pressed to fund such desperate and costly schemes.

While we waited for Sister Hoa to grease the proper wheels, I began to live with Ed—to become the kind of wife that he desired. At first, our jobs kept us apart a good deal of the time, which was okay with me. My shift at the Navy EM club ended about eleven, which was when Ed's night shift at the outlying camps was beginning. Although this didn't bother me at all (the idea of ministering to an old, fatherly man as a husband was still too queer to appeal to me), it was not what Ed had in mind for our relationship, so, shortly after we moved in together, he told me to quit my job. Ed's conception of a wife was not someone who worked shoulder to shoulder with her man "in the fields," which was the Vietnamese way, but a queen on a pedestal who spent her days at the beauty shop or overseeing the full-time maid he hired to do all the housework and so kept her long, red fingernails from getting broken. It was a curious role for Phung Thi women, who, for a thousand years, had never been without a day's work before them. Although I tried to please him and play the role he had in mind (idleness was infectious, I discovered—as though every day was New Year's!), I felt more guilt than pleasure. It was as if I had become Lien—an icy princess who seemed to have nothing better to do than read magazines and lord over her servants. Nevertheless, the gift of time was one I could now pass on to my son, and Jimmy began to rediscover his mother just as I began to rediscover what families were all about. Shortly after I accepted Ed's proposal, in fact, I was told by the doctor that my family was about to get a little bigger.

One Sunday, after my clothes began getting tight again at the belly, Sister Hoa came with the one-eyed policeman, an armful of papers— including a marriage certificate and a birth certificate for little Jimmy— and a justice of the peace, to the nice house Ed had rented. While we filled out the forms, Ed sent for his friends, who had agreed to be our witnesses, and told our maid to prepare for a little party to celebrate our marriage. To mark the occasion, I had borrowed one of Lan's fancy cocktail dresses, which (with a few pins and a short veil cut from a sun hat), I quickly turned into a makeshift, Western-style bridal gown.

Within an hour Ed and I were married in a civil ceremony. I had invited my sisters Ba and Lan to come, but they refused; so Hoa cried on behalf of my absent relatives. Although Lan's objections to my marriage seemed more to do with envy than principle (her American boyfriend, Robert, was a friend of Ed's and I think it nettled her that I received a marriage proposal first), Ba's complaints were more traditional. Custom demanded that a bride wait three years after the death of her father before she gives herself to a man, and even in wartime many people thought I was acting too rashly.

"Phan boi," Ba Xuan said one day after a particularly heated discussion of my situation. "You betray your ancestors!" She then sang a little song for my benefit, which I remembered singing myself with other girls in derision of a woman who left the village to marry a man in the city:

Da Da birds live only in Da Da trees,
They sing: Why do you marry and go far away,
Instead of loving a man nearby?
Your father gets weak;

Your mother gets old;
Who will be around
To bring them a bowl of rice,
Or serve them tea?

"Do you see now what you're doing?" Ba asked, genuinely concerned for my soul. "Americans are *thu vo thuy vo chung*—they have no beginning and no end. They don't care about their ancestors. Because they don't know what reincarnation is, they think they're free to do any cruel thing they want in this life—no matter how much it hurts others."

"Can't I be married to Ed without becoming an American myself?" I replied sincerely. "Can't I keep an altar in my house and pray to our father and to Sau Ban and to Grandma and Grandpa Phung, even if Ed doesn't believe in it himself?"

"Sure you can—of course you can—" Ba was really angry. "But secretly, he'll scorn you—and that scorn will come out later in cruelty and disrespect. I'm older than you, Bay Ly. I've been married a long time and know how men act. Why do you think all those little Amerasian bastards are shunned by our people, eh? Not because we don't think they're cute or need help, but because they're tainted with the invader's karma. You don't have to be Viet Cong to know that and hate them for it. Now you want your next child to become one of them! Honestly, Bay Ly—what gets into your head sometimes? And what will our mother think?"

That, of course, is what I regretted most: that my mother could not be with me anymore, even in spirit. Although I did not have the courage to speak to her directly about my plans, I believed the simple fact that I was marrying outside my race, let alone to an American invader, was enough to threaten her motherly love. Sadly, Lan kept me well apprised of my mother's black moods:

"Dua con hu, she calls you, Bay Ly," Lan told me shortly before the wedding. "A spoiled rotten child! She says you're acting ungrateful toward your parents and soiling the family name. She says that even though our father's dead, you have made him sad with your decision. It's not too late to call things off, you know."

I felt like challenging Lan—for her years of ignoring our customs herself and her own easy ways with Americans—but I knew it would be fruitless. Our mother usually sided with Lan because Lan had money and was a mature woman and was not the "baby of the family," which is how I gradually realized I would always be viewed, no matter what I did in life. Although Vietnamese are raised to respect their ancestors and love their nation, they are not above civil war. In the triangle formed by our family's sad situation—Lan's contest with me for our mother's affection, our struggle against the tide of a changing society, and our different feelings about Americans—I could almost see a fishpond version of the Viet Cong war itself. If I could not make peace with my family in such matters, how could the real fighters on both sides expect to resolve their differences?

When the short ceremony was over, Ed shook the officials' well-greased palms and complimented them on their sense of duty—working on a Sunday just to help an American get married! Their attitudes, he said innocently, were what Vietnamese-American cooperation was all about. We then had a fine party with Ed's friends, but they, too, left quickly, as if embarrassed by their old friend's child bride. Later, my little niece Tinh, Hai's daughter, came over with sweet rice to wish me good luck and tell me that she loved me. We hugged and cried and I told her I would never forget her.

Unfortunately, our quest, which had begun so hopefully, soon bogged down in obstacles thrown up by destiny or luck—or the government.

First, there was the problem of marriage counseling, a requirement mandated by the American consulate in Danang. Now that his own child was on the way, Ed said he wanted to adopt Jimmy, which was fine with the Americans; but the Vietnamese counselor—a short, fat, greedy woman about Ed's age—raised a long list of objections. While Ed was at work, I attended sessions with this woman and negotiated a price for each objection. Unfortunately, the more I paid, the more she wanted, and each dispensation cost more than the last. After several of these "conferences," I was running out of the money Ed allotted for our paperwork. (He gave me two hundred dollars a month to run our household, fifty of which went to pay rent. The rest was to buy food and wrap up our affairs with the government.) Because Ed didn't want me to work after we were married, I had nothing to draw on for the difference but my savings— most of which I had already given to my mother. For several weeks, the officials at the chief district headquarters dined well while my mother and Jimmy and I practically starved. Still, I made sure my husband never suspected our situation. His plate was always full and our refrigerator was always stocked with cold beer. I didn't want my American savior to know the depth of corruption into which my homeland had sunk.

Finally, just when the counselor was getting ready to sign our release, she paused, and said, "Oh yes, about my bonus—"

"What bonus are you talking about?" I asked, amazed. "I've already paid you almost every dollar to my name—including every cent my husband gives me to run our house. What more could you possibly want?"

"Oh, it's not for me," she said, as if she were asking for church donations. "It's for our 'coffee fund' here at the office. You know, we have lots of volunteers who come in and help us with our cases. We can't afford to pay them, so we offer them coffee and tea and meals when they work overtime—the way they had to work for your application. And you know how long *that's* taken us!"

I couldn't believe what I was hearing. "So—how much coffee are we talking about?" I asked guardedly.

"Well, to tell you the truth," she gazed pensively out the window, tapping her yellow teeth with the end of a pencil, "cash loses its value quickly these days, have you noticed? Even American greenbacks. I was thinking more in terms of merchandise—something that holds its value. You know, like diamonds—"

"Diamonds!"

"Now, don't get excited." She opened her desk drawer and produced a page torn from a Sears catalogue. "I don't mean raw gemstones or anything like that. Just something nice that will keep its value better than paper money. Like this nice diamond watch, for example"—she pointed to a pretty lady's watch on a much-handled page—"or maybe a nice dinner ring—like this!" While she shopped from the catalogue, I wondered how many other poor applicants had spent their life savings just to furnish this greedy lady's home, wardrobe, or office on the eve of their departure. We finally decided that a genuine pearl necklace would be just what the volunteers needed for breakfast, so I used up my last favors from old black market partners and obtained one for half-price. I had now completely exhausted my reserves and prayed there would be no more surprises. In the world's shortest adoption ceremony, I slid the black velvet jewelry case across her desk, received Jimmy's papers in return, and was out of the office before the price could go up again.

Unfortunately, like a frog trying to jump from a table by leaping half the distance remaining on each try, my victories always fell just short of my goal. When I brought the signed papers back to Hoa, she informed me that my plans had hit another snag.

"Of course," she said, as if it were nothing, "we'll need your mother's signature. You're still under age, and even if you're married, you'll need your parents' consent before leaving the country."

Up to this point, I had been able to avoid the whole issue of what to do about my mother. As far as she was concerned, Ed was just another

American "boyfriend" (marriage to an outsider was not valid in her eyes) and my life and future, whatever they would be—as well as the life and future of my son—would always be in Vietnam. Although I knew my mother must eventually learn what was going to happen to me, I was not so sure that I had to be the one to tell her; or that she should even know before I left. Now, my procrastination had caught up to me. I would have to be either an exceptionally brave and honest daughter or a very skillful liar. Like many young girls that age, I decided to be the latter.

"Here, Mama *Du,*" I said casually, shoving a form and a pen at her one day after lunch. "You have to sign this."

"What is it?" I knew she couldn't read or write, although, like many peasants, she had been taught to make her mark when it was required on legal papers.

"It's nothing; just an application for a bank account. You've probably wondered where all our savings went, right? Well, I deposited them in a safe place. What if the house burned down? All our money would go up in smoke! With my second baby on the way, I have to be more responsible."

She looked at the mysterious form a long moment, and for a guilty instant, I thought that maybe she had learned to read and would discover what I was up to. As independent as I had become over the last few years, I knew I could never stand up against my mother if she made a really big fuss over things. If the choice came down to leaving the country or destroying my mother's love for me, I knew I would have no options—even if it meant raising a hated Amerasian baby as an outcast among our people. Fortunately, I had a lifetime of peasant's habits on my side.

"Okay, if you really think it's wise." She made her mark and gave me the form. "I still wouldn't trust anyone outside the family with my money, though. Why don't you just give it to Uncle Nhu's son? He's helped us before—"

I gave her a long, tight hug and kissed the top of her graying head. "Thanks, Mama *Du.* You won't regret it!"

On February 11, 1970, my second son was born in a clean hospital run by Americans for U.S. dependents. Although Ed already had two grown sons he greeted the arrival of this new spirit like a brand-new father. He passed out cigars to his friends and told them how proud he was of "Thomas"—a good Christian name for a strong and spirited little boy.

Alone in the hospital room, I sang a song of welcome to the little soul I called "Chau"—one who was destined to wander—who lay nursing at my breast:

> Go out every day and you will learn,
> Each step that you take will make you wiser.
> Go here, go there, go everywhere—
> How can you be smart by staying home?
> In the world you will find many nations
> And many people all over the land;
> You'll cross deep oceans and tall mountains,
> And roads that crisscross the sand.
> You'll find people that come in four races:
> Yellow, white, red, and black;
> You'll float through the sky in four directions:
> East, west, north, and south;
> But you will never know all these things, my son,
> Unless you get out of your house.

When I got out of the hospital, my mother came to stay with us at Ed's house and help me through my period of *buon de*. Although Ed always tried to treat her kindly, she was content to behave like a servant when he was around—grunting only when spoken to and showing indifference to his favors. She was mostly concerned about how little Tommy (she always called him Chau) would get by when the war was over. If the Communists won, she knew his invader's blood—*con lai*—would put all of us in danger. If the Republicans won, she knew that same foreign blood—his light skin and American features—would cause him to be shunned in the village as soon as the Americans withdrew. As a result, she spent hours pressing his nose against his face, hoping to flatten it like a Vietnamese. She fed him dark juice and rubbed the juice on his body and kept him outdoors in hopes that his skin would darken like ours. I didn't know if these things would work or not, but I could see in them the desperation that was rising inside my mother; desperation that made it harder for me even to think about telling her the truth: that Ed and I and my two fine boys would one day step on an airliner and, very likely, never be seen by her again.

A few months after Tommy was born, Ed's overseas contract expired and it was time for him to return to the States. The plan was for Ed to go to San Diego first and prepare his home and local relatives for our arrival. After seeing him off at the airport, I moved my things to Lan's apartment where I would live until my own departure, now less than a week away.

During my last few weeks in Danang, when word of my marriage spread through the neighborhood and I dealt with people as "Mrs. Ed Munro" rather than Phung Thi Le Ly, the world around me began to change. Certainly, I was the same person I had always been, but now I was labeled in a different way. I was no longer completely Vietnamese, but I was not quite American either. Apparently, I was something much worse. Even people I had expected to understand me, to be sympathetic to my dreams, looked down on me and called me names—not always to my back: *Di lay My! Theo de quoc Ve My! Gai choi boi!* Bitch! Traitor! American whore! During many endless hours spent standing in line or sitting in waiting rooms or by desks of minor officials, I found myself on the receiving end of dirty glances from Vietnamese clerks, secretaries, errand boys, and janitors. No citizen of Danang was so poor or humble that he or she was not superior to Le Ly *Munro*—turncoat to her country. Teenagers and a few Republican soldiers who lived in our neighborhood gave me cat-calls and sang derisive songs when I passed and, on two occasions, threw stones at me when I appeared on the street alone. In one instance our home was broken into, burglarized (which was understandable), and vandalized (which was not).

Even people who forgave me my new American name could not excuse me for accepting an older man as my savior. On many occasions Ed and I were openly cheated—charged two or three times more than even the black market price for food or supplies—just so people could show us their indignation. It seemed as though the more we accepted their wrath, the more contempt they showed us. In private conversations, I was often pleasantly (and sometimes not so pleasantly) reminded that in America, people hated anyone—even other Americans—who came from Vietnam, and quoted the war protestors' slogans. They were a gallery of sullen, unforgiving faces that I often saw in my sleep: tattered victims on Vietnam's foundering ship of state watching jealously as I abandoned them for the lifeboat of America. I was experiencing, I discovered, not only what foreigners had faced in my own land for generations; but the ultimate price of my own independence. It made Sister Hoa's demands seems paltry by comparison.

In any event, after paying more bribes to obtain my passport, I was finally ready to depart Danang for Saigon; to get a visa at the American embassy—the last hurdle standing between my sons and me and our flight to a better life.

On March 20, 1970, Jimmy, Tommy, our maid, and I boarded the shuttle flight for Tan Son Nhut. All through the flight, I thought about my mother and how she would react when my maid (she drew the short straw—none of my sisters would do it!) returned to Danang and broke the news of our departure to my mother. Part of me wanted to believe she already knew the truth—learning it, perhaps, from a neighbor or by that intuition through which every mother knows her daughter—and that the truth had been in her eyes the last time I looked into her face: a benediction for my new life. Of course, unless I was to come back someday, I would probably never know.

During the two-nonth stay before our overseas flight, I had no trouble saying farewell to Saigon. As the capital of our country as well as Anh's home, it had become the symbol of everything I wanted to leave behind—to let go of and cut loose from my life. In the three years since I had been here, Saigon had become even bigger and noisier and dirtier and more wealthy and more wealth-driven and more cosmopolitan than it had ever been before. Rather than being less Vietnamese, which is how the Viet Cong described it, Saigon now seemed to be more and more what the Vietnamese people themselves were becoming: vicious, grasping, estranged, desperate, and dangerous—mostly to themselves. Still, I had one last piece of business to attend to before these chains were broken.

The great U.S. embassy was busy as a marketplace—full of staff and visitors. After a long wait, a junior American clerk received me only to tell me that Vietnamese citizens seeking visas were supposed to report to a different building, where such requests were processed by the Vietnamese Immigration and Naturalization Department. This distressed me greatly—not just for the extra step—but because dealing with Vietnamese bureaucrats always meant more cost and trouble.

The emigration office was located in a two-story white apartment building that was near the main post office and the Nha Tho Duc Ba Catholic Church. I was not encouraged when I walked through the door. Instead of a businesslike office, the apartment was the residence of a well-heeled Republican woman who had refined the art of administrative extortion to a science.

"How badly do you want to go to America?" she asked, cutting right to the heart of the matter. "You'll need documentation from the Vietnamese embassy in Washington. It's going to be expensive. How much do you have to spend?" Perhaps she phrased it this way so that if anybody ever challenged her, she could say she was simply separating the charity cases from those who could pay the government's fee.

I replied with a good, cheap guess.

"That's not enough," she said flatly. "Come into my house. We'll have to discuss your case."

After brief negotiations, accelerated by my early admission that my American husband was no longer around to pay my bills and that I could only raise more cash by selling my airline ticket, which would defeat the purpose of a visa, we agreed upon a price.

"Okay," she said, ushering me back outside. "You'll have to wait out here while I prepare your letter. My house isn't a bus station, you know. And by the way, there'll be a small surcharge for our tea fund—"

I spent the next few hours hoping that tea was cheaper than coffee—even at Saigon's inflated prices. By the end of the day, though, I went home with the all-important letter.

On May 27, 1970, my sons and I stood in line to board the big American jetliner to Honolulu. As the passengers shuffled forward, juggling their carry-on bags and jackets, they showed their tickets to one last Republican official. The Americans passed quickly. The Vietnamese, however, usually had to stop and delay the line while they fumbled through their purses or pockets. When my turn came, the official did not ask for passports or visas or certificates of any kind. He asked only a single question—the last phrase I would hear in my native tongue on the soil which held my father's bones:

"Are you carrying Vietnamese money? If so, please drop it in the basket before you go."

LATE EVENING, APRIL 10, 1986:
TINH's HOUSE AT CHINA BEACH

We finish my farewell dinner quietly—in a different mood, certainly, from the one in which we sat down. Before, tension between Bon Nghe and sister Ba was thick enough to stew. Now, with their feelings out in the open but not trampled on, they seem able to find peace with each other. Even brother Chin joins the conversation at the end, sounding not so dispirited after all. Perhaps his original slow-witted manner was his defense against the insanity around him, both in and out of prison. He had never seemed a particularly strong person, and the weak shouldn't be grudged their protectors. Like any other living thing, he flourishes best when he's not dodging someone's boot.

Tinh and my mother and Ba clear the table and Anh announces he has to go—he is late for his sister's in Danang. Bon Nghe, to my mildly aching heart, gets his hat and raincoat too (he'll need them this time; it's been pouring rain for an hour!). After Anh leaves, Bon walks to the kitchen and says good-bye to the women, then shakes hands with Bien and Chin and finally turns to me.

"Nhi is waiting for me and the weather's turned sour," he says, taking my hand. "Say hello to your children for me. Tell them I'd like to meet them one day. Give my love to Lan and her sons as well."

"It was wonderful seeing you, brother Bon." Tears sting my eyes. I can't think of anything clever to say—only what's in my heart. "I love you. I don't want to lose you again."

He hugs me and we walk together to the door.

"Keep me informed about your progress on the clinic," he says. "When the time comes, I'm sure I can help you over here."

Despite my desire to look him full in the face, to burn his image into my memory, he keeps averting his glance. He puts on his floppy rain hat and my long-lost brother Bon returns to the shadows from which he came. "Have a safe trip home," the half-hidden face says, reminding me that, despite my current feelings, that home is no longer Vietnam.

We open the front door and are enveloped by the smell of wet earth and the sound of silver rain in puddles and on tin roofs. He walks his bike from the porch, mounts, and after a few wobbly yards, pedals strongly into the night. When I turn back to the house, I see that everyone has silently gathered around me.

I wipe a tear from my cheek and smile. "Why all the long faces? The party isn't over yet. Come on, let's have some tea!"

"I don't think so," my mother says grimly. "I have a bad feeling about tonight. Look how dark it is—and all this bad weather. It isn't safe to be outside."

"It's just a little rain, Mama *Du,*" I reassure her.

"It's not just the rain. The police stay indoors in bad weather, so that's when the criminals come out. I think you'd better get back to the hotel before it gets too late."

My voice catches in my throat, "But it's still early, Mama *Du!* Let me stay a little longer—please! After I go, who knows when I'll see everyone again?"

"Maybe Bay Ly's right, Grandma Phung," Tinh says. "Maybe she should spend the night with us."

"Oh no!" my mother says, shaking her head. "People would really talk then! I think she should go right now. And you too, Ba Xuan. Take Chin home. See to your children. Go on!"

"Yes, Mama *Du,*" Ba says obediently, and her family quickly gets their things. Chin shakes my hand—it's a strong shake this time, not an invalid's trembling paw. I share a brief hug with my older sister—we clutch each other's face momentarily to remember it with our hands—and her family files from the house, disappearing into an alley beyond the street lamp's misty glow.

I feel Bien's hand on my shoulder.

"Don't cry, Bay Ly. Everyone had a fine time. Get your things and I'll run you back on my bike before the storm gets worse."

"No!" I look at my mother, who is just a blur now through my tears. "I don't want to go! It's all ending too soon!" I can hear my own voice, sobbing like a little girl's—distant like somebody else's—but I can't help it. *Poor, spoiled Bay Ly,* I can see them thinking, *she always has to have her way, doesn't she? And now she wants to have her way again, despite everyone's feelings. Who does she think she is, anyway?*

"Come along, Bay Ly." I hear my mother's voice. "Straighten up and be a lady. It's really best that you leave now."

"Okay—all right!" I shout at her, rushing past all their shocked faces to get my jacket in the kitchen. "I'm leaving!"

By myself in the other room, I pull a handkerchief from my jacket pocket and wipe my eyes. Quietly, Tinh appears in the doorway.

"Are you all right, Bay Ly?" she asks.

I blow my nose loudly. "Yes! No. I don't know. It's just that—" Something inside claws at my vitals to get out.

She steps up and puts her arm around me, "I know." Tinh smooths my hair. "You're going to miss everyone so much—"

"It's not just that," I sniff. "It's too much like—you know, when I was a little girl. It's too much like New Year's when everyone would come home for Tet—Sau Ban, Lan, Ba Xuan, you and Hai. Everyone would be so happy, then everyone would leave. I watched Bon Nghe walk out the door just now like Sau Ban did so many years ago. *Only he never came back!*" I break down again and Tinh holds and comforts me. "I don't want to lose my brother that way! I don't want to lose my mother! I don't want to lose any more of you like that!"

After a minute I compose myself and Tinh lets me go.

"Thanks," I smile at her. "You must think I'm pretty silly, right? Some big lady from America! Got the answers for everything, don't I?"

"Well, one thing you don't have," Tinh says, "is a rain hat. Let me give you mine for the trip to the hotel. And look—Grandma brought a couple of your suitcases by mistake. You'll have to take those too—"

"No, no mistake," I say, putting on my jacket. "I can replace everything easily enough at home. You keep them and wear whatever fits. We're about the same size now, after all these years!"

We hug again and I go back to face my hosts. My poor mother is pacing the room like a worried old hen, wringing her hands.

"Don't fret, Mama *Du,*" I smile at her. "You're right. It's best that I go now."

It hurts me a little to see my mother look so relieved, but I know it's relief for me as well. I say good-bye to Hai and Tinh and her children while Bien puts on his jacket and takes out his bike. The little seat behind his own looks less comfortable than Anh's motorbike, but it is still a limousine compared with the way most people get around this unhappy town. Being grateful for what you get, whatever it may be, is an old Buddhist creed and I'm glad I'm finally remembering it.

"I'll walk you out," my mother says, taking my hand. We stand on the porch and watch Bien prepare the bicycle.

"How long until you're back in the States?" my mother asks.

"About a week," I reply, still dabbing my eyes, relaxing after my cry. "Anh's sister has invited me to stay with her a few days in Saigon; then I thought I'd drop by and see how Lien is getting along. I'd like to remember her happier than the last time we saw her, eh?"

"That would be a blessing," my mother says. She is quiet a moment, then adds, "I'm very proud of you, Bay Ly. You've grown up to see the side of things that's hidden from most people."

"You taught me that, Mama *Du.*" I squeeze her hand.

"No. You got that from your father. I'm still learning. Take tonight, for example. If it hadn't been for you, Ba Xuan and I would still be fighting; and the wall between her and her brother would be higher than ever. Who knows—maybe next trip I'll even feel okay about your spending the night with us here at Tinh's. But that's asking too much of this old heart right now. I've lived a long time, Bay Ly, but tonight my life seems way too short. We're born and we're taught by our parents and then all of a sudden we have to figure everything out again for ourselves. It's like doing your homework when you were a little girl, eh? Each stage of life has its lessons and we either learn them or play hooky—"

"I was pretty good at playing hooky, Mama *Du,* remember?"

"Yes, but I never worried about you. Now I know my faith was justified. You've done your homework, Bay Ly. The rest of us—well—our whole world turned upside down because we didn't learn our lessons about getting along. And we're still in trouble for it, aren't we? We need to listen to our higher selves, Bay Ly—as you have done—and not so much to each other."

"Papa talks to me, do you know that?"

My mother sighs. "Yes, and he used to talk to me, too. It's just that

—well, it's always been hard for me to listen. That's why I need teachers to come and tutor me, eh?—every so often, like you and Anh!"

"I have nothing to teach you, Mama *Du*. And you have nothing to be ashamed of."

"Oh, I wouldn't say that. Remember what you and Bon Nghe were talking about tonight? About how stupid it is to give up the important things in life for somebody else's promise about tomorrow? Well, I have to admit something to you. All I could think about while you were saying that was how I kept Sau Ban's new bride from following him to the South. If she had gone, I probably would have had two *chau noi*—two grandsons by sons—near me now, instead of only one. But no—I decided that if Sau Ban had a wife with him, he might not join the Viet Cong. Can you believe it? I gave up a grandson to gain a soldier—and wound up losing both. Your father always wanted her to go—to let your poor brother know at least some of the joys of married life. But I kept her from it in the name of war. At the time, I thought I was doing the right thing. I *knew* I was doing the right thing! Now, I can see how wrong it was."

"It was Sau Ban's choice, too, Mama *Du*." I try to make her feel better.

She waves my words away, "He was just being a good son. And that was his mistake, too, wasn't it? If I'd had my way, I would've prevented you from going to America, did you know that? You were smart not to tell me, Bay Ly—more than smart, you were wise. Who knows what would've happened to you and your sons if you'd stayed in Vietnam?" My mother sighs, "Well, all that's in the past. You see, I'm just like everyone else around here—much better at digging up old bones than planting new seeds. That's your job: work for you and Anh and Bon Nghe and Nam and all the others. Just remember, though, that all those connections in your life, with the living and the dead, are also like that roof you talked about. A thatched roof starts out green, then dies and turns brown—but that doesn't mean it was never alive, or can't shelter you in your old age. Without it, you'd be worse than the stones: left out in the rain and forever by yourself."

Bien rings the bicycle bell and yells, "All aboard! The train is leaving!"

"Good-bye, Mama *Du*." I hug my mother one last time.

"Bye, bye," my mother whispers. "You'll always be my baby."

It is morning, April 11, 1986—the day I must leave Danang. Anh and Bien arrive and after breakfast, we set off for the Air Vietnam bus station. I ride with Anh while Bien follows with my one remaining tote bag and Anh's suitcase. When the shuttle bus pulls out, Bien rides alongside for some time, waving good-bye while we drive down Thong Nhat Street—the street of independence—on our way to the airport. As his lifeline to the outside world, Bien seems as reluctant to let me go as I was to say good-bye to my family. It helps us both to know there are loving hands now on both sides of the ocean.

At the Danang airport, Anh and I get off the bus and shuffle into line with the other Saigon passengers. Although I have virtually no luggage, I still feel bogged down and heavy.

The ride from Tinh's house the night before was as depressing as the weather. Not only did we have to sneak around like Viet Cong before we left, but as soon as we pulled away, my mother and Tinh went back into the house and shut everything up—I could almost hear the door lock in my face.

"I was worried about you last night," Anh says while we wait. "You seemed upset by your brother and sister fighting."

"That was nothing." I smile. "You should have seen me when it was time to leave. I acted just like a baby. Be glad you weren't there."

"Well, don't worry. I think everything went extremely well—far better than I expected. How did you sleep?"

"It was hot and muggy in the room," I reply, "and I had lots of bugs for company."

"I'm sorry to hear that," he says.

"Why? It was wonderful. I don't want to go. It's too early. I want to go pull weeds in the paddies and nap in my old hammock and chop onions for my mother's supper."

"Well, the officials were very specific about how long you could stay. You don't want to wear out your welcome with the *Ban Viet Kieu*. If it's worth anything, I think your timing is perfect. You accomplished almost everything you set out to do. The longer you hang around, the more chances there are for trouble. Besides, you can use the extra days in Saigon to look into that clinic you and Bon Nghe talked about. You can start making contacts and find out what approvals you're going to need. Yes, I think everything turned out just fine, Bay Ly"—he pats my hand for reassurance—"very fine indeed!"

We board the old aircraft—it's as dirty and crowded as the one that brought us north five days before—and find our seats. In a few minutes it starts to taxi, and with no other airplanes around, we are soon climbing high into the gray-matted sky. As we push the earth away, I feel my family—not my ancestors or the love I will always feel for my parents and brothers and sisters, but the people themselves—slip from my grasp. It is as if the thatchwork of helping hands that raised and nurtured me now turns palms up, fingers interlaced, to boost me to someplace else: to another world, another existence, into another life circle. Instead of feeling dull and depressed, as I did when I boarded, exhilaration fills my body —the way my spirit soared on that first airplane ride from this very spot so many years ago.

Gray cloudlets, weeping rain that does not touch the ground, slip past the window as we climb. In April 1949, a disembodied soul slipped through the universe on unknown rays to find a vehicle on earth. Nine months later, the entity called Le Ly was brought with great pain by Huyen and Phung Trong into the world of brothers and sisters and harsh and loving lessons. The first words her tiny ears heard, beyond her own natal scream, was the midwife saying, "Suffocate her!" but Huyen gave them both a lesson in compassion and did not. In the East, she traveled roads that led inward to man's soul and learned the ways of the heart and spirit. In the West, she learned the ways of the heart and mind, and learned of roads that led outward to the stars.

By coming back to her place of landing, she completed the first circle of her life. By reencountering her companions on that journey, she recited to them the lessons she had learned, and was judged by universal law— that more-than-physical bond between beings everywhere and at all times—and was told the purpose of her life.

I look over to Anh, who is happily lost in his newspaper, and feel unbounded joy. His life force glows and embraces me with a strength and beauty that make my body and spirit melt together. We will have a lot to share over the next few days: brave talk about hospitals and helpers and how to catch the ears and tug the hearts of people much bigger than I am—politicians, philanthropists, and others who have shared our journey all over the world. I look over the tops of the seats and up and down the shabby airliner and the bright aura of the humanity around me— Oriental and Occidental commingled and indistinguishable—bathes the walls in golden light.

I glance out the window to cool my eyes on the soggy clouds and luscious greens of Mother Earth. As we bank toward the south, climbing over the sandy coastline, I see the upturned thimbles of Marble Mountain and the lazy snakes of the Song Han delta. As if suspended in time, knowing the engines will momentarily carry me above and beyond the screen of clouds, I spot a loamy patch of ground covered with thatch-roofed houses rising among the paddies like a mother's knee. There is a scraggly jungle on two sides—fighting, even as I watch, with sap and flowers to come back after a decade of fire and poison to become the lush paradise I once knew. There is a swamp just to the north, with scruffy shrubs and misshapen trees and footless sand concealing a thousand secrets. To the east, there is a small, bald hill overlooking the rest, where an older, wiser entity—almost finished with its quest for perfection—bestowed on a younger spirit the object of her journey.

For a glistening instant, Ky La dances before my eyes, then vanishes into memory.

EPILOGUE

A Song of Enlightenment

A LONG TIME AGO, in a fight for justice—a fight over strong beliefs about right and wrong—a proud boy chopped off another boy's arm with his family's sword. The victorious boy, believing the battle was over, gave thanks, sheathed his weapon, and went home.

The boy lived with his grandmother, who taught him to always be good and honorable; and with an orphan girl, whom the grandmother had raised to be an honorable wife for her grandson.

Not long after the fight, a call to battle reached their house. The king's messenger told them a great war was beginning that would test the power of good against evil. Understandably, the boy had two minds about responding. He believed in goodness and virtue, of course, and had proved it in his fight with the wrong-headed boy whom he had maimed. But he was soon to marry his fiancée, too, and was anxious to begin a family.

To resolve his dilemma, the boy consulted his wise old grandmother (who had taught him everything about the past), and his fiancée (who shared his dreams about the future), and asked them what to do. Because the grandmother loved virtue and justice above all things, she said the boy should go to war without hesitation. Because the girl loved the boy and also respected the grandmother's opinions, she too said the boy should go and promised to wait faithfully for him no matter how long the war should last.

So the boy went with the messenger and was gone a long time, during which he distinguished himself in many battles. When he returned, however, he found his home in shambles. The crops had failed, the animals had run away, and the house itself lay in disrepair. When he opened the door, he was greeted by his fiancée, who now looked as old as the grandmother he remembered.

"What happened?" he asked in astonishment. "Why has my home been ruined? Where is my grandmother? What's happened to you?"

"It was horrible," the fiancée said, falling weeping in his arms. "After you left, the boy whose arm you cut off came back and took revenge against us. He killed your grandmother and chopped her into pieces, then he raped me, pillaged our house, and burned our farm."

The boy-turned-soldier already had his ancestral sword half drawn in rage when he cried, "I will avenge this atrocity! Justice and virtue must prevail!"

On his way down the road, he stopped at his grandmother's grave and prayed for the strength and courage he would need to avenge her. While he was praying, his old enemy appeared. But instead of striking him from behind or calling him to combat, the enemy fell to his knees and begged the soldier to behead him for the wrong he had committed.

The soldier, believing his prayer for justice had been answered, drew his sword and prepared to strike, when a bell sounded in a nearby temple. The soldier paused as a song, born on the wind in a chorus of ghostly voices—now his grandmother's, now the victims he and his ancestors had killed in war, now the voices of his own children yet-to-be-born—filled the air around him:

> Late afternoon—
> Hear the bell—
> The bell wakes up
> My soul—
>
> We must hurry to become
> Enlightened—
> We must kneel beneath the tree of
> Buddha—
> We look into the face of god and
> Forget the past—

To forgive our brother is to forgive
Ourselves—
We abandon our revenge;
Our lives have seen suffering enough.
We are tired and worn out with
Ourselves—

If I take revenge, it will be the cause;
The effect will follow me into my next life.
Look into the mirror: see the compassion in your heart.
Avoid all resentment and hatred for
Mankind—

The soldier, having had his passion interrupted by the bell and his spirit awakened by the song, put away his sword and helped his enemy get up.

"Go your own way," the soldier said. "I took your arm, and that cannot be replaced; but I could have had your life, and this I have returned to you."

"Go your way in peace," the one-armed man replied. "I took your loved ones, it's true, and what's done cannot be undone; but I, too, have returned to you your life: for my brothers would have avenged me even though you had my head."

So the two men, no longer boys, parted and began new lives. To commemorate the breaking of the circle of vengeance, the temple bell now rings twice each day and reminds the people to arrest their passions long enough to think; and having thought, to hear the song of enlightenment.

* * *

IN THE SPRING OF 1970, my sons and I joined our American savior, Ed, in San Diego, California. By winter 1973, emphysema had claimed my husband's life and I was left a widow—a stranger in a foreign land. Despite my ignorance of America, however, I was still determined to find the better life we sought. But that is another story; another life circle.

In this book, I have tried to show how we peasants survived—and still survive today—as both makers and victims of our war. I have shared with you the face of battle, the shape of terror, the shades of love, and the colors of joy as I have seen them.

Today, I am very honored to live in the United States and proud to be a U.S. citizen. I do my best to honor the American flag, which I have seen not only raised in battle against me but flying proudly over the schools where my wonderful boys have learned to be Americans.

Most of you who read this book have not lived my kind of life. By the grace of destiny or luck or god, you do not know how hard it is to survive; although you now have some idea. Do not fell sorry for me—I made it; I am okay. Right now, though, there are millions of other poor people around the world—girls, boys, men, and women—who live their lives the way I did in order to survive. Like me, they did not ask for the wars which swallowed them. They ask only for peace—the freedom to love and live a full life—and nothing more. I ask only that you open your heart and mind to them, as you have opened it to me by reading this book, and do not think that our story is over.

Most of you learned about life in school, from your friends and families, from your jobs, and from books and television. Although I learned most of what I know from life itself, I think we can all agree on at least one thing: that nobody has a perfect view of everything. Our job is to share what we know so that our wisdom—our vision of the common truth— can become common knowledge for the world.

The Vietnam war will not be over until it ends for everyone. Over four hundred thousand U.S. veterans are still recovering from wounds inflicted on their bodies and their spirit. Sixty-three million souls in Vietnam are still suffering from their "victory." Some of these souls inhabit infant bodies born misshapen from Agent Orange. Others are doomed to die of cancer and other illnesses related to wartime chemicals which have contaminated the supply of water in many places. Sixty thousand have lost limbs and over three hundred thousand are unable to work because of war-related disabilities. By some counts, as many as twenty-five thousand Amerasian children—the fruit of the union of so many beautiful white- or dark-skinned American men and dark-haired, dark-eyed Vietnamese women—are still waiting to find a future with families they've never seen. Some observers estimate that between six and seven million Vietnamese men, women, and children are dying slowly of starvation, malnutrition, and disease because food and other necessities cannot be produced or imported in sufficient quantities from Western countries, some of which, like the United States, continue a wartime embargo. The circle of vengeance persists.

I can only say what I myself have learned: that life's purpose is to grow. We have time in abundance—an eternity, in fact—to repeat our mistakes. We only need to correct them once, however—to learn our lesson and hear the song of enlightenment—to break the chain of vengeance forever.

If we can do this personally, no matter how many others follow, our own hearts will at least find peace.

In the name of my father and all the other victims of war, I founded an agency in 1987 to help my brothers and sisters in Vietnam while helping my brothers and sisters in the United States come back from their wartime experience. The East Meets West Foundation seeks support from the U.S. Government, Vietnamese Government, the American and Vietnamese people, corporations, charitable groups, religious organizations, and individual benefactors in all nations to heal the wounds of war and break the circle of vengeance that perpetuates suffering in the name of justice around the world. As I write these words, work is beginning in Xa Hoa Qui to build a Victims of War Center for the homeless and rural poor. These clinics, built in cooperation with Vietnam veterans groups from across America, will be staffed and supported by volunteer physicians, dentists, and other health professionals from the United States and other countries involved in America's longest—and Vietnam's costliest—war. We are making special efforts to "reenlist" medical corpsmen, nurses, and physicians who have previously served in this and other combat zones. If you are a veteran of any war, you are especially encouraged to sign on for another "tour of duty" in service to humanity and yourself—to heal the wounds that may linger in your spirit and help the Vietnamese people, who, like war victims anywhere, are the spiritual partners of your journey.

If this book has been the bell that breaks the pattern of hateful feelings in your life, use the quiet that's now in your heart to hear the song of enlightenment. It's the song your spirit has been singing since the moment of your birth.

If you would like to help, please write or call:

Asia Resource Center
P.O. Box 15275
Washington, DC, 20003
(202) 547-1114

East Meets West Foundation
12540 Oaks North Drive Suite 4
San Diego, CA 92128
(619) 673-3734

U.S.-Vietnam Friendship and Aid Association
P.O. Box 453

Murrieta, CA 92362
(213) 395-4702
(714) 677-5905

Veterans-Vietnam Restoration Project
P.O. Box 69
716 Locust Avenue
Garberville, CA 95440
(707) 923-3357

World Vision
919 West Huntington Drive
Monrovia, CA 91016
(818) 357-7979